## The Roman Provinces, 300 BCE–300 CE

Provincial coinage gives us a unique insight into the Roman world, reflecting the values and concerns of the elites of the many hundreds of cities in the Roman Empire. Coins offer a very different perspective from written history, which usually represents the views of the senatorial class, and which was usually composed long after the events that are described. The coins, in contrast, provide evidence without hindsight, and uniquely allow a systematic examination across the whole Roman world. This volume makes it possible for instructors and students and scholars to deploy a complex set of material evidence on many historical topics. It includes over two hundred illustrations of coins with detailed captions, so providing a convenient sourcebook of the most important items, and covers topics such as the motivation for Roman conquest, the revolution of Augustus, the world of the Second Sophistic and the crisis of the third century.

**Andrew Burnett** was Deputy Director of the British Museum from 2002 to 2013, having begun his career at the Museum in 1974 in the Coins and Medals department as a research assistant. He went on to become Deputy Keeper in 1990 and Keeper in 1992. He is a past president of the Royal Numismatic Society, the Roman Society, and of the International Numismatic Commission, and is currently an honorary research associate at the Ashmolean Museum, Oxford. His main research interests are in the coinage of Roman Britain, the early Roman coinage of the third century BCE, Roman provincial coinage, and the history of numismatics.

## Guides to the Coinage of the Ancient World

General Editor

Andrew Meadows, *University of Oxford*

Coinage is a major source of evidence for the study of the ancient world but is often hard for those studying and teaching ancient history to grasp. Each volume in the series provides a concise introduction to the most recent scholarship and ideas for a commonly studied period or area, and suggests ways in which numismatic evidence may contribute to its social, political and economic history. The volumes are richly illustrated, with full explanatory captions, and so can also function as a numismatic sourcebook for the period or area in question.

Titles in the series

The Roman Provinces, 300 BCE–300 CE: Using Coins as Sources
*by Andrew Burnett*
The Roman Republic to 49 BCE: Using Coins as Sources
*by Liv Mariah Yarrow*
The Athenian Empire: Using Coins as Sources
*by Lisa Kallet and John H. Kroll*
From Caesar to Augustus (c. 49 BC – AD 14): Using Coins as Sources
*by Clare Rowan*
The Hellenistic World: Using Coins as Sources
*by Peter Thonemann*

Headquartered in New York City, the American Numismatic Society serves an international community dedicated to the study and public appreciation of coins, currencies, medals, and other related objects. Since its founding in 1858, the ANS has assembled a permanent collection with over 800,000 objects dating from 650 BCE to the present and a numismatic library, which houses approximately 100,000 books, documents, and artifacts. These resources are used to support research, publications of books and periodicals, lectures, academic seminars, and exhibitions. The ANS invites researchers to visit one of the largest collections of coins from the ancient world either in person by appointment or through its open access databases online.

# The Roman Provinces, 300 BCE–300 CE

Using Coins as Sources

ANDREW BURNETT
*The British Museum*

Shaftesbury Road, Cambridge CB2 8EA, United Kingdom

One Liberty Plaza, 20th Floor, New York, NY 10006, USA

477 Williamstown Road, Port Melbourne, VIC 3207, Australia

314–321, 3rd Floor, Plot 3, Splendor Forum, Jasola District Centre, New Delhi – 110025, India

103 Penang Road, #05–06/07, Visioncrest Commercial, Singapore 238467

Cambridge University Press is part of Cambridge University Press & Assessment, a department of the University of Cambridge.

We share the University's mission to contribute to society through the pursuit of education, learning and research at the highest international levels of excellence.

www.cambridge.org
Information on this title: www.cambridge.org/9781009420136

DOI: 10.1017/9781009420099

© Andrew Burnett 2024

This publication is in copyright. Subject to statutory exception and to the provisions of relevant collective licensing agreements, no reproduction of any part may take place without the written permission of Cambridge University Press & Assessment.

When citing this work, please include a reference to the DOI 10.1017/9781009420099

First published 2024

*A catalogue record for this publication is available from the British Library.*

*A Cataloging-in-Publication data record for this book is available from the Library of Congress*

ISBN 978-1-009-42013-6 Hardback
ISBN 978-1-009-42010-5 Paperback

Cambridge University Press & Assessment has no responsibility for the persistence or accuracy of URLs for external or third-party internet websites referred to in this publication and does not guarantee that any content on such websites is, or will remain, accurate or appropriate.

# Contents

| | |
|---|---|
| *List of Figures* | *page* ix |
| *List of Maps* | xxviii |
| *List of Boxes* | xxix |
| *Preface* | xxxi |
| *Acknowledgements* | xxxix |
| *Chronological Tables* | xl |
| *List of Abbreviations* | xlii |

**1 Precious Metal Coinages at Rome and in the Provinces**     1
    1.1   Silver     4
    1.2   Gold     32
    1.3   The Emergence of the Late Roman System of Precious
         Metal Coinage     41

**2 The Beginnings of an Empire in Italy and the Western**
**Mediterranean (300–200 BCE)**     44
    2.1   The Adoption of Coinage at Rome     45
    2.2   Coinage in Roman Territories     52
    2.3   The Changing Use of Coinage in the Early Roman
         World     68
    2.4   Roman Imperialism: Iconography     70
    2.5   Continuity and Change: The End of Non-Roman
         Coinage in Italy     72

**3 The Growth of an Empire during the Late Republic**
**(200–31 BCE)**     77
    3.1   Italy     79
    3.2   Sicily     82
    3.3   Spain     84
    3.4   Africa     89
    3.5   Cyrenaica     90
    3.6   Gaul     90
    3.7   Greece and the Balkans     91
    3.8   Asia Minor     97
    3.9   Bithynia     101
    3.10   Cilicia     102

**viii** Contents

| | |
|---|---|
| 3.11 Syria | 103 |
| 3.12 Patterns across the Roman World | 106 |
| 4 Whose Coins? A Model for City Coinage in Imperial Times | 110 |
| 5 The Revolution of Augustus – and Becoming More Roman in the First Century | 129 |
| 5.1 Trends | 131 |
| 5.2 Roman Interventions | 157 |
| 5.3 'Two Empires': The End of Local Coinage in the West | 168 |
| 6 Reinforcing Greek Identity in the Golden Age of the Second Century CE | 174 |
| 6.1 Changing Consciousness and the Pattern of Coinage | 175 |
| 6.2 A New Mode of Production | 178 |
| 6.3 The End of Small Denominations | 182 |
| 6.4 East and West and Latin and Greek | 187 |
| 6.5 A Liminal Zone: From Moesia to Cyrenaica | 191 |
| 6.6 Designs | 197 |
| 6.7 Antinous | 218 |
| 7 'From a kingdom of gold to one of iron and rust' in the Third Century CE | 222 |
| 7.1 Political and Security Problems | 224 |
| 7.2 Economic and Monetary Problems | 237 |
| 7.3 Fragmentation | 246 |
| 7.4 The End of Provincial Coinage | 257 |
| *Guide to Further Reading* | 271 |
| *Bibliography* | 272 |
| *Appendices* | 304 |
| 1. Numismatic Glossary *(by Andrew Meadows, updated and revised by the author)* | 304 |
| 2. Denominational Systems *(by Andrew Meadows, updated and revised by the author)* | 309 |
| 3. The Production of Ancient Coinage *(by Andrew Meadows)* | 311 |
| *Notes* | 313 |
| *Index* | 347 |

# Figures

P.1  A view of the city of Amasea, in Pontus (northern Asia Minor), minted under the emperor Severus Alexander. RPC VI temporary number 6467. Robert Hoppensteadt collection. *page* xxxiii

P.2  The city council in session. Trebonianus Gallus (251–3), Alexandria Troas, as RPC IX 432. Münzkabinett der Staatlichen Museen zu Berlin, 18265746. Photographs by Bernhard Weisser. xxxvi

1.1–1.2  The first Roman silver coins. 6

1.1  Roman silver didrachm, about 300 BCE, as *RRC* 13/1. Münzkabinett, Staatliche Museen zu Berlin 18200980. Photographs by Dirk Sonnenwald.

1.2  Roman silver obol, about 300 BCE, as *RRC* 13/2. Numismatica Ars Classica 72, 16 May 2013, lot 396 (0.66 g).

1.3–1.7  Silver coinage in Sicily in the Second Punic War. 9

1.3  Philistis, wife of Hiero II, king of Syracuse, silver 16 10-litrai coin. Münzkabinett der Staatlichen Museen zu Berlin, 18203199. Photographs by Dirk Sonnenwald.

1.4  Syracuse, Fifth Democracy (214–12 BCE), silver 12 litrai coin. Bibliothèque nationale de France Luynes 1392.

1.5  Carthaginian silver half-shekel minted for Sicily about 214–212 BCE. Bibliothèque nationale de France FG 663.

1.6  Roman silver quadrigatus, minted in Sicily, about 213–210 BCE, as *RRC* 42/1. Münzkabinett, Staatliche Museen zu Berlin 18271447. Photographs by Bernhard Weisser.

1.7  Roman silver denarius, about 210 BCE, as *RRC* 44/5. Bibliothèque nationale de France REP-2693.

1.8–1.11  Roman silver coins of the denarius system, about 200 BCE. 11

1.8  Roman silver denarius, about 210 BCE, as *RRC* 44/5. Münzkabinett, Staatliche Museen zu Berlin 18225771. Photographs by Reinhard Saczewski.

# List of Figures

| | | |
|---|---|---|
| 1.9 | Roman silver quinarius, about 210 BCE, as *RRC* 44/6. American Numismatic Society 2002.46.33. | |
| 1.10 | Roman silver sestertius, about 210 BCE, as *RRC* 44/7. Bibliothèque nationale de France REP-1960. | |
| 1.11 | Roman silver victoriate, about 210 BCE, as *RRC* 44/1. Bibliothèque nationale de France REP-1977. | |
| 1.12 | Iberian silver denarius, from Osca (Bolscan). Second century BCE. Bibliothèque nationale de France FG 290. | 14 |
| 1.13–1.15 | Silver coins struck under Roman Republican rule in the Eastern Empire. | 18 |
| 1.13 | Athens, silver tetradrachm, late second century BCE. Münzkabinett, Staatliche Museen zu Berlin, 18204002. Photographs by Dirk Sonnenwald.1. | |
| 1.14 | Silver cistophorus minted at Apamea, Asia, in the name of Cicero as proconsul, 51/0 BCE. Münzkabinett, Staatliche Museen zu Berlin, 18204062. Photographs by Reinhard Saczewski. | |
| 1.15 | Silver tetradrachm, Antioch, Syria, minted in year 19 of Roman rule = 31/30 BCE, as *RPC I*, 4136. Bibliothèque nationale de France 1541bis. | |
| 1.16–1.17 | Provincial silver coins of the early imperial period. | 21 |
| 1.16 | Augustus (31 BCE–14), silver cistophorus, about 25 BCE, as *RPC I*, 2208. American Numismatic Society 1944.100.39182. | |
| 1.17 | Augustus, silver tetradrachm, Antioch, 4/3 BCE, as *RPC I*, 4153. Bibliothèque nationale de France 1984.746. | |
| 1.18 | Silver coin of Tyre. *RPC I*, 4672. American Numismatic Society 1944.100.72874. | 22 |
| 1.19–1.20 | Nero's reformed provincial silver coins. | 24 |
| 1.19 | Nero, Antioch, silver tetradrachm, as *RPC I*, 4185, 62/63. Bibliothèque nationale de France Chandon 1834. | |
| 1.20 | Nero, Alexandria, silver tetradrachm, as *RPC I*, 5295, 66/67. Bibliothèque nationale de France Vogüé 612 = SNG 504. | |
| 1.21–1.25 | Coordinated silver issues made for Trajan. | 27 |
| 1.21 | Trajan (98–117), silver denarius, Rome. Bibliothèque nationale de France Imp-2591 = BNC 52. | |

# List of Figures — xi

1.22 Trajan, silver cistophorus, Asia, as *RPC III*, 1315. Bibliothèque nationale de France Imp-3501.

1.23 Trajan, silver drachm, Lycia, as *RPC III*, 2676. Bibliothèque nationale de France FG 18.

1.24 Trajan, silver didrachm, Caesarea in Cappadocia, as *RPC III*, 2991. American Numismatic Society 1985.39.60.

1.25 Trajan, silver tetradrachm, Antioch, Syria, as *RPC III*, 3564. American Numismatic Society 1944.100.58454.

1.26 The spoils captured at the Roman victory over the Carthaginians at the Battle of Mylae in 260 BCE. Rome, Musei Capitolini. Photograph by the author.   35

1.27–1.28 Carthaginian and Roman gold coins.   36

1.27 Carthaginian gold coin, about 250 BCE. Bibliothèque nationale de France Luynes 3746.

1.28 Roman gold coin, about 215 BCE, as *RRC* 28/1. Bibliothèque nationale de France REP-21346.

1.29–1.31 Gold coins of Julius Caesar and Vercingetorix.   37

1.29 Gold coin of Julius Caesar, 48 BCE, as *RRC* 452. Münzkabinett, Kunsthistorisches Museum, ID54486. Photographs by Margit Redl, KHM.

1.30 Gold coin of Julius Caesar, 46 BCE, as *RRC* 466. American Numismatic Society 1980.109.152.

1.31 Gold coin of Vercingetorix, about 50 BCE. Bibliothèque nationale de France 3780A.

1.32–1.33 Hadrian and the Provinces.   39

1.32 Hadrian, aureus, as *RIC II.3* no. 1530. Münzkabinett der Staatlichen Museen zu Berlin, 18204508. Photographs by Dirk Sonnenwald.

1.33 Hadrian, aureus, as *RIC II.3* no. 1478. Münzkabinett der Staatlichen Museen zu Berlin, 18204515. Photographs by Dirk Sonnenwald.

1.34–1.35 Provincial silver coins in Egypt.   42

1.34 Tiberius (14–37). Silver tetradrachm, Alexandria, Egypt, as *RPC I*, 5089. Münzkabinett, Staatliche Museen zu Berlin, 18233708. Photographs by Dirk Sonnenwald.

1.35 Diocletian (284–305). Bronze tetradrachm, Alexandria, Egypt. American Numismatic Society 1944.100.68386.

xii List of Figures

1.36 The last gold coins of the early imperial system.   42
Gallienus (260–268), debased gold coin, as *RIC V.1*,
no 81 var. Bibliothèque nationale de France FG 1374.

2.1–2.2 Bronze coins of Rome and Naples, late
fourth century BCE.   45
2.1 Rome, bronze coin, late fourth century BCE, as *RRC* 1.
Münzkabinett, Staatliche Museen zu Berlin, 18214344.
Photographs by Lutz-Jürgen Lübke.
2.2 Naples, bronze coin, late fourth century BCE, as *HN* 584.
Bibliothèque nationale de France FG 371.
2.3 Roman currency bar.   46
Mid third century BCE, as *RRC* 11. Bibliothèque
nationale de France REP-423.
2.4–2.6 Struck silver, bronze coins and cast aes grave.   48
2.4 Roman silver didrachm, mid third century BCE,
as *RRC* 25/1. Münzkabinett, Staatliche Museen zu Berlin,
18214584. Photographs by Lutz-Jürgen Lübke.
2.5 Roman bronze coin, mid third century BCE, as *RRC* 25/3.
Münzkabinett, Staatliche Museen zu Berlin, 18214623.
Photographs by Lutz-Jürgen Lübke.
2.6 Roman *aes grave* as, mid third century BCE, as *RRC* 25/4.
American Numismatic Society 1969.83.459.
2.7–2.8 Silver and bronze coins of Metapontum, southern Italy,
late fourth century.   50
2.7 Metapontum, silver didrachm, late fourth century BCE,
as *HN* 1574. Bibliothèque nationale de France FG 1168.
2.8 Metapontum, bronze coin, late fourth century BCE, as *HN*
1640. Bibliothèque nationale de France 2016.80.
2.9 Naples, bronze coin, mid third century BCE.   54
As *HN* 589. Bibliothèque nationale de France FG 429.
2.10 Scipio Africanus at Canusium?, late third century BCE.   54
As *HN* 660. Bibliothèque nationale de France Luynes 226.
2.11 Silver coin of Populonia, early third century BCE.   56
As *HN* 152. American Numismatic Society 1949.100.14.
2.12–2.13 Bronze coins of Etruria.   57
2.12 Populonia, bronze coin, mid third century BCE, as *HN* 195.
Münzkabinett, Staatliche Museen zu Berlin, 18220286.
Photographs by Reinhard Saczewski.

# List of Figures xiii

2.13 Cosa, bronze coin, mid third century BCE, as *HN* 210.
Münzkabinett, Staatliche Museen zu Berlin, 18220381.
Photographs by Reinhard Saczewski.

2.14 Silver drachm made in the Po Valley, northern Italy, late third
century. 58
Münzkabinett, Staatliche Museen zu Berlin, 18204768.
Photographs by Dirk Sonnenwald.

2.15–2.16 Roman coins minted in Sardinia. 61

2.15 Roman Sardinia, silver quinarius, 211 BCE, as *RRC* 65/1.
Numismatica Ars Classica 61, 2011, lot 287.

2.16 Roman Sardinia, bronze sextans, 210 BCE, as *RRC* 64/6.
American Numismatic Society 1944.100.140.

2.17 Carthaginian five-shekel silver coin, minted in Sicily, during
the First Punic War. 62
Bibliothèque nationale de France Luynes 3758.

2.18–2.19 Bronze coins of King Hiero of Syracuse. 65

2.18 Hiero, King of Syracuse (275–215 BCE), bronze coin.
Bibliothèque nationale de France FG 1880.

2.19 Hiero, King of Syracuse (275–215 BCE), bronze coin.
Bibliothèque nationale de France FG 1917.

2.20 Carthaginian silver coin, minted in Spain, late
third century BCE. 66
Numismatica Ars Classica 84, 2015, lot 534.

2.21–2.23 Roman silver coins minted in Spain. 67

2.21 Roman silver quadrigatus, minted in Spain, about 215
BCE, as *MIB* 215/01. Bibliothèque nationale de
France Rep-1577.

2.22 Roman silver drachm, minted in Spain, about 215 BCE,
as *MIB* 215/04. Madrid, Real Academia de
la Historia, 2bis.

2.23 Roman silver diobol, minted in Spain, about 215 BCE,
as *RRC* 28/5 and *MIB* 215/05. Numismatica Ars
Classica 27, 12 May 2004, lot 206.

2.24 Rome and Locri. 70
Locri, silver stater, about 280 BCE, as *HN* 2348.
Bibliothèque nationale de France FG 1891.

2.25–2.26 Roman coinage and aggressive imperialism. 71

2.25 Roman silver didrachm, mid third century BCE,
as *RRC* 20. American Numismatic Society 1944.100.15.

xiv List of Figures

2.26 Roman cast *aes grave* as, about 225/20 BCE, as *RRC* 35/1.
Bibliothèque nationale de France REP-20.

3.1–3.3 The Roman denarius coinage. 78

3.1 Roman silver denarius, about 210 BCE, as *RRC* 44/5.
Münzkabinett, Staatliche Museen zu Berlin, 18225771.
Photographs by Reinhard Saczewski.

3.2 Roman bronze as, about 210 BCE, as *RRC* 56/2. Bibliothèque
nationale de France Rep-751.

3.3 Carthaginian silver coin, Sicily, struck over a Roman silver
victoriate. Hersh Collection (now British Museum
2002,0102.5499). Photographs by the author.

3.4–3.5 Bronze coins of Paestum, southern Italy. 80

3.4 Mineia, Paestum, bronze semis, first century BCE,
as *HN* 1258. Classical Numismatic Group 106, 19 January
2005, lot 103.

3.5 Paestum, bronze semis, first century BCE, as *HN* 1238.
Numismatica Ars Classica 27, 12 May 2004, lot 41.

3.6 Uncertain mint in Italy, first century BCE. 81
As *HN* 2672. Bibliothèque nationale de France E58.

3.7–3.8 Romano-Sicilian coins, second century BCE. 82

3.7 Roman Sicily, bronze as. Bibliothèque nationale de France
Rep-20742.

3.8 Roman Sicily, bronze coin. Bibliothèque nationale
de France FG 996.

3.9 Accounts from Tauromenium, first century BCE. 83
Antiquarium del Teatro Antico, Taormina, ISic002986,
25–30. Photograph by Jonathan Prag. Su concessione del
Parco Archeologico di Naxos Taormina.

3.10–3.11 Iberian denarii and bronzes. 85

3.10 'Iberian denarius' of Arsaos, Spain, as *MIB* 85/15b, late
second century BCE. Bibliothèque nationale de
France K 863A.

3.11 Iltirta, Spain, bronze coin, as *MIB* 67/78c, late second
century BCE. Bibliothèque nationale de France 212.

3.12 Bronze coin of Ebusus (modern Ibiza). 86
Bibliothèque nationale de France Delepierre 3224.

| | | |
|---|---|---|
| 3.13 | Saguntum, Spain, bronze coin. | 87 |
| | As *MIB* 34/62. Formerly Hispanic Society of America, Jesús Vico 09–10–2012, 131, lot 75. | |
| 3.14 | M. Cato, silver denarius, about 46 BCE. | 89 |
| | As *RRC* 462/1. American Numismatic Society 1937. 158.268. | |
| 3.15–3.16 | Silver and bronze coinage of Gaul, late first century. | 91 |
| 3.15 | Silver quinarius from Gaul, inscribed Ateula and Ulatos, first century BCE. Bibliothèque nationale de France 7202. | |
| 3.16 | Bronze coin of the Lexovii from Gaul, first century BCE. Bibliothèque nationale de France 7163. | |
| 3.17–3.18 | Greek silver coins for the Romans? | 93 |
| 3.17 | Roman Macedonia, silver tetradrachm inscribed Aesillas, first century BCE. Bibliothèque nationale de France FG 112. | |
| 3.18 | Leucas in Acarnania, silver stater inscribed Bathyos, first century BCE. Bibliothèque nationale de France FG 69. | |
| 3.19 | The Thessalian *diorthoma*. | 94 |
| | Thessalian League, silver stater, first century BCE. Bibliothèque nationale de France Delepierre 1154. | |
| 3.20 | Bronze coin of Thessalonica with Janus head. | 95 |
| | American Numismatic Society 1944.100.10742. | |
| 3.21 | Mark Antony, 'fleet coinage'. | 95 |
| | As *RPC I*, 1454. Münzkabinett der Staatlichen Museen zu Berlin, 18215848. Photographs by Dirk Sonnenwald. | |
| 3.22–3.24 | Coins of the triumvirs from Thessalonica. | 96 |
| 3.22 | Thessalonica, bronze coin, 37 BCE (?), as *RPC I*, 1551. American Numismatic Society 1944.100.11863. | |
| 3.23 | Thessalonica, bronze coin, 37 BCE (?), as *RPC I*, 1552. American Numismatic Society 1944.100.11859. | |
| 3.24 | Thessalonica, bronze coin, 37 BCE (?), as *RPC I*, 1553. Numismatica Ars Classica 123, 9 May 2021, lot 202. | |
| 3.25–3.26 | Pergamene and Roman cistophori. | 97 |
| 3.25 | Kingdom of Pergamum, silver cistophorus, mint of Ephesus, about 150 BCE. Bibliothèque nationale de France Waddington 6869. | |
| 3.26 | Roman Asia, silver cistophorus, mint of Ephesus, with date 49 = 86/5 BCE. Bibliothèque nationale de France 2667. | |

**xvi** List of Figures

| | | |
|---|---|---|
| 3.27–3.28 | Bronze asses from Lampsacus (about 45 BCE) and an uncertain mint in Asia Minor (about 40 BCE). | 100 |
| 3.27 | Lampsacus, Roman colony, about 45 BCE, as *RPC I*, 2273. American Numismatic Society 2015.20.1180. | |
| 3.28 | Mark Antony, Roman Asia Minor, uncertain mint, signed by Atratinus augur, about 40 BCE. *RPC I*, 2226. American Numismatic Society 2015.20.1935. | |
| 3.29 | The invention of brass. Brass coin of Apamea, mid first century BCE. British Museum 1889,0710.3 = BMC Apamea 44. Photographs by the author. | 100 |
| 3.30 | Roma on a bronze coin of Nicaea. American Numismatic Society 2015.20.2703. | 101 |
| 3.31 | Veni, vidi, vici. Bronze coin of Nicaea, as *RPC I*, 2026, with date 236 = 47/6 BCE. Classical Numismatic Group 112, 11 September 2019, lot 421. | 102 |
| 3.32 | Tarcondimotus of Cilicia. As *RPC I*, 3871. Naville 54, 2019, lot 234. | 103 |
| 3.33 | Bronze coin inscribed 'year 1 of Rome', 64/3 BCE. American Numismatic Society 2015.20.3542. | 104 |
| 3.34 | Roman Syria, silver tetradrachm with the monogram of Aulus Gabinius, governor in 57–55 BCE. As *RPC I*, 4124. Bibliothèque nationale de France Luynes 3427. | 105 |
| 3.35 | Cleopatra and Mark Antony, *c.* 36 BCE. Silver tetradrachm, as *RPC I*, 4094. American Numismatic Society 1977.158.621. | 105 |
| 3.36 | Augustus and Actium on a coin of Pella. As *RPC I*, 1548. Leu WA 3, 25 February 2018, lot 506. | 108 |
| 4.1–4.2 | Coins signed by Roman quaestors. | 111 |
| 4.1 | Roman Macedonia, L. Fulcinnius quaestor, second century BCE. Bibliothèque nationale de France FG 105. | |
| 4.2 | Octavian (?), Amisus, Pontus, anonymous quaestor, late first century BCE, as *RPC I*, 2156. Classical Numismatic Group 374, 18 May 2011, lot 368. | |
| 4.3–4.4 | The Bronze coinage of Antioch. | 112 |

List of Figures  **xvii**

4.3 Galba (68–9), Antioch, bronze coin, as *RPC I*, 4314. Bibliothèque nationale de France FG 251.

4.4 Galba (68–9), Antioch, bronze coin, signed by the imperial legate C. Licinius Mucianus, as *RPC I*, 4313. Münzkabinett, Staatliche Museen zu Berlin, 18257569. Photographs by Bernhard Weisser.

4.5 Coin of the League of 13 Cities. 113
As *RPC IV.2* temporary number 1019. Bibliothèque nationale de France FG 1111.85.

4.6–4.7 Competition between cities. 114

4.6 Gordian III (238–44), Magnesia ad Maeandrum, Lydia, as *RPC VII.*1, 552. American Numismatic Society 1944.100.46489.

4.7 Gallienus (253–68), Nysa, Lydia. CGT Collection.

4.8–4.9 Portraits and autonomy. 115

4.8 Demos, Eucarpia, Phrygia, about 150 CE, as *RPC IV.2*, temporary number 2010. Bibliothèque nationale de France Waddington 5988.

4.9 Boule, Accilaeum, Phrygia, third century CE, as *RPC VII.1*, 678. Münzkabinett, Staatliche Museen zu Berlin, 18202001. Photographs by Reinhard Saczewski.

4.10 Lucian and the false prophet Alexander. 116
Lucius Verus (161–9), Abonoteichus, as *RPC IV.1*, temporary number 5364. Bibliothèque nationale de France FG 485.

4.11–4.12 *Damnatio memoriae.* 117

4.11 Nero (54–68), Tripolis, Phoenicia, bronze coin, countermarked for Otho (69), as *RPC I*, 4520. Bibliothèque nationale de France Babelon 1905.

4.12 Caracalla (198–217) and Geta, Stratonicea, Caria, bronze coin, as BMC 70. Bibliothèque nationale de France FG 967.

4.13–4.14 Proposing a Coinage at Ancyra. 118

4.13 Nero (54–68) and Poppaea, Ancyra, Phrygia, bronze coin, as *RPC I*, 3111. Münzkabinett, Staatliche Museen zu Berlin, 18201913. Photographs by Reinhard Saczewski.

4.14 Senate, Ancyra, Phrygia, reign of Nero (54–68), bronze coin, as *RPC I*, 3113. Bibliothèque nationale de France Waddington 5629.

# xviii List of Figures

4.15 Antinous and Polemo at Smyrna. 119
Bronze coin, as *RPC III*, 1975. Bibliothèque nationale de
France FG 2253.
4.16 The mint building of Alexandria. 120
Lucius Verus (161–9), bronze drachm, mint of
Alexandria. As *RPC IV.4* temporary number 14030.
American Numismatic Society 1944.100.61693.
4.17–4.18 Coins of Chios with denominations. 125
4.17 Chios, bronze 3-as coin, signed by Aur. Chrysogonos,
third century. Münzkabinett, Staatliche Museen zu Berlin,
18202607. Photographs by Lutz-Jürgen Lübke.
4.18 Chios, bronze dichalkon, second century, as *RPC III*,
1899. Münzkabinett, Staatliche Museen zu Berlin,
18202619. Photographs by Lutz-Jürgen Lübke.

5.1 *Pax Romana* established. 129
Augustus, silver cistophorus, as *RPC I*, 2203/2,
Münzkabinett der Staatlichen Museen zu Berlin,
18202459. Photographs by Dirk Sonnenwald.
5.2 Gabinius at Nysa-Scythopolis. 132
As *RPC I*, 4828A. American Numismatic Society
2015.20.1724.
5.3 Julius Caesar at Lampsacus. 133
As *RPC I*, 2269/3. Münzkabinett der Staatlichen
Museen zu Berlin, 18270435. Photographs by Bernhard
Weisser.
5.4 The triumvirs at Ephesus. 134
As *RPC I*, 2569. Münzkabinett der Staatlichen Museen zu
Berlin, 18203581. Photographs by Lutz-Jürgen Lübke.
5.5 Mark Antony at Ptolemais. 135
As *RPC I*, 4740. American Numismatic Society
2008.24.9.
5.6 L. Sempronius Atratinus, Sparta, 30s BCE. 135
As *RPC I*, 1101A. Naumann 119, 7 August 2022,
lot 422.
5.7–5.8 The adoption of the portrait of Augustus. 136
5.7 Augustus (31 BCE–14 CE), Ebora, Spain, as *RPC I*, 51.
Münzkabinett der Staatlichen Museen zu Berlin,
18237441. Photographs by Lutz-Jürgen Lübke.

| | | |
|---|---|---|
| 5.8 | Augustus, with Gaius and Lucius, Amisus, Pontus, 2/1 BCE, as *RPC I*, 2148/8. Numismatica Ars Classica 72, 16 May 2013, lot 1419. | |
| 5.9 | Augustus and the *lituus*. | 138 |
| | Augustus, bronze coin of Laodicea, as *RPC I*, 2894. Münzkabinett der Staatlichen Museen zu Berlin, 18240968. Photographs by Lutz-Jürgen Lübke. | |
| 5.10–5.11 | Agrippa on provincial coins. | 139 |
| 5.10 | Augustus and Agrippa, Nemausus, Gaul, as *RPC I*, 525. Münzkabinett der Staatlichen Museen zu Berlin, 18202605. Photographs by Dirk Sonnenwald. | |
| 5.11 | Augustus and Agrippa, Apamea, Bithynia, as *RPC I*, 2008. Nomos obolos 5, 26 June 2016, lot 516. With thanks to Nomos AG. | |
| 5.12 | Caesonia, the wife of Caligula. | 140 |
| | Bronze coin minted by Agrippa I, King of Judaea, as *RPC I*, 4977. Classical Numismatic Group 531, 25 January 2023, lot 634. | |
| 5.13–5.14 | Female members of the imperial house. | 141 |
| 5.13 | Livia and Julia, Pergamum, Mysia, as *RPC I*, 2359. Münzkabinett der Staatlichen Museen zu Berlin, 18265750. Photographs by Lutz-Jürgen Lübke. | |
| 5.14 | Messalina, third wife of Claudius (41–54), Nicaea, Bithynia, as *RPC I*, 2038. Bibliothèque nationale de France 794. | |
| 5.15–5.16 | Coins of Laodicea and Hierapolis with similar portraits. | 143 |
| 5.15 | Nero (54–68), Laodicea, Phrygia, as *RPC I*, 2917. Classical Numismatic Group 327, 28 May 2014, lot 822. | |
| 5.16 | Nero, Hierapolis, Phrygia, as *RPC I*, 2975. Classical Numismatic Group 90, 23 May 2012, lot 1090. | |
| 5.17 | Nero and the freedom of the Greeks. | 143 |
| | Bronze coin of Patras, as *RPC I*, 1279. Bibliothèque nationale de France 1249. | |
| 5.18 | A long and abbreviated inscription. | 145 |
| | Domitian, bronze coin of Nicaea, as *RPC II*, 637. Bibliothèque nationale de France Waddington 810. | |
| 5.19–5.20 | The temple of Augustus at Pergamum. | 149 |

xx List of Figures

5.19 Augustus, Pergamum, as *RPC I*, 2358. Münzkabinett der Staatlichen Museen zu Berlin, 18207868. Photographs by Lutz-Jürgen Lübke.

5.20 The Demoi of Pergamum and Sardis, minted by Pergamum, about 1 BCE, as *RPC I*, 2362. Münzkabinett der Staatlichen Museen zu Berlin, 18266356. Photographs by Lutz-Jürgen Lübke.

5.21 Claudius at Mopsus, Cilicia, south-east Turkey. 150
As *RPC I*, 4054. Classical Numismatic Group MBS 64, 24 September 2003, lot 666.

5.22–5.23 Augustan coins from north Africa. 151

5.22 Augustus, Lepti Minus, Africa, as *RPC I*, 784. Bibliothèque nationale de France 2007.52.

5.23 Augustus, Hadrumetum, Africa, as *RPC I*, 777. Bibliothèque nationale de France 1067.

5.24 The first Roman coins to use brass in the west. 153
Julius Caesar with C. Clovius, as *RPC I*, 601. American Numismatic Society 1969.222.63.

5.25 Tiberius and the deified Augustus, Mytilene. 154
As *RPC I*, 2343. British Museum 1875,0404.1 = BMC Mytilene 186. © The Trustees of the British Museum.

5.26–5.31 Some regional bronze coinages under Augustus. 160

5.26 Coin inscribed Avavcia, Gaul, late first century BCE. Bibliothèque nationale de France 8868 (GAU-9309).

5.27 Augustus, sestertius, mint of Lugdunum, as *RIC I*, Augustus 231. Münzkabinett der Staatlichen Museen zu Berlin, 18202597. Photographs by Dirk Sonnenwald.

5.28 Augustus, sestertius, mint of Rome, signed by the moneyer M. Sanquinius, about 20 BCE, as *RIC I*, Augustus 341. Bibliothèque nationale de France BNC Auguste 281.

5.29 Augustus, Alexandria in Troas, as *RPC I*, 1656. Münzkabinett der Staatlichen Museen zu Berlin, 18241718. Photographs by Lutz-Jürgen Lübke.

5.30 Augustus, 'CA' sestertius, Asia, as *RPC I*, 2233. Münzkabinett der Staatlichen Museen zu Berlin, 18202464. Photographs by Dirk Sonnenwald.

## List of Figures    xxi

5.31  Augustus, Antioch, Syria, SC bronze, as *RPC I*, 4248.
Münzkabinett der Staatlichen Museen zu Berlin, 18215627.
Photographs by Dirk Sonnenwald.

5.32  Domitian and the grant of coinage to Achaea.   164
Bronze coin of Patras, as *RPC II*, 219. Bibliothèque
nationale de France 1230.

5.33–5.34  Base metal coins made in Rome, intended for circulation
in the east.   166

5.33  Domitian, on a coin of Agrippa II, King of Judaea,
dated 85/6, as *RPC III*, 2269. American Numismatic Society
1944.100.62891.

5.34  Hadrian (117–38), orichalcum coin for Syria, as
*RPC III*, 3674. American Numismatic Society
1953.171.624.

5.35  The last provincial coins in the west.   170
Claudius, bronze coin of Ebusus, as *RPC I*, 482.
Bibliothèque nationale de France B 511.

5.36–5.37  Agrippa at Caesaraugusta and Rome.   171

5.36  M. Agrippa, Caesaraugusta, Spain. Reign of Caligula
(37–41), as *RPC I*, 386. Münzkabinett der Staatlichen
Museen zu Berlin, 18222478. Photographs by Reinhard
Saczewski.

5.37  M. Agrippa, Rome, reign of Caligula, as *RIC I*, Gaius 58.
American Numismatic Society 1937.158.461.

6.1  Aureus of Hadrian proclaiming a Golden Age.   175
As *RIC II.3*, Hadrian 297. Bibliothèque nationale
de France IMP-70.

6.2–6.3  The first die link between cities.   178

6.2  Trajan, Colophon, Ionia, as *RPC III*, 2005.
Münzkabinett der Staatlichen Museen zu Berlin,
18269317. Photographs by Karsten Dahmen.

6.3  Trajan, Metropolis, Ionia, as *RPC III*, 2010. British
Museum BMC Metropolis 56.2. © The Trustees of the
British Museum.

6.4–6.6  Coins of Julia Domna, the wife of Septimius Severus,
struck with the same obverse die.   180

## List of Figures

6.4 Julia Domna, wife of Septimius Severus (193–211), Smyrna, Ionia, British Museum BMC Smyrna 389. © The Trustees of the British Museum.

6.5 Julia Domna, Clazomenae, Ionia. British Museum 1845,1217.20 = BMC Clazomenae 126. © The Trustees of the British Museum.

6.6 Julia Domna, Ephesus, Ionia. Classical Numismatic Group 217, 26 August 2009, lot 272.

6.7 The last small denomination coins from Egypt.  183
Antoninus Pius, as *RPC IV*, temporary number 16083. Bibliothèque nationale de France 2380 = SNG 2737.

6.8 The last small denominations in Asia Minor.  187
Cyme, bronze coin, reign of Valerian and Gallienus (253–60). American Numismatic Society 1944.100.44144.

6.9 Commodus from Coela in Thrace.  189
As *RPC IV*, temporary number 10949. Münzkabinett der Staatlichen Museen zu Berlin, 18235374. Photographs by Reinhard Saczewski.

6.10 Marcus Aurelius from Cyrenaica.  192
As *RPC IV*, temporary number 6852. Bibliothèque nationale de France Caesarea FG 465.

6.11 Trajan, from Cydonia, Crete.  192
As *RPC III*, 110. Bibliothèque nationale de France FG 245.

6.12 Trajan from Tomi.  194
As *RPC III*, 779. Bibliothèque nationale de France 2001.503.

6.13 Bilingual coin of Domitian from Philippopolis, Thrace (modern Plovdiv).  195
As *RPC II*, 351. Münzkabinett der Staatlichen Museen zu Berlin, 18247974. Photographs by Lutz-Jürgen Lübke.

6.14 Claudius, Koinon of Cyprus.  195
As *RPC I*, 3928. Bibliothèque nationale de France FG 793.

6.15 The coinage of Hadrian from Elis.  198
As *RPC III*, 308. Münzkabinett der Staatlichen Museen zu Berlin, 18200646. Photographs by Reinhard Saczewski.

6.16 The Temple of Artemis at Ephesus – one of the Seven Wonders of the Ancient World.  199
Hadrian, as *RPC III*, 2073. Bibliothèque nationale de France FG 673.

|       |                                                      |     |
|-------|------------------------------------------------------|-----|
| 6.17  | Vows for the imperial cult at Ephesus.               | 200 |

Macrinus, Ephesus. Bibliothèque nationale de France FG 866.

6.18 The early Greek philosopher Heraclitus celebrated on imperial coins of Ephesus. 201
As *RPC IV*, temporary number 1125. Bibliothèque nationale de France M 4432.

6.19 Pergamum under Commodus as Caesar. 202
As *RPC IV*, temporary number 3244. Münzkabinett der Staatlichen Museen zu Berlin, 18231822. Photographs by Lutz-Jürgen Lübke.

6.20–6.21 The great altar of Zeus at Pergamum. 203

6.20 Septimius Severus and Julia Domna, Pergamum.
Numismatica Ars Classica 88, 8 October 2015, lot 664.

6.21 Great Altar of Pergamum, second century BCE.
Pergamonmuseum, Berlin, Pe 1. Photo: Staatliche Museen zu Berlin, Antikensammlung. https://id.smb.museum/object/829881.

6.22 The sophist Attalus at Smyrna. 205
Marcus Aurelius, as *RPC IV*, temporary number 2943.
Bibliothèque nationale de France FG 2262.

6.23 Anazarbus, adorned with Roman trophies. 205
Julia Maesa, grandmother of Elagabalus (218–22), as *RPC VI*, temporary number 7264. Classical Numismatic Group EA 129, 21 December 2005, lot 198.

6.24 'Concord' between Philadelphia and Ephesus. 206
Trajan Decius (249–51), as *RPC IX*, 722. Bibliothèque nationale de France FG 1033.

6.25 The 'pseudo-autonomous' coinage of Tyre, Phoenicia, 152/3. 207
As *RPC IV.3*, temporary number 2258. American Numismatic Society 1944.100.73058.

6.26 Dido and the foundation of Carthage. 209
Gordian III (238–44), Tyre, Phoenicia, as *RPC VII.2*, 3565. British Museum 1970,0909.242. © The Trustees of the British Museum.

6.27 The invention of the Greek alphabet by Cadmus. 209
Philip (244–49), Tyre, as *RPC VIII*, temporary number 2767. Triton XXII, 8 January 2019, lot 729.

**xxiv**  List of Figures

6.28 A Victory temple of Domitian at Loadicea. 210
As *RPC II*, 1284. British Museum 1872,0709.314 = BMC
Laodicea 185. © The Trustees of the British Museum.

6.29 Temple enclosing the 'Dacian Victor', i.e., Trajan,
celebrated on coins of Silandus under Lucius Verus. 211
As *RPC IV*, temporary number 1757. Yale University
Art Gallery 2009.110.57.

6.30 Coin of Amasea in Pontus, minted for Lucius Verus and
showing the emperors Marcus Aurelius and Lucius
Verus in civilian dress and clasping hands. 211
As *RPC IV*, temporary number 1255. Bibliothèque
nationale de France FG 894.

6.31 Trajan in triumph. 213
Trajan, Alexandria, Egypt, as *RPC III*, 4798. Fritz
Rudolf Künker GmbH & Co. KG, Osnabrück Auction
182, 14 March 2011, lot 645. Photographs by Lübke &
Wiedemann, Leonberg.

6.32 Tutu or sphinx? 214
Hadrian (117–38), Alexandria, Egypt, as *RPC III*, 5909.
Münzkabinett der Staatlichen Museen zu Berlin,
18201166. Photographs by Reinhard Saczewski.

6.33 Hadrian and the bear hunt. 215
Hadrianotherae, Mysia, as *RPC III*, 1626. Leu 24, 3
December 2022, lot 2126.

6.34 Veterans at Berytus. 216
Hadrian, as *RPC III*, 3855. Bibliothèque nationale de
France FG 1234.

6.35 Marsyas with a wineskin, depicted at the colony of
Laodicea in Syria in the reign of Macrinus. 217
Bibliothèque nationale de France Laodicea Y 23879.179.

6.36–6.37 The problem of Antinous, Hadrian's lover. 219

6.36 Antinous, Amphictyons, Greece, as *RPC III*, 444/1.
Bibliothèque nationale de France 218a (Luynes 2308).

6.37 Antinous, Tarsus, Phoenicia, as *RPC III*, 3285.
Münzkabinett der Staatlichen Museen zu Berlin,
18200843. Photographs by Reinhard Saczewski.

## List of Figures    **xxv**

7.1   Crude engraving in the third century.    223
Gallienus (253–68), Salonina and Valerian II, Panemoteichus,
Pisidia. British Museum 1974,0102.40. © The Trustees of the
British Museum.

7.2–7.3   Aemilian and Supera    224

7.2   Aemilian (253), Alexandria, as *RPC IX*, 2332. Classical
Numismatic Group 481, 2 December 2020, lot 275.

7.3   Cornelia Supera, wife of Aemilian, Iulia Gordus, Lydia, as
*RPC IX*, 896. Bibliothèque nationale de France 1403.

7.4   Severus Alexander, from Byzantium.    225
As *RPC VI*, temporary number 900. Münzkabinett der
Staatlichen Museen zu Berlin, 18235869. Photographs by
Reinhard Saczewski.

7.5   The divine ruler as protector of the empire.    226
Gordian III (238–44), Tomi, Pontus, as *RPC VII.2*, 1676.
Münzkabinett der Staatlichen Museen zu Berlin, 18278165.
Photographs by Bernhard Weisser.

7.6   Coins of Tium, in north-west Asia Minor, show a portrait of
Julia Maesa, the grandmother of Elagabalus (218–22), holding
a poppy flower.    228
Tium, Bithynia, as *RPC VI*, temporary number 2874. Classical
Numismatic Group 90, 23 May 2012, lot 953.

7.7–7.8   Caracalla at Pergamum and Laodicea.    229

7.7   Caracalla (198–217), Pergamum, Mysia. Numismatica Ars
Classica 54, 24 March 2010, lot 504.

7.8   Caracalla, Laodicea, Phrygia. British Museum 1872,0709.315
= BMC Laodicea 226. © The Trustees of the British Museum.

7.9   Caracalla at Laodicea.    230
Münzkabinett der Staatlichen Museen zu Berlin, 18225044.
Photographs by Lutz-Jürgen Lübke.

7.10   Coins of Elagabalus from Nicomedia celebrate its award of
three neocorate temples for Augustus, Septimius Severus
and Elagabalus.    231
As *RPC VI*, temporary number 3354. Fritz Rudolf Künker
GmbH & Co. KG, Osnabrück Auction 273, 14 March 2016,
lot 853. Photographs by Lübke & Wiedemann, Leonberg.

7.11   Prize crowns at Side.    232
Valerian. Classical Numismatic Group EA 413, 31 January
2018, lot 256.

**xxvi** List of Figures

7.12 Elagabalus, Laodicea (Asia). 233
As *RPC VI*, temporary number 5498. Bibliothèque nationale de France 1696.

7.13 Trajan Decius, Philadelphia. 233
As *RPC IX*, 716. Bibliothèque nationale de France 1034.

7.14 Coins of Philip from Bizya in Thrace (in European Turkey) give a simplified bird's eye view of the city. 234
As *RPC VIII*, temporary number 306. Bibliothèque nationale de France 2013.208.

7.15 Noah's Ark. 235
Philip I, Apamea, Phrygia, as *RPC VIII*, temporary number 1630. Leu 7, 24 October 2020, lot 1457. On loan to the Israel Museum.

7.16–7.17 Myth and history at Abydus. 236

7.16 Septimius Severus (193–211), Abydus, Troas. Münzkabinett der Staatlichen Museen zu Berlin, 18221501. Photographs by Bernhard Weisser.

7.17 As 7.16. Boston, Museum of Fine Arts 2002.24 (photo from Triton 5, 15 January 2002, lot 176).

7.18 An acclamation for the emperors at Prusias, Bithynia. 237
Caracalla. Ashmolean Museum. Image © Ashmolean Museum, University of Oxford.

7.19–7.20 Coins of Sparta with value marks. 243

7.19 Julia Domna, wife of Septimius Severus, Sparta, Peloponnese. British Museum 1885,0606.44 = BMC Sparta 83. © The Trustees of the British Museum.

7.20 Gallienus (253–68), Sparta. Classical Numismatic Group 442, 17 April 2019, lot 648.

7.21 A bronze denarius? 245
Gallienus, Sinope, Paphlagonia. American Numismatic Society 1944.100.41884.

7.22–7.23 Values at Colybrassus. 248

7.22 Valerian (253–60), Colybrassus, Cilicia. American Numismatic Society 1973.191.115.

7.23 Salonina, wife of Gallienus, Colybrassus. British Museum 1874,0716.93 = BMC Colybrassus 12. © The Trustees of the British Museum.

7.24 Large bronze coin minted for Antoninus Pius by Pautalia in Thrace. 251

|        |                                                                                                 |      |
|--------|-------------------------------------------------------------------------------------------------|------|
|        | As *RPC IV*, temporary number 3925. American Numismatic Society 1975.249.1.7.21.                |      |
| 7.25   | Gordian III, from Daldis in Lydia.                                                               | 252  |
|        | As *RPC VII.1*, 200. Triton 20, 10 January 2017, lot 455.                                        |      |
| 7.26–7.27 | Sestertii from Rome and Viminacium for Gordian III, 239 CE.                                   | 254  |
| 7.26   | Gordian III, sestertius, Rome, as *RIC IV.3*, Gordian III 259A. American Numismatic Society 1995.11.1373. | |
| 7.27   | Gordian III, sestertius, Viminacium, as *RPC VII.2*, 1. Classical Numismatic Group 360, 30 Sept. 2015, lot 237. | |
| 7.28   | Syrian tetradrachms minted in Rome.                                                             | 254  |
|        | Philip I. As *RPC VIII*, temporary number 2379. American Numismatic Society 1944.100.59072.     |      |
| 7.29   | The Asian Games at Smyrna.                                                                      | 260  |
|        | Gallienus. Münzkabinett der Staatlichen Museen zu Berlin, 18202508. Photographs by Reinhard Saczewski. | |
| 7.30   | Perge under Tacitus: The last city coins of the Roman Empire.                                    | 261  |
|        | Münzkabinett der Staatlichen Museen zu Berlin, 18268139. Photographs by Bernhard Weisser.        |      |
| 7.31   | The last provincial coins from Egypt.                                                           | 263  |
|        | Constantius I, as Caesar (293–305). American Numismatic Society 1965.32.39.                       |      |
| 7.32   | Countermarking to revalue coins.                                                               | 266  |
|        | As *RPC VI*, temporary number 3569. Münzkabinett der Staatlichen Museen zu Berlin, 18221296. Photographs by Dirk Sonnenwald. | |
| 7.33   | The coming of Christianity.                                                                     | 269  |
|        | British Museum 1906.1010.1. © The Trustees of the British Museum.                               |      |
| 7.34   | Diocletian, mint of Ticinum (modern Pavia).                                                     | 270  |
|        | As *RIC VI*, Ticinum 27a. Münzkabinett der Staatlichen Museen zu Berlin, 18235385. Photographs by Reinhard Saczewski. | |

# Maps

| | | |
|---|---|---|
| 1.1 | The Roman provinces | *page* 3 |
| 1.2 | The main silver mints in Italy *c.* 300 BCE | 5 |
| 1.3 | 'Iberian denarii' | 15 |
| 1.4 | The principal provincial silver mints under the Empire | 20 |
| 2.1 | Hoards of bronze and silver in third-century Italy | 52 |
| 5.1 | Cities making coins with the portrait of Mark Antony | 135 |
| 5.2 | Cities making coins with the portrait of Augustus | 136 |
| 5.3 | Cities in the Maeander valley with a common style of portraiture, first century CE | 142 |
| 5.4 | The incidence of brass on provincial city coins in the Julio-Claudian period | 156 |
| 5.5 | The main bronze mints under Augustus | 159 |
| 6.1 | Die- and style-links between cities, in the reign of Gordian III (238–44) | 181 |
| 6.2 | Changes to the 'numismatic border' between the western and eastern parts of the Empire | 196 |
| 6.3 | Cities (24) making coins which portrayed Marcus Aurelius and Lucius Verus standing together and clasping hands | 212 |
| 6.4 | Cities minting coins for Antinous | 218 |
| 6.5 | Cities making coins for Antinous of medallic size | 220 |
| 7.1 | Silver mints in the late third century CE | 256 |

# Boxes

| | | |
|---|---|---|
| 1.1 | Silver minting in Italy during the third century BCE | *page* 8 |
| 1.2 | The 'Hopkins graph' | 12 |
| 1.3 | 'Iberian denarii' | 14 |
| 1.4 | Nero's reforms of the coinage | 23 |
| 1.5 | The value of silver coins in imperial Asia | 30 |
| 1.6 | The production and use of gold coinage in the ancient world | 33 |
| 1.7 | The scale of Roman gold in the 40s BCE | 38 |
| 1.8 | A gold or silver monetary economy? | 39 |
| 1.9 | The wide circulation of Roman gold | 40 |
| 2.1 | The pattern of bronze minting in Italy during the third century BCE | 54 |
| 2.2 | The hoard from Nora, Sardinia | 60 |
| 2.3 | The minting of bronze coinage in third-century BCE Sicily | 63 |
| 2.4 | The currency of the western Mediterranean in the third century BCE | 73 |
| 2.5 | The currency of the western Mediterranean during the Second Punic War | 74 |
| 3.1 | The Cordova hoard | 85 |
| 3.2 | The Thessalian *diorthoma* | 94 |
| 3.3 | The coinage of Ephesus in the first century BCE | 98 |
| 3.4 | The Roman silver coinage from Antioch at the end of the Republic | 104 |
| 3.5 | The changing patterns of currency in the Roman world during the Republican period | 106 |
| 4.1 | Portraits and autonomy | 115 |
| 4.2 | Provincial mint buildings | 120 |
| 4.3 | Coins for Sestus, Thrace | 124 |
| 4.4 | Moneychangers' abuses | 126 |
| 4.5 | The pattern of coins found in excavations | 127 |
| 5.1 | The portrait of Augustus | 136 |
| 5.2 | Emperors as gods | 141 |
| 5.3 | The number of words on the obverses of early imperial provincial coins | 146 |
| 5.4 | The increasing diversity of reverse designs | 148 |

| | | |
|---|---|---|
| 5.5 | Buildings on coins | 149 |
| 5.6 | Augustan coins from Spain | 152 |
| 5.7 | The quality of brass | 155 |
| 5.8 | The increasing size of provincial coins of Asia in the first century CE | 157 |
| 5.9 | The number of cities producing coinage in Achaea in the later first century CE | 164 |
| 5.10 | The approximate diameters and average weights for orichalcum coins made in Rome 'for the East' | 167 |
| 5.11 | The end of city coinage in the west | 169 |
| 6.1 | The increase in production of provincial coins | 176 |
| 6.2 | Possible denominations at Smyrna | 184 |
| 6.3 | The changing pattern of denominations at Smyrna | 184 |
| 6.4 | Latin and Greek at Roman colonies | 190 |
| 6.5 | Temples on coins | 199 |
| 6.6 | The imperial neocorate | 200 |
| 7.1 | Games on third-century coins | 231 |
| 7.2 | Calculating the output of provincial coins in the third century CE | 238 |
| 7.3 | Obverse dies used by Smyrna and in Lydia | 241 |
| 7.4 | The numbers of coins for each *RPC* volume from the 'core collections' | 241 |
| 7.5 | Value marks on coins of Sparta | 244 |
| 7.6 | New values under Valerian | 246 |
| 7.7 | The declining weights of coins | 247 |
| 7.8 | Values present on coins of cities in Pamphylia and Pisidia in the reigns of Valerian and Gallienus | 250 |
| 7.9 | New silver mints in the third century | 255 |
| 7.10 | The number of cities whose coinage ceased, by reign, before Valerian | 265 |

# Preface

## The Roman Empire and Its Coinage(s)

> In Gratidianus' praetorship the tribunes of the people summoned the college of praetors to council, so that in order that the matter of the coinage should be settled . . . For at that time the coin was being thrown about so much that no one could tell what he had. They drafted an edict, defining the penalty and the legal process . . . Gratidianus went straight to the rostra and gave out the edict on his own . . . And the affair brought him great honours; statues in every street, with incense and candles. No one has ever been more popular with the masses.
>
> (Cicero, *de Officiis* III.80)

Coinage was an essential part of the fabric of Roman life: what happened to it mattered. The history of Roman coinage is part of the history of Rome. The growth of Roman power and the establishment of a Roman Empire in the Mediterranean and northern Europe is reflected in the growing spread of Roman coinage and its adaptation to meet the reality – and the changing realities – of the new empire. The coinages used in the expanding Roman territories can be explained by the history of the times and, in turn, can add significantly to our understanding of those times.

Some of this is well understood. The so-called 'mainstream' Roman coinage – the silver, bronze and, later, gold coins, produced mainly in the city of Rome and which circulated throughout all or most of the Empire – has been studied for centuries. Its production, designs, physical composition and expanding areas of circulation mirror the changing politics and economic expansion of the Roman state from its emergence as a world power in the third century BCE until the fall of the Empire many centuries later. The 'crisis' of the third century CE – a crisis whose existence it is fashionable today to query – is, in fact, all too evident in the coinage: the collapse of the silver coinage, the pressure on the gold, the dispersal of minting and the ending of bronze coinage are all effects of the military and economic disasters of the period. The new political order of the later Empire, most commonly associated with the names of the emperors Diocletian (284–305) and Constantine (306–37), started to emerge from the reign of Aurelian (270–5), and saw a fundamental change in the coinage system of the Roman world: from a fairly stable system with a clear relationship between coins made from the different metals to one where gold predominated, and the base metal coinage floated in value against it.

The late Roman coinage was wholly under centralised control. A network of imperial mints, established essentially in or near the frontier zones, produced coins in a unified system of denominations and a common set of designs. The coins could, in principle, circulate anywhere in the Empire, and their production reflected the government's need to protect the frontiers and pay for the soldiers who were required to defend them. The coinage and tax systems were aligned to guarantee a ready supply of gold, and, in turn, to ensure the loyalty of the army.

The previous five centuries – since the introduction of the first Roman coins in around 300 BCE – had been very different. As Roman armies conquered new territories and the overwhelming nature of Roman power saw others cede their sovereignty, the Romans encountered and inherited a kaleidoscope of different coinages and financial systems. One of the characteristics of Roman imperialism – perhaps one of the pillars of its success – was to preserve local systems of government or political organisation as far as they remained compatible with the intentions of the elite – the Senate in the Republican period and subsequently the emperor. This was also true of the coinage in what became, after annexation or conquest, the provinces of the Roman Empire.

## Coinage in the Provinces

The increasing specialisation of studies of the past in the nineteenth century led to quite a sharp divide between 'the Roman Imperial Coinage proper' (the gold, silver and bronze produced mainly in Rome) and 'Greek Imperial Coinage'. The latter term was applied to most of the other coinages used in different parts of the Empire. They had a limited circulation and, in the Roman east, they were inscribed in Greek, the standard language of the eastern part of the Roman Empire: hence 'Greek'. 'Imperial' meant produced under the Roman Empire, generally with a portrait of the reigning emperor. The last thirty years or so have seen the gradual erosion of this split between the two categories of coinage, reflecting the less legalistic and more fluid approach of many modern Roman historians. Out of the window have gone concepts such as a rigid distinction between 'imperial' and 'senatorial' provinces, or the intense studies of the legal basis of the power of the emperor. They have been replaced by a greater emphasis on what actually happened, rather than any theoretical system which may or may not have underlain it. So too with the coinage: few scholars nowadays believe that the prominent letters SC (*Senatus consulto* = 'by decree of the Senate') mean that the Roman Senate exercised any real power over the bronze coinages which were marked with these letters. So too, few nowadays believe in a system of 'the right to coin', whereby a community might be permitted by the central power to produce its own coinage: a medieval and early modern concept that had only a limited validity in the ancient classical world. Of course, the Roman government could intervene – and intervene dramatically – if it wanted to, and several examples will be discussed later in this book. However, such interventions were unusual, and for the most part the local coinages in the areas taken over by the Romans were left to develop without intervention or any effective control beyond the cities which produced them. As a result, they give us a view from the perspective of one slice of the Roman population – the elites who ran the hundreds of individual cities which were the backbone of Roman society.

**Figure P.1** A view of the city of Amasea, in Pontus (northern Asia Minor), minted under the emperor Severus Alexander.
The circuit of defensive walls rises up the mountain and surrounds a selective view of the interior. Two temple facades can be seen, as well as other buildings. The coin has the inscription ΑΔΡ ϹΕΥ ΑΛΕΞ ΑΜΑϹΙΑϹ ΜΗΤ ΝΕΩ ΠΡ ΠΟΝ ΕΤ ϹΚΗ. It is highly abbreviated, to get as much boastful information on to the coin as possible, and refers to the favours granted to the city by the emperors Hadrian, Septimius Severus and Severus Alexander; that it was the mother city (metropolis) of the region; that it was the city which had won the right to have a temple of the emperor ('neocorate'); and that it was the first city of Pontus: 'Of the Hadrianic, Severan and Alexandrian Amasia, metropolis, neocorate, and first city of Pontus, in year 228 [= 225/6 CE]'. Amasea was also the home city of the Roman writer Strabo, who described it much earlier in his *Geography* (12.3.39) as being 'wonderfully appointed both by human design and by nature, and at once being able to provide the benefits of both a city and a fortress'. (*RPC VI* temporary number 6467)

xxxiv    Preface

They give us a picture below that of most written history, written by famous authors like Tacitus or Cassius Dio, who were Roman senators, or like Livy and Suetonius, who mixed with the highest echelons of Roman society. The picture from coins is, at the same time, above that which archaeology can reveal about the lives of ordinary people. Thus the perspective of these city coins is unique, and needs to be valued and interpreted as such.

The 'developments' which the provincial coinages underwent were gradual, but cumulatively fundamental. By adopting a largely chronological analysis,[1] this book seeks to explore and explain them, and in this way show how the provincial coinage as a whole can be explained by the changes which took place in the Roman world, and how, in turn, the coinages can throw new light on those changes. It must be admitted straightaway that this approach is experimental – previous accounts have been for the most part mostly descriptive, and often from a limited geographical or thematic viewpoint – and ideas will be put forward here that may not withstand the test of future criticism.

Parts of this model are familiar in description, though for the most part lacking in explanation. This is true of three of the four big themes of change which underlie the discussions in subsequent chapters. The first is the gradual decline of some of the coinages in the areas which fell under Roman power. This is most obvious in the case of locally produced silver coinage. In almost every new territory which came under Roman rule, whether in the provinces of Gaul in the west or of Asia and Syria in the east, silver coinage slackened in production, and eventually came to an end. Sometimes it did so at an early date, as in Gaul, and sometimes at a very late date, as in Egypt. Why did it come to an end? And why did it end at such different times?

Similar to – and different from – the pattern of silver was that of bronze coinage. The first century CE saw a complete break between west and east. Locally produced bronze coinage in Spain, Africa, Gaul, Sicily and even Italy (where it was on a tiny scale) came to an end in the second quarter of the first century. This is such a familiar picture to numismatists and historians alike that it hardly attracts any serious discussion or attention. Yet it would have fundamentally affected the visual and monetary world of millions of people. Why did this change happen? And how? And what effect did it have?

From a chronological perspective, the third main change was to the character of the locally produced coinage in the eastern part of the Empire (the territories to the east of the Adriatic Sea). It did not cease in the first century CE, as in the west. On the contrary, it not only continued, but it thrived for another two hundred years, and the cities there produced thousands of coin designs. Yet the nature of the provincial coinage was by no means static during this period. The model that is put forward in later chapters is one of chronological development; how a wide range of diverse coinages with diverse characteristics nevertheless underwent similar changes. Change affected the designs of the coins, as well as their form and physical appearance. They came to look more like 'Roman' coins: the words 'Roman' and 'Romanisation' are used here to denote the process whereby coins minted at places other than Rome came to resemble those minted at Rome. They did so with the adoption of the emperor's portrait, by using longer and abbreviated inscriptions and by becoming physically larger (much like the sestertii produced for centuries at Rome). However, these changes happened at different times (e.g., earlier in the province of Asia than in that of Syria) and to different degrees (e.g., Egypt became the most 'Roman'). Why, again, did these changes take place and why at different times?

This phase of 'Romanisation' did not, however, last throughout the period under consideration. The later second century and the third century represent a fourth phase in the development of the provincial coinage, a phase that has not previously been clearly identified. Different parts of the Empire, even different parts of the same province, started to behave differently and buck the trends observable elsewhere. For example, most of the Empire – all of the west, and Syria and Egypt – saw the end of very small denominations in the middle of the second century CE, but in the province of Asia such small coins flourished until the end of the coinage in the middle of the third century. If the former pattern was the product of a gradual inflation of prices (even though this is denied by some historians), why would this not also have affected one of the most central and prosperous parts of the Empire? At the other end of the spectrum, as it were, the same is also true – a number of communities in Asia made very large and heavy coins which departed from Roman norms. Why were coins produced which were much bigger and heavier than any ever made at the mint of Rome? Designs also changed. The coinage took on, to some extent, a more military character during the military crises of the third century, and, perhaps due to the changing economic climate, the concerns which the city elites projected on their coins shifted away from expensive building projects.

This lessening unity and growing diversity of the coinage in the later second and third centuries can be seen as a reflection of the greater

**Figure P.2** The city council in session.
Some rare coins of the colony of Alexandria in the Troad (north-west Asia Minor) show the decurions (the town councillors of a colony) in session. All of its members would have been elected from the leading families of the town. Colonies would often add the letters D D to their coins, standing for *decreto decurionum* (by decree of the decurions) showing that it was they who made decisions about the city's coinage. (*RPC IX* 432)

political and economic fragmentation of the Empire at the time. It was becoming too difficult to control it from a single point and economies were becoming more localised.

These are some of the themes which will be explored in this book. Answers and explanations will be offered, some perhaps more convincing, some less so. Most important of all, however, is to remember that almost any generalisation about the provincial coinage will have exceptions, often substantially so. City coinage was mostly produced in over 700 cities by small groups of prominent citizens, not as the result of an imposed imperial policy. Even at a provincial level (rather than that of individual cities), different regions behaved differently. A province like Egypt maintained its closed currency system until the time of Diocletian; elsewhere, in Asia or Syria, such systems were eroded and abandoned much earlier. The province of Lycia, in south-west Asia Minor, chose to have a very different currency system from the rest of Asia and the Roman east, choosing a monetary system much like that of the Roman west: in this case, it is as if the western system had leapfrogged over Greece and set up a bridgehead in Asia. Some – but not all – of the coinages of the so-called 'client kings' (theoretically independent rulers but under the strong influence of Rome) produced coins that were more 'Roman' than even the coins of the Roman colonies which were scattered around, like little Romes, throughout the Empire. Some, however, did not. Explanations can be offered for such characteristics, but the reader should constantly bear in mind that there were many exceptions to any generalisation. This makes it different to give a convincing and simple overview of the complicated patchwork of provincial coinage. It is a complex subject. Trying to understand it and explain its complexities, and what they tell us about the working of the Roman Empire (and vice versa), is, however, at the same time the attraction and interest of the topic.

## Provincial Coins and History

Much has been written about individual provincial coinages, but fewer attempts have been made to interpret them as a single phenomenon. As a result, this book has the dual aim of trying to set out a general account of the development of these many separate coinages over a long period of time, while at the same time highlighting the many debates to which they can contribute. What does the behaviour of gold and silver in the provinces tell us about the degree to which Rome was connected with other parts of the ancient world, or the extent to which the Romans sought to impose their own institutions and ideology on their newly acquired territories (Chapter 1)? What was the impact of the adoption of Roman coinage on Roman society in the third century BCE, and what does the way that the Romans engaged with the various coinages, which they found in the provinces they acquired, tell us about how they regarded their newly acquired empire during the period of the Roman Republic (Chapters 2 and 3)? What was the impact of the new political order imposed by Augustus, and can it help explain the fundamental division which emerged between the western and eastern empires in the first century CE (Chapter 5)? How did the cities reconcile the reality of empire with their own internal concerns and their desire to compete with each other (Chapters 4 and 6)? How can the provincial coinages help us understand the third century crisis (Chapter 7)? In each chapter, many other themes will be considered, such as the economic implications of monetisation, the Roman approach to provincial administration, or identity and cultural change in the provinces. As a result, the treatment is at times dense and the detail may seem overwhelming, but any attempt to understand the complexities of provincial coinage amply repays the effort involved.

## A Living Subject

Finally, a word about the material. These provincial coinages were produced by some 700 cities of the Empire: however, each of this large number of cities produced relatively small amounts of coinage (currently there are 70,000 different varieties in the *RPC* database, which deals only with the imperial period, and so the 'average' city is represented by 100 types over a period of many centuries). As a result, the coins are often rare today, and not infrequently unique. The rarity of many of the coins also means that our knowledge often relies on poorly preserved specimens – as will be clear from many of the illustrations in this book. Holdings in many museums, including coins from excavations, are not always easily accessible and still remain unpublished in many cases. In addition, there is a large market for unprovenanced coins, where new designs still turn up almost every week, and any picture painted here is therefore subject to modification and updating. Since nowadays museums cannot acquire material without documentation concerning their origin, the only way to keep up to date with new discoveries is to monitor their appearance on the art market. In turn these new discoveries may also prompt a reconsideration of what was previously known. As a result, provincial coinage is a living and lively subject.

# Acknowledgements

I am grateful to Roger Bland, Philip Kay, Fiona Haarer, Andrew Meadows, Ute Wartenberg and especially George Watson for reading through all or part of the text and offering comments and corrections. The three anonymous readers at Cambridge University Press also made many helpful criticisms and comments. Many thanks for their help also go to Marta Barbato, Chiara Chiantini, Andrew McCabe, Jerome Mairat, Maria Cristina Molinari, Jonathan Prag, Pere Pau Ripollès, Arnaud Suspène and Paolo Visonà. Thanks also to the curators at the Bibliothèque nationale de France (Frédérique Duyrat, Dominique Hollard, Julien Olivier) and the Staatliche Museen zu Berlin (Bernhard Weisser, Karsten Dahmen) for their help with the illustrations, most of which are drawn from those two institutions, along with the American Numismatic Society. Jerome Mairat was kind enough to help with high-resolution versions of the maps, using the *RPC* mapping facility.[2] Many thanks also to Gordon Lee for his painstaking work in the copyediting of the text. His rigorous approach has greatly improved the coherence and navigability of the book.

The text began life as a series of annual lectures to the Royal Numismatic Society over the years 2014–18, and I am also grateful to those who attended and made helpful comments.

# Chronological Tables

## Roman Republic (third to first centuries BCE)

| | |
|---|---|
| **290 BCE** | Final defeat of Samnites in south central Italy |
| **280–275 BCE** | Pyrrhic War and conquest of most of southern Italy |
| **264 BCE** | Final defeat of Etruscans in central Italy |
| **264–241 BCE** | First Punic War and conquest of Sicily and Sardinia |
| **218–201 BCE** | Second Punic War, also called the Hannibalic War. Conquest of Spain. |
| **197 BCE** | Creation of Spanish provinces |
| **149–6 BCE** | Third Punic War and destruction of Carthage. Annexation of Africa |
| | Creation of the Province of Macedonia |
| **133 BCE** | Kingdom of Asia bequeathed to Rome |
| **121 BCE** | Conquest of southern Gaul |
| **91–88 BCE** | Social War, between the Romans and their Italian allies or *socii* |
| **88–63 BCE** | Three wars against Mithradates, King of Pontus |
| **63 BCE** | Kingdom of Bithynia bequeathed to Rome |
| | Conquest of Syria by Pompey |
| **58–50 BCE** | Julius Caesar's conquest of northern Gaul |
| **49–4 BCE** | Dictatorship of Julius Caesar |
| **44–31 BCE** | Civil Wars, ending with the defeat of Mark Antony by Octavian/Augustus at the Battle of Actium |
| **30 BCE** | Conquest of Egypt |

## Roman Emperors (first to third centuries CE)

| | |
|---|---|
| **Augustus** | 31 BCE–14 CE |
| **Tiberius** | 14–37 CE |
| **Caligula** | 37–41 CE |
| **Claudius** | 41–54 CE |
| **Nero** | 54–68 CE |
| **Galba** | 68–69 CE |

(cont.)

| | |
|---|---|
| **Otho** | January–April 69 CE |
| **Vitellius** | July–December 69 CE |
| **Vespasian** | 69–79 CE |
| **Titus** | 79–81 CE |
| **Domitian** | 81–96 CE |
| **Nerva** | 96–98 CE |
| **Trajan** | 98–117 CE |
| **Hadrian** | 117–138 CE |
| **Antoninus Pius** | 138–161 CE |
| **Marcus Aurelius** | 161–180 CE |
| **Lucius Verus** | 161–169 CE |
| **Commodus** | 177–192 CE |
| **Pertinax** | January–March 193 CE |
| **Didius Julianus** | March–June 193 CE |
| **Septimius Severus** | 193–211 CE |
| **Caracalla** | 198–217 CE |
| **Geta** | 209–211 CE |
| **Macrinus** | 217–218 CE |
| **Elagabalus** | 218–222 CE |
| **Severus Alexander** | 222–235 CE |
| **Maximinus** | 235–238 CE |
| **Gordian I** | March–April 238 CE |
| **Gordian II** | March–April 238 CE |
| **Pupienus** | April–July 238 CE |
| **Balbinus** | April–July 238 CE |
| **Gordian III** | 238–244 CE |
| **Philip** | 244–249 CE |
| **Trajan Decius** | 249–251 CE |
| **Trebonianus Gallus** | 251–253 CE |
| **Aemilian** | 253 CE |
| **Valerian** | 253–260 CE |
| **Gallienus** | 253–268 CE |
| **Claudius II** | 268–270 CE |
| **Quintillus** | 270 CE |
| **Aurelian** | 270–275 CE |
| **Tacitus** | 275–276 CE |
| **Florian** | June–September 276 CE |
| **Probus** | 276–282 CE |
| **Carus** | 282–283 CE |
| **Diocletian** | 284–305 CE |
| **Maximian** | 286–305 CE |
| **Constantius I** | 293–306 CE |
| **Galerius** | 293–311 CE |

# Abbreviations

| | |
|---|---|
| *AE* | *L'Année Épigraphique* |
| *GIC* | *Greek Imperial Countermarks* (Howgego 1985) |
| *HN* | *Historia Numorum: Italy* (Rutter 2001) |
| *IGCH* | *Inventory of Greek Coin Hoards* (Thompson *et al.* 1973) |
| *IG* | *Inscriptiones Graecae* (Berlin-Brandenburgische Akademie der Wissenschaften, 1860–) |
| *IGRR* | *Inscriptiones Graecae ad res romanas pertinentes* (Cagnat 1906–28) |
| *MIB* | *Moneda Ibérica* (Ripollès & Gozalbes) |
| *OGIS* | *Orientis Graeci inscriptiones selectae* (Dittenberger 1903) |
| *RIC I* | *Roman Imperial Coinage* Vol. I (Sutherland 1984) |
| *RIC II.1* | *Roman Imperial Coinage* Vol. II.1 (Carradice & Buttrey 2007) |
| *RIC II.3* | *Roman Imperial Coinage* Vol. II.3 (Abdy & Mittag 2019) |
| *RIC IV.3* | *Roman Imperial Coinage* Vol. IV.3 (Mattingly, Sydenham & Sutherland 1949) |
| *RIC V.1* | *Roman Imperial Coinage* Vol. V.1 (Webb 1927) |
| *RIC VI* | *Roman Imperial Coinage* Vol. VI (Sutherland 1967) |
| *RPC I* | *Roman Provincial Coinage* Vol. I (Burnett, Amandry & Ripollès 1992) |
| *RPC II* | *Roman Provincial Coinage* Vol. II (Burnett, Amandry & Carradice 1999) |
| *RPC III* | *Roman Provincial Coinage* Vol. III (Amandry & Burnett 2015) |
| *RPC VII 1* | *Roman Provincial Coinage* Vol. VII Part I (Spoerri 2006a) |
| *RPC VII 2* | *Roman Provincial Coinage* Vol. VII Part II (Mairat & Spoerri Butcher 2022) |
| *RPC IX* | *Roman Provincial Coinage* Vol. IX (Hostein & Mairat 2016) |
| *RRC* | *Roman Republican Coinage* (Crawford 1974) |
| *RRCH* | *Roman Republican Coin Hoards* (Crawford 1969) |

# 1

## Precious Metal Coinages at Rome and in the Provinces

This book is essentially chronological, and adopts a chronological approach to the bronze coins made by the cities of the Empire. However, the coins of gold and silver which were used and sometimes made in the provinces differ in one very important respect: they were mostly under imperial rather than civic control. As such, they call for a separate treatment.[1]

The way that the gold and silver behaved allows us to illuminate a number of historical issues: for example, the degree to which the Romans imposed a monetary supremacy over their provincial populations for major payments; the extent of monetary and economic integration of the different parts of the Empire; or how the Roman Empire was connected to other parts of the ancient world across the globe. The relatively rare interventions into the gold and silver coinage made by emperors such as Nero throw additional light on their regimes and the effectiveness of their administration. The picture for gold is different from that for silver, and hence this chapter is divided into two parts.

The Roman world was essentially a monetised society, at least from about 200 BCE until the end of the Empire. There were sophisticated banking systems, and credit was generally available. Coins were available for high and low-value transactions, but not all transactions were made in coin. Other precious items, like bullion or jewellery, could sometimes have a monetary role, and, more significantly, many transactions took place without coins changing hands, both across long distances and more locally. The fragmentary nature of the evidence – papyri or occasional references in classical authors – means that it is hard to estimate the quantum of such 'paper' transactions, but it is clear that they represented a substantial proportion of monetary activity.[2] As in other pre-industrial economies, however, such transactions were redeemable in coin, and gold and silver coins were by far the most important elements, by value, of the monetary economy of the Roman world.

## 1 Precious Metal Coinages

Silver had been the staple medium of exchange, in uncoined form, in the urbanised societies of the Middle East in the second and first millennia,[3] and hence from the sixth century BCE it became the most important metal for coinage. In the west, in Italy, however, this role was initially played by bronze.[4] Gold had become a common coinage metal in the Greek world from the time of Alexander the Great, and, although it played little or no role in the Roman state before the time of Julius Caesar, the Romans encountered it in some of the territories they took over. However, once gold coinage had become a staple part of the Roman monetary system in the time of Julius Caesar, minting was concentrated in the city of Rome,[5] and little was minted in the provinces, except in times of civil war.

Silver coinage was minted in large quantities throughout the period, largely at Rome, but there were also substantial issues from several mints in the eastern provinces, notably Caesarea in Cappadocia, Antioch in Syria and Alexandria in Egypt. The resulting system seems complicated to us, and it would have worked only if it had been controlled by the Romans. Generally speaking, silver minted in the provinces was more over-valued than the denarius minted in Rome, and so would have required regulation to maintain its value and stop the effect of 'Gresham's Law' (bad money drives out good). This reveals an important aspect of Roman provincial administration.

As precious metals, gold and silver behaved differently from the lower value bronze and other copper alloy coinages. The copper alloy coins had restricted areas of circulation. Gold and silver, however, travelled much more widely. Although they have tended in the past to be studied as phenomena within the Roman Empire, their high value meant that they also played a wider role beyond the frontiers of the Empire, playing a part in the ancient global economy of precious metals. Roman gold and silver coins, for instance, are often found in ancient India or in Germany, across the Rhine frontier. A very recent hoard from Norfolk shows that some also came to Britain before the invasion of 43 CE.[6] As such, gold, in particular, has a place in current debates about globalised Rome, in which the Roman Empire is studied in the wider context of the history of the ancient world beyond modern Europe and the Mediterranean.[7]

Many different sorts of silver coinage were made within the Empire, creating a number of different patterns of circulation. The silver denarius, minted from about 200 BCE, was the most important, dominating the currency of the western half of the Empire from the time of Augustus, and gradually replacing the many provincial silver coinages in existence in

**Map 1.1** The Roman provinces

# 4    1 Precious Metal Coinages

the east. By the later third century CE, virtually all the provincial silver coinages had disappeared. From that time the denarius and its radiate successor, known today as the antoninianus or radiate, came to be used throughout the Empire, setting the scene for the very different monetary system of the later Roman Empire.

The existence of these local silver coinages and the long-term tendency for them to disappear have some parallels with the patterns that existed for the more diverse – but less monetarily important – bronze coinages. There were, however, substantial differences, in the scale of production, in government control and, above all, in the timing of decline. Local production of both silver and bronze coinage declined and then ended in the western provinces, but at very different times: during the first century BCE for the silver, but a hundred years later for the bronze. The pattern of the minting of silver in the eastern Empire is similarly one of decline and cessation; and, once again, the provincial silver came to an end substantially earlier than the bronze. These patterns demand different explanations about the working of the Roman economy and the way change took place.

## 1.1  Silver

### 1.1.1  Silver Coinage in the Third Century BCE: Italy and Sicily

The pattern of silver production in the Roman world is more complicated than that of gold, reflecting a looser control by the central government and the survival of some of the many different systems of silver coinage which were in place when the various territories fell under Roman control. Their survival illustrates the attitude of the Roman government to the administration of its empire. The Romans did not, on the whole, practise monetary imperialism and try to impose their own model of currency on the territories they acquired. In some places, local systems continued to flourish. In others, they withered and were occasionally brought to an end. Such direct intervention was rare, but there was a general tendency for the local systems to die out and to be replaced by the silver denarius (and its successor, the more debased antoninianus or radiate). The process of this change allows us to see that, despite an acquiescence or laissez-faire attitude towards the continuance of local systems, changes were nevertheless brought about by wider changes in the economy of the Roman world.

**Map 1.2** The main silver mints in Italy *c.* 300 BCE

Roman silver coinage was first made in about 300 BCE,[8] on the model of the silver coinages of other Italian states, and using the same sort of silver.[9] By then, silver coinage had been produced by the Greek colonies in the very south of Italy for over two centuries, and in the late fourth century the monetary economy of southern Italy had expanded in three senses: the volume of coinage had increased; new smaller denominations, in both silver and bronze, were introduced; and the use of coinage spread to central Italy, further north and inland, in areas such as Etruria and Samnium. One consequence was the first production of silver coinage at Rome.

The economic and cultural background to its introduction has been much discussed (see also Chapter 2), and it is clear that the coinage was, at first, on a small scale and isolated chronologically. Rome may have started to make coins, but it did not become a fully monetised society for a hundred years, until the end of the third century.[10]

After an initial issue (Figures 1.1–1.2), no more silver was minted for some forty or fifty years, when a more regular production began. Later, in the early years of the Second Punic War (218–01), the scale of minting grew with the coins known today as the 'quadrigati'. Their greater production perhaps exploited, in part, silver from Spain.[11] Large quantities of silver were also passing from Carthage to Rome: at least 100,000 – and perhaps 200,000 or even 300,000 – Carthaginian silver coins were captured at the Battle of Mylae in 260 BCE (Figures 1.26–1.28). Enormous indemnities, amounting to a total of some 100 tonnes of silver, were imposed by Rome on the Carthaginians after their defeat in the First Punic War. By the middle years of the devastating Second Punic War, however, the quality of the coinage declined and then it

**1.1**  **1.2**

**Figures 1.1–1.2** The first Roman silver coins.
The first Roman silver coins were made in about 300 BCE at a weight standard (the didrachm of 7.2 g) and silver fineness that was borrowed from the silver coinage of Neapolis (modern Naples), where they may even have been made. They show a head of the god Mars and the head of a horse, probably an allusion to the festival of the *October Horse*, a chariot race that was held in honour of Mars, at the end of which the head of the lead horse from the winning chariot was sacrificed to the god. Very few coins were made at the time, however, and only four obverse dies are known. At the same time, some very small fractional silver pieces (obols) were made, reflecting the way that the monetary economy of Italy had expanded into smaller transactions. The date of their production has been hotly debated for many years, the principal problem being a clash between the archaeological evidence of hoards, which point firmly to about 300 BCE, and a literary tradition, above all in the much later author Pliny (*Natural History* 33.42–44), which placed the first Roman use of silver in 269. Over the last few decades the archaeological evidence has become stronger, while it has been pointed out that Pliny's text is full of errors (Burnett & Crawford 2014). Various attempts have been made to reconcile the two sources, all predicated on some misrepresentation by Pliny. The debate continues. Figure 1.2 is enlarged × 1.5. (1.1 *RRC* 13/1; 1.2 *RRC* 13/2).

collapsed: the weight and fineness of the silver coinage was reduced, and, as will be described below, an emergency coinage of gold was briefly introduced. This was the end of the first phase of Roman silver production.

The War against Pyrrhus (282–71 BCE) saw the decline and end of many of the large silver coinages of the other city states in southern Italy. During that war, most of the mints reduced the weight of their coins by almost 20 per cent, and at Tarentum, the largest mint, the purity of the silver was also reduced by some 5 per cent.[12] Metapontum, Heraclea, Thurii, Croton and Velia all ceased to strike silver. Silver production continued only at Tarentum and Naples until about 250, when both coinages seem to have come to an end.[13] The principal Etruscan silver coinage, of Populonia, also ended at about the same time. The coins of all these mints, however, remained in circulation for the rest of the third century.

Subsequently some other communities, typically in Campania and most of them colonies of Rome, produced issues of silver (Cales, Suessa, Teanum, Paestum, Nuceria and Teate) (Box 1.1). The production of these allied coinages may be related in some way to the First Punic War (264–241), and they were perhaps intended to support the Roman war effort. But the chronology of the coinages is not certain, and some or all of them may have been made after the war.

Thereafter, no more silver was minted in Italy, except at Rome, until the Second Punic War. During that war some silver coins were made in Italy by the Carthaginians, and by their allies, the Brettii, Tarentum and Metapontum (Figure 2.7). Silver was also minted in northern Italy, in the Po Valley, where coins imitating those of Marseilles were minted at about this time (Figure 2.14), although their date cannot be determined with any precision.

Sicily also had a long tradition of using coins. In addition, after the Carthaginians occupied Sicily in the fifth century, they made and used gold, electrum and silver coins, down to the first half of the third century. Their territory was finally taken over by Rome with the Carthaginian defeat at the end of the First Punic War (264–41). In eastern Sicily, coinage was provided by Syracuse, but Syracusan coinage is hard to date, and much of it, both in silver and gold, may well date from the end of the century. As a result, the nature of the precious metal currency of Sicily immediately after the war remains unclear, though there is some slight evidence that, as in Sardinia (see Section 2.2.5), Roman silver may have replaced that of Carthage.[14]

**8**     1 Precious Metal Coinages

## Box 1.1 Silver minting in Italy during the third century BCE

| | 300–272 BCE | 272–230 BCE | 230 BCE–00 |
|---|---|---|---|
| Large silver coins | Populonia | Rome | Po Valley |
| | Cora | Cales | Rome |
| | Arpi | Suessa | Capua |
| | Rome | Teanum | Tarentum |
| | Neapolis | Neapolis | Metapontum |
| | Tarentum | Nuceria | Bretii |
| | Velia | Teate | |
| | Heraclea | Tarentum | |
| | Metapontum | Paestum | |
| | Thurium | | |
| | Croton | | |
| | Locri | | |
| Small silver fractions | Alba | Nola | Rome |
| | Norba | Rome | Arpi |
| | Signia | Caelia | Bretii |
| | Peripoloi P | Tarentum | |
| | Saunitai | | |
| | Allifae | | |
| | Nola | | |
| | Fistelia | | |
| | Arpi | | |
| | Canusium | | |
| | Rome | | |
| | Neapolis | | |
| | Canusium | | |
| | Tarentum | | |
| | Heraclea | | |
| | Metapontum | | |
| | Thurium | | |
| | Croton | | |

During the Second Punic War, much silver, and some gold, was made by Syracuse, which was at first allied with the Romans. These coins continued to be minted after Syracuse had switched to the Carthaginian side, and other Carthaginian allies, Agrigentum and the 'Siceliotai', also made some silver during the war. The Romans brought substantial amounts of their own silver coin into Sicily from at least 214, and also minted silver there.

## 1.1 Silver

A fundamental change to the silver currency of both Italy and Sicily took place in the middle of the Second Punic War. It was a rare example of change being imposed by the Romans. By this time, the Romans had come to control Spain and the silver mines, which had supplied the bullion for

**Figures 1.3–1.7** Silver coinage in Sicily in the Second Punic War. The silver coinage of Syracuse (1.3–1.4) consisted of denominations expressed in multiples of *litrai* (here 16 and 12). King Hiero made coins in his own name, and also for his wife Philistis (1.3) and his son Gelon. They form a hierarchy: the largest for the King, the medium for the Queen and the smallest for their son. The fine coins of Philistis, who is also known from an inscription in the theatre at Syracuse, have her veiled portrait and a chariot driven by Victory. When Hiero's successor was deposed in 214, a 'democracy' was established, and made silver coins in many denominations: this one (1.4) depicts the head of the goddess Athena, and a figure of Artemis. The Carthaginian issues included half *shekels*, showing a head of the god Melqart and an elephant, with the Punic letter A below (1.5). The Romans made several different series, some of which used a corn ear as a symbol of Sicily. The earlier ones showed a head of Janus (compare Figure 1.28) and a chariot (1.6), and the later ones (1.7) belonged to the new system of the *denarius* (for which see below, Figures 1.8–1.10). (1.6 *RRC* 42/1; 1.7 *RRC* 44/5)

**10**  1 Precious Metal Coinages

their Carthaginian enemies. The Romans introduced their new silver coin, the denarius – and its related fractions, the victoriate, the quinarius and the sestertius – and analyses suggest that much of the required bullion came from Spain.[15] The introduction of this new coinage was also accompanied by the disappearance of all earlier Italian and Sicilian silver – of all the Italian city states, of Syracuse and of Carthage. The Romans had clearly decided to remove the precious metal coinage of Carthage, the potent symbol of a hated enemy, and at the same time also removed all the earlier silver of Italy, Sicily and indeed Rome itself. At that moment, shortly before 210 BCE, the silver currency of Italy and Sicily changed completely and thereafter consisted only of Roman silver of the new denarius system.[16]

### 1.1.2 The Silver Denarius

The reforms of *c.* 212–11 introduced the denarius, one of the most successful coins of antiquity.[17] It endured for almost five centuries, although its status, appearance and physical nature changed greatly over this period; by 240 CE it was barely recognisable as the descendant of its predecessor of many generations before. For its first 150 years it was the principal precious metal coin of the Roman state, being minted in large quantities, and it was only reduced to playing a more subsidiary role with the introduction of the gold coin in the later first century BCE, as described below. However, it never ceased to be of great importance, and the massive inflow of wealth which Rome received as more and more territory was conquered – in the form of booty, indemnities and taxes – will have provided a plentiful supply of metal for minting, supplemented by the mining of new silver.

It was, at first, accompanied by subsidiary denominations, the quinarius and sestertius, worth a half and a quarter, respectively, and marked as such with the numerals V and IIS for the values of 5 and 2½ asses. It is not at all clear why so many of the smaller denominations were minted. They were also accompanied by an even more enigmatic coin, the victoriate (Figure 1.11). It had no mark of value and was minted at two-thirds of the weight and about two-thirds of the fineness of the denarius, and so contained about half as much silver as the denarius.[18] The only ancient source to explain the coin, a much later text of Pliny, says that this coin 'was brought from Illyria and reckoned in place of trade' (*Natural History* 33.46). It did not, however,

## 1.1 Silver

**Figures 1.8–1.11** Roman silver coins of the denarius system, about 200 BCE. The principal coin of the new silver coinage, introduced in the middle of the Second Punic War, was the denarius ('*tenner*'), named after the value mark X, standing for its value, 10 (asses). It was accompanied by two closely-linked denominations, marked with the values of 5 (the 'quinarius') and 2½ (the 'sestertius'). They all have a helmeted head of the goddess Roma and, on the other side, the two Dioscuri brandishing spears on horseback (the Dioscuri were the legendary helpers of the Romans in battle). There was also a coin of less pure silver, with a head of Jupiter and no value mark, known as the 'victoriate' from the figure of Victory on the reverse. (1.8 *RRC* 44/5; 1.9 *RRC* 44/6; 1.10 *RRC* 44/7; 1.11 *RRC* 44/1)

have any role in Illyria and Pliny's text notoriously contains a number of errors, so we cannot regard the remark about trade as being reliable. It seems a better idea to consider parallels in other states which produced coinages of differing finenesses. In the Attalid state in Asia Minor a generation later, coins of a lower silver content were used with an artificially high value imposed by the state for internal transactions:[19] almost exactly the opposite of what Pliny says! However, the victoriate's production did not last long and ceased sometime early in the second century.

From 200 to about 150 BCE, most of Rome's coin production – if not all[20] – consisted of large numbers of bronze 'asses', whose weight declined and then stabilised. There is a consensus that they were produced as the medium for paying soldiers, and that the decline of bronze after the middle of the century indicates a switch to paying in silver.[21] The large quantity of bronze minted at the time is presumably also the reason that the denarius was retariffed from ten to

**12**     1 Precious Metal Coinages

sixteen asses in about 140 BCE: a major adjustment that was probably a reflection of changing market prices. As bronze had become more plentiful, more bronze coins were needed to make up the value of a silver one. Physically, in terms of its fineness and weight, the denarius remained mostly stable for the next 150 years, until the civil wars of the late Republic, when Mark Antony reduced its fineness in the late 30s BCE.[22] His debased coins then circulated together with their finer predecessors, an indication of the subsidiary nature that by then characterised silver coinage. Antony's great enemy, Octavian/Augustus, however, maintained the quality of his silver coinage, which remained high, if somewhat reduced in weight, until the reforms of Nero, as discussed in Section 1.1.5 below.

Even if there were an expansion of the money supply (Box 1.2), there were still severe financial crises, caused by a lack of liquidity: in the 80s BCE; in 63 BCE, when it seems that gold in the form of bullion was needed to supplement the silver coinage; and above all in the 40s BCE, when Cicero complained of a 'lack of coins'. We learn that gold bullion could also be used then: Cicero was expecting a debt to be repaid in gold

---

**Box 1.2  The 'Hopkins graph'**

There has been some debate over whether or not the large production of denarii caused a growth (followed later by a shrinkage) in the 'Roman money supply' in the late second and first centuries BCE The idea was first put forward by Hopkins 1980 (see also Hopkins 2002). Although the statistical basis is quite fragile, the general picture of an increase and then fall in the number of denarii in circulation has some plausibility. One cannot, however, necessarily conclude that there had there had been 'an increase in the use of money for more activities' (Kay 2014: 93), relative to the sizes of the population and territory of the Empire, since they had both grown enormously during the period. Although the denarius was not used throughout the Empire, its area of circulation did expand greatly: the Italian peninsula and the central Mediterranean islands from 210; northern Italy and Spain from the second century; Africa from 146; and Greece from the first century BCE. However, other silver coinages were also made in some of these and in other areas, such as the Iberian denarii in Spain. Ideally, their size and scope would be factored into an empire-wide calculation of the Roman monetary stock, but the statistical basis of doing so would be very weak.

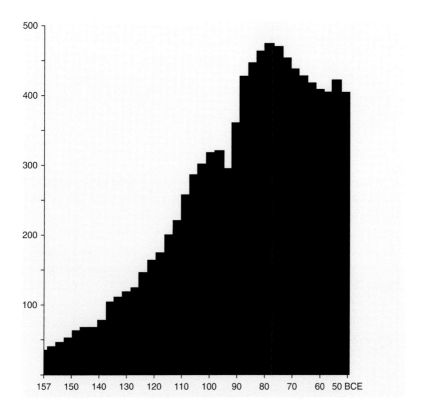

(*Letters to Atticus* 12.6). The problems of silver availability provide the background to the introduction of the massive issues of gold under Julius Caesar.

### 1.1.3 Silver Coinage in the Western Mediterranean in the Second and First Centuries BCE

Some silver coinage had been made by the Greek colonies in Mediterranean Spain from the sixth to the third century BCE, but the monetary stock of Spain initially consisted mainly of silver bullion, often chopped up into very small pieces. This changed in the third century. The Carthaginian conquest at the time saw the production of coinage in electrum (an alloy of gold and silver), silver and bronze, a production which came to an end with their defeat by the Romans in the Second Punic War. Some communities, such as Gadir or Ebusus, also minted bronze from the fourth century. For their part, the Romans imported coinage into Spain and

## Box 1.3 'Iberian denarii'

**Figure 1.12** Iberian silver denarius, from Osca (Bolscan).

These coins are characterised by a male head on the obverse and a horseman with a spear on the reverse. The inscriptions, in 'Levantine Iberian' script, give the name of the issuing community (here Bolscan = ancient Osca, modern Huesca). The uniformity of denomination and design across a wide geographical area is hard to explain without some Roman agency. It remains unclear, however, if the coinages were local initiatives tolerated and moulded by the Romans, or if their production was stimulated by the Romans, whether to meet some fiscal need, such as the payment of taxation, or simply to support the needs of a greater monetisation arising from greater urbanisation.

made some small silver issues there during the war. The very large scale of contemporary silver coinage from the city of Emporion suggests that it too may have been used by the Romans to pay their expenses. It was accompanied by silver 'imitations' of Emporitan coins, some with recognisable place names in Celtiberian script.[23]

With the Roman occupation of the Iberian peninsula, coin use spread inland from the Mediterranean area (the province of Hispania Citerior), especially with the growing urbanisation of the region, but coinage remained scarce until the second half of the second century BCE. From that time on, there was a flowering of diverse coinages (mostly, however, in bronze), minted by more than 180 communities, across north-west, central and southern Spain. These coinages reveal the cultural and ethnic diversity of the region, with the names of their communities, for example, appearing in Greek, Punic, Latin, and in several local scripts. The designs also reflected local religious diversity. In one large area, however, north-western Spain, a uniformity of designs was introduced for an extensive silver coinage in the middle of the second century, the so-called 'Iberian denarius' (Box 1.3).

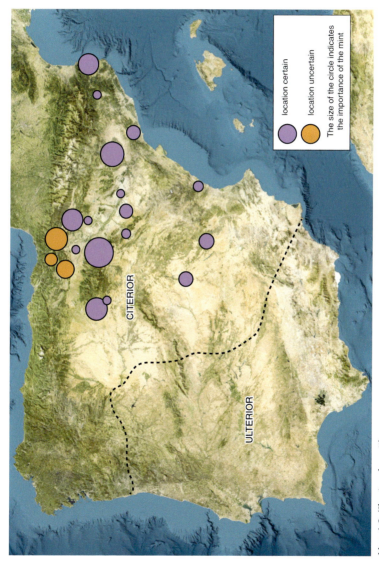

Map 1.3 'Iberian denarii'

Silver coinage production in Spain came to an end in about 70 BCE – a hundred years before the end of provincial bronze production there – but it continued to circulate until the end of the first century. Roman denarii had continued to arrive in Spain during the second and first centuries, and hoards show that the two sorts of coin circulated together. From the end of the first century BCE, however, the Iberian coins disappeared from circulation and Roman denarii formed a monopoly of silver in circulation. All were imported from Rome, apart from a few issues made during the civil wars at the end of the Republic and in 68–69 CE.

Between Spain and Italy lay the islands of Corsica and Sardinia, both of which had become part of the Carthaginian Empire and had used Carthaginian coins from the late fourth century. Corsica was captured by the Romans in 259. We have little information about the silver coinage in use before or after that date, apart from the slightly unexpected presence of two silver coins of Populonia at Aléria. Roman coins of the denarius system were, however, used from the end of the third century.

For Sardinia, seized by the Romans in 238, the documentation is much better. Carthaginian gold and electrum (and presumably silver) coins circulated in the late fourth and early third centuries. The Roman annexation in 241, however, was swiftly followed by their replacement by Roman and Italian silver coins, as a hoard from Nora now shows,[24] complementing an earlier find from Cagliari (Box 2.2). As we shall see in Chapter 3, this contrasts with Carthaginian bronze, which continued in circulation until the Second Punic War. The Roman decision to abolish Carthaginian gold and silver foreshadows the similar change in Italy during the Second Punic War, and is another example of a rare Roman intervention.

To the north lay Gaul: Cisalpine Gaul, between the Po and the Alps, was conquered at the end of the third century; across the Alps, southern Gaul (Gallia Narbonensis) was annexed in 121 BCE; and the huge area of Transalpine Gaul to the north was conquered sixty-five years later by Julius Caesar, in the 50s.

Before the Roman conquests, the various regions of ancient Gaul had made gold and silver coins in imitation of Greek coins and, as in other regions, they continued to circulate for a while. In northern Italy, the silver coins imitating the coins of the Greek city of Massalia (modern Marseilles) (Figure 2.14) followed the same pattern as the Spanish coins, remaining in circulation from the third to the second century. In southern Gaul, the currency of Massalia and other local communities continued, but In both cases they were accompanied by Roman coins. The conquest of the rest of Gaul by Julius Caesar brought the production of gold there to an end (see Section 1.2), but coinage in silver and bronze continued until the reign of Augustus (Figures 3.15–3.16).[25] It was only then that Roman coins began to play an important role in the currency of the region.

### 1.1.4 Silver Coinage in Greece and the Eastern Mediterranean in the Second and First Centuries BCE

The Romans acquired large tracts of territory as they conquered Greece and the eastern Mediterranean. Macedonia was conquered in 168 BCE, and Achaea in 146 BCE; Asia was bequeathed to Rome by its last king in 133 BCE; Syria and the Levant were annexed by Pompey in 64 BCE; and Egypt fell under the control of the Romans with the death of Cleopatra in 30 BCE.

As their empire grew in the east, the Romans inherited and maintained the fiscal and monetary systems which had been in force before their conquest, such as taxation and coinage. Silver coinages in Greece, Asia, Syria and Egypt continued to be produced much as they had been before Roman rule. It has been argued that some of them were manipulated by the Romans to meet their own needs, especially the cost of warfare.[26] When large issues have been identified, they have been associated by modern scholars with periods of conflict, such as the wars against Mithradates, for which the Romans would have needed cash to pay and supply their armies. This explanation seems likely in many cases, as we saw with the coinage of Emporion in Spain, but, as in Spain, we should not assume that warfare was the only explanation for minting.[27] Warfare does not account for the production of silver coinage in subsequent centuries, when there is little or no correlation between periods of minting and of warfare, and the particular needs of the individual communities would have continued, as well as those of their new Roman masters.

Two general trends can be observed. The first is the gradual cessation of some, though not all, locally produced silver, the same pattern as we have seen in Spain and Gaul. In Greece the last substantial silver coinages (of Athens and of the Thessalian League) came to an end in

1.13

1.14

1.15

**Figures 1.13–1.15** Silver coins struck under Roman Republican rule in the Eastern Empire.

After the Roman conquest of Greece, Athens continued to make plentiful silver coins (1.13), exactly as before. They use the traditional Athenian coin designs: a helmeted head of the city's patron deity, Athena, and her sacred bird, the owl. The coins also have the names of officials responsible for the coinage. However, there is no sign of the Romans, and it is only thanks to the detailed studies of modern numismatists that we can date some of the coins to the Roman period, in this case to the 130s. In Asia Minor, the former kingdom of Attalus and his successors had seen the introduction of a coin called the cistophorus ('basket-bearing', after the design). Initially they too showed no sign of the Romans, but in the 50s BCE the Greek inscriptions were dominated by ones in Latin, giving the name of the Roman provincial governor. In this case (1.14) he is M. CICERO M.F. PROCOS, the famous orator Cicero, who was governor of the Roman province of Cilicia in 51–50 BCE. In Syria, the Romans even revived the earlier coins of the King Philip, with his portrait and inscription (1.15). The only clue to Roman domination is the date at the bottom of the back of the coin: the number 19 in Greek numerals (ΘΙ) denoting the 19th year of the Roman province = 31/30. (1.15 *RPC I*, 4136)

the middle of the first century BCE. Further east, the old royal coinages of Asia (cistophori) and Syria (tetradrachms) continued for a long time and were gradually transformed into the coinages of Roman Asia and Roman Syria, only to peter out and eventually cease, much later, in the imperial period. In parallel, the Roman denarius spread east, arriving in Greece in large quantities in the first century BCE, in Asia (perhaps) from the same time or at least from the early imperial period, and in Syria from the late first century CE.

As the denarius gradually came to dominate all these areas and replace locally produced silver, accounting systems started to change from their earlier, local systems to the Roman. 'Denarii', instead of local denominations, were specified for payment in Thessaly by a directive of Augustus.[28] Far to the east, Germanicus ordered that taxes should be reckoned in 'Italian asses', as is preserved in an inscription from Palmyra.[29] The great diversity of coinage in use must, indeed, have caused practical problems. This might be at the highest level, as when Augustus drew up his 'accounts of the Empire', or at the individual level, when it exposed its users to the necessity of changing money from one type to another. Cicero, for example, was desperate not to be paid in cistophori when he was appointed governor in Asia Minor.

## 1.1.5 Provincial Silver under the Empire

The coinage system of the Republic continued into the Empire. Monetarily, the political break of the reign of Augustus brought little change: cistophori were minted in Asia by Augustus in much the same way as before, even if their appearance had been transformed by the new designs of the imperial portrait and symbols. A similar cosmetic change took effect on the coinage of silver tetradrachms minted at Antioch in Syria, but their fineness and weight were again much the same as before. From the reign of Tiberius, silver coinages were also made in the new territories of Cappadocia and Egypt on the model of their previous royal coinages, as had been the case in Syria seventy years earlier.

A very few smaller silver civic coinages survived into imperial times: in Africa (Leptis), Greece (Nicopolis), Asia (Chios, Stratonicea, Mylasa, Tabae, Rhodes), Cilicia (Aegeae, Seleucia, Mopsus, Tarsus) and Syria (Seleucia, Apamea, Laodicea, Sidon), but

## 1 Precious Metal Coinages

**Map 1.4** The principal provincial silver mints under the Empire

most of these coinages did not survive for long. They were all made in very small amounts. It is probably better to think of them just in terms of being high-value civic coins, made exceptionally in silver rather than bronze, rather than as a significant phenomenon of civic silver.[30] Perhaps only rich cities, or rich individuals in those cities, could afford to make them.

The exception is the silver coinage of Tyre (Figure 1.18), whose nature has been much debated. It preserved its non-imperial appearance and was minted in substantial, if declining, quantities, until the time of the First Jewish War (66–70 CE), when it ended. At that point the silver coinage of the area was reformed, with minting being concentrated on Antioch.

**Figures 1.16–1.17** Provincial silver coins of the early imperial period. Provincial silver coins were made with different sizes, shapes, finenesses and designs, depending on their predecessors. Silver *cistophori*, worth three denarii, were made in the province of Asia, probably at Ephesus. They were inscribed in Latin and have designs which reflect both local and Roman cults, and the person of the emperor, here (1.16) the Capricorn, Augustus' natal sign. Silver *tetradrachms*, worth four denarii, were minted at Antioch. Some of the earliest (1.17) were minted with the portrait of the emperor Augustus, named by a Greek inscription, and a figure of the city goddess of Antioch on the back; the coins have a reference to his 12th consulship and the date 'year 27' (= 4/3 BCE) of an era starting with the Battle of Actium. See also Figure 1.18. (1.16 *RPC I*, 2208; 1.17 *RPC I*, 4153)

In all areas of the Empire, there was a tendency for earlier coinages to decline, and then to disappear and be replaced by denarii. It is clear that the civil wars at the end of the Republic had a particularly significant effect. They saw many local silver coinages come to an end and be replaced by silver denarii, made by the various factions in the provinces.

Other changes are harder to document and date. For example we do not know when Republican cistophori fell out of use, but from time to time we can see the intervention of the Roman authorities. On the rare occasions they intervened the process was accelerated. The clearest case concerns the coinage of Egypt in the reign of Nero. His predecessors had minted silver in large quantities, but all of it, together with the last silver coins of Cleopatra, jointly known as coins 'of imperial and

**Figure 1.18** Silver coin of Tyre.
The silver coinage of the city of Tyre was one of the most important silver coinages in the Levant. It was produced continuously from the late second century BCE until the time of Nero's reforms (Box 1.4). Its designs never changed, and the imperial portrait was never adopted, perhaps reflecting Tyre's status as a free city (the inscription calls it 'Tyre, the sacred and inviolable'). The obverse has a head of the city's patron deity, Heracles (or his Phoenician 'equivalent', Melqart) and the reverse shows an eagle with a palm branch over its shoulder in front of a club. The reverse also has the number POB = 172, referring to the year of production according to the city's era (i.e., 46/47 CE), and the enigmatic letters KP. The coinage was so important that it has been suggested that it was, in fact, minted by the Kings of Judaea, but this seems unlikely. However, it was used by Jewish people to pay their tax to the temple in Jerusalem. (*RPC I*, 4672)

Ptolemaic silver', was removed from circulation and replaced by new coins in the name of Nero, which were consequently minted in very large numbers.[31]

### Reforms of Nero

The change in Egypt was not isolated. Precious metal coinages were reformed, across the Empire, in the reign of Nero.[32] It has been known for a long time that, although the gold and silver coinage remained stable for almost a century from Augustus to Nero, nevertheless in about 64 Nero reduced the weight of the gold and reduced both the weight and the fineness of the silver. Our understanding of what happened in Nero's reign has benefitted greatly from recent analyses of the silver content of the coins, both the denarii made at the main imperial mint and the silver made at a number of other mints in the eastern Mediterranean.[33]

Nero's profligacy, and consequent shortage of money, has traditionally been the most popular explanation of his debasement of the coinage. Other

## Box 1.4 Nero's reforms of the coinage

In the reign of Nero (54–68) many changes were made to the monetary system of the Empire. They took place at different times in the course of the reign, and were different, if complementary, in nature:

1. The weight of the gold coin was reduced in *c.* 64 from 7.70 g to 7.35 g, so that the post-reform coins contained 95% of the gold in pre-reform coins.

2a. The weight of the silver denarius was reduced in *c.* 64 from 3.65 g to 3.45 g, from 90 to 96 coins per libra (a reduction in weight of about 6%). The purity of the silver was at first reduced from 99% to 80%, but in 68 it was increased up to 90%. Therefore, the reduction in the weight of pure silver in a denarius was at first from 3.65 g to 2.76 g, and then to 3.10 g. This means that the denarius contained, at first, 75% and then, 85% of the silver in pre-reform coins.

2b. Various changes occurred on the provincial silver coinage during the reign, at the following dates:

| Crete | *c.* 60 | weight reduced, no good analyses |
| Caesarea | *c.* 64 | weight and fineness (70%) unchanged |
| Tyre | 65 | the coinage of pure silver shekels and half-shekels petered out and then ceased |
| Antioch | 59 | fineness improved 50 to 70% (Figure 1.19) |
| Alexandria | 54 | fineness reduced from 25 to 20% (Figure 1.20) |

3. A new system for sourcing the metal for minting into coins was introduced. Previously, newly mined silver had been used, but from 64 old silver coins were recycled.

4. The principal mint for gold and silver was moved from Lugdunum, where it had been located since the reign of Augustus, to Rome in 64.

5. Some of the earlier silver coins were removed from circulation:

| Rome | recycling of earlier silver coin inaugurated |
| Tyre | removal of all from circulation |
| Antioch | removal of earlier issues |
| Alexandria | removal of Ptolemaic and earlier imperial issues. |

**Figures 1.19–1.20** Nero's reformed provincial silver coins.
Under Nero, a new silver tetradrachm was introduced at Antioch (1.19), combining the emperor's portrait with an eagle with a palm branch, taken from the coinage of Tyre (which was now discontinued). The coins also bear the dates AIP (111) and Θ (9), referring to the year according to the era of the city and the ninth year of Nero's reign. They were more fine than their predecessors at Antioch, but less fine than the coinage of Tyre, indicating that the reform was making a complicated change to the currency of the area. The reformed silver tetradrachm from Alexandria was made at a lower fineness than its predecessors. Some pieces depict the emperor Tiberius (ΤΙΒΕΡΙΟΣ ΚΑΙΣΑΡ), which were intended to keep Tiberius' image in circulation, even though the common coins made earlier during his reign were now demonetised see Figure 1.34). (1.19 *RPC I*, 4185, 62/63; 1.20 *RPC I*, 5295, 66/67)

suggestions have been made more recently; for example, that Nero was attempting to harmonise the denarius with the standards of provincial silver coins.[34]

No doubt the debate will continue, but the explanation that seems to account best for all the relevant changes is to see them as a series of measures designed to deal with a problem of an endemic shortage of silver in the first centuries BCE and CE. A shortage is known from the 40s BCE, when Cicero refers to a 'lack of coins' (*Letters to Atticus* 9.9), and it has been suggested that the patterns of coin issue and hoarding can substantiate the decline in the availability of silver coinage at the time.[35] A drop in silver extraction during the first century BCE is suggested by geological evidence from the drop in the amount of lead (a by-product of silver production) discovered in ice cores extracted in Greenland.[36] Tacitus also refers to a shortage of cash in 33 CE (*Annales* VI, 16–17). It is also well known that few silver denarii were minted between the 30s and 64 CE, even though minting had been plentiful under Augustus and Tiberius. Much of it, moreover, may have flowed out of the Empire, especially to India and Germany.

The various changes to the silver fineness of the coins (described in Box 1.4) and the removal of purer silver coins from circulation are all acts which provide evidence for a concerted effort to save silver all over the Empire, and so to make the existing stock of metal go further. The change from using newly-mined silver to recycling old silver coins in 64 suggests that the problem of new supply had become severe. It can also account for the transfer of the mint from Lugdunum back to Rome. This has never been properly explained, but a move of the mint back to Rome would have located it near the *aerarium*, the destination of coinage paid as taxation, and so would have facilitated the reminting of recycled coinage.

The scope of the logistical changes that took place during these years of change was enormous. Operations to recover silver or to enhance minting were undertaken across the whole empire: in Lyons, Rome, Thrace, Crete, Antioch, Tyre and Alexandria. Geographically, this was a remarkably wide set of changes, without parallel at any other time in the Empire, whether for the coinage or anything else.

If the geographical scope seems huge, so does its scale, especially when we consider the practicalities of the minting and supply of coinage. Any statistics rest on a fragile basis, but, for the gold coinage under Nero, annual minting has been estimated at eight million coins, and bigger figures are also possible. The minting of silver will also have run into the millions of coins. A lot of wagons would have to have made their way up the *clivus Capitolinus* to bring the required metal to the mint: at least some two to four wagons of metal every single day. None of these figures should be regarded as having any great accuracy, but they may serve as a very rough indication of the likely scale of the operations required.

In addition, the changes to the various supply chains for the issue of new coinage to and from Lugdunum and to its destinations in the provinces would have needed a correspondingly massive re-organisation.

That all this happened, apparently without mishap, is a sign of an extraordinarily effective administrative system, one requiring much careful planning and a large cast of personnel to put it into operation. It was an exercise,

## 26   1 Precious Metal Coinages

however, which was never repeated by any other emperor. Nero had a bad press, and was remembered for his tyrannical acts, but his reform of the coinage shows that he presided over an extremely effective administration.[37]

### A Period of Empire-Wide Cooperation

The civil wars of 68–69 CE saw a proliferation of minting, as the various contenders for power set up mints in many locations in the western and eastern parts of the Empire. As had happened previously, the pattern of less centralised minting continued for a few years after the end of the conflicts. As a result, many provinces saw a brief production of denarii: Spain, Gaul, Africa, the Balkans, Asia and Syria. As Vespasian asserted his control, however, he, like Augustus a century earlier, re-established the centralisation of denarii.

A complex system for the production of provincial silver (and some bronze) then emerged, in which three main mints – Rome, Antioch and Alexandria – cooperated, or were coordinated, to make silver coinage for other provinces.[38] The mint at Rome seems to have made 'local' silver for Crete, Asia, Cappadocia, Lycia, Syria and Arabia; the mint at Antioch made coins for Crete, Cyprus and Arabia, as well as for Syria; and the mint at Alexandria made coins for Syria, as well as for Egypt. The pattern is even more complicated when we also take into account that some bronze coins were similarly made 'outside' their province at Rome: bronzes for Cyrenaica, Cyprus, Syria and even for Agrippa II in Judaea were also produced there. Some aspects of this pattern are, however, disputed and care needs to be taken in drawing any conclusions.

If the scale of this distributed minting does not seem to be as great as the changes made by Nero, as described in Box 1.4, the geographical extent was equally empire-wide, and the system seems, in some sense, to be a legacy of Nero's actions. It has been suggested that the new system should be seen as a way of reminting earlier silver, and if so, then it would also seem to be a means of saving silver, since that was the purpose of such reminting. The metal was presumably in short supply as the reductions in the fineness of the denarii imply. The situation was made more complicated by Domitian's attempt to restore the quality of the silver denarius in 82, a change which – unlike Nero's debasement – found little or no reflection in the provincial silver. Nor, apparently, did Trajan's subsequent reduction of the silver content of the denarius. Presumably because the provincial silver coinages were already considerably overvalued in its areas of circulation (see Section 1.1.6 later in

**Figures 1.21–1.25** Coordinated silver issues made for Trajan.
During Trajan's short second consulship (98–99), the mint of Rome made silver coins for circulation in different parts of the Empire, as is shown by their similar style and other common technical details, such as die axis. Denarii (1.21) circulated throughout the western Empire. Cistophori (1.22) were made for circulation in the province of Asia, with a value of three denarii. Drachms (1.23) were made for Lycia (SW Turkey), didrachms for Cappadocia (1.24), and tetradrachms for Syria (1.25). They were inscribed in both Latin and Greek, and with a variety of sizes and designs that demonstrate a knowledge of the traditional designs in use previously in the targeted areas of circulation.
(1.22 *RPC III*, 1315; 1.23 *RPC III*, 2676; 1.24 *RPC III*, 2991; 1.25 *RPC III*, 3564)

this chapter), there was no urgency to change their already relatively insignificant nature.

The system of empire-wide coordination remained in force during a fairly short period of fifty years from the reign of Vespasian to that of Hadrian, when decentralised minting of provincial silver returned. Thereafter, there were only a few isolated cases of the mint of Rome producing provincial silver coinage: under Lucius Verus (161–9) for Mesopotamia; under Severus Alexander (222–35) for Egypt; and under

**28**    1 Precious Metal Coinages

Philip (244–9) for Syria. The great bulk of provincial silver was, once again, normally made in the region in which it circulated.

An extreme example is provided by the province of Asia late in the reign of Hadrian, when many cistophori were made and a very large number of different mints was involved, probably some 25–30.[39] In his reign also, the provincial minting of denarii was resumed to some extent, in Antioch and Asia (perhaps related to the recoinage of cistophori), but this was a short-lived phenomenon which did not continue after his reign.

The reason for this change of approach, from centralised back to localised production, is not easy to fathom. Did the wide coordination of coinages just seem too complicated a system to administrate? The Neronian and subsequent changes show what was possible, but also suggest that the effort required to bring them about was just too great. As a result, the 'system' returned to its previous character, from the middle of the second century CE.

### The Decline of the Imperial and Provincial Silver Coinage

The next major change to the denarius took place in the reign of Septimius Severus (193–211). In about 194, its silver content was reduced further, to about 45 per cent. We cannot say, at the moment, how this change affected the provincial silver coinages, since not enough reliable analyses of the coins have yet been published. However, the introduction of a new silver coin – the antoninianus or radiate – by Caracalla (211–17) does seem to have had a response in the coinage of Caesarea in Cappadocia, where new denominations were also introduced, but we do not know enough about the silver content of the coins to form a definitive judgement.

The staple silver coin of the Empire, the denarius (and its successor, the antoninianus or radiate), underwent further decline in its silver content in the third century CE, and we know from geology that silver production slumped at the time.[40] Provincial silver coinages were now fewer in number and became more spasmodic in production. Almost no silver was minted in Egypt for thirty years, but it resumed in 219. A few cistophori were made for Asia under Septimius Severus, but they were the last issue of locally produced silver in the province of Asia. The silver coinage of Cappadocia continued after the reign of Caracalla into that of his short-lived successor Macrinus (217–8), but thereafter nothing was produced for twenty years until Gordian III (238–44), whose issues marked the end of Cappadocian minting. Silver minting at Antioch, which had been sparse in the second and early third centuries, resumed on a large scale – perhaps a recoinage of earlier Syrian silver[41] – from about 213 to 219, when silver production switched to Egypt. It resumed twenty years later, with Gordian III, and then continued off and on until 253. From then on, however, only antoniniani were minted, as discussed below, and it remains unclear how long the provincial silver may have remained in circulation.

## 1.1.6   The Imperial System of Silver Coinage

The provincial silver coinages were on a small scale, when compared with the output from Rome, and most remained in the provinces or areas in which they were produced. This is clear in the case of Egypt, where the Romans continued the strictly controlled monetary system of their Ptolemaic predecessors, and in Syria, where the tetradrachms produced at Antioch, and sometimes elsewhere, never left the area. Cistophori too were confined to Asia. The 'client' kings of Mauretania set up a similar system in the early first century CE.

There were some exceptions, such as the silver 'drachms' minted in Lycia (Figure 1.23), which turn up in hoards from all over the Empire; and the same may be true of the smaller silver denominations minted at Caesarea in Cappadocia, and most of the tiny silver output from Petra under Caracalla has been found in the west.[42]

These patterns raise the question of how the dual systems worked. The characteristic difference between the two sorts of coin – denarii and local silver denominations – was that the locally produced coins contained lesser amounts of silver, compared with the amount in the denarii minted mainly in Rome. The exact proportions of silver in provincial silver coins are still the subject of detailed study, as older investigations have been found to have methodological flaws, and our understanding of the phenomenon is developing all the time.[43] But only coins containing the same amount of silver as denarii, like the Lycian drachms, regularly left their region of origin.

The lower level of silver in provincial coins was known widely at the time, as instanced by Cicero's complaint in 59 BCE: 'See what they say, whether there may be hope for denarii or whether we will be rubbished with Pompeian cistophori?' (*Letters to Atticus* II, 6, 2). A sharp distinction was also made at the time between, on the one hand, Roman/Italian/'our' coins and, on the other, 'their' coins,[44] or ones described by a local adjective to make a contrast with the Roman ones. 'Rhodian drachmae', for example, are contrasted with the 'Roman denarius' in a Flavian inscription from Cibyra (*iKibyra* 42), and the aristocratic jurist Volusius Maecianus, writing

**30** 1 Precious Metal Coinages

in the middle of the second century, remarked that the tetradrachm and the drachm could be regarded as 'foreign' coins (*Distributio* 45).

The different amounts of silver in denarii and provincial coins means that they cannot have circulated together without some regulation. An official exchange rate between the different sorts of coin must have been enforced by the Roman provincial authorities. Only some such mechanism would have blocked the operation of 'Gresham's Law', which would otherwise have seen 'bad money drives out good' from the provinces.[45] Traces of this regulation can be seen in Asia (Box 1.5) and Egypt, where the value of the local tetradrachm was probably initially fixed at 1¼ denarii, and later at one denarius.[46]

It is a pity that we cannot document this process of regulation more fully, but the general picture prompts the questions of why such a system existed and why it came to an end. The first question is easier to answer than the second. Put simply, the Romans inherited coinage systems when they took over new territories, such as in Asia or Egypt. It was characteristic of Roman expansion to take over existing arrangements, both of taxation and coinage, rather than undertake their reform. Perhaps we can also infer that such systems of coinage were continued because they were profitable: if the Romans were able to make payments in coins containing less silver, then they too, like their predecessors, would have made a good saving. In turn, they would expect to receive payments in purer denarii or, as in Egypt, be

---

### Box 1.5  The value of silver coins in imperial Asia

A series of inscriptions was set up prominently on the wall of the theatre in the city of Ephesus in 104 CE, to record the gift of a foundation to the city by C. Vibius Salutaris. They use the terms 'of twelve silver asses' and 'of a drachma' interchangeably, showing that a cistophoric drachm was officially tariffed at three-quarters of a denarius (*iEph* 1a.27, ll. 221, 301–2). Recent analyses show, however, that a cistophoric drachm contained about 2 g of pure silver, compared with about 3 g for a denarius. Three quarters of the weight of silver in a denarius would have been about 2.25 g, so the cistophori must have had an overvaluation of 10% relative to the denarius. As a result, they were worth more in the province of Asia, where their value was fixed at this artificially high rate. This explains why they did not leave the province, since outside the artificially high value would not have applied.

able to enforce a favourable exchange of denarii into locally produced coinage. Pre-Roman Egypt, at the end of the fourth century BCE, is the clearest example of a local 'closed currency system' using coins of lesser silver. It was a monopoly system, and only Ptolemaic coins were allowed to be used in Egypt.

However, there was also another version, in which the currency of an area might consist of coins of different fineness. Examples of this mixed system are Rome in about 200 BCE (the denarius and the victoriate) and the Attalid kingdom in Asia Minor in the middle of the second century BCE, where coins with more silver were used for external purposes, and those of less silver were used internally.

Before the coming of the Roman Empire, such a system would have only worked well between autonomous states if there was a strong balance of trade, as in the case of Egypt. People needed to trade with Egypt, and, since using the local coinage was the only way of doing so, they had to change their own coins into Egyptian ones when they entered the province.

The system must, however, have been either only marginally profitable, or else (which amounts to much the same thing) difficult to maintain, as otherwise it would surely have continued much longer and not broken down in the gradual ways we have seen. Egypt seems to stand at the end of the spectrum of its successful operation, and so it was maintained there over six centuries. Elsewhere, however, there was a tendency for the similar monopoly systems of overvalued coins first to be eroded into a mixed system (of poorer local coins and finer denarii), and later to peter out entirely.

The use of coins containing different amounts silver within a single political unit suggests that some direct profit was derived from the exchange of coins from one sort to the other, and also that an additional indirect profit was derived from the lower cost of making some of the coins with less silver. Such a system, however, could only overcome market forces if it were enforced by official regulation.

The Roman province of Asia provides an example of the change from a monopoly of baser silver to a mixed system of denarii and local silver. Cistophori were made there in large quantities in the Republican period, and they were at that time the only substantial silver coins in circulation. They continued to be minted in the 20s BCE, and then in the reigns of Claudius and Hadrian. Smaller issues were made at other times, in the Flavian period, under Trajan or under Septimius Severus, when the last cistophori were made. Denarii, which seem to have been used in the

## 32  1 Precious Metal Coinages

province since the middle of the first century BCE (as shown by a hoard from Halicarnassus and by a new Augustan hoard from Aezani)[47] must have played an increasingly important role, and some were even minted there in the reigns of Augustus and of Hadrian, alongside the cistophori.

In Cappadocia, similarly, local silver was minted in the second century CE and under the Severans; there was then a gap of twenty years before the last issues, under Gordian III.

These changes in Asia and Cappadocia are examples of a more general pattern. Local silver came to have less and less importance, and in many areas it began to be mixed with and subsequently replaced by Roman denarii or antoniniani. Such changes have already been discussed for Republican Spain and Greece during the second and first centuries BCE. The phenomenon continued over a long arc of time: the process was similar, but it might take place at very different times in different areas.

The breakdown of the mixed system makes sense as a consequence of a gradual transfer of precious metals from the provinces to the centre. As a city like Athens or a league like the Thessalian League gradually became impoverished, they would have lacked the resources to make their own silver coinage. When such local coinages were taken over by the Romans, their continuation would have required the transport of silver back to the provinces, a costly operation that could hardly have been justified by the profit it would bring (except perhaps in Egypt). Although this happened to some extent in the late first and early second centuries, as we have seen, it may well have seemed pointless to continue such a system. Minting more denarii and exporting them was much simpler. This explains the rare mention of the official transport of coin into the provinces: of the 'money of the empire' in a Trajanic inscription from Asia,[48] or of the 'struck silver and counted coin', which was exempt from the customs tax that was normally payable on the transfer of goods between provinces.[49] The state did not tax itself.

## 1.2 Gold

Precious metal coinage in the Greek world, from the sixth century to the time of Alexander the Great was predominantly made of silver. Gold and silver were, exceptionally, both minted in the Persian Empire. After Alexander's conquests, the use of gold coins became more common and for a hundred years they circulated widely across Eurasia and north Africa. Gold coins were not made or used in China, where gold and silver bullion might be used for high-value transactions,[50] but the pattern of gold coinage across the rest of the world reveals interesting chronological and geographical patterns.

If we look at Eurasia and north Africa as a whole, then several different chronological phases can be identified (Box 1.6).

The earlier of these phases are not relevant here, although they show that gold coinage had been established in some areas well before the coming of Rome. Those who produced it were able to manage a bimetallic system, whereby a mixed coinage of gold and silver would be subject to the strains

## Box 1.6 The production and use of gold coinage in the ancient world

| Phase | Date | North Europe | West Mediterranean | East Mediterranean | Persia, etc. | Indian Subcontinent | East Asia |
|---|---|---|---|---|---|---|---|
| 1 | 550–350 | No | No | Yes | Yes | No | No |
| 2 | 350–250 | Yes | Yes | Yes | Yes | No | No |
| 3 | 250–50 | Yes | No | No | No | No | No |
| 4 | 50 BCE–100 CE | Yes | Yes | Yes | No | No | No |
| 5 | 100–250 | Yes | Yes | Yes | No | Yes | No |

The production and use of gold coinage can be divided into five main phases.

1. Persian phase (550–350 BCE). Gold coinage starts in Lydia, and is adopted by Persia.
2. Expanding phase (350–250 BCE). Alexander the Great and his immediate successors made gold, as had the Persian kings; the production of gold coinage expands to the western Mediterranean (Carthage) and north-west Europe (the 'Celtic world').
3. Northern phase (250–50 BCE). The period saw a flight of gold to Gaul (where the massive numbers of dies show how it was minted in very large quantities) and the Black Sea area (where many hoards have been found). Gold does, exceptionally, continue as part of the monetary system of Egypt until about 150 BCE.
4. Roman phase (50 BCE–100 CE). The Roman Empire permanently adopts gold, starting under Julius Caesar. Parthia and India use silver.
5. Bipolar phase (100–250 CE). The production of gold coinage spreads to India, but misses out Parthia.

**34** 1 Precious Metal Coinages

created by the changing market price of the two metals. Balancing the two was the greatest concern of European governments in the early modern period, and no less a figure than J. M. Keynes was puzzled as to how the ancient Persians were able to do so in the ancient world.[51] The Persian Empire, however, did change the weights of some silver coinages to allow them to maintain their value relative to gold.[52]

It may be that the virtual disappearance of gold coinage from the Mediterranean world in about 250 BCE, after the massive issues of the Macedonian kings Philip II and Alexander III, could be seen as a consequence of a similar difficulty, but no general explanation has yet been found. The observable flows of gold to the north in the last centuries BCE may perhaps be the result of gold having different values (whether monetary or social) in different areas. For example, gold might have had a higher metallic value in India than in the Mediterranean, and the so-called Celtic peoples of northern Europe seem to have placed a considerable social premium on gold, as witnessed by the prestige they attached to gold objects such as torques.

After 250 BCE, gold coinage survived in the Mediterranean only in Ptolemaic Egypt, where the monetary system was manipulated and closely controlled by the government. This would have allowed the possibility of imposing a *fiat* system, which would have fixed the relative value of gold to silver coinages by royal decree, but even that must have broken down by 150 BCE. Thereafter, gold was minted and used only in north-west Europe, while the earlier gold found its way into hoards around the northern Black Sea. For example, all the late hoards of gold coins in the name of Lysimachus are found in modern Bulgaria, Romania or Ukraine. As a result, when Rome emerged on to the world scene in the third century BCE and started to make coinage, the only precious metal coinage in common use for coinage was silver, and silver remained the principal precious metal for Roman coinage for the next 250 years.

Some very small gold issues had been made by the city states of southern Italy in the late fourth and early third century BCE, at Metapontum, Heraclea and especially Tarentum. They were one aspect of the great increase in coin production at the time, fuelled partly by the need to pay large mercenary armies to fight against Rome, and partly by the new vogue for the ostentatious display of wealth, made fashionable at the time by the Macedonian kings. Tarentum's last gold was produced in the Pyrrhic War (280–75 BCE), when the Tarentines had called in Pyrrhus to help them in their fight against the Romans.

Rome's other great enemy of the time, Carthage, minted gold and electrum (the alloy of gold and silver) in large quantities in the third century, but it similarly came to an end with the defeat of Carthage in 201

BCE. Syracuse in Sicily, long a Roman ally, had also minted gold, but Syracuse changed sides in the course of Second Punic War (218–201 BCE), and its defeat and capture by the Romans in 212 saw the end of its coinage in precious metals and the transfer of its assets to Rome.

The Romans themselves did not make any gold coinage until the Second Punic War (218–201 BCE), when the financial problems caused by the scale of the war forced them to reduce the weight and fineness of their silver coinage and introduce a supplementary coinage in gold, an indication of the financial emergency they were facing. Recent analyses made in France show that this Roman gold was made from Carthaginian gold coins, no doubt including those captured at Mylae (Figures 1.27–1.28).

The Roman conquest of the lands of the eastern Mediterranean, in the second and first centuries BCE, saw the continuance of the coinages previously made and used there. There was by then, as we have seen, no area in the eastern Mediterranean with any significant gold coinage. A few minor issues were minted – in the name of the Roman general Flamininus in

**Figure 1.26** The spoils captured at the Roman victory over the Carthaginians at the Battle of Mylae in 260 BCE.
This fragmentary inscription (ILS 65) is a later copy of the one which adorned a victory monument and column set up to the Roman consul C. Duilius, who commanded the Roman fleet at its victory over the Carthaginian fleet at the Battle of Mylae (modern Milazzo), off the coast of Sicily, in 260 BCE (*cf.* Figure 2.26). The last six lines summarise the wealth he captured, including '[aur]om captom numei MMMDCC' ('gold captured: coins: 3700'), and '[argen]tom captom praeda numei M[]' ('silver captured as booty: coins: [the figure has not survived]') (see also Figure 2.17).

1.27                                    1.28

**Figures 1.27–1.28** Carthaginian and Roman gold coins.
Carthage had made many gold coins, composed of gold or gold mixed with silver (an alloy known today as electrum). Many were captured at the Battle of Mylae (see Figure 1.26) and others may have been paid as part of the huge indemnity which Rome imposed on Carthage at the end of the First Punic War. The Carthaginian coin (1.27), made during the First Punic War, shows the head of the principal state deity, Tanit, and a standing horse with a solar symbol above. The Roman coin (1.28) was made in the Second Punic War. It shows the double-head of Janus, perhaps a symbol of the closure of the temple of Janus in 235 BCE, to mark the end of the war. The oath swearing scene on the reverse may allude to the way that Hannibal broke the provisions of the treaty sworn between Rome and Carthage, under which Carthage would not cross the Ebro river in Spain: *Punica fides* ('Carthaginian faith') would take on the ironic meaning of treachery. Recent analyses show that the Roman coins have the same trace elements as the Carthaginian, demonstrating their origin (Suspène, Artru, Nieto-Pelletier *et al.* 2023). (1.28 *RRC* 28/1)

Greece or Macedonia in about 196 BCE,[53] or by the city of Ephesus in the late second and early first centuries BCE.[54] A few Roman coins were also minted in gold, for instance, by Sulla in Greece and Rome during the late 80s BCE, at a time of financial crisis,[55] or by Pompey in Spain in 71 BCE. Their exceptional nature is indicated by their rarity today.

Julius Caesar's conquest of Gaul in the 50s BCE ended the production of 'Celtic' gold there, and saw the transfer of massive amounts of gold to Rome. Recent analyses have shown that it was refined and minted into gold coins,[56] perhaps partly to help relieve a shortage of silver and certainly to finance political bribery on a massive scale. It was well known, for example, that Caesar 'was secretly working on the magistrates with his money and corrupting them' (Plutarch, *Pompey* 58).

From the time of Caesar onwards, gold became once again a staple coin metal in the Mediterranean, and it became a more important part of the monetary system than silver, especially as it seems that the Romans were

## 1.2 Gold

**Figures 1.29–1.31** Gold coins of Julius Caesar and Vercingetorix. Julius Caesar started to produce a regular gold coinage in 48 BCE. The first coins (1.29) bear the number 52, which, remarkably, can only be a reference to his age. The largest issues were made in 46 and signed by the *praetor* called A. Hirtius (1.30), and were continued in the next year by the urban prefect L. Plancus. The unusual identity of the magistrates who signed it and the crude style evident from 46 makes it stand apart from the coinage produced at the main mint of Rome. One suspects that Caesar had set up his own mint somewhere else in Rome, as a means of protecting the security of the gold: the publicity given to his own age marks it out as his private property. Caesar seized the gold in the Treasury in 49, and brought more back from Gaul. Some of the Gallic gold would have been in the form of gold coins acquired as booty in Gaul, which recent analyses have shown to have the same trace elements, even though they were made of gold that was much less pure (Suspène, Blet-Lemarquand, Nieto-Pelletier *et al.* 2023). This one (1.31) was inscribed VERCINGETORIX, the name of the Gallic chieftain who was Caesar's great enemy in Gaul. (1.29 *RRC* 452; 1.30 *RRC* 466)

often faced with a shortage of silver, as discussed in the Reforms of Nero section earlier in this chapter (pp. 22–26). As a result, the production of gold was closely controlled and centralised. Its importance lay in its value, and it probably accounted for the largest amount of coined money in circulation (Box 1.8). When Roman emperors subsequently reduced the weight or fineness of the silver,[58] the gold was left largely unaffected, or if it did change – as happened under Nero – its reduction was not proportionate, illustrating the primacy of gold over silver. In that sense, the Roman Empire was on the gold standard. The value of the silver was fixed in relation to the gold: initially perhaps at 20 denarii to the aureus, but for most of the imperial period at 25.[59]

# 38  1 Precious Metal Coinages

> **Box 1.7  The scale of Roman gold in the 40s BCE**
>
> Caesarian gold was minted on an enormous scale. A die study of the coins of Hirtius (Figure 1.30) identified 111 obverse dies in 535 specimens, suggesting a total original number of dies of about 130. At an average of 30,000 coins per die would mean some four million coins, each weighing 8 g, and totalling over 30,000 kg of gold. Calculations such as this cannot be regarded as at all accurate, but they can be compared with the 6,675 kg of gold that was carried in Caesar's triumph of 46 BCE.[57] Some enormous hoards have also been reported. In 1714, one hoard (or perhaps two), said to be of 80,000 coins, was found at Brescello in northern Italy (*RRCH* 441), and in 1877 another was found at Caiazzo (inland from Naples, Italy), probably consisting of more than 1–2,000 coins (*RRCH* 423).

Thereafter, the gold coins in later circulation in any part of the Roman Empire were the aurei produced centrally at Rome,[60] illustrating a different attitude to the control of gold from other metals. Aurei were, exceptionally, produced outside Rome, but only at times of civil war, when political authority broke down – in 44–31 BCE, following the death of Caesar; in 68/9 CE, following the murder of Nero; and in 193–4 CE, following the murder of Commodus. These coins were, however, minted on the same model as those minted at Rome, and their production in the Roman provinces reflects political fragmentation and the location of the various contenders for the imperial power – Mark Antony in Greece, Galba in Spain or Pescennius Niger in Cappadocia and Syria. Generally speaking, and curiously, the fragmented pattern of gold production would usually continue for a few years after a period of civil war had ended, before centralisation was once again restored (perhaps after a slow recovery of supply lines).

Roman gold coins have been found in hoards in nearly all the provinces of the Empire, particularly in western Europe, where there has been a long modern tradition of recording coin finds. Hoards and other finds of gold are also known from other areas, such as Greece, Turkey, Syria, Israel and Egypt, even though the documentation is less strong there. There is, however, a debate about the importance of gold in the monetary economy of

## Box 1.8 A gold or silver monetary economy?

Duncan-Jones (1994: 70–2) estimated that gold represented about 70 per cent of the value of coinage in circulation in the Empire. The basis of the calculation was fragile, but it was, at least, indicative. Bland & Loriot (2010: 109–10) pointed out that, although gold coins represent only a tiny proportion of coins recovered from sites, they represent a very large amount by value: for example, the seventeen gold coins from Richborough would have had the same value as the other 50,000 coins recovered; and of course, we can assume that gold coins would have had a relatively lower loss rate, since their owners would surely have searched harder for any losses. Bransbourg 2022, however, has recently criticised the basis of Duncan-Jones' calculation, halving his estimate of the proportion of gold and preferring to see silver as the more important metal being minted, by value, during the second century. But the enormous amounts of first-century gold, minted especially by Nero, continued to circulate in the second century, and they seem to have represented a much greater value than any newly minted coins. No doubt, the debate will continue.

**1.32**   **1.33**

**Figures 1.32–1.33** Hadrian and the Provinces.
Hadrian issued a series of coins, including gold, celebrating the geography of the Empire, and twenty-five provinces or cities appear, ranging from Spain (*Hispania*) to Egypt (*Aegyptos*). His interest in all the regions of the Empire is also apparent from the journeys he made around the Empire, which celebrated the regions, his visits (*Adventui Aug* …), the regional armies (*Exercitus* …), and his restoration of their fortunes (*Restitutori* …). In the words of Jocelyn Toynbee, they represented 'the idea of the Empire as a vast unity, a brotherhood of fellow-citizens of the world living together on an equality in prosperity and peace, under the aegis of a beneficial central government, to which the well-being of each member was a matter of vital interest' (Toynbee 1934: 156). (1.32 *RIC II.3* no. 1530; 1.33 *RIC II.3* no. 1478)

# 40    1 Precious Metal Coinages

Roman Egypt – there are very few finds, and almost no mentions in the plentiful records of transactions that have survived in papyri. It seems possible that the Romans continued to control the monetary economy of Egypt in the same way as their late Ptolemaic successors, and operated there with a precious metal coinage only in silver, as had been the case for the last hundred years of Ptolemaic rule. If gold was not used there, it would be the only exception to the common acceptability of gold throughout the Empire, which was otherwise the clearest – and only – aspect of full monetary integration across the Empire.

The tight control of gold, implied by centralised minting, continued well into the third century CE. From then, some gold started to be produced from mints outside Rome, and, in addition, its fineness was sometimes reduced. Considerable amounts of gold were minted at Antioch and perhaps Nicomedia under Elagabalus (218–22) and a few pieces may also be known from Antioch for Gordian III (238–44) and Philip (244–9).[61] During the joint reign of Valerian and Gallienus (253–60), however, gold was also minted at in Gaul, Milan, Antioch and perhaps Samosata.[62] Dispersed minting and reduced

---

**Box 1.9  The wide circulation of Roman gold**

Roman gold coins circulated widely throughout the Roman Empire and beyond, and played many different roles. An interesting example is provided by two coins of the emperor Claudius (41–54). They were originally made at the same time, as is shown by the fact that they were struck from the same dies. One was found in a hoard lost at Bredgar, Kent, UK (British Museum 1957,1010.32), and the second at Pudukkottai, Tamil Nadu, India, 10,000 km distant (British Museum 1898,0803.12). The Bredgar coin comes from a hoard which may have been lost during the Roman invasion of Britain, and was presumably in the possession of a rich officer who was killed in the fighting. The Pudukkottai coin probably travelled to India as an object of trade, perhaps in exchange for some of the luxuries whose purchase was a source of enormous wealth leaving the Empire, a trade worth 25 million denarii a year, according to Pliny (*Natural History* 12.84). However, Pliny's figure is either corrupt in the text or an underestimate, since we know from a papyrus record that a single cargo was worth 2 million.[63]

fineness are symptoms of the beginnings of the break-up of the early imperial monetary and administrative system. By the fourth century, a different system of gold production was established across the Empire, reflecting the more fragmented nature of the late Roman economy. Gold was then minted locally at several imperial mints, from Trier in the north-west to Alexandria in the south-east.

The system of gold coinage in the later Empire was fundamentally different from that of the early Empire, since the gold coin was then worth its bullion value (the meaning of 'solidus', as shown by its occurrence in the Greek version of Diocletian's price edict as having the same value as gold in the form of bars).[64] As a result, the value of a gold coin could float upwards against the denarius (by then purely a nominal unit of account) as prices of all commodities, including metals, rose. This system perhaps started sometime earlier, probably under Aurelian (270–75), when the uncoupling of gold from other coinage metals would account for the monetary inflation that took place from his reign onwards.

## 1.3 The Emergence of the Late Roman System of Precious Metal Coinage

There was only one type of gold coinage in circulation in the early Empire, and, as we have seen, the multiplicity of local silver coinages gradually came to an end. They were replaced by the denarius and its successor, the antoninianus or radiate, which was first introduced by Caracalla (211–17) and became the staple 'silver' coin of the Empire from 238.

The continuing debasement of the radiate is well known, from 45 per cent fine in about 200 to only about 1 per cent by 275. In the 250s, gold too began to be debased,[65] and both metals were increasingly minted at more centres throughout the Empire, as the monetary economy of the Empire became fragmented. Gold was increasingly recycled, and left the Empire through wars and trade.[66] Efforts were made to stabilise the situation towards the end of the third century, and they saw the new, late Roman monetary system emerge. It was based on a coin of pure gold whose value was fixed at its gold content, and it seems likely that it was free to float in value against the silver coinage (both pure and alloyed).[67] An abortive attempt was made to fix the value in Diocletian's price edict of 301, but

**Figure 1.34–1.35** Provincial silver coins in Egypt.
The mint at Alexandria had produced the only 'silver' coinage in use in the province of Egypt. It had started to do so, on the model of its Ptolemaic predecessors, from the seventh year of the reign of Tiberius (20/21 CE) (1.34). Large silver looking coins were produced with the portrait of the emperor and the deified Augustus, although they contained only about 25% silver. Production continued for almost 300 years, right up to the reign of Diocletian. The last issues (1.35), made in the twelfth year of his reign (295–6), retain the character of their predecessors: the inscriptions are still in Greek, but the coins are much reduced in size from their earlier predecessors, and contained almost no silver. (1.34 *RPC I*, 5089)

**Figure 1.36** The last gold coins of the early imperial system.
In the middle of the third century, the weight and fineness of the gold coin dropped significantly. This poorly made and thin coin, dating from late in Gallienus' sole reign (260–268), weighed only 1.36 g and was only 88% fine. Other coins of the time are similarly small, and some even more debased. (*RIC V.1*, no 81)

the continuing price inflation of gold meant that a cyclical pattern of reform and debasement became the hallmark of the later third and fourth centuries.

The new ideology of the later Empire, as a single territory despite being divided into several separate parts, also brought about a unified currency in all the provinces. Even the apparently successful local coinage of Egypt was brought to an end and replaced with coins which had the same composition and designs as those in use in the rest of the Empire. The late Empire saw a monetary system that was very different from the one that had preceded it and had lasted and evolved for the previous four hundred years. The coinage was now uniform in content, appearance and value across the Empire, and it had entirely lost the local diversity that had characterised its predecessor.

# 2

## The Beginnings of an Empire in Italy and the Western Mediterranean (300–200 BCE)

The third century BCE saw Rome emerge from a position of being only one among several city states in central Italy to one of being the dominant power of the western Mediterranean.[1] The Samnite Wars brought control of central Italy, while the defeat of Pyrrhus added southern Italy and ushered in the great struggle with Carthage and its empire. The First Punic War (264–241 BCE) ended with the Roman defeat of Carthage and saw Sardinia and Sicily fall to Rome. A generation later, the Second Punic War, the great war against Hannibal (218–201 BCE), led to the breaking of Carthaginian power and the annexation of its provinces in Spain. It was a war on an unprecedented scale with fighting in Italy, Spain and north Africa, and it had lasting effects on the economy, monetary system and psyche of the Romans. The phrase 'Hannibal at the gates' became proverbial, meaning that disaster threatened, and it was used to make children behave.

Roman coinage had taken its first tentative steps in around 300 BCE, and it developed into a distinct and unusual system, before collapsing during the Second Punic War, a hundred years later. The early Roman coinage then fell to pieces. It was subsequently revived and reformed with the introduction of a new coinage system, based on the denarius. The reform (see Chapter 3) brought about a fundamental change in the coinage system of the Roman world, which was by then beginning to reach out beyond Italy, to Sicily, Sardinia, Cisalpine Gaul and Spain. This chapter looks firstly at the development of a coinage system in third-century Rome; secondly, at the pattern of coinage in its newly acquired provinces and dependent territories; and then, finally, at the collapse of the system at the end of the century.

The coinage can throw much light on two crucial aspects of the contemporary development of Roman society and ideology. Firstly, it can give us guidance about the aspirations of Rome at the time: the old debate about the nature

**Figures 2.1–2.2** Bronze coins of Rome and Naples, late fourth century BCE. The first Roman coins were made in bronze (2.1), copying from the contemporary coinage of Neapolis (2.2) (modern Naples) the designs of a head of Apollo and the forepart of a man-headed bull (a reference to a river). The only difference was in the inscription, which was in Greek and read ΡΩΜΑΙΩΝ ('of the Romans') instead of ΝΕΟΠΟΛΙΤΩΝ ('of the Neapolitans'). Few such coins were made, and only a handful have survived today. Late fourth century BCE. Figure 2.1 is enlarged × 1.5. (2.1 *RRC* 1; 2.2 *HN* 584)

of Roman expansion. Did the Romans conquer the western Mediterranean in self-defence or was their success born from an aggressive imperialism, both ideological and economic? As the coinage is virtually the only contemporary source for the period, its 'evidence without hindsight' means that it can play a central role in this debate.

Secondly, the period saw a transformation of Roman society from one without coinage, reliant on other forms of monetary transactions, to one which, by the end of the third century, had an extensive coinage and seems to have been a society that was as monetised as any ancient state, with a plentiful and full range of denominations available. How did this change come about, and what are its implications for the social and economic development of Rome?

## 2.1 The Adoption of Coinage at Rome

Let us start with the very beginning. The first point to look at is indeed why the Romans started to make coinage at all. Not all ancient states did so, and there was no tradition of coinage in central or northern Italy. Rome itself seems to have used money in the form of weighed bronze (*aes rude*) for several centuries, as suggested by the descriptions of the reforms of Servius Tullius, and mentions in the Twelve Tables.

**Figure 2.3** Roman currency bar.
Large cast bars were produced in the early/mid third century, with varying designs. Here we can see a trident and a caduceus, both tied with a fillet and probably alluding to a naval victory in the First Punic War. See also Yarrow 2021, 17–19. This piece weighs 1680 g, and it and other bars were perhaps intended to be at a standard of five Roman pounds. Original size: 98 × 188 mm.
(*RRC* 11)

## 2.1 The Adoption of Coinage at Rome 47

**Figure 2.3** (cont.)

To try and understand why the Romans introduced the change from weighed out bronze to coined bronze and silver, we need to look at the nature of the earliest Roman coinage, and examine how it fits into its Italian context.

The early Roman coinage had four main elements:

1. the struck silver didrachms (Figures 1.1, 2.4 and 2.25);
2. the struck bronze (Figures 2.1 and 2.5);
3. the cast heavy bronze or *aes grave* (Figures 2.6 and 2.26);
4. and, at first, currency bars (Figure 2.3), sometimes wrongly and misleadingly called '*aes signatum*' today.[2]

The silver was mostly used in southern Italy because there had been for long a circulation of silver coins there (with south Italian Greek coins). Bronze predominated in central Italy, where there had previously been a metallic currency based on uncoined bronze.

At first, these monetary objects were produced only sporadically and in small amounts, and not in any clear relationship to each other; but from about 250 BCE, a series of changes were made to the weights and fineness of the different elements in a way that brought them together into a single system, which we might call 'the first Roman coinage system'. The relationship between the different elements was marked by the use of common symbols, two of which – the sickle and the club – link the struck bronze, the struck silver and the *aes grave* together; currency bars now disappeared. The final change took place in about 225 BCE, when the designs were altered so that the different elements were characterised by the presence of a janiform head on both the silver and the *aes grave*. This was the coinage system with

2.4    2.5

**Figures 2.4–2.6** Struck silver, bronze coins and cast *aes grave*.
All three were integrated in the later third century, and can be seen from the use of a common symbol, in this case a sickle. The silver and bronze repeat the designs of earlier coins, with a horse's head and a helmeted head of Mars, now adapted to show the features of Alexander the Great (no beard, and long sideboards). The *aes grave* as, a large coin weighing 234 grams, shows the heads of a double-headed god (perhaps Janus or the Dioscuri) and of Mercury, who wears a winged helmet. (2.4 *RRC* 25/1; 2.5 *RRC* 25/3; 2.6 *RRC* 25/4)

## 2.1 The Adoption of Coinage at Rome

**2.6**

**Figures 2.4–2.6** (cont.)

which the Romans entered the Second Punic War (218–201 BCE). The war caused such problems for Roman resources and finances that it destroyed this early currency system.

As discussed in Chapter 1, Italy had undergone the same three fundamental changes to its currency as the wider Mediterranean world of the Hellenistic period. The first was a big increase in the amount of coinage being minted and circulating. We can see this in several ways in Italy; though here 'Italy' means only southern Italy, the part of the peninsula from Naples southwards, since further north there was no tradition of making or using coinage (bronze bullion was the medium of money there). The principal silver denomination of the time is conventionally called the stater or didrachm, and we can see from the numbers of coins in hoards and from the numbers of dies used to make them that there was a big increase in their output in the last third of the fourth century. This was a pattern common to all the principal mints of the region: Neapolis, Velia, Metapontum, Heraclea, Croton, Thurii and especially Tarentum, the wealthiest city in southern Italy (Maps 1.2 and 2.1). In addition, some mints made some unusually large silver coins, which can be called double staters or tetradrachms, and we find examples at both Thurii and Metapontum. There was also some production of gold, most regularly at Tarentum, but also on a small scale from Metapontum, Heraclea and Locri. Gold coinage had previously been a sign of emergency in the Greek world, but with the large production of gold staters by the Kings of Macedon, Philip II and Alexander the Great, it started to become a more regular feature of the ancient monetary systems.[3]

**Figures 2.7–2.8** Silver and bronze coins of Metapontum, southern Italy, late fourth century.
The silver coin depicts a helmeted head labelled as *Leucippos*, a legendary founder of the city. Both have a corn ear on the reverse, referring to Metapontum's agricultural wealth. The bronze coin is inscribed with its denomination, *obolos*. (2.7 HN 1574; 2.8 HN 1640)

## 2.1 The Adoption of Coinage at Rome   **51**

The second main change was the beginning of an extensive fractional coinage. Small silver coins and bronze had indeed been minted in Italy since the fifth century, but only, it seems, on a small scale. In the late fourth century, many small silver and bronze coins were minted. One mint, Tarentum, produced almost no bronze but a coinage of silver fractions which one gets the impression was on a vast scale, to judge from the hundreds and indeed thousands recovered in hoards today. The chronology of these coins is not well established, but the main lines seem clear: the surge in production taking place at the end of the fourth century and the first half of the third. The bronze has been less studied, with notable exceptions at Neapolis and Metapontum, and also Velia.[4] The pattern of bronze seems slightly different from that of silver, since its production seems to have continued until the end of the third century, at least at Neapolis.

It is hard to see how this second change could not have led to a change in the monetary habits of the south Italians. There was now an extensive availability of small denominations, and this must imply a more intensive use of coinage in the lives of the citizens of the communities that made them.

The third change was the spread of coinage to new areas. Many new communities, often non-Greek, now started to make coinages, both in silver and bronze. Examples are Cora, Fistelia, Allifae and Arpi, and also Populonia in Etruria. It seems that such coins were produced on irregular occasions between the late fourth century and the middle of the third.

The first Roman coins fit perfectly into this pattern. Rome was, like a number of other communities, adopting coinage, in silver didrachms and crucially also in low-value pieces, like silver fractions and bronze.[5]

Viewed in this way, we can see that the adoption of coinage at Rome was part of the shifts that were affecting not just Rome, but which were having an impact more widely in Italy. It was this monetary change, rather than a military or economic transformation, that seems to be the best explanation of the peculiarly erratic, infrequent and small-scale nature of early Roman coinage.

The changing cultural outlook of Rome is another factor. Roman society was enjoying, as it emerged onto the world stage, an intense hellenisation and it was adopting many Greek institutions and Greek aesthetics: painting, town planning, tomb architecture, pottery, equestrian statues . . . and coinage. It was even possible to describe Rome as a 'Greek city' at the time.[6] As some aspects of Roman society adopted Greek models, shared values and outlook included the adoption of the Greek institution of coinage, while the ideological changes in attitude towards wealth and money among the Roman senatorial elite would have encouraged that development.[7] In many ways, including the coinage, 'Greece herself conquered her ferocious conqueror'.[8] But there were different attitudes, and such differences might help explain the spasmodic nature of Rome's early coinage.

## 2.2 Coinage in Roman Territories

So far, we have seen how the Roman coinage arose, and described how, by roughly the middle of the third century, it took on its own characteristic and, one might say, Roman identity. Until the end of that century, it consisted of fairly small quantities of silver and large amounts of bronze, both heavy cast

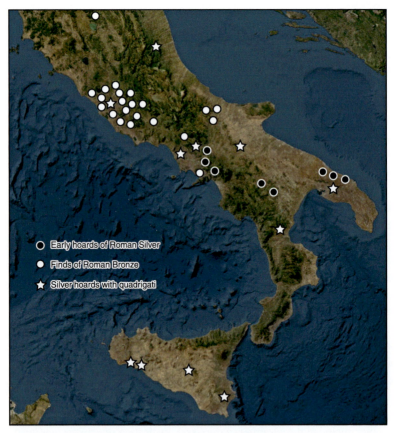

**Map 2.1** Hoards of bronze and silver in third-century Italy
The white dots represent bronze finds; the black dots represent silver finds before the quadrigati; and the white stars represent the finds of quadrigati.

pieces and lighter stuck pieces. The silver circulated predominantly in the south, and the bronze is found mainly in central Italy. Silver was not, it seems, much used at Rome or anywhere in central or northern Italy until the very end of the century, when there was a step change.[9] Until then bronze, in the form of *aes grave* or uncoined metal (*aes rude*) predominated and would have been used for exchange and payment.[10]

Roman coinage was, however, only one of many Italian coinages in the third century. The next section of this chapter looks at what was happening in the rest of Roman territory, as Roman power expanded throughout peninsular Italy and into Sardinia, Corsica, Sicily and, at the end of the century, Spain. This is a complex story and the material is not well published or easy to interpret, but some generalisations can be made. They illustrate how the Romans reacted to the situation they found in their newly conquered territories and how the communities in those territories responded to the new *realpolitik*.

For each area below, a brief survey is given of the production and circulation of coinage and its interaction with the new Roman coinage. The picture is drawn together at the end. The main changes to the silver coinage have already been discussed in Chapter 1, and are only summarised here to provide a context for the discussion of the bronze.

## 2.2.1 Southern Italy

The great increase in the production of Italian silver coinage in the late fourth century continued into the third century. However, with the Roman defeat of King Pyrrhus and the capture of Tarentum in 272 BCE, after which Rome was in control of the whole of southern Italy, changes began to happen. As described in Chapter 1, the war against Pyrrhus saw the end of most of the large silver coinages of Italy, and only a few communities, typically in Campania, thereafter produced issues of silver. After the First Punic War, which ended in 241 BCE, no more silver was minted in Italy, except at Rome.[11]

Bronze, however, continued to be produced, and the fullest study we have, for Neapolis (Naples), suggests that it continued until the late third century (Figure 2.9).[12] Bronze coinage was also made by many other communities. These bronze coinages may have been produced in connection with the war efforts (during the Pyrrhic and the First and Second Punic Wars), but the role of bronze coinage at the time is not clear. Box 2.1, however, shows that some of the issues may have coincided with periods of warfare, although most of them cannot be dated with any precision.

## Box 2.1 The pattern of bronze minting in Italy during the third century BCE

**Figure 2.9** Naples, bronze coin, mid third century BCE. (*HN* 589)

**Figure 2.10** Scipio Africanus at Canusium?, late third century BCE. (*HN* 660)

The dates are from *Historia Numorum: Italy* (*HN*; Rutter 2001), but are often uncertain. Naples made plentiful bronze coinage throughout the third century, and some of the coins can be dated from overstrikes. The coins with the enigmatic letters IΣ (2.9) belong to the middle of the century and show a head of Apollo and a man-headed bull, symbolising the local river (see also Figure 2.2). Most of the coinages in the third column (230–200 BCE) were probably made during the Second Punic War. One issue, from Canusium in Apulia (Figure 2.10), has been thought to depict the Roman general Scipio Africanus, who took refuge there in 216 BCE after the Roman defeat at the Battle of Cannae, as described by the historian Livy in his Book 22. This is probably fanciful, although the 'portrait' does seem unusually lifelike.

| 300–272 BCE | 272–230 BCE | 230–200 BCE |
|---|---|---|
|  | Aesernia |  |
|  | Aquinum |  |
|  | Caiatia |  |
|  | Cales |  |
|  | Compulteria |  |
|  | Beneventum |  |
|  | Suessa |  |
|  | Teanum |  |
| Neapolis | Neapolis | Neapolis |
|  |  | Meles |
|  |  | Atella |
|  |  | Calatia |
|  |  | Capua |

## 2.2 Coinage in Roman Territories 55

### Box 2.1 (cont.)

| 300–272 BCE | 272–230 BCE | 230–200 BCE |
| --- | --- | --- |
| Akunniadad | | |
| | Nuceria | |
| | Frentani | |
| Larinum | Larinum | Larinum |
| Arpi | | Arpi |
| Ausculum | Ausculum | Ausculum |
| Luceria | | Luceria |
| | Canusium | |
| Grumum | | |
| Silvium | | |
| | Salapia | |
| Tarentum | | |
| | Teate | Teate |
| | Venusia | Venusia |
| | | Brundisium |
| | | Caelia |
| | Butuntum | |
| | Graxa | Graxa |
| | Orra | Orra |
| | Rubi | |
| | | Mat(eola?) |
| | Paestum | Paestum |
| | Sturni | |
| | ?Velia | |
| | | Lucani |
| Metapontum | Metapontum | ?Metapontum |
| Croton | | |
| Hipponium | | |
| Locri | | |
| | | Bretii |
| | | Nuceria |
| | | Petelia |
| Rhegium | Rhegium | Rhegium |

The bronze currency of southern Italy in the late third century consisted, then, of the issues of especially Neapolis, supplemented by smaller coinages as described. However, they (and all the silver), disappeared from circulation during the Second Punic War, when they were replaced by Roman denarii and bronzes. Little bronze coinage was made thereafter in Italy, apart from some small issues of locally produced bronze (e.g., Paestum, Vibo), as well as the local (and perhaps unofficial) responses to the crisis of small change in late Republican Italy, which is discussed in Chapter 3.

### 2.2.2 Etruria

The Roman conquest of Etruria is not documented in any great detail. Fighting had taken place from the fourth century and continued for thirty years after the Battle of Sentinum in 295 BCE. We hear of various conflicts thereafter; northern Etruria was subjugated by 280 BCE, and the Romans then turned their attention to southern Etruria, and their final victory seems to have been that celebrated by M. Fulvius Flaccus *de Vulsiniensibus* in 264 BCE.

In Etruria, the minting of silver seems mainly to have been confined to one mint. Populonia was responsible for the extensive series of uniface coins and (probably) gold coins in the fourth century and especially in first half of the third century. They are very hard to date. There seems nowadays to be an emerging consensus that the majority of them were made around *c.* 300–250 BCE (Figure 2.11), but it is not at all clear whether minting continued after 280 BCE. The Ponte Gini hoard seems to show that the Etruscan silver coinage of Populonia continued in circulation until the second half of the third century. But presumably it did not survive much longer, since there is no trace of it in the hoards from the Second Punic War, although (again) there is not much evidence.[13]

Bronze *aes grave* was made by casting at a few centres: at Volaterrae, Tarquinii and elsewhere (the wheel series), and struck bronze coins were made at Populonia, Vetulonia and Cosa. The dating of most Etruscan and

**Figure 2.11** Silver coin of Populonia, early third century BCE.
The rather crude facing head of Medusa is accompanied by the number XX, presumably indicating a value of 20 (though the name of the units is not known); other amounts also appear on other coins. The coins are often one-sided, with blank reverses, showing that the normal coinage conventions were not adopted in Etruria. They are hard to date: in the past their style has been used as a criterion, and there is now some hoard evidence (as from Ponte Gini) suggesting a third-century date. (*HN* 152)

other northern *aes grave* is very difficult,[14] and it is not clear whether *aes grave* arose autonomously in pre-conquest Etruria and Umbria, or if it was inspired by the existence of Roman *aes grave*. There is no direct evidence for dating, and the dubious criterion of weight standards has been deployed in the past (the use of different standards at Etruscan centres does not necessarily imply different dates). If these series were made after the Roman conquest, as seems more likely, should we regard them as at least being tolerated by the Romans, or possibly even produced under Roman direction or encouragement?

In the part of Etruria nearest to Rome, Roman bronze coins from all of the third century are found, but further to the north of Etruria only Roman coins of the later third century occur.[15] This suggests that until about 250 BCE the currency of Etruria excluded Roman coins, and that they only arrived later, after the Roman conquest.

The picture that, tentatively, emerges for Etruria is as follows: silver was minted at Populonia before (and possibly after) the Roman conquest, and remained in circulation until the end of the century. Etruscan bronze continued to be made after the Roman conquest, and it continued in use into the later part of the third century. After the conquest, it was joined in circulation by Roman coins. However, none of these coinages circulated much after the Second Punic War, after which the currency of the area consisted solely of silver and bronze of the Roman denarius system.

2.12           2.13

**Figures 2.12–2.13** Bronze coins of Etruria.
The coin of Populonia depicts the head of Vulcan, the god of metalworking, together with his hammer and tongs. The territory of Populonia was rich in metals. The inscription is in Etruscan characters (reading backwards), *PVPLUNA*. The coin of the colony of Cosa copies the head of Mars and the horse's head from the first Roman silver coin (compare Figure 1.1). It can be dated after 273 BCE, the date of the foundation of the colony, but its exact date remains uncertain. (2.12 *HN* 195; 2.13 *HN* 210)

## 2.2.3 Northern Italy

The Romans had come into contact with Cisalpine Gaul – roughly the area of northern Italy in the Po Valley – in the late third century, and they had defeated the Gauls at the Battle of Telamon in 225 BCE. The Gauls mostly joined the Carthaginians after Hannibal's crossing of the Alps, and the area was finally subdued in the early second century.

**Figure 2.14** Silver drachm made in the Po Valley, northern Italy, late third century. The designs (a female head and a lion) and the garbled legend are taken from coins of Massalia (modern Marseilles).

Some silver coins were made and circulated in this area, based on the drachms of Massalia (Marseilles).[16] Their chronology is very uncertain, but they have been found with Roman coins (quadrigati) in hoards from Monte Bibele, near Bologna, and Rome (from the Capitoline), suggesting that they were made in c. 225–215 BCE. The Monte Bibele hoard is the earliest find of Roman coins from the area. There are also a number of slightly later finds which combine the Po Valley drachms with Roman coins of the early denarius period. Thereafter, the drachms soon disappeared from circulation, presumably being removed by the Romans, just as they removed other southern Italian silver coinages. The support given by the Gauls to the Carthaginians would provide a specific reason for this removal, although it can also be seen as part of the general change which took place over Italian currency in about 200 BCE.

## 2.2.4 Corsica

The Roman victors acquired several new territories from their struggle with Carthage: Corsica, Sardinia, Sicily, and later Spain, were all taken over, although north Africa was not annexed until the middle of the second century. Corsica was captured from the Carthaginians by the Romans in 259 BCE by L. Scipio.

Punic coins circulated in Corsica,[17] and, although no hoards seem to be known, over a hundred coins found at Aléria have been published, all bronze and mostly from Sardinia, minted in the first half of the third century.[18]

One would also expect Punic silver (and gold) to have been present before the Roman capture, but, strangely, the only silver finds which have been recorded are two silver coins of Populonia, both from Aléria, one apparently countermarked.

For the Roman period, there are a several reports of Roman bronze and silver coins from the period of the Second Punic War, including a large number of victoriates.[19] The currency of Corsica, then, switched from Punic to Roman, but the chronology and details cannot be established at the moment.

### 2.2.5 Sardinia

Just after the end of the First Punic War in 241 BCE, the Carthaginian mercenaries in Sardinia rebelled in 238 BCE, and offered the island to the Romans. Carthage thus lost control of Sardinia, and it became Roman territory. There was a major revolt against the Romans in 215 BCE, led by Hampsicoras, the Sardinian leader who after the Battle of Cannae in 216 BCE invited the Carthaginians to retake Sardinia, but it was soon crushed.

Our understanding of the Punic currency in Sardinia during the third century is better than for Corsica. It depends partly on excavation coins and chance finds, principally from Tharros,[20] and more particularly on the twenty or so hoards which have been published, including the important find made at Nora in 2008. Several hoards of Punic gold and electrum were deposited during the late fourth and early third century BCE. There are no recorded hoards of silver coins from this period, but we might reasonably assume that any silver currency was also provided by Carthage.

For the period immediately after the Roman conquest, the hoard of about fifty silver quadrigati from Cagliari suggested that Roman silver coins entered the island only ten–twenty years after its annexation,[21] but the hoard of eighteen Italian and Roman silver coins discovered at Nora has transformed our understanding.[22]

Although it is only one hoard, it shows that Roman (and some Italian) silver coinage entered the island shortly after its annexation. The absence of any Punic silver (or indeed gold) coins suggests that by this date they had been demonetised by the Romans. The silver

## 60  2 Beginnings of an Empire

> **Box 2.2  The hoard from Nora, Sardinia**
>
> The hoard from Nora, Sardinia (on the southern coast of the island, near Pula) was found during the excavations of a temple. The hoard consisted of the following silver coins:
>
> > 5 Neapolis
> > 1 Cales
> > 1 Campano-Tarentine
> > 11 Rome
> > > 1 Hercules/wolf and twins ROMANO
> > > 4 Roma/Victory ROMANO
> > > 2 Mars/horse head ROMA
> > > 4 Mars/horse ROMA
>
> As this new hoard is complete, we can be sure that it was deposited before the beginning of the quadrigati, and the latest Roman coins show that it was probably deposited in the 230s BCE, since there are no quadrigati, which are usually dated from 225 onwards.

currency of Roman Sardinia consisted then of Roman coins, as evidenced by the Nora and Cagliari hoards. After the Second Punic War, as in Italy, they were replaced by Roman coins of the denarius system.[23]

A different picture emerges for the bronze, however.[24] A first group belongs to the period of the first half of the third century, consisting of the same Carthaginian coins as are found throughout Carthaginian territory, together with issues which were made in Sardinia. A second group of hoards has previously been connected with the revolt under Hampsicoras, but are nowadays dated rather earlier, to the time of the mercenaries' revolt.[25]

Roman bronze coins seem to have arrived in any quantity only in the Second Punic War and bronze coins were made by the Roman praetors governing Sardinia in 211–209 BCE (Figures 2.15–16).

Therefore, in Sardinia, the evidence suggests that, at the time of conquest, the Romans demonetised the Carthaginian precious metal coinage and replaced it with their own. However, they allowed the Carthaginian bronze to continue in circulation until the time of the Second Punic War. Carthaginian bronze disappeared shortly thereafter, to be replaced by Roman bronze.

**Figures 2.15–2.16** Roman coins minted in Sardinia.
The Roman praetors who governed Sardinia in 211–209 BCE made some silver and many bronze coins, which bear their abbreviated names: here AVR for C. Aurunculeius and MA for Manlius Vulso. Many of them are struck over earlier Punic coins: a deliberate act of defacement? (2.15 *RRC* 65/1; 2.16 *RRC* 64/6)

### 2.2.6 Sicily

Sicily is more complicated. Its eastern part remained under the control of the rulers of Syracuse, most notably Hiero II, while the rest of the island – much the greater part – passed from Carthaginian to Roman control at the end of the First Punic War in 241 BCE. What happened to its coinage?

We have much more evidence for Sicily than for Corsica or Sardinia, although it is not, in fact, as plentiful or helpful as one might have hoped. Collections of material have been published, and there are in-depth studies for two sites, one in eastern Sicily, Morgantina, and one in western Sicily, Monte Iato, just south of Palermo.[26]

Roman quadrigati are well known from Sicily, especially western Sicily, and indeed some were even made there, characterised by a small corn ear, the symbol of Sicily's agricultural wealth (Figure 1.6). The earliest datable hoard context is the Syracuse hoard, which had coins of Hieronymus but not of the following 'Democracy', and so was presumably buried by 214 BCE.[27] But what happened before, during the thirty years between 241 and 214 BCE?

First, let us look at silver (and gold). The early third century saw a break from the earlier coinage which consisted of gold (and electrum) from Carthage and Syracuse (Agathocles, Hicetas, Pyrrhus), the silver currency of Siculo-Punic tetradrachms and the similar issues of Agathocles and imported *pegasi* from Corinth and its colonies. All these were replaced by new issues, especially in the reign of Hiero II. Hiero reigned for a very long time (270–215 BCE), and this makes the dating of his coinage (and that in the name of his wife Philistis – Figure 1.3 – and his son Gelon) very difficult.

We have a number of hoards from SE Sicily with coins in their names, but they are very difficult to date. At the end of the century, coins of Hiero and his family are found in hoards with coins of Hiero's successor Hieronymus (215–214 BCE) and the subsequent 'Democracy' (214–212 BCE), as well as Roman coins (quadrigati). Even at this late date, many of them seem to be in very good condition, suggesting that minting continued until the end of the reign, during the Second Punic War.[28]

The Carthaginians minted electrum and silver coins in Sicily, and there are now several hoards of them from the island.[29]

Thus there is a gap in the evidence. No hoards of precious metal coins are known from Sicily for the second half of the third century, apart from those containing coins of Hiero and his family, which, as we have seen, may date from the Second Punic War and are found only in SE Sicily. However, it seems very unlikely that there was no silver coinage in circulation in Sicily between the First and Second Punic wars. We should, however, recall that, until the discovery of the Nora hoard, the same was true of Sardinia. All we can say at the moment is that there is no evidence in hoards of the arrival of any Roman silver coins before the quadrigati, but it is possible that Sicily will produce a 'Nora hoard' at some time in the future.[30]

We are on somewhat stronger ground with the bronze, although the evidence is also limited. Roman bronze certainly came to Sicily during the

**Figure 2.17** Carthaginian five-shekel silver coin, minted in Sicily, during the First Punic War.
This large silver coin has the head of Tanit, the patron deity of Carthage (see also Figure 1.27), and, on the reverse, the winged horse Pegasus, copied from earlier coins of Corinth and its colonies (which had circulated extensively in Sicily). The Punic inscription reads B'RST (meaning perhaps 'in the land'), possibly implying that Carthage had formally annexed the parts of Sicily which it controlled. Such coins may have formed part of the booty captured by the Romans at the Battle of Mylae (Figure 1.26), and they disappeared from circulation after the war.

Second Punic War. Two hoards containing them may have been deposited in the first years of the war, as were several others, which closed in the middle years of the war.[31] The same coins are present among the excavation finds from Morgantina and Monte Iato. At this time, the Romans also made bronze coins in Sicily, characterised by the presence of a corn ear.

There is some evidence for the presence of Roman bronze before the Second Punic War, but not much. There is a single small 'hoard' of *aes grave* from Sicily, found in Naxos or Piazza Armerina,[32] and a series of rare Roman bronzes was also made in the island in about 240 BCE.[33] A few early Roman bronzes were found at Morgantina, but we cannot be sure of their dates of circulation and loss.

One might consequently assume that the bronze currency between the Punic wars consisted of Carthaginian coins, as in Sardinia, but this does not seem to be true. The contextual analysis of the finds at Morgantina and Monte Iato indicates that the presence of Carthaginian coins was reduced in the middle of the third century.[34]

What, then, constituted the bronze coinage of Sicily in the later third century? There was almost no Roman and little Punic. And, apart from Syracuse (see Figures 2.18–2.19), no other Sicilian towns minted anything very much at this period, as the summary in Box 2.3 shows.

---

### Box 2.3 The minting of bronze coinage in third-century BCE Sicily

Only a few Sicilian cities minted bronze coinage in the mid to late third century BCE.

| | Latest pre-mid-third-century minting | Next minting |
| --- | --- | --- |
| Abakainon | 280–270 BCE | post 241 BCE |
| Adranon | – | – |
| Agyrion | – | 208–205 BCE |
| Aitna | – | 211–200 BCE |
| Akragas | 287–279 BCE | 213–210 BCE |
| Akrai | – | post 212 BCE |
| Alaisa | – | 211–208 BCE |
| Alontion | 280–270 BCE | post 210 BCE |
| Ameselon | – | – |
| Amestratus | – | 215–213 BCE? |

**64** 2 Beginnings of an Empire

### Box 2.3 (cont.)

| | Latest pre-mid-third-century minting | Next minting |
|---|---|---|
| Enna | – | 217–214 BCE |
| Entella | – | late C1 |
| Eryx | – | – |
| Gela | – | 208–200 BCE |
| Herakleia Minoa | – | – |
| Herbessos | – | – |
| Himera/Thermai H | – | 206–205 BCE |
| Hybla Megale | – | 190–186 BCE |
| Iaitia | 330–260 BCE | post 210 BCE |
| Kalakte | – | 215–200 BCE? |
| Kamarina | 310–290 BCE | – |
| Katane | – | 216/5–206 BCE |
| Kentoripai | – | 214–210 BCE |
| Kephaloidion | – | late C1 |
| Leontinoi | early third century/post 210 BCE | post 210 BCE |
| Lilybaion | – | 208–180 BCE? |
| Menai | – | 204–190 BCE |
| Messana (Mamertini) | 264–241 BCE | 215–202 BCE |
| Morgantina | – | 210–185 BCE (Hispani) |
| Motye | – | – |
| Nakone | – | post 216 BCE |
| Naxos | – | – |
| Panormos | – | 211–200 BCE |
| Segesta | – | post 210 BCE |
| Selinous | – | – |
| Solus | before 254 BCE | post 210 BCE |
| Syrakosai | 286–276 BCE (Pyrrhus) | Hiero |
| Tauromenion | 265–263 BCE? | 210–208 BCE |
| Tyndaris | 276–253 BCE | post 210 BCE |
| Lipara | post 289 before 252 BCE | – |

This table of third century minting in Sicily is based on Puglisi 2009 (minor mints omitted). The dates are mostly taken from Carroccio 2004.

We are drawn to the conclusion that, as the Romans conquered Sicily, they abolished the bronze coinage of Carthage and replaced it with the bronze coinage of Syracuse, not just in the area of Syracusan control, but also in western Sicily, which was under their direct rule.

**Figures 2.18–2.19** Bronze coins of King Hiero of Syracuse. The only coins of the period, made and found in quantity, are the two main types of Syracuse, minted under Hiero II, with a cavalryman and with a trident. They occur in a number of hoards from all over the island in large numbers and without any other coins (Puglisi 2009 H22–23, H93, H160, H162, H166, H251–3, H374 and H376–77). Large quantities were recovered from Morgantina (more than 200), and some from Monte Iato (71), the latter suggesting that 'the new flow of Syracusan coins from east to west is therefore not unconnected with the Roman occupation of west Sicily from 254 BCE, and the collapse of Punic hegemony' (Frey-Kupper 2013: 709).

To summarise the picture of the currency of Sicily in the third century: Carthaginian coinage in all metals disappeared from circulation in the middle of the century, and was replaced, as regards bronze, with the coinage of Syracuse. As for the silver, we cannot be sure: Roman silver certainly entered the island late in the century, and in SE Sicily it is found in hoards together with the coinage of Syracuse, but, as we have seen, the evidence for the nature of the silver currency of the island during the years between the Roman conquest and the Second Punic War is not good.

After the Second Punic War, the silver currency changed, and only Roman silver denarii were present on the island. The pattern for bronze currency is more complicated, but essentially the earlier coins also disappeared, and Roman bronzes arrived in considerable quantities. However, they were accompanied by the strange 'Roman-Sicilian' coinage and by some locally produced civic bronze. We shall return to this complicated picture in the Chapter 3.

### 2.2.7 Africa

It may seem surprising that Africa has been included in this survey, since, even after the defeat of Carthage in 201 BCE, the Carthaginian state continued to exist, and to produce coinage, now of much debased silver. However, curiously, there is some evidence for the presence of Roman coinage there before 200.[35] A quadrigatus was found at Kerkouane, a site probably abandoned in the middle of the third century, but the quadrigatus and the two bronzes also reported from the site were probably lost there at the end of the third century or the beginning of the second. Even more intriguing are the three Roman quinarii from Carthage, perhaps part of a hoard. These finds, however, are exceptional, perhaps betraying the occasional presence of Romans, and the bulk of the currency in use in north Africa continued to consist of Carthaginian coins.

### 2.2.8 Spain

Roman involvement in Spain only began in the Second Punic War. Before then, the silver currency of third-century Spain was confined to the eastern part of the country, especially the coastal areas. It consisted of coins minted by the Carthaginians in Spain, together with very large numbers of coins of Emporion with the design of a pegasus and 'Emporion' imitations, supplemented by substantial amounts silver in uncoined form.[36] The imitations have a variety of enigmatic inscriptions, but some are recognisable place names, implying a widespread production. Bronze coinage consisted of some locally produced coins, such as of Gades and Malaga, together with Hispano-Punic coins, of which we have a few hoards dating to the time of the Second Punic War.[37]

**Figure 2.20** Carthaginian silver coin, minted in Spain, late third century BCE. The Carthaginian conquest of Spain gave access to the rich silver deposits there, and they were exploited to make coins. This one depicts the Carthaginian god Melqart, who had affinities with Hercules, and so carries a club. It has sometimes been thought to have the features of Hannibal, but this seems unlikely. The reverse showed an elephant, perhaps representing one of the ones which Hannibal took with his army when he crossed the Alps to invade Italy.

## 2.2 Coinage in Roman Territories

**Figures 2.21–2.23** Roman silver coins minted in Spain.
As well as importing coins into Spain, in support of their war effort, the Romans also made a few silver coins there, as has recently been discovered. The characteristically crude style of the quadrigatus (2.21) is typical of finds made in Spain (contrast Figure 1.6). Specimens of its very rare half-piece (2.22) have also been found in Spain; they retain the head of Janus, while the reverse is a copy of the oath scene on Roman gold (see Figure 1.28). The ⅙ piece (2.23) also has Janus, and a horse, perhaps copied from other early Roman coins. Figure 2.23 is enlarged × 1.5. (2.21 *MIB* 215/01; 2.22 *MIB* 215/04; 2.23 *RRC* 28/5 and *MIB* 215/05)

The earliest context for Roman coins in Spain is the series of (mostly) metal detector finds made at the site of La Palma in the Ebro delta, which was probably a Roman marching camp and which dates to 215 BCE.[38] Otherwise, however, only a very few Roman coins seem to have entered Spain before the period of the denarius. There are only one or two quadrigati in hoards,[39] and only a very small number of silver coins were made in Spain by the Romans.[40]

After the war, however, there was a change in the currency of Spain. The earlier Punic, Emporitan and Roman silver disappeared, as did the earlier Punic bronze. Roman denarii and bronzes are found during the second century, but were supplemented by the extensive series of locally produced 'Iberian denarii' and bronzes, which will be discussed in Chapter 3. Hoards of the second century consisted of some Roman and many locally produced bronzes; the earlier material had all gone.[41]

**68** 2 Beginnings of an Empire

## 2.3 The Changing Use of Coinage in the Early Roman World

The beginning of this chapter described the growing use of coined money in southern Italy, and how the earliest Roman silver and bronze coins fitted into the new and expanding Italian and Mediterranean model of more coinage and smaller denominations. Yet, as we have seen, Roman coinage was at first episodic and on a small scale. Moreover, Roman silver at first circulated only in the south of Italy, where an economy which used silver coinage had been long established by Greek cities there. There is almost no sign of silver coinage being used in Rome until the end of the third century, and only a little more in central and northern Italy.[42] Silver coin can have played little or no part in the economy of these areas, and it was anyway small in scale compared with what we know of other amounts of silver coming into Rome through booty and indemnities.[43] This picture challenges the traditional accounts of the development of banking in the late fourth (and so third) century, and indeed the earlier existence of a monetised economy of the sort that can be found in the plays of Plautus. None of this would be problematic in the second century, even the early part of the second century, when a silver-using monetised economy seems well enough attested both by the written sources and by the archaeological finds.[44]

What of bronze and the bronze coinage? Central Italy had long enjoyed a currency of bronze by weight, often today called *aes rude* or 'uncoined bronze'. Its antecedents as a form of currency go back a long way, as has been argued for the Bronze Age Europe in general.[45] *Aes rude* continued in use into the third century, and, apart from an isolated issue in the late fourth century (Figure 2.1), Roman bronze coins started to be made only during the third century. The larger pieces were cast in moulds and consisted of large bronze discs (*aes grave* = 'heavy bronze') or bars. The small hoard from Santa Marinella is one of the earliest hoards to contain them, and several large deposits are known, for example from Vicarello and Carsoli.[46]

There is no obvious way to assess the scale of the cast bronze coinage since its technique of manufacture precludes the estimation of its size by counting dies, as is used for other (struck) coinages. It is clear, however, that the early bronze survives in much smaller numbers than the bronzes (including the cast prow *aes grave*) that were made at the end of the century, so there is no compelling reason to suppose that bronze coin was in widespread use in the Roman economy. That is not to say that it was not used for some purposes such as the payment of fines ('ex aere moltatico' = from the fine money), attested from the fourth century (and perhaps earlier) both from Rome and elsewhere in central Italy.[47] Dedications of bronze coins in sanctuaries are also well attested, where the coins started to replace dedications in uncoined metal (*aes rude*).[48] It is less clear that it could be used for other purposes. A few third-century coins have been recovered from the Roman Forum,[49] allowing the possibility of some very restricted use in retail trade. Military pay is a possibility, but the date of its introduction is uncertain, and the two likely dates (about 400 or 340 BCE) are far too early for it to have been paid in coin. The first big issues of struck bronze were not minted before about 270–250, and there is no reason to suppose that the production of *aes grave* began before about 280 BCE.[50]

During the third century there seems to have been a strange imbalance in the different parts of Roman territory, from the point of view of the use of coined money. It seems likely that southern Italy and Sicily, the areas which had long used silver and bronze coins, continued to do so, but a monetised economy did not develop further north or in Mediterranean Spain until much later.

It was only from the period of the Second Punic War that silver came into widespread use throughout the Roman world, and then a sudden change took place from a society that essentially used only bronze and, to some extent, bronze coinage, to one which enjoyed a fully monetised system of both silver and bronze coinage. The picture in the plays of Plautus shows a society that must suddenly have become more or less fully monetised. The increase in coined money allowed a greater use in daily activities, as can also be seen, for example, in the construction of new shops (*tabernae*).[51] At the macro level, the availability of an increased amount of money and capital encouraged the development of economic activity, seen for example, in the increase of the number of shipwrecks recorded in the Mediterranean in the second century CE.[52]

The wider impact of the adoption of coined money in early Greece has been explored in a number of studies, which have sought to consider its effect on social and political, as well as economic, behaviour, and indeed on the intellectual and literary life of the societies that produced it.[53] Rome in the late third century invites a similar investigation.

## 2.4 Roman Imperialism: Iconography

The surveys presented above give an idea of the changes that occurred in the new Roman territories. Sometimes 'inherited' coinages continued, but sometimes the Romans intervened to bring about change.

One of the curiosities of these changes, which was also to remain a feature of the next two centuries, was how little the iconography of the coins of various communities was influenced by Roman ideology. This is the principal reason why it is often difficult to tell which coins were produced before and which after the establishment of Roman rule: they look more or less exactly the same and they avoid any reference to contemporary events. There was only one isolated exception in Italy, on the coins of Locri, which date to the time of the Pyrrhic War (Figure 2.24).

Cosa in coastal Etruria and Ausculum in northern Apulia imitated contemporary Roman coins (Figure 2.13),[54] but other colonies and independent cities did not, and they continued the tradition of designs that referred in some way to their own religious or civic identity. This traditional approach of the Italian communities was in stark contrast to the practice of the Romans themselves. They constantly changed the designs on their coinage, emphasising war and victory, as well as the iconography of Alexander the Great (Figures 2.4–2.5, 2.25), whom they must have seen as some sort of precedent to their own role as conquerors. the coinage of the

**Figure 2.24** Rome and Locri.
Some rare coins of Locri, in the very south of Italy, break the traditional mould of Italian coinage and refer to Rome. The reverse depicts two figures labelled as PΩMA and ΠΙΣΤΙΣ, the personifications of Rome and of Good Faith. This may be a reference to the *deditio in fidem*, the voluntary surrender in 282 BCE, under which Locri put itself under the protection of Rome, and when a Roman garrison was installed. This is the earliest personification of Rome to have survived, and only later did the Romans adapt her iconography to resemble the war goddess Minerva (Burnett 1986): see also Figure 3.30. (*HN* 2348)

## 2.4 Roman Imperialism: Iconography

**Figures 2.25–2.26** Roman coinage and aggressive imperialism (continued on p. 72).

**72** 2 Beginnings of an Empire

One of the changing motifs used by the Romans was this forcefully imperialist design on a silver coin (2.25), depicting Hercules and the wolf and twins. It shows Hercules, regarded at the time as a god of Victory, in the guise of Alexander the Great: he has Alexander's hairstyle and wears his royal diadem. The reverse depicts the symbol of Rome, the wolf and twins, perhaps based on a statue group set up on the Capitoline Hill. Together they make the visual claim that Rome was Alexander's successor. Some years later the Romans introduced the new designs for the bronze, the head of Janus and a prow (2.26), a design which was to remain in use for over a century (see also Figure 3.2). The coins are marked with a prominent I, denoting the denomination of one as, and they were among the last Roman coins made by the casting method. As the coins became smaller, they would usually be struck from dies, a technique which would not work for very large coins. The most likely reference of the head of Janus is to the closure of the gates of the Temple of Janus in 235 BCE. This act symbolised the end of war and the establishment of peace. It had been achieved principally through the Roman naval victories of the First Punic War, such as that of the Battle of Mylae. The captured prows were probably proudly displayed in the Forum on the victory monument of the Roman commander C. Duilius (*cf.* Figure 1.26). (2.25 *RRC* 20; 2.26 *RRC* 35/1)

later third century seems particularly politicised: the figure of Jupiter on a chariot hurling a thunderbolt refers to the legendary battle of the gods and the giants, probably an allegory for the conflict of Rome against Carthage; the prow on the bronze coinage marks the Roman achievement of naval supremacy in the western Mediterranean from the time of the First Punic War (Figure 2.26); while the oath scene on the gold coins minted at the start of the conflict with Hannibal (Figure 1.28) may evoke the *Punica fides*, the later Roman catchphrase for the treachery of the Carthaginians, who brought about the war by breaking a treaty.[55] No such approach is visible at all on the allied or enemy coinages of the third century.

## 2.5 Continuity and Change: The End of Non-Roman Coinage in Italy

As we have seen, however, the Romans brought about many changes to the currency of the third century. We can summarise the previous discussion in Box 2.4 for the mid third century and Box 2.5 for the Second Punic War.

There are some clear examples of Roman intervention, such as the changes to the silver currency of Sardinia at the end of the First Punic War, or to the silver and bronze currency of Sicily at the same time. These

## Box 2.4 The currency of the western Mediterranean in the third century BCE

| Region | Roman 'conquest' | SILVER | BRONZE |
|---|---|---|---|
| **Etruria** | 280 BCE | Etruscan silver minting continues until *c*. 280 + BCE | Etruscan bronze continues Joined by Roman after 1PW[*] |
| **S Italy** | 272 BCE | Minting stops except at Tarentum and Neapolis where it continues till *c*. 250 BCE New small mints (e.g. Cales) Some Roman silver | Bronze continues to be made until 2PW[†] (e.g. Neapolis) New small mints Some Roman bronze |
| **N Italy** | 225 BCE | Some minted at the end of the century | Bullion? |
| **Corsica** | 259 BCE | No evidence Roman coins start in 2PW | Punic coins continue? Roman coins start in 2PW? |
| **Sicily** | 241 BCE | Punic gold and silver disappear; replaced (?) by Roman (and Syracusan) silver Roman coins arrive by 2PW, some minted there | Punic and Sicilian bronze replaced by bronze of Hiero II Roman bronze arrives only in 2PW, some minted there |
| **Sardinia** | 238 BCE | Punic gold and silver replaced by Roman silver | Punic bronze remains in circulation until 2PW Some Roman bronze arrives in 2PW |
| **Spain** | 207 BCE | Mostly Punic and Spanish Some Roman silver arrives in 2PW | Mostly Punic and Spanish Some Roman bronze arrives in 2PW |

[*] First Punic War; [†] Second Punic War

# 74  2 Beginnings of an Empire

## Box 2.5  The currency of the western Mediterranean during the Second Punic War

| Region | | SILVER | BRONZE |
|---|---|---|---|
| **Etruria** | 280 BCE | Roman denarii | Roman |
| **S Italy** | 272 BCE | Roman denarii | Roman |
| | | | Some tiny issues, e.g., Vibo, Paestum |
| **N Italy** | 225 BCE | Roman denarii | Roman |
| **Corsica** | 259 BCE | Roman (victoriati) | Roman coins start in 2PW? |
| **Sicily** | 241 BCE | Roman denarii | Roman |
| | | | 'Romano-Sicilian' issues |
| | | | Revival of civic coinage |
| **Sardinia** | 238–7 BCE | Roman denarii | Roman; some local bronze in C1 |
| **Spain** | 207 BCE | Roman denarii | Roman bronze |
| | | Revival of civic silver | Revival of civic bronze |

changes can be interpreted as a wish to destroy symbols of the enemy. We can, however, also see that any such political intervention could vary from metal to metal, as the survival of Punic bronze in Sardinia after 238 BCE (and perhaps southern Italy) makes clear, and this pattern will also be observed on other, later occasions.

We find a similar pattern for silver and bronze in both Etruria and southern Italy, though it is hard to be sure if we are dealing with political intervention.[56] The ending of silver coinage in most Italian cities at the time of the Roman conquest suggests that Roman intervention was at least a factor. At the same time, we should not ignore economic factors. There was undoubtedly a transfer of wealth from the Etruscan and Italian cities to Rome, and this may have been a factor in the decline of those silver coinages at Tarentum and Naples that survived the Roman conquest but then came to an end sometime later.

In some other cases, such as the beginning of Roman coinage or – to jump a long way forward – the ending of Roman provincial bronze in the west in the first century CE, it has been suggested that we should think principally in terms of cultural rather than political or economic factors. We have already seen how changes in Italian and Roman society made the

Romans want to have a coinage in *c.* 300 BCE. Much later, differing attitudes in the western and eastern parts of the Empire caused the inhabitants of one half of the Empire to abandon locally produced coinage but encouraged the inhabitants of the other half to produce it with increasing vigour. It may be that similar cultural factors were also at work in southern Italy or Etruria.

The Second Punic War had two main effects. On the one hand, it stimulated coinage on both sides, for Rome and for Carthage. Both Rome and Carthage themselves produced much more coinage to pay the expenses of the war, and the period saw many new local coinages, some in silver but mostly in bronze. It is not difficult to see them as contributions to the cost of the war effort, on both sides, whether made willingly or under coercion.

Towards the end and after the war, however, there was a change in the currency, in all areas. In peninsular Italy no third-century silver or bronze survived into the second century. It was all replaced (with one or two exceptions, as described in Chapter 3) by Roman denarii and Roman bronze. The war also saw the same change in Sicily. Roman denarii became the only silver in circulation there, and they were accompanied by Roman bronze, supplemented (as we shall see in more detail in Chapter 3) by some locally produced coinage. The coinage of independent Syracuse, not only in gold and silver, but also in bronze, disappeared from circulation immediately after the fall of the city in 212 BCE.[57] Syracuse, long a Roman ally, had demonstrated its treachery by switching sides to support the Carthaginians. It fell after a long and bitter siege, and its coinage, a symbol of its treachery, was destroyed, just as Carthaginian coinage was destroyed.

In Sardinia, the change to Roman silver had already taken place. The same may have been true in Corsica. Both areas, probably, changed from Punic to Roman bronze from the time of the Second Punic War.

In Spain, the situation was similar, but different. After the war, most of the earlier silver disappeared from circulation, whether Punic, Roman or Spanish (Emporion and Emporitan imitations). But the pattern for the bronze is more complicated. It seems that the earlier bronze remained in circulation for some time. Then, only later in the second century, did the coinage of Iberian denarii and bronzes begin.

However, in all the areas we have discussed we see a common pattern, though one that was applied to a greater or lesser degree, either during or after the war. Nearly all the previous coinage of the third century was swept away, and replaced with new coinages, and principally that of

Rome. 'Did Rome conquer Italy or did Italy overcome Rome?'[58] The history of the coinage at the end of the third coinage gives decisive evidence for the former.

Political motivation seems the most likely explanation, although we should be careful not to exaggerate it. Carthage – and now, also Syracuse – was the hated enemy, and we can understand a wish to obliterate its coinage, a symbol of the Carthaginian state and sovereignty. But the coinage of allies, and, indeed, Rome itself, also disappears at the same time, to be replaced by new coinages. The picture was more complicated, and, as with the introduction of coinage a hundred years earlier, politics, economics and ideology all played a part in the transformation of the currency of the western Mediterranean from that of a series of independent and dependent states to one dominated by a single power. However, the new pattern was one which, nevertheless, retained a great plurality, as we shall see in Chapter 3. Rome may have been the single, dominant power, but it did not impose its own coinage on all of its new, growing empire. The Romans may have had an imperialist ideology, but it had only a limited practical effect. Hostility had to be very strong to generate the destruction of coinage, and, as we have seen, continuity was more of a common theme.

# 3

## The Growth of an Empire during the Late Republic (200–31 BCE)

'In less than fifty-three years the Romans have brought nearly the whole inhabited world under their sole rule, a thing which cannot be found ever to have happened before'. As the words of Polybius state (*Histories* 1.1), the years from 220 to 170 BCE saw great changes in Roman rule. Rome defeated Carthage in Spain and Africa, and quickly dominated the remaining powers of the eastern Mediterranean – Macedon, Syria and Egypt. Territorial annexation followed in the west, but, in the east, the establishment of direct Roman rule was delayed for several decades. Roman territory did, however, gradually increase and new provinces were established: Macedonia was conquered in 168 BCE, and Achaea in 146 BCE; Asia was bequeathed to Rome by its last king in 133 BCE; Syria and the Levant were annexed by Pompey in 64 BCE; Gaul was conquered in the 50s BCE; and Egypt fell under the control of the Romans with the death of Cleopatra in 30 BCE. Thus by the end of the Republican period and the establishment of the monarchy by Augustus, the Roman Empire was territorially largely complete.

The coinage produced during the Republican period reflects these changes, and it can help us understand how Rome wished to administer its newly subjected peoples.[1] In particular, it has a relevance to the debate about Roman imperialism – how aggressive was Rome in seeking to impose its own institutions like coinage on its newly acquired territories and populations? The new Roman currency, based on the denarius, was not imposed on all the provinces of the new and growing empire. It did spread rapidly through Spain, but arrived east of the Adriatic only later: to Greece in the late second or first century BCE, and to Asia and Syria only in the first century CE. Even in the west, it did not have a monopoly. Spain saw a curious experiment in the second and early first centuries, the production of the so-called Iberian denarii and bronzes, modelled partly on Roman coins and circulating with them. A similar phenomenon took place in Gaul in the first century: the production across a wide area of silver 'quinarii'. There was an intention to continue, or even prop up, 'non-Roman' coinages

**Figures 3.1–3.3** The Roman denarius coinage.
The principal coins of the new denarius system were the silver denarius (3.1) and the bronze *as* (3.2). The silver coin was marked with the numeral X, and called the 'tenner' because it was worth ten asses (until about 140 BCE, when it was retariffed at sixteen asses: on which see Lo Cascio 2016, 340–2). Additional denominations were initially made in silver and gold, including the victoriate (Figure 1.11). The bronze *as* was accompanied by a range of smaller bronze denominations. They all had the prow of a ship on the reverse, and different obverses: in the case of the *as* the double head of Janus (see also Figure 2.26). At first, minting was dispersed in a number of centres in Italy, Sicily and Spain, but, after the Second Punic War, production was confined to the mint at Rome. The date of the first coins of the new system was long debated, but there is nowadays a consensus that it began in the first half of the Second Punic War. The exact date, however, is still uncertain. It was definitely before 211 BCE, as is shown by the finds from Morgantina in Sicily and overstrikes such as the one illustrated here (3.3): this Carthaginian coin was minted in Sicily before 210 BCE and was struck over a Roman victoriate. The Carthaginian coin shows traces of the Roman coin (*cf.* Figure 1.11): the back of the head of Jupiter can be seen in front of the chin on the obverse; on the reverse, the letters RO, part of ROMA, can be seen at the bottom of the coin. (3.1 *RRC* 44/5; 3.2 *RRC* 56/2)
Figure 3.3 is enlarged × 1.5.

and indeed monetary systems, just as the Romans tended to take over other aspects of administration from the territories they conquered. Exceptions were violent and rare: only Carthage, which 'must be destroyed' (*delenda est*), saw its gold and silver currency obliterated after the Third Punic War in 146 BCE, like the city itself, just as earlier Carthaginian coinage had been expunged in the third century.

As well as Roman coins, Roman units of account started to spread across the new territories, but they were by no means universally imposed. The course of their spread is hard to document, depending as it does on the occasional inscription that has relevant information, and the evidence is not sufficient to allow us to understand the full extent of the adoption of Roman denominations throughout the Republican (and, indeed, Imperial) periods. Equally fragile are the attempts which have been made recently to see a more indirect influence of Roman coins ('Roman' in the sense used in this book to mean like those made at the mint of Rome) on the physical appearance of local coinages during the Republican period.

The most surprising feature of the coinage in the provinces is (to the modern mind) the almost complete lack of references to the new power, Rome or even (at first) the new dominant personalities like Sulla, Pompey and Caesar. Few, indeed, were the 'imprints of Roman imperium', as they have been called (Galani 2022).

All these themes are explored in more detail below, region by region, and at the end of the chapter some generalisations are drawn which provide a clearer understanding of the patchwork of monetary systems that existed across the Roman world in the Republican period, and the changes to them that took place. In turn, they allow us to see more clearly how the Roman imperial monetary system evolved.

## 3.1 Italy

In Chapter 2 we saw how, in the third century BCE, Roman coinage was at first confined to Italy. The silver remained mostly in southern Italy, where it circulated with south Italian Greek coins, and the bronze in central Italy. By the end of the century, Roman bronze had spread southwards, while Roman silver started to be used further north, as well as also being found in Sicily, and, in fairly small quantities, in Sardinia and Spain. In some of these areas it circulated beside locally produced silver.

The Second Punic War against Hannibal and the introduction of the denarius, however, brought a fundamental change in the circulating medium. All the earlier silver, including all the non-Roman silver, was swept away and in most of these areas (except Spain) the denarius became the only silver coin in circulation.

At the same time, the amount of silver coinage in circulation increased greatly, presumably a reflection of an increasing monetisation of society. During the third century, silver coinage had been minted and used on a sparse scale, but the archaeological and literary evidence indicates a step change at the end of the century. From this time, Rome and its dependencies started to look like the other monetised economies of the Mediterranean world.[2]

Roman silver and bronze was used through Italy in the last two centuries BCE. Small amounts of bronze coinage continued to be minted at a few cities in southern Italy, such as Brundisium, Paestum, Copia or Vibo Valentia.[3] They seem to have followed the Roman system of denominations, but on a lighter weight standard.

3.4                                  3.5

**Figures 3.4–3.5** Bronze coins of Paestum, southern Italy.
The coinage of Paestum is particularly interesting, since it bears inscriptions which show it was produced under many different people, some of whom held the civic offices of *quinquennalis*, *duovir* (and later *quattuorvir*), and *praetor*. The coinage even continued into the reigns of Augustus and Tiberius, when it was also signed by *duoviri*, and even on one occasion by a woman called Mineia (3.4), a known benefactor of the colony. The coinage also adopts a new diversity of designs, presumably echoing the model of Roman denarii, and depicts a variety of deities and views of buildings, such as temples or the basilica which had been restored by Mineia. There is even a rare instance of a depiction of a coining scene on a coin signed by the *praetor* Q Laur .... (3.5) It is accompanied by the inscription S P D D S S MIL, which has been interpreted as standing for 'sua pecunia dono dedit senatus sententia milia' ('he gave, from his own money, thousands [of such coins], with the consent of the senate [of Paestum]'). This is an explicit and early reference to the system of city liturgy, whereby a prominent individual would provide some benefit to the citizens, including that of coinage. (3.4 *HN* 1258; 3.5 *HN* 1238)

**Figure 3.6** Uncertain mint in Italy, first century BCE.
An enigmatic series of coins were made somewhere in Italy in the first century BCE. They have a head of Bacchus, and on the reverse his sacred animal, a panther with a thyrsus (the sacred staff of Dionysus) in its mouth. The coins have no inscription which identifies their origin. They are found widely in Italy and southern France, and were made from a very large number of dies. (*HN* 2672)

From about 80 BCE, almost no bronze was produced at the mint of Rome for many decades: there were a few exceptions, such as the rare bronzes of a reduced weight standard made for several years from 91 BCE,[4] or the heavier but equally rare pieces made by Sulla in 82 BCE.[5]

The problems created by an increasing lack of official coinage prompted three main responses. The first was the production of imitations of the official bronzes in Italy and elsewhere.[6] The second was the influx of coins such as those of Massalia and Ebusus.[7] The third was the production of imitations of Massalia and Ebusus in Italy, together with the manufacture of coins with new designs, such as those with Bacchus and the panther (Figure 3.6), whose makers perhaps deliberately avoided adding any inscription which might have identified the authority, perhaps not officially sanctioned, responsible for minting them.[8] This mass of official, imitative and 'foreign' coinage comprised the bronze currency throughout the first century and until the reign of Augustus, and it was one of the monetary problems that he tried to address, as will be discussed in Chapter 4.

It may well have been not just a matter of inconvenience, but one that had a real impact on society. We hear in 85 BCE that 'the coin was being thrown about so much that no one could tell what he had'.[9] The meaning of the passage is much debated, but it might refer to a changing ratio between the silver and bronze coinage, perhaps caused by the confusing farrago of the latter and the debasement of the former.[10] The solution of Marius Gratidianus – whatever it was – brought him 'great honours; statues in every street, with incense and candles. No one has ever been more popular with the masses' (Cicero, *de Officiis* III.80).

## 3.2  Sicily

Western Sicily became Roman territory after the First Punic War, whereas the kingdom of Syracuse continued to exist in the eastern part of the island, and was taken over by the Romans only after their successful siege of Syracuse in 212 BCE. Thereafter, for the last two centuries BCE, the currency in use there differed from that of both Italy and Spain. As in Italy, only Roman denarii were used as silver currency. Roman bronzes also came to Sicily, but, as in Spain, they represented only a small part of the bronze currency. As in Spain, they were accompanied by substantial quantities of locally produced bronzes, many made by city authorities. The circulation of the city coinages was usually limited to their local region, as is shown by the coins recovered in the excavations at Monte Iato and Morgantina.[11]

Very occasionally some of these city issues bear the names of Romans. There were also two series of 'Romano-Sicilian' coins, made during the second century and probably to be attributed to Panormus and Lilybaeum. They prominently display Roman names, occasionally with the letter Q, standing for *quaestor*, which demonstrates that the names refer to men in the Roman provincial government.[12] The Lilybaeum series have a prominent Janus head on their main denomination and a value mark I, which suggests that they were tariffed in terms of the Roman *as*, even

3.7                                            3.8

**Figures 3.7–3.8** Romano-Sicilian coins, second century BCE.
The Romans made two series of bronze coins for circulation in western Sicily. One series (3.7) has the head of Janus and a wreath enclosing the name of a Roman official (here the *quaestor* Mn. Acili. Q. = the *quaestor* Manius Acilius). The other (3.8) has a head of Jupiter and the standing figure of a warrior, who is accompanied by a monogram standing for Panormus (modern Palermo) as well as a Roman name (here Cato, probably another *quaestor*). Altogether some 20–25 men are named, sometimes in highly abbreviated monograms (whose expansion is not clear). It seems likely that they were all Roman officials in Sicily, probably *quaestors* like Manius Acilius. Their names are not preserved in any other source, and they were presumably minor members of the same families which produced more famous Manii Acilii and Porcii Catones (Frey-Kupper 2013, 248–53).

though they were made on a much lighter weight standard and are found together in hoards. However, a few of their smaller denominations have value marks, expressed by two pellets or one pellet with the letter *X*, which stands for *chalkous*. It is not clear how coins of one or two *chalkoi* might relate to an as.

Other city coins also have value marks, if only infrequently. They may be expressed either as dots, apparently representing ounces (*onkiai*), or as straight lines, where the pattern of marks indicates that they express the number of *chalkoi*.[13]

The fullest source of information is derived from the inscriptions from Tauromenium that preserve the financial accounts of the city.[14] These accounts, which date from the second and first centuries BCE, show, at first, a system of a talent worth 120 *litrai*. Later, sometime between 61 and 46 BCE, the system changed (at the same time that the accounts stopped using Greek months and adopted Roman ones), to a new one of *nomoi* and litrai. The talent was replaced by the *nomos* at a rate of 1 talent = 3 *nomoi*. The *nomos*, which then was also = 40 *litrai*, seems plausibly to be the same as a Roman denarius. There are also occasional mentions in the accounts of other units, called a *heminomos* (half-nomos) and *tetralitron* (4-*litrai*).

**Figure 3.9** Accounts from Tauromenium, first century BCE.
The first six lines of this section read: 'Income to the Stewards during June: 7851 nomoi, 31 litrai. Expenditure: 8757 nomoi, 38 litrai. Balance: 2567 nomoi and a half nomos'.

**84** 3 The Growth of an Empire during the Late Republic

However these different Sicilian systems may have been related to the Roman, their very existence meant that there was need for a system of exchange between them. It was open to abuse, as Cicero complained in 70 BCE in relation to the abuses carried out by C. Verres, the Roman governor of Sicily. In his speech against Verres (2 *Verr.* 3.181), Cicero asked, no doubt disingenuously, 'what exchange commission can there be when all use one kind of money?' The denarius may have prevailed as the only silver coin in circulation, but the existence of so many different sorts of coins – and perhaps systems – in Sicily meant that their exchange must have been facilitated by moneychangers. As discussed in Chapter 4, their activities were open to misuse, and Verres may well have invented some sort of scam which allowed him to get personal gain.

## 3.3 Spain

During the Second Punic War, the silver currency of Hispania (modern Spain and Portugal) had consisted of a mixture of many Punic and a few Roman coins, along with locally produced issues, from mints such as Gades (Cádiz), Arse (Sagunto) and Tarraco (Tarragona).[15] There was a considerable amount of coinage from Emporion (Empúries), and, in addition, much uncoined silver was also used as money. Although coinage was produced on a large scale during the war, its use was largely confined to a broad strip of land along the Mediterranean coast, and coinage did not yet appear in the vast areas of central, western or northern Spain. However, its growing use seems to have stimulated a wider subsequent production and a growing social monetisation, coupled with increasing urbanisation.

After the war, the Romans gradually extended their power and control, and, in 197, Spain was divided into two provinces, each ruled by a Roman praetor. Carthaginian coinage disappeared and Roman denarii and bronzes increased in circulation. Some twenty-five hoards of Roman denarii are known from ancient Spain from the last two centuries BCE.[16]

Some of the hoards also include 'Iberian denarii' (Figure 3.10), which were made in the name of about twenty communities, all located in the more northerly province (Hispania Citerior). They copied the shape and weight of the Roman denarius and have a fairly standard pair of designs with a characteristically archaising style – a male head and a galloping horseman holding a spear, designs which might perhaps have been derived from early Roman denarii. Some of the earliest were made at Kese (the later Tarraco), and production generally seems to have been most intensive in

## 3.3 Spain

**3.10**                         **3.11**

**Figures 3.10–3.11** Iberian denarii and bronzes.
The silver coin is inscribed *Arsaos* in Iberian script, referring to the place near modern Pamplona where it was made. The bronze is inscribed *Iltirta*, referring to the modern Lleida in northern Spain. Both have a male head on the obverse (accompanied by dolphins) and a horseman on the reverse, who holds an axe (?) on the silver and a palm branch on the bronze. (3.10 *MIB* 85/15b; 3.11 *MIB* 67/78c)

### Box 3.1  The Cordova hoard

A chance find was made in 1915 at Molino de Marrubial, on the outskirts of Cordova in southern Spain. It was deposited in about 110–100 BCE, and contained 222 Roman silver denarii and 82 locally produced 'Iberian denarii', as well as several pieces of silver bullion. The relative wear of the two sorts of coin has been used in the past as an argument for an early date for the beginning of the production of Iberian denarii. Some mints started to make them before about 170 BCE, but the chronology is fragile.

the late second and early first century BCE (Map 1.3). Although made only in northern Spain, they circulated over a much wider part of the Iberian Peninsula. They occur in many hoards, on their own (mostly in the interior) or in association with Roman denarii (as in the Cordova hoard). Their production ended in the 70s BCE, but they remained in circulation until the end of the century.

Roman bronze coinage occurs widely across Spain. For example, it has been found in the hoards from Torelló d'en Cintes in Menorca, Écija and El Saucejo near Seville in Andalusia, and Pinos Puente in Granada;[17] at the Roman military camps at Numantia in Soria and Cáceres el Viejo in Extremadura; and also in the indigenous city of Kelin near Valencia.[18] It was supplemented by imitations of Roman coinage. The wide diffusion of

Roman and imitative coinage was not, however, restricted to Roman or military contexts. The imitations never accounted for more than a relatively small proportion of the bronze coinage in circulation. Locally produced coinage flourished, and was produced in large quantities by over 180 communities, but there were many different patterns of coinage production in each of the two provinces.

The communities in the north which produced 'Iberian denarii' also made similar coins in bronze (Figure 3.11). They had the same designs (male head, horseman) on the larger denominations, while smaller bronze coins had other standardised designs – a horse or a pegasus on the halves and a half-pegasus or a dolphin on the quarters. They are inscribed with Iberian letters referring to the Iberian name of the community that produced them. Their production continued later, though on a smaller scale, indeed into early imperial times.

In the more southerly province (Hispania Ulterior) no silver was minted, and the bronze coinage of the area was much more varied. It used a wider variety of scripts, both local (Tartessian, Iberian), Punic and Latin, and an extremely wide variety of designs. The designs include many animals, fish and plants, and they have been interpreted both as economic and religious symbols. The weight standards are hard to understand, as are their denominational systems, but they are perhaps to be related to Roman ones; there must have been some sort of means of allowing the different coinages to exist side by side.

Most of the bronze coinages were produced on a small scale, and it seems that little was minted in the first century BCE. A shortage of small change is suggested by the worn state of locally minted coinage, and the production of imitations of Roman Republican coins, especially the smaller denomination (the semis), which also circulated until the end of the century.

**Figure 3.12** Bronze coin of Ebusus (modern Ibiza).
Ebusus meant 'island of Bes', the squat Egyptian god who is depicted on the coinage. The neo-Punic inscription on the reverse names the island ('ybshm) and prominently displays the numbers 20–20–10, perhaps indicating a local system of denominations.

The presence of bronze asses minted by Rome influenced the choice of large bronze coins in Spain. The Spanish issues did not adopt the same standards as Rome – the early issues tend to be about 20–24 g, only about two-thirds of the standard of the earliest Roman asses, which tended to be about 30–35 g in the early second century, but which soon descended to much the same weight as the heavy Iberian coins. The 'Iberian asses' of Hispania Citerior were even lighter, at about 9–13 g, at a time when the Roman standard was about 18 g. The rare Roman asses of the first century were produced at a standard of about 13 g, and by that time they were much the same in size and shape as the bronzes made in Spain. However, the latter were produced at such a variety of sizes and weights that it is it difficult to identify any common standards. The Spanish coins, then, follow the same general trends as the Roman coins, but they were not closely linked to them, and there was much local variation.

The worn bronze currency was eventually supplemented on a large scale by the plentiful issues of the Augustan period, a picture that can be seen elsewhere (see Chapter 4).

**Figure 3.13** Saguntum, Spain, bronze coin.
The coins of Saguntum (previously called Arse) minted in about 100 BCE are the exception to the rule that the coins did not follow Roman styles and iconography. They are big coins, about the same size as Roman *asses*, and the prow on the reverse is copied from a Roman prototype. Although their obverses depart from the Janus head so familiar on the Roman coins, they use a helmeted head of Roma, derived from Roman denarii. The choice of designs reflects the increasing Romanisation of the city, since the Celtiberian script was soon accompanied by Latin and the new name Saguntum. The coins are bigger and heavier than their predecessors (when the city used only Celtiberian script and called itself Arse), and the choice of size and shape looks as if they were deliberately chosen to emphasise this cultural change (*cf.* Adams 2003, 279–81). They demonstrate how closely a community could embrace an institution of its powerful master, if it so chose. However, the other Spanish communities did not follow this course, and the influence of Rome was more indirect and the changes more gradual. (*MIB* 34/62)

**88** 3 The Growth of an Empire during the Late Republic

This complex pattern of minting raises many questions, few of which can be answered with any degree of certainty. Many mint attributions and chronologies have become more definite as new finds are made and more studies are undertaken, but the fundamentals still lack clear explanations. The most important concern the Iberian denarii. How did this coinage come about? How was it regulated? Why was it minted only in the north, and especially near the Pyrenees, far from the silver mines in the south? What was its purpose? Why did it come to an end? Why was it eventually taken out of circulation, long before Roman Republican denarii were removed from circulation?

The discussion of broad issues in Chapter 1 may provide some pointers. It was noted there that the cessation of the coinage was part of the same trend across the whole Mediterranean for local silver coinages to come to an end. Similar patterns can be seen in other areas, particularly Greece, at about the same time, and the same explanation may apply to the ending of the production of Iberian denarii. Similarly, their removal from circulation at the end of the century may be another aspect of the shortage of silver discussed there.

The beginning of the coinage, however, seems a unique phenomenon, and there is no other silver coinage which 'springs fully formed' in this way. However, once again we should look elsewhere. A parallel can be found in the inauguration of the cistophori in the independent Attalid kingdom in Asia at much the same time. Should we regard the introduction of the 'Iberian denarii' as part of a more widespread Mediterranean phenomenon (as was discussed in Chapter 1 regarding the creation of the Roman victoriate, a generation or two earlier), whereby coinages of different fineness were recognised as having different functions, one essentially internal and one essentially external?

Whether or not this is so, the political structure behind the creation of the Iberian denarii (and bronzes) is intriguing, though obscure. The introduction of the Iberian denarius was not part of a general reform (and so, different from the case of the victoriate), and it is very hard to see how so many similar coinages could have arisen without some role of the Roman authorities – in this case presumably the Roman praetorian governor (or governors: is the absence of the coinage from Ulterior also the result of a positive decision?). There is no other obvious candidate to have initiated and developed the coinage, with its common approach across a wide area of production. This, then, may well be an instance of a Roman intervention intended to create an additional circulating medium in silver. The temptation to see a single guiding mind is very strong, but who and why? And why then, and why in this manner?

## 3.4 Africa

After its defeat in the Second Punic War, the Carthaginian state was permitted to continue in Africa, until it was finally removed in 146 BCE at the end of the Third Punic War. Carthage was then physically devastated, and all the remaining Punic gold and silver coinage was also destroyed and replaced with Roman silver denarii: Punic precious metal coinage was a symbol of the defeated state, and like the city, had to be destroyed.

Thereafter, Roman denarii provided the only silver in circulation in the new Roman province of Africa, but the bronze currency seems to have been different (see Chapter 2). Some Roman bronze travelled there, and some local bronze coinage seems to have been produced there, but the earlier Carthaginian bronzes seem to have continued in circulation until the imperial period, although we do not have a great deal of evidence.[19] Some system must have been established to enable them to circulate together with Roman bronzes, as well as the locally produced bronze.

The few bronzes made in Africa are often large, like the coins made in Spain. There is no trace of the influence of Roman designs in the province before the reign of Augustus, although there is in the adjacent dependent kingdoms: rare large bronze coins of Bogud (c. 49–38 BCE), a king in western Mauretania, have a very Roman prow for their reverse, while in eastern Mauretania, his elder brother king Bocchus II (c. 49–33 BCE) adopted a Janus head for his even larger bronzes.[20]

**Figure 3.14** M. Cato, silver denarius, about 46 BCE.
During the Civil Wars at the end of the Republic, some denarii were also made in Africa. This one was probably minted at Utica, and is signed by Cato. It has the head of the goddess Roma and a seated figure of Victory, and expressed Cato's conservative wish to see Republican Rome victorious over Julius Caesar (Devoto & Spigola 2020). After the defeat of the Republican forces in Africa, Cato famously committed suicide at Utica. (*RRC* 462/1)

## 90    3 The Growth of an Empire during the Late Republic

## 3.5    Cyrenaica

Further east, Cyrenaica became Roman property in 96 BCE, and was organised as another new province by 75 BCE. The nature of its currency in the first century BCE is difficult to determine, as there is very little evidence. A very small amount of Roman Republican coinage has been recorded from Cyrene and Ptolemais, both silver and bronze.[21]

The province of Cyrenaica was enlarged into a new joint province of Cyrenaica and Crete after the conquest of Crete in 67 BCE, and from *c.* 40 BCE a series of connected bronzes was produced. Soon thereafter, however, each part of the province made its own issues, and they have been found at many sites. Their initial relationship to the Roman system of denominations is not certain, but by the reign of Augustus it seems that they were responding to the Roman system, and the relatively heavy weight of several of the previous issues points in a similar direction.[22]

## 3.6    Gaul

The rise and disappearance of the Po Valley silver drachms from Cisalpine Gaul, and the arrival of the first Roman coins in the region, were discussed in Chapter 2. Thereafter, Roman silver and bronze coinage predominated in the area, as in other parts of Italy.

Across the Alps (Transalpine Gaul), the Roman conquest was in two main phases. The first province to be occupied was in the south (hence the modern name Provence, from the Latin 'provincia') in 121 BCE, and the long series of wars fought by Julius Caesar in 58–50 BCE led to the seizure of the remainder of Gaul to the north.

As described in Chapter 1, Caesar's conquest saw the end of gold coinage in Gaul and the transfer of massive amounts of gold to Rome, where it became an important source for the first systematic Roman gold issues under Caesar. 'Gallic' silver and bronze continued to be struck after Caesar's conquest, and many Gallic silver coins were made at the same weight as Roman quinarii;[23] and some quinarii in a Roman style were certainly made at Lugdunum by Mark Antony. Gallic bronze coinages may also have been influenced to some extent by the Roman system, as suggested by the coins of the Lexovians inscribed with 'simissos publicos' ('official semisses').[24]

Gallic coins were probably all translatable into Roman denominations, as perhaps implied by Cicero in 69 BCE, when he said, 'no Gaul transacts any business without a Roman citizen, and no coin circulates in Gaul without

**3.15**   **3.16**

**Figures 3.15–3.16** Silver and bronze coinage of Gaul, late first century. Silver coins inscribed ATEVLA and VLATOS were made in north-eastern France and Belgium. The inscriptions presumably refer to one or more rulers, otherwise unknown (although the first name was, in the distant past, attributed to Attila the Hun!). The designs loosely copy Roman coins, and the coins were made at the weight of the Roman quinarius, although their silver content looks more debased. Further east, near the mouth of the Seine river, the Lexovii made bronze coins inscribed *simissos pvblicos lixovio*, meaning 'official semis of the Lexovians'. They have reverses with other words, in this case *cisiambos cattos vercobreto*. The first two words are the names of a local magistrate(s), whose office of *vergobretus* is known as the principal magistrate of other Gallic peoples.

being recorded in the account books of Roman citizens'.[25] However, the Gallic bronze coins were small in module, perhaps just influenced by the similarly small size of the silver,[26] and there was no attempt to make large bronze coins like the Roman ones.

Towards the end of the late first century BCE, a number of Roman colonies in the south produced large bronzes, generally with two heads on the obverse, recalling the head of Janus, and sometimes a prow on the reverse.[27] They were variations on the bronze asses previously minted so commonly at Rome.

## 3.7   Greece and the Balkans

The Romans had first intervened in Illyria in 229 BCE, and it became the scene of many Roman conflicts and interventions. Little coinage had been made in the area, but large quantities of silver were minted by Dyrrachium and Apollonia in the second and first centuries, together with an increasing amount of bronze from several cities.[28] Roman silver denarii also travelled to the region, in increasing numbers from the late second century, and particularly during the civil wars of the later first century. A few denarii were minted at Apollonia in 49 BCE, and they were followed by large issue of Apollonian silver, copying the general appearance and weight of the denarius, but with local designs. No silver was subsequently produced in Illyria, but bronze continued into the imperial period.

When the Romans conquered Macedonia (168 BCE) and southern Greece (146 BCE) they encountered areas with long traditions of using gold, silver and bronze coinage.[29] The conquests brought the royal coinages of Macedonia to an end, although the federal coinages of leagues of Aetolian and Achaean cities seem to have continued.[30] There was not, however, a change to using Roman coins. Roman bronze coins did not travel to Greece, and silver denarii arrived in Greece in quantity only during the first century BCE.

Instead, a number of 'local' silver and bronze issues were made (Figures 3.17–3.18). It has long been realised that these coinages were made during the period of Roman rule, and traditionally they were interpreted in terms of the local history of the communities involved: for example, paying for wine or slaves. More recently, however, they have been seen in terms of meeting Roman needs.[31] Since many of them are found in hoards from further north, in modern Bulgaria and Romania, it was thought that they represented plunder from warfare, but it has now been suggested that a function for paying Roman auxiliary soldiers is more likely. For example, when the Roman general Sulla landed with his army in Greece in 87 BCE, he called 'for money, allies and provisions from Aetolia and Thessaly'.[32] Thessaly itself produced a well-organised silver and bronze coinage, with multiple denominations and many names of magistrates, suggesting a substantial coinage. Some of the extensive series of Athenian coins of the early first century bear monograms which have been interpreted as standing for the name of the Roman quaestor Lucullus in about 85 BCE.

However, in the case of Athens, it has been doubted whether the whole coinage should be explained by Roman manipulation, and some of it, at least, seems to be connected with Athens's pre-eminent trading position. And we should not rush into assuming that any large silver coinage must necessarily be explained by war or Roman manipulation (as discussed in the Asia Minor section below).

A similar argument has been used to explain some at least of the bronze coinages made in the area during this period. In Macedonia, for example, very large quantities of bronze coinage (perhaps from more than 1,000 dies) were minted at Amphipolis, Pella and Thessalonica.[33] Sometimes, at Thessalonica and Amphipolis, they also borrow Roman iconography (the Janus head) (Figure 3.20), and other issues show a helmeted head (presumably the goddess Roma) with the names of a Roman magistrate (quaestor) in Greek, for example

**Figures 3.17–3.18** Greek silver coins for the Romans? Several series of coins were made in the Roman province of Macedonia in the first decades of the first century c. 90–75 BCE, during and just after the First Mithradatic War: a large issue of tetradrachms with the name of the Roman AESILLAS Q(uaestor) (3.17), and silver tetradrachms made by Thasos (ΘΑΣΙΩΝ) and Maronea (ΜΑΡΟΝΕΙΤΩΝ). Further west, silver drachms were made at Dyrrhachium and Apollonia, both in Illyria, in the late second and early first centuries BCE. Further south, silver was also minted by the island of Leucas (ΛΕΥΚΑΔΙΩΝ) (3.18), as well as the Thessalians (ΘΕΣΣΑΛΩΝ) and the Aenianes (ΑΙΝΙΑΝΩΝ). The members of the federal Achaean League made silver triobols. Above all, there was a very large 'new style' silver coinage from Athens, in the second and first centuries BCE (see Figure 1.20). The iconography of these coins is, for the most part, not Roman, and such Roman names as appear on them have a subsidiary position (De Callataÿ 2011: 64).

ΜΑΚΕΔΟΝΩΝ ΤΑΜΙΟΥ ΛΕΥΚΙΟΥ ΦΟΛΚΙΝΝΙΟΥ ('Of the Macedonians, in the quaestorship of Lucius Fulcinnius') (Figure 4.1).

Very few of the 'Greek' silver coinages (except those from Athens and Thessaly) seem to have continued after 75 BCE, probably because Roman denarii started to circulate in Greece from about this time. Athens and Thessaly, however, continued to mint silver until the 40s BCE, and the end of their production coincides with the spread of minting of Roman silver denarii (and gold aurei) to Greece in the time of the civil wars after the death of Caesar (see Chapter 1). The silver was probably repurposed to mint denarii, many of which were minted there, including the enormous issue of

Mark Antony's 'legionary' denarii. From this time onwards denarii were the only silver coins in circulation.

However, even during the period in which denarii are found in Greece, there is little sign of the Roman system of accounts being adopted. Polybius tells us that 'a half-as is the fourth part of an obol',[34] but this seems to be more of an approximation, intended to explain the term to his readership, than the reflection of an official rate. There are mentions of small quantities of denarii in the accounts of the temple treasuries on Delos; apart from them, accounting in Roman denarii may perhaps first occur in the inscription from Messene which describes the amounts of money raised by a tax to pay tribute to Rome.[35] The inscription, which has been dated to the first century BCE (although later dates have also been suggested) lists payments in talents, minae, staters, obols and chalkoi, and then converts them to amounts of denarii (δειναρίου) and obols and chalkoi, suggesting a means of accounting that could use Greek or Roman terms for silver coins, but Greek for smaller amounts.[36] The *diorthoma* from Thessaly (Box 3.2) records the official establishment of the use of Roman denominations in the reign of Augustus.

### Box 3.2 The Thessalian *diorthoma*

'Fifteen staters according to law, which became twenty two and a half denarii according to the amendment' (Bouchon 2008, Zelnick-Abramowitz 2013). Several inscriptions from Thessaly concerning a tax on freeing slaves refer to a change in accounting from 15 staters to 22½ denarii kata to diorthoma ('according to the amendment'). Occasionally, 22½ denarii are also referred to as 22 denarii and 1 quinarius (tropaikon), but sometimes as 22 denarii and 4 obols, suggesting that Greek terms remained in use for smaller amounts.

**Figure 3.19** The Thessalian *diorthoma*.
This coin of the Thessalian League has the name Italos on both sides, as well as Diocles on the reverse. An Ita[] also signed coins for Augustus and Livia, but is probably a different man.

The coins of Thessalonica and Amphipolis with the Janus head also seem to copy the numeral I and the letter S from their Roman prototypes, apparently implying the use of the *as* and *semis* in Macedonia.[37] The 'fleet coinage' of Mark Antony, some of which was made in Greece, uses Roman denominations for bronze coins from the sestertius to the quadrans, expressed in Greek and Latin, and so shows that the terms could be understood and used by the 30s BCE (Figure 3.21).

**Figure 3.20** Bronze coin of Thessalonica with Janus head.
The value mark I, copied from Roman Republican asses (as Figure 3.2) is above it. The reverse design (the two Dioscuri on prancing horses) was also copied from Roman coins, the denarii of C. Servilius (RRC 147–8).

**Figure 3.21** Mark Antony, 'fleet coinage'.
In the early 30s BCE, three series of bronze coins were made in Greece and Syria by Mark Antony and his lieutenants. They have an elaborate set of designs, intended to help the user understand Roman denominations. This coin was made somewhere in Syria or Cyprus by L. Calpurnius Bibulus. It was a coin of three asses, as indicated by the prominent Greek numeral Γ (=3) at the bottom of the reverse. The numeral is accompanied by a three-legged symbol and the obverse has three portraits (Mark Antony with Octavian/Augustus on the left; Octavia, Octavian's sister who was married to Antony to cement their alliance, on the right. The coins were so poorly made that in the past it has been suggested that they were struck on ships in Antony's fleet. This seems unlikely but the name 'fleet coinage' has stuck, as a convenient label. (*RPC I*, 1454)

The impact of Rome becomes a little more visible in the time of the Civil Wars at the end of the first century. Coins of a little-known 'Koinon of the Lacedaemons' depict the head of the goddess Roma, while Thessalonica declared its freedom (*Eleutheria*), reflecting the new status granted to it by Rome.[38]

**3.22**

**3.23**

**3.24**

**Figures 3.22–3.24** Coins of the triumvirs from Thessalonica.
A remarkable series of coins were minted by Thessalonica during the Second Triumvirate, of Octavian, Antony and Lepidus. The reverses name Mark Antony and Octavian (M ANT AYT Γ KAI AYT (= Marcus Antonius Imperator, Gaius Caesar Imperator) on 3.22, or simply ANT KAI (Antonius, Caesar) on 3.23. There is no mention of Lepidus, the third – and clearly irrelevant to the Thessalonicans – triumvir. The largest coins depict *Eleutheria* (Freedom), the medium ones have *Agonothesia* (Institution of Games) and the smallest *Homonoia* (Concord), which is made explicit on the reverse as being between Thessalonica and Rome. The games were presumably instituted to celebrate the granting of freedom. (3.22 *RPC I*, 1551; 3.23 *RPC I*, 1552; 3.24 *RPC I*, 1553)

## 3.8 Asia Minor

The Romans acquired the province of Asia in 133 BCE, when it was bequeathed to Rome by its last king.[39] The coinage of the previous kingdom of Pergamum had consisted of civic and regal issues; the latter had been reformed in the earlier second century with the introduction of coins called cistophori, which were made at several mints.[40]

In the case of the mint of Ephesus, the years of the new Roman era were recorded on the coins as Greek numerals. Occasionally the names of Roman governors were also added, and they appeared regularly in the 50s BCE, even including the famous Cicero (Figure 1.14). Indeed it was Cicero himself who complained, when appointed to be the governor of the province of

3.25

3.26

**Figures 3.25–3.26** Pergamene and Roman cistophori.
The cistophori ('box-bearing') had no royal portrait but showed a depiction of a box with a snake on one side, and bow case with snakes on the other, the symbols of the supposed divine ancestors of the royal house, Heracles and Dionysus. The minting of similar coins continued after the Roman annexation of the province, and indeed there was an increase in the number of mints issuing them. It is not easy to distinguish coins made before (3.25) or after the Roman annexation (3.26), a characteristic that underlines how the Roman administration simply continued what they found in place. Cistophori did not leave their area of production in western Asia Minor, which formed a 'closed currency area' using coins which were greatly overvalued.

Cilicia (southern Turkey), that he would make a loss changing denarii into cistophori: 'but there is certainly enough of a loss in the exchange' (*Letters to Atticus* XII.6.1). The cistophorus contained less silver than an equivalent value in denarii,[41] and this was the mechanism by which its circulation was restricted to the province, as described in Chapter 1.

The increasing production of cistophori was matched by a reduction in the number of cities issuing their own civic silver coinage.[42] By the reign of Augustus, only five cities still made silver coinage (Chios, Rhodes, Tabae, Stratonicea and Mylasa), and, of these, only that of Rhodes were on more than a tiny scale.

As with the coinages in Greece, it has been suggested that the Romans manipulated the coinage of Asia to meet their own needs, such as paying their soldiers. The best way of looking at this idea is through the coinage of Ephesus, since, as we have seen, it is dated by the Roman era. The mint of Pergamum was more important than Ephesus in terms of its

### Box 3.3 The coinage of Ephesus in the first century BCE

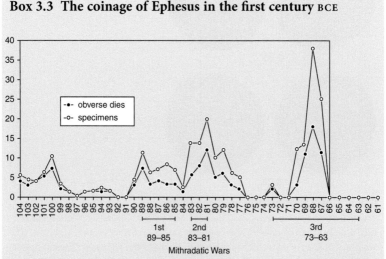

The output of the dated coinage of Ephesus has been analysed to show the peaks of production coincided with the wars fought by the Romans against Mithradates (De Callataÿ 1997: 171-9), with production at Ephesus being highest in 84–80 BCE and 70–68 BCE. There is clearly a link, but it is not an exact link, since there were periods of high production when there was no fighting, and similarly periods of war when there was no production, most notably the last few years of the war, from 66 to 63 BCE (Burnett 2021a: 23).

volume of production,[43] but its coins can be dated only approximately. However, the relative numbers of coins of each mint in one well-documented hoard suggest that output increased well before the First Mithradatic War and may well have been high between the Second and Third Mithradatic Wars.[44]

Roman influence on the silver coinage of Asia increased in the middle of the first century BCE. Denarii are first known from that period, as shown by a hoard from Halicarnassus and by a new Augustan hoard from Aezani,[45] but the cistophori continued long into the imperial period. Some denarii were also minted there in the same period, starting in 49 BCE.[46] It has also been suggested that Roman weight standards were used by the few remaining silver coinages and that the weights of many of the more plentiful bronzes were standardised to make them fit with Roman denominations.[47] However, it is difficult to distinguish, in the case of silver, between a putative Roman standard and a declining Greek (Attic) standard. On the other hand, the adoption of Roman weights would match the similar trend further west, in Gaul and Illyria, and also further south, in Lycia. The bronzes are harder to assess. Later, in the imperial period, there was no common standard for bronze denominations, let alone a Roman one, and the only provincial coins which seem probably to have been tariffed as asses during the later Republican period were made at very different standards.[48]

There is little evidence about the denominations in use. The word 'drachma' occurs in some inscriptions of the Roman period, and the first appearance of 'denarius' seems to be in one of the provisions of 75 BCE (or earlier), incorporated into the later customs law from Ephesus.[49] Even more remarkably, the term 'as' also appears in the same inscription, probably from about the same date.[50] The designs used on the coinage of the short-lived Caesarian colony at Lampsacus (head of Janus and prow) imply a knowledge of Roman denominations in *c.* 45 BCE,[51] and a few years later coins were made at an uncertain location in Asia Minor by Atratinus under Mark Antony, which also had a Janus head and a prow (Figures 3.27–28).[52]

No Roman bronze coins travelled to the province of Asia, but bronze coinage had been minted in very large quantities by the cities in Asia during the late second and first centuries BCE. Most of them were made from bronze, an alloy of copper and tin, with varying amounts of cheap lead. However, one of the most interesting developments was the introduction of the new metal, orichalcum. Much the same as modern brass, it was an alloy of copper and zinc, and was manufactured by the novel 'cementation' process (in which metallic copper was heated with zinc ore in a closed

**3.27**  **3.28**

**Figures 3.27–3.28** Bronze asses from Lampsacus (about 45 BCE) and an uncertain mint in Asia Minor (about 40 BCE).
Both copy the head of Janus and the prow from Roman Republican asses (Figure 3.2) but they are much smaller and lighter than the Roman prototype. The Lampsacus coin, though slightly earlier, is much smaller than that of Atratinus. See also Figure 5.3 for a larger denomination from Lampsacus. (3.27 *RPC I*, 2273; 3.28 *RPC I*, 2226)

**Figure 3.29** The invention of brass.
Brass, as well as copper and bronze, started to be used for coinage in Asia Minor in the first century BCE. Its ancient name was *orichalcum* ('golden bronze'), reflecting its shiny new yellowish appearance. Some coins of Apamea were made, presumably as special presentation pieces, on very large flans and sometimes with elaborate borders. This coin depicts Athena and her owl.

vessel). It first appeared at the beginning of the first century on some of the coins of Mithradates in the Pontic region.[53] The new brass coins were accompanied by some made out of pure copper, and from this period, the three metals of brass, bronze and copper were the main metals used for base metal coinage. Some fine orichalcum pieces were produced in the Roman province of Asia, in the region of Phrygia. Sometimes they had an elaborate border (Figure 3.29), showing that the new gold-like metal was appreciated aesthetically, as well as being used to distinguish one denomination from another. The extent of the use of this new alloy for coinage is not yet well defined, due to a lack of analyses, but it is clear that it provided a model for the system of brass and copper coins which was adopted at Rome by Augustus (see Chapter 4), and which thereafter became the norm for the base metal coinage made at Rome for three centuries

## 3.9 Bithynia

The kingdom of Bithynia (modern northern Turkey) was bequeathed, just as Asia had been two generations before, by its last king to Rome in 74 BCE. In the aftermath of the final defeat of Mithradates, it was formed into a new province with the region of Pontus in 63 BCE.

After the formation of the new province, no silver coinage was produced until the reign of Hadrian, well into the imperial period, when cistophori were made there, perhaps implying that the cistophorus had been used previously in this area.

The area had, however, maintained the legacy of Mithradates of a common set of designs for the base metal coinage at several different mints.[54] This common approach is found for Amisus, Apamea, Bithynium, Nicaea, Nicomedia, Prusa and Tium.[55] In the middle of the century, the names of three Roman governors appeared (C. Papirius Carbo in 61–59; C. Caecilius Cornutus in 56; and Vibius Pansa in 47), together with a depiction of the goddess *Rome* (Roma), who was shown seated on shields and holding a figure of Victory (Figure 3.30). They can

**Figure 3.30** Roma on a bronze coin of Nicaea.
The coin has a head of the god Dionysus on the obverse, together with the date of BKΣ = year 222 of the era of the city = 61/60 BCE. On the reverse a figure of Roma (labelled ΡΩΜΗ) is shown seated on pile of shields, holding a figure of Victory in her right hand and spear in her left. The inscription reads ΕΠΙ ΓΑΙΟΥ ΠΑΠΙΡΙΟΥ ΚΑΡΒΩΝΟΣ (under Gaius Papirius Carbo). The representation of Roma as a military goddess like Athena was formulated in the third century BCE (Burnett 1986), and is derived from similar Greek depictions of Athena.

**Figure 3.31** Veni, vidi, vici.
Caesar's famously quick victory was over Pharnaces, the youngest son of Mithradates, who had killed his father after his father's defeat by the Romans in 63 BCE. Pharnaces was rewarded by Pompey with a kingdom based on the Crimea, and later took advantage of the civil war between Pompey and Julius Caesar. He hoped to restore his father's kingdom in Asia Minor, with himself as king. However, he was defeated by Caesar at the Battle of Zela in northern Asia Minor in 47 BCE after Caesar's whirlwind march from Egypt, and the three-word slogan was used in Caesar's later triumph. It seems no accident that it is precisely at this date that Caesar's portrait appeared on the coinage of Nicaea, which Caesar might have visited on his return to Italy. The coins bear the date of ϛΛΣ = year 236 of the era of the city = 47/46 BCE and have the first definite portrait of a Roman ruler on the city coinage of the Roman Empire. (*RPC I*, 2026)

be contrasted with the other city coinages in the western Mediterranean, which continued to deploy religious and other symbols of their own identity. This more innovative approach, with a greater focus on Rome, helps to explain the sudden appearance of the head of Roma on the obverse of Cornutus' coins and then a portrait of Julius Caesar on the coins of Papirius Carbo from Nicaea in 47/6 (Figure 3.31).

## 3.10 Cilicia

The province of Cilicia, in the south-east part of modern Turkey, was organised by Pompey after the Mithradatic Wars, and underwent a number of later changes. Parts were ruled by 'client kings', such as Tarcondimotus or the priest kings of Olba. Much was controlled by the kings of Commagene, one of whom (Antiochus IV) made many coins throughout his kingdom. The capital of the Roman province was Tarsus, but its coinage, like that of other Cilician cities, showed no signs of the Roman presence until the reign of Augustus.

**Figure 3.32** Tarcondimotus of Cilicia.
Tarcondimotus ruled a small territory in Cilicia, based on Hierapolis Castabala. Little is known about him, but he was perhaps installed there by Pompey. In the following years of civil wars he regularly changed his allegiance, finally siding with Mark Antony. He may have been given the royal title by Antony, and he proudly proclaimed it together with his loyalty on his coins: ΒΑΣΙΛΕΩΣ ΤΑΡΚΟΝΔΙΜΟΤΟΥ ΦΙΛΑΝΤΩΝΙΟΥ = 'King Tarcondimotus, the friend of Antony'. He chose Roman models for his portrait, and incorporated features from the portrait of Antony. He was killed in the campaign that led to Antony's defeat at the Battle of Actium. His coinage is exceptional in Cilicia for reflecting the new power order. (*RPC I*, 3871)

## 3.11  Syria

The Romans created the province of Syria in 64 BCE at the end of the Third Mithradatic War (73–63 BCE), when Pompey defeated Tigranes of Armenia. The period of fighting at the end of the war has been connected with the production of silver coinages at Aradus and Laodicea, which peaked in 65–63 BCE, but they were not very extensive and employed only a few obverse dies. The principal mint in the area was Antioch, although it was closed for silver production during the first few years of the Roman province.[56] When a major reorganisation of the province was carried out in *c.* 57–55 BCE by the Roman governor Aulus Gabinius, coinage was produced in huge quantities (Figure 3.34), for reasons that are not clear.

Little coinage was made at Antioch for the subsequent 100 years: there was a big production in the name of Cleopatra and Antony (if it was made at Antioch) (Figure 3.35),[57] but most of the years of the Roman civil war are remarkable for their very low production, which continued into Augustus' reign. There is no sign either of any extensive minting in connection with Augustus' expedition to recover the Parthian standards in 19 BCE, and hardly any coinage was made there at all under his successor

**Figure 3.33** Bronze coin inscribed 'year 1 of Rome', 64/3 BCE.
A series of bronzes, from an uncertain mint city, proclaim that they were made 'in the first year of Rome' (L A PΩMHΣ). The few provenances recorded and the designs (a head of Hercules and the ram of a galley) have not as yet provided an exact attribution for these cities, which originate from somewhere in modern Jordan. The 'year of Rome' will refer to a new city era adopted by the mint town, presumably as a result of the conquest and reorganisation of the area by Pompey.

## Box 3.4 The Roman silver coinage from Antioch at the end of the Republic

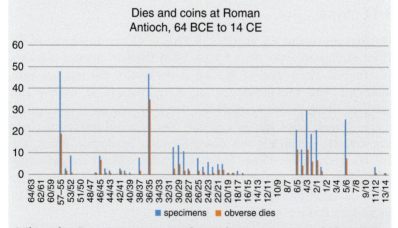

When the Roman governor Aulus Gabinius reorganised the newly founded province of Syria in 57–55 BCE, he made a huge number of silver tetradrachms, whose designs and inscriptions were copied from those of one of the last Syrian kings, King Philip Philadelphus. The only clue to the Roman origin of the coins is the small monogram of Gabinius' name on the reverse. The continuing pattern of these anonymous coins was interrupted only once, to allow the spectacular coins minted for

## Box 3.4 (cont.)

Cleopatra and Antony (36/35 BCE). In this chart, the blue bars denote the number of surviving specimens, and the red bars the number of obverse dies used to produce them. The two sets of numbers are broadly consistent, and suggests peaks of production. However, most years of the wars after Caesar's death (44 to 31 BCE) were marked by a very low level of production, and very little was produced during the middle years of Augustus' reign.

**Figure 3.34** Roman Syria, silver tetradrachm with the monogram of Aulus Gabinius, governor in 57–55 BCE.
The designs are copied from one of the last Syrian kings to rule the area before the Roman conquest. The obverse has a stylised head of King Philip Philadelphus, and the reverse a seated figure of Zeus holding a small figure of Victory. The inscription to either side refers to the Syrian king, but the small monogram to the left of Zeus is of the Greek letters AY ΓB (= Aulus Gabinius). (*RPC I*, 4124)

**Figure 3.35** Cleopatra and Mark Antony, *c.* 36 BCE.
Silver tetradrachms were made in the names of Cleopatra and Mark Antony somewhere in Syria (perhaps Antioch). We know that Cleopatra was on the obverse because there are many fewer dies for her than Antony, and normally obverses have fewer dies. The Greek inscriptions read ΒΑCΙΛΙCCΑ ΚΛΕΟΠΑΤΡΑ ΘΕΑ ΝΕWΤΕΡΑ ('The younger Queen Cleopatra Thea' or perhaps 'Queen Cleopatra, the younger goddess'), and ΑΝΤWΝΙΟC ΑΥΤΟΚΡΑΤWΡ ΤΡΙΤΟΝ ΤΡΙWΝ ΑΝΔΡWΝ ('Antony Imperator, Triumvir') (*RPC I*, 4094)

**106**  3 The Growth of an Empire during the Late Republic

Tiberius. There is no obvious way to explain this pattern of coinage; once again, some can be explained by periods of warfare, but only to a very limited extent.[58] Both silver and bronze have no overt reference to Rome and the Romans until well into the reign of Augustus.

We know nothing about the denominations used in the early Roman province. Although some denarii seem to have been made there in the Roman civil war, denarii did not commonly circulate until the end of the first century CE. From the reign of Augustus we have some evidence for the introduction of Roman denominations (denarius and as) alongside the local ones (drachm, obol and chalkous), but the date of this change is not clear (see Chapter 4).

## 3.12   Patterns across the Roman World

We have seen that, at the end of the third century, a big change came over currencies of the territories which Rome took from the Carthaginians, at least as concerning gold and silver coins. The demonetisation of these Carthaginian coins took place in Italy, Sicily, Sardinia, Spain and probably Corsica.

As Roman power spread east of Italy, however, the same did not happen, and the currencies of the new Roman territories in Greece, Asia Minor and later Syria remained largely unchanged, even though they evolved. This was the more usual pattern.

---

**Box 3.5 The changing patterns of currency in the Roman world during the Republican period**

| Region | Approx. date of Roman control (BCE) | Denarius from | End of local silver | Local bronze | Roman accounting |
|---|---|---|---|---|---|
| **Italy** | 270 | 210 | 250 | a little | yes |
| **Sicily** | 241/210 | 210 | 210 | mixed | c. 50 BCE (Tauromenium) |
| **Sardinia** | 241 | 210 | 241 | ? | ? |
| **Spain** | 210 | 210 | 70 | mixed | yes |

## Box 3.5 (cont.)

| Region | Approx. date of Roman control (BCE) | Denarius from | End of local silver | Local bronze | Roman accounting |
|---|---|---|---|---|---|
| **Africa** | 146 | 146 | 146 | all | ? |
| **Cyrenaica** | 96 | ? | none | all? | ? |
| **Gaul** | 123/50 | 118 | Augustus? | all | by 69? (Fonteio)? |
| **Macedonia** | 168 | 70 | Augustus? | all | ? |
| **Achaea** | 146 | 70 | 40 | all | C1 BCE (Messene, Thessaly) |
| **Asia** | 133 | Augustus | continues (imperial) | all | C1 BCE? (Ephesus) |
| **Bithynia** | 63 | ? | some imperial | all | ? |
| **Syria** | 64 | Flavian | continues (imperial) | all | Augustus (Germanicus) |

It is not clear why the Romans adopted a different policy in the east. It may be that the greater monetary sophistication of the east was regarded as needing little change, unlike the west, where coinage had come to be in common use only a relatively short time before. There is, however, no direct evidence to explain the change in the west. It has been observed that the Romans had a more ambivalent attitude to their engagement with the territories in the east,[59] and one can certainly argue that the pattern of coinage in the late Republic reflects a different attitude to the states in the east. When Flamininus proclaimed the 'freedom of the Greeks' in 196 BCE, he was setting the scene for a less aggressive policy towards annexation and conquest. That is not to say that the Romans were any less violent than any other ancient state, but that they treated the eastern states that fell under their domination in a different way from those they conquered in the west.

However, perhaps it is a mistake to think too simply in terms of a contrast between west and east. It was a normal feature of Roman policy to allow institutions and systems to continue in the areas they conquered. This may partly explain their encouragement (if that is a correct understanding) of the silver coinage of 'Iberian denarii' in Spain, and the creation of the 'Romano-Sicilian' bronze coinages in western Sicily at the same time. We should regard the more violent changes that took place after the Punic wars (the First, the Second against Hannibal and the Third in 149–146 BCE) as the exceptions and look for a special reason to explain them. As we have seen, it is not hard to find one.

By the end of the Republic, Roman denarii made up the exclusive silver currency of Italy, Sicily and Africa. They were dominant in Spain, and starting to circulate in Gaul and Greece. The production of local silver, whether or not it had previously been instigated by Rome, generally petered out, even though it might continue to circulate into imperial times. It was only in the third century CE that 'Roman' coinage formed the exclusive silver currency of the whole Roman Empire. There was no early Roman repetition of the revolution which had overtaken the silver coinage of the Hellenistic world around 330 BCE, when coinage in the name of Alexander was minted across all his vast new territories and which left as its legacy the lasting adoption of the new Attic weight standard for silver.[60]

The evidence for the spread of Roman units of account is very thin, but we have seen that they started to be recognised, initially perhaps only for the silver, as the evidence from Tauromenium in Sicily and Messene in Greece suggests. Roman units of bronze seem little used in the provinces until the end of the Republican period.

The most important theme of this chapter has been how little change took place.[61] If the coinage was the only evidence that had survived and an otherwise uninformed observer had tried to write the history of Roman expansion, she or he would not have realised that the Romans had

**Figure 3.36** Augustus and Actium on a coin of Pella.
The defeat of Mark Antony at the Battle of Actium in 31 BCE left Augustus as the undisputed sole ruler of the Roman world. The veteran colony of Pella in Macedonia celebrated the event on coins which showed Augustus as *Imp Divi f.* ('Son of the divine ruler' [Julius Caesar]) and standing on a prow, signifying his naval victory at Actium (*Actio*). (*RPC I*, 1548)

conquered Spain or any territory to the east of Italy. Earlier approaches to coin iconography continued without change almost everywhere, and there were only one or two diminutive signs of the Roman presence. The very few examples include: the designs of a denarius copied at the colony of Valentia in Spain (Figure 3.13); a head of Roma copied from silver denarii on the bronze coins made (and signed by) the Romans in Macedonia (Figure 4.1); Roman symbols on the reverse of the AESILLAS coinage (but which chose to present the Macedonian king Alexander the Great on the obverse) (Figure 3.17); a helmeted head of Roma at Gortyn; or the depiction of the goddess Roma on the bronze coinage of Bithynia – and even there it was again felt necessary to clarify the representation by adding the word *Rome* in Greek (Figure 3.30). Efforts have been made to find more examples which might have reflected the new reality of power, such as the presence of a wolf on some Iberian coins, but, even if one accepts that cities might deliberately or subconsciously oscillate between themes of local and Roman significance, the examples of Roman themes are few and far between.[62] They hardly impact at all on the tradition of using motifs which referred to some aspect, usually a religious one, of the identity of the city that produced them. They have no overt reference to the new world in which the cities were subject to the power of Rome. There is not, either, much sign of Roman sensibilities, such as the preference on their coins for subjects like buildings. The characteristic language of the 'Greek' coins which were made when their communities were subject to the new power of the Romans continued to be drawn from their own religious or natural world (see Chapter 4). Certainly, no overarching concept of empire was imposed or adopted on the coinage. That would not change until imperial times, and then only gradually, as we shall see in the next chapters.

Changes picked up pace under Augustus, when virtually every community in the Empire placed his portrait, or that of a member of his family, on their coinage. In that sense, provincial coinage then became recognisably 'imperial', although it was otherwise very slow to lose its Hellenistic roots. But, from the reign of Augustus, the new world was plainly there for all to see.

# 4

## Whose Coins? A Model for City Coinage in Imperial Times

This chapter departs from the chronological approach adopted for most of this book, to provide a general model of the nature of provincial coinage under the Empire and how it best helps the historian understand the concerns of the cities which produced it. However, the city coinages were never in a 'steady state', and the historical changes which took place to them will be analysed in the subsequent Chapters 5–7.

During the Republic, the coinage minted at Rome was under the control of three annual magistrates, the *tresviri auro argento aere flando feriundo* ('the three men for casting and striking gold silver and bronze': Figure 5.28). They were presumably controlled by the more senior financial magistrates, the quaestors, themselves subject to regulation by the higher magistrates and the Senate. The *tresviri* survived well into the imperial period, but their office became honorary, and the imperial coinage was controlled by one of the emperor's senior freedmen, the *a rationibus*, the secretary of finance.[1]

A distinction was also made in antiquity between the two categories which we call Roman and provincial coins. It is formulated in different ways in our sources. Roman coins – coins minted in gold, silver and bronze, mostly at Rome – are variously described as 'Roman', 'Italian' or 'our', even 'of the government'; provincial coins – coins minted by the cities of the Empire, nearly all in bronze – as 'foreign', 'their' or sometimes by a more specific name, such as 'Rhodian'.[2] These opposing categories overlap and were not rigidly distinguished. For example, the silver coinage of Syria could be regarded as 'foreign' even though it was clearly subject to some imperial control, as is clear from the reforms of Nero discussed in Chapter 1.

There is little evidence about the control of the coinage produced in the provinces during the Republic. From time to time, coins are signed with a Q, standing for quaestor, and referring to the Roman provincial financial official (Figures 4.1–4.2; see also Figures 3.7 and 3.17). The city coins of

**Figures 4.1–4.2** Coins signed by Roman quaestors.
During the second century BCE, Roman quaestors made a series of bronze coins in Macedonia. On one side they depict the head of the goddess Roma, based on Roman denarii (cf. Figure 3.1), and on the other they set out their name: 'Of the Macedonians, during the quaestorship of Leukios Folkinnios (= Lucius Fulcinnius)'. Later in the century, an unknown quaestor (Q) signed the coins which showed the fetial (FETIA) ceremony of sacrificing a pig, in this case to sanctify the treaty made between Rome and Amisus (see Sánchez 2021). (4.2 RPC I, 2156)

Greece and Asia Minor often include Greek personal names in their inscriptions. These names may refer to the holder of a city magistracy, such as the *exetastai* ('examiners') who had signed some pre-Roman coins of Erythrae in Ionia,[3] but they may also refer to individuals who had sponsored the costs of a coinage, under the 'liturgy' system whereby wealthy citizens were supposed to support many aspects of civic life. An exceptional case is the coinage of Athens, whose silver coins regularly have two or three names, but the nature of any office they may have held is unclear.

In the imperial period, most provincial coinage consisted of low-value bronzes minted by some 700 cities, especially by those located in the eastern part of the Empire.[4] As described in Chapter 1, locally produced silver had declined during the second and first centuries BCE, a process that continued in the imperial period. The denarius, and its successor the antoninianus, gradually came to play a more and more dominant role in the silver currency of the Empire, although local silver continued to be minted on a regional basis in the eastern provinces and to have a monopoly in Egypt.[5]

Some bronze coinages also played a regional role. For example, Antioch produced large quantities that circulated widely in Syria.[6] No doubt Roman provincial officials, such as the Syrian governors whose names sometimes appear on the Antiochene coins (Figure 4.4), played a role in the regulation of these provincial silver and bronze coins. Some similar arrangement may have applied to the few 'civic' coinages, like those of Nemausus or Alexandria Troas, which were manipulated by the Romans to be more

**Figures 4.3–4.4** The Bronze coinage of Antioch.
The coinage of Antioch refers to different authorities. These examples have the portrait of the emperor Galba (68–9), and reverses which refer to a Decree of the Senate (SC) and the Roman governor of Syria C. Licinius Crassus Mucianus (= *epi Moukianou*). The decree may have been passed to introduce a reform of the coinage under Augustus. (4.3 *RPC I*, 4314; 4.4 *RPC I*, 4313)

than just simple city coinages, partly, perhaps, for military purposes and partly to improve the state of the low-value currency (see Chapter 5). Similarly, the rare countermarking of coins with a reference to a Roman legion was presumably done on the initiative of the Roman military.[7]

The name of one other provincial body sometimes also appears on provincial coinage, and may well also have played some role in its regulation: the Koinon or federation of cities of a particular region. Several such Koina, which also seem to have played a role in the development of the provincial cults of the emperor,[8] are mentioned explicitly on the coinage: Crete, Thessaly, Macedonia, Bithynia, Paphlagonia, Lesbos, 'the thirteen cities', Phrygia, Galatia, Lycia and Cyprus. Sometimes the coinage might have been made on behalf of a Koinon by an individual city, but, if no city is mentioned, one might suppose that the coinage was authorised by the Koinon. A role for the Koinon may also be suspected when one finds a coordination of designs and denominations between different cities in the same region, as for example in Bithynia.[9] It also seems likely that it was

**Figure 4.5** Coin of the League of 13 Cities.
A series of magnificent coins were made at Sardis for the emperor Antoninus Pius (138–61) on behalf of the 'League of 13 Cities'. The League has recently been identified as a league created by the cities in Asia Minor which were devastated by an earthquake in 17 CE (Hallmannsecker 2020). The long inscription on the coins states that the coins were 'provided for by M. Claudius Fronto, asiarch [chief priest of the provincial cult of the emperor] and high priest of the 13 cities, the Koinon of the 13 Cities'. The scene on the reverse is drawn from the mythological history of Sardis, and shows a seated Heracles reaching out to the legendary Queen Omphale, for whom Heracles was said to have laboured. (*RPC IV.2* temporary number 1019)

the Koinon of Lycia which agreed that city coins should not be made in the province of Lycia, but to import western style coins instead, since we know that the Koinon was in charge of the region's financial affairs (see Chapter 5).

Most of the bronze coinage was, however, produced in the names of the cities and other communities (such as the 'tribal' groupings in Gaul), although none was produced in the western half of the Empire after 50 CE. From that time, the western provinces of Spain, Gaul, Britain, Italy, north Africa and the western Balkans were supplied with bronze on a massive scale, mostly from Rome. In contrast, the cities in the eastern half of the Empire continued to mint coins with a low value and very restricted areas of circulation,[10] until the general cessation of bronze coinage throughout the Empire in the middle of the third century CE.

City life is much better documented in the imperial period than earlier, especially in the province of Asia. As the 'epigraphic habit' grew, the number of inscriptions increased greatly, and the same cultural change overtook the coinage. The inscriptions and designs used on it became longer and more varied, and began to give more and more information. As a result, we can document quite fully how the system of control and production worked. Most of the evidence comes from the province of Asia and from the second and third centuries, and we must be cautious in applying the same model(s) to earlier periods and different regions. It seems reasonable to suppose, however, that many of the aspects which can be established for Asia may well have applied more widely, in other less well documented regions and in earlier periods.

**4.6**

**4.7**

**Figures 4.6–4.7** Competition between cities.
The coinage often reveals the competition between cities to assert prominence over their near and distant neighbours. Cities might claim to be the principal city (metropolis) of an area, or boast about the award of an imperial temple (neocorate), especially when they had more than one. Nicaea announced it was 'first city of the province [of Bithynia and Pontus]' (Figure 5.18), a claim disputed by its neighbour Nicomedia, whose coins called it 'first and metropolis'. Ephesus, the provincial capital of Asia, stated from the second century that it was the 'first in Asia'. An extreme example of such claims is provided by Magnesia on the Maeander which proudly issued coins (4.6) declaring that it was the 'seventh of Asia' (ΕΒΔΟΜΗ ΤΗС ΑϹΙΑϹ) (here for Gordian III). The response from its neighbour Nysa, further up the Maeander Valley (4.7), was to trump the claim by declaring it was number 6 (ς) (here for Valerian). This may seem a slightly absurd claim to us, but there were more than 300 cities in the province (Habicht 1975: 67), many of them tiny, so being in the premier division was important. (4.6 *RPC VII.1*, 552)

## Box 4.1 Portraits and autonomy

From the time of Augustus, the obverses generally have the portrait of the emperor, or sometimes a member of his family. Heads of gods or personifications (such as the Roman Senate in Figure 4.14, or the city's Council or People) also occur instead of an imperial portrait, frequently so in Asia (Martin 2013). Sometimes, but not always, their images were used as a marker of a smaller denomination (as was the practice of the mint of Rome in the first and early second centuries), but not always. The coins are often very hard to date, unless they can be linked to an imperial issue in some way (for example, by the presence of a known magistrate). Because they lack an imperial head, these coins have traditionally been called 'pseudo-autonomous', a term that is convenient, but should not be taken to imply any sense of autonomy.[11]

**4.8**

**4.9**

**Figures 4.8–4.9** Portraits and autonomy.
The examples illustrated here were minted for Eucarpia (4.8) and Accilaeum (4.9), showing Demos and Boule. (4.8 *RPC IV.2*, temporary number 2010; 4.9 *RPC VII.1*, 678)

The 'People' and the 'Council' were the essence of city secular identity, and preface almost every civic decree. Some cities never produced such 'pseudo-autonomous' coins, such as the major city of Ephesus; others, such as Termessus Major in Pisidia, produced only such coins. A few cities were specially favoured by the emperor, and given privileged status; some such 'free' cities produced only coins without imperial heads (Athens, Chios, Rhodes or Tyre), but this was not the case everywhere, as the coins of Aphrodisias show.

Much has been written on the subject of the authority by which city coinages could be made and how they were controlled.[12] Commentators in the nineteenth and early twentieth centuries had a strong belief in 'the right to coinage' which might be withdrawn at any time, such as was thought to have happened in 89 BCE in Italy or 146 BCE in Greece. These views reflect their authors' understanding of contemporary attitudes to coinage, but today such a right is regarded as being of little significance in the Roman world. Of course, at the most general level, coinage – like everything in the Roman Empire – required at least imperial acquiescence. This is shown by the rare (only?) example we have when that acquiescence was withdrawn.[13] When Vespasian revoked the grant of Freedom (*libertas*) which Nero had made to Achaea, the city coinages there all stopped (see also Chapter 5). They resumed only under Domitian when some of the coins of Corinth declared that they were produced with the permission of the emperor (*perm Imp*) and some from Patras referred *indulgentiae Aug moneta inpetrata* ('to the gracious favour of the Emperor for the concession of coinage': see Figure 5.32).

**Figure 4.10** Lucian and the false prophet Alexander.
A man called Alexander is recorded as having 'petitioned of the emperor to change the name of Abonoteichus and call it Ionopolis, and to strike a new coin bearing on one side the likeness of Glycon and on the other that of Alexander, wearing the fillets of his grandfather Asclepius and holding the harpa of his maternal ancestor Perseus'. This story appears in a work by the second-century author Lucian, who regarded Alexander as a fake and a swindler (Lucian, *Alexander* 58). The story finds some confirmation from coins: if we look at the rare coins of Abonoteichus (a small town in what is now northern Turkey), we find that it did change its name to Ionopolis (ΙΩΝΟΠΟΛΕΙΤΩΝ) by the joint reign of Marcus Aurelius and Lucius Verus (161–9), and that its coins do show the human-headed Glycon snake (ΓΛΥΚΩΝ). They do not, however, show any image of Alexander, so that part of the request, if the story is true, must have been denied. The anecdote is another example of asking the emperor for permission to make coins, even if such permission was not actually needed. (*RPC IV.1*, temporary number 5364)

We have also seen in earlier chapters how the Romans intervened to destroy Carthaginian coinage. But these examples are exceptions to a more general pattern of laissez-faire. A limiting case is provided by the condemnation of the memory of an unpopular emperor. His statues were then changed and his name erased from inscriptions (and even papyri), but such a 'condemnation of the memory' (*damnatio memoriae*, as it is often called today) did not touch the provincial coinage on more than a local level.[14] Similarly, when countermarks were applied to civic coins, the operation was directed by a city, either the one that had originally issued the coin or by another one, to validate it in some way.[15]

4.11

4.12

**Figures 4.11–4.12** *Damnatio memoriae.*
When the memory an unpopular emperor or a member of his family was condemned, their names were often erased on official inscriptions (and sometimes papyri documents). Unlike inscriptions, however, coins were only occasionally erased. In 68–9, Tripolis in Phoenicia obliterated Nero's name with that of his three successors, Galba, Otho (4.11) and Vespasian. Stratonicea in southern Asia Minor erased the portraits of Geta from many of its coins (4.12), after Caracalla had murdered him in 211 and ordered his name to be removed from inscriptions. However, all such interventions took place only locally, and were probably carried out on the initiative of the individual town councils, perhaps promoted by a single individual (the instances of Geta follow more or less down the coast of Asia Minor, suggesting only a casual intervention, perhaps spread by word of mouth). There is no sign of any more general actions, which would have required the involvement of bigger organisations, such as provincial councils, Roman governors or even the emperor. (4.11 *RPC I*, 4520)

**Figures 4.13–4.14** Proposing a Coinage at Ancyra.
Coins minted by Ancyra in Phrygia for Nero and his wife Poppaea record how Tiberius Basillos had proposed the issue of coins (αἰτησαμένου Τι Βασίλλου) when the proconsul P. Volasenna (Οὐολασέννα ἀνθυπάτῳ) was the Roman governor of the province of Asia. The smaller denomination depicts the Senate on the obverse, and shows the stele on which the decision was recorded. (4.13 RPC I, 3111; 4.14 RPC I, 3113)

Early in the Empire, several African cities inscribed the proconsul's name on their coins, preceded by a more or less abbreviated version of the word *permissu*.[16] In Spain the same word is found preceding that of the name of the emperor (Figure 5.7), as in *perm Imp Caesaris Augusti* (and sometimes referring to the emperor after his death: *perm divi Aug*).[17] Permission could certainly be sought and granted, though it does not seem to have been a requirement. Perhaps it was more of a way of attracting the emperor's attention (or that of the Roman governor: Figures 4.13–4.14) and flattering him.

Other formulae include references at colonies to the agreement of the local magistrates, by Decree of the Decurions (D D or EX D D = *ex decreto Decurionum* = by decree of the decurions, the colony's governing councillors), who had provided the funds for the coins (P P = *pecunia publica*, 'from the public purse').[18]

A similar formula, αἰτησάμενος, occurs in Greek on several coins of the eastern part of the Empire, and has been interpreted in a similar way, as referring to a grant of permission. But, while the verb αἰτεῖσθαι could be used of asking a ruler for permission for coinage,[19] its occurrence on city coins belongs to the sphere of local city government, and refers to the making of a proposal to the city council.[20] The same is true of other related formulae such as ψηφισάμενος ('put to the vote')[21] and εἰσαγγείλαντος ('submitted a proposal').[22]

The verb ἀνέθηκε ('endowed' or 'dedicated') also occurs, only rarely in the first century,[23] but more frequently in the second century from the reign of Hadrian. It implies that an individual had paid for a coin issue, and is a particular feature of many of the unusual coins of Hadrian's favourite Antinous (on which see Section 6.7). Its use remained fashionable down to the reign of Caracalla, but thereafter became rare again,[24] following the trend apparent in inscriptions, of a reduction in civic patronage.[25] Benefactions by individuals, such as the provision of coinage, were becoming less common.

A slightly different explanation seems likely for the related words which refer to a person who 'took care of the coinage' (ἐπιμελητής, ἐπιμεληθέντος or variant: an example is Figure 4.8).[26] This occurs mostly in the first and very early second century, and probably also has the sense of the person who paid for the coinage, rather implying that there was a 'special officer', who was appointed to oversee the coinage.[27] This seems the most likely interpretation of a joint issue by a husband and a woman (presumably his wife) from Eucarpia in the reign of Hadrian: the husband 'proposed' the issue (αἰτησαμένου), while the wife 'took care of it' (ἐπιμεληθείσης).[28] It is

**Figure 4.15** Antinous and Polemo at Smyrna.
The famous sophist (a term that did not carry its modern scornful connotation; more like our 'intellectual') from Smyrna, Marcus Antonius Polemo, signed coins of Smyrna. The inscription reads ΠΟΛΕΜΩΝ ΑΝΕΘΗΚΕ ϹΜΥΡΝΑΙΟΙϹ ('Polemo dedicated it to the people of Smyrna'). Polemo was a friend of the emperor Hadrian, and he made coins which portray Hadrian, the empress Sabina and also Hadrian's lover Antinous. The reverses of the coins for Antinous depict a prow and various animals: a panther, a ram and a bull. The first two refer to the gods Dionysus (as does the prow: Kuhn 2011) and Hermes, to whom Antinous might be likened; the significance of the bull is debated, and an allusion has been suggested to Attis, with whom Antinous was also linked (Klose 1987: 17–18). The bull has a faint crescent moon on its flank, which also suggests the Apis bull of Egypt, another association of Antinous. (*RPC III*, 1975)

less common in the second century than ἀνέθηκε, and, similarly, fell out of use in the third century.[29]

As we have seen, the practice of adding personal names, mainly in the province of Asia, was a continuation of an earlier Greek tradition. These names are today collectively – but misleadingly – often known as 'magistrates' names'.[30] Sometimes, indeed, they are the names of local officials or, more rarely, Roman governors, but in most cases the names are not qualified with any further information, and we have no way of establishing their identity, except by inference or if we are lucky enough to have some other evidence.

Titles accompanying the names were rare in the Hellenistic period (the *exetastai* at Erythrae being an exception), but they start to appear more frequently in the imperial period. In no case, however, is there an example of someone who was specifically a 'monetary magistrate', like the *tresviri* at Rome. Presumably the generally small scale of city coinage meant that there was no reason to make any provision for such a role.[31]

## Box 4.2 Provincial mint buildings

**Figure 4.16** The mint building of Alexandria.
Only at Alexandria, where there was a massive mint supplying coinage for the whole of Egypt, do we get a glimpse of a mint building on a series of coins made in 162/3. They show the figure of Moneta (MONHTA), the personification of the mint (perhaps here a real statue), standing in front of a two-storey building. The top has a small statue of Hermes, the god of commerce, and the bottom is decorated with a prancing lion. Three bags of money are shown in front of the first floor, before a free standing column, perhaps representing a portico. (*RPC IV.4*, temporary number 14030)

We have very little evidence for provincial mint sites. The imperial coinage of Athens was made in different places at different times. In the first century, a building located near the SE corner of the Agora was used, and, in the third century, a different one in the SW corner. The

4 Whose coins? **121**

---

**Box 4.2 (cont.)**

location of minting in the second century Athens has not yet been discovered (Kroll 1993: 292–5). In both cases, the buildings had originally been constructed for other purposes, and it seems that parts of them were taken over to make coins when the decision to mint coins was made. This was probably the general pattern, although later cities often combined to produce coins on a more cooperative basis, as described in Chapter 6.

---

The presence of a name does not necessarily imply the individual's involvement in the coinage, even though it may occur with the title of a magistracy, such as the *strategos* (general), *archon, grammateus* (secretary) or that of a religious position, such as priest or high priest. Sometimes, these are the names of the eponymous officials of a city, used to denote a particular year: 'in the time of *x* [name] the *y* [magistracy]'. When eponyms, for example the *stephanephoroi* (crown bearers) at Smyrna or the *hieromnemones* (sacred registrars) at Byzantium, occur on coins, they probably had no role in relation to the production of the coinage. The name merely appears as it might do on any official city document.

Similarly, the presence of the names of a Roman governor on city coins does not necessarily imply his involvement. At Smyrna, for example, the names of governors sometimes appear, together with those of the city's *stephanephoros* and *strategos*. This does not mean that all three were involved in decisions about the coinage. The mention of the *stephanephoros* is a way of dating the issue, and the presence of the Roman governor's name should probably be interpreted in the same way. Such names often also appear on weights or inscriptions, similarly without necessarily indicating any personal involvement, but rather just as a means of giving the date.[32]

In the early imperial period, a wide variety of positions are mentioned, but by the Flavian period, the most commonly mentioned ones were the *strategos*, the *archon* and the *grammateus*; and, by the second century, the *strategos* and the *archon* predominate.[33]

As time went on, titles might proliferate. In the third century, several people refer to themselves as being of equestrian rank (ἱππικός).[34] The urge to promote one's status even led Domitius Rufus at Sardis to proclaim on his coins that he was not only an 'Asiarch and son of a twice-Asiarch', but

**122**  4 Whose coins?

also 'the most powerful first archon',[35] while Aurelius Aelius Phoebus of Iulia Gordus states a greater claim to notice. He tells us that he was 'of equestrian rank, and a relative of Senators'.[36]

Occasionally, more than one name appears on a coin, and sometimes it is clear that several persons were acting together, perhaps as a board: ten names appear at Hierapolis in the year that Fabius Maximus was governor of Asia (10–9 BCE), while the names of thirteen *grammateis* appear at Magnesia in Ionia during the short six-year reign of Gordian III. Early imperial coins of Antioch in Caria use the phrase συναρχία ('joint administration'), with a personal name.[37]

At first, during the Julio-Claudian period, the names were generally in the nominative case, as they had been earlier. From the middle of the first century, however, a variety of formulae started to appear, until the pattern of names settled down in the second century to the usual format ἐπί (or some other preposition) followed by the genitive case ('under . . .').[38] The preposition ἐπί is often ambiguous concerning the role (if any) of the individual named after it. Other prepositions, such as διά ('through')[39] or παρά ('from')[40] seem to be largely localised Carian and Phrygian variants, being in use at some cities over a long period of time, and not necessarily having any different sense. In all these cases, as with the similar use of names on city weights, we may suspect that the individuals were responsible for the coinage. Sometimes – at least – they may have paid for it, but in most cases we cannot be exactly sure of the nature of their involvement.[41]

One special and very small group of names are those of women. There are very few of them, less than 1 per cent of the total recorded on imperial provincial coins.[42] They start to appear in the time of Augustus, reflecting the greater prominence of women in civic life from that time. Although barred by their gender from membership of the city assemblies and councils, they played an important role as benefactors in their own right, sometimes through holding priesthoods and sometimes holding an official position of a symbolic kind in the city, such as the eponymous position of *stephanephoros* (wreath bearer) or *prytanis* (president). In the latter case, their names appear symbolically, without implying any role in the coinage, as was the case with their male equivalents. Examples are the three female eponymous *stephanephoroi* who appear on the first- and second-century coinage of Smyrna or the six female *hieramnemones* at third-century Byzantium (Figure 7.4). The last case is interesting since they all appear named with men, presumably their husbands, and a woman's participation in civic life was often linked to that of her husband. An example occurs at Eucarpia, already mentioned above, where the husband P. Cl. Max. Marcellianus 'proposed' their issue (ΑΙΤΗCΑΜΕΝΟΥ), and the wife Pedia Secunda, 'took care' (ΕΠΙΜΕΛΗΘΕΙCΗC) of the issue. Such issues might be coordinated in other ways: at Acmonea, L. Servenius Capito added his name to the larger denomination coins struck with the portrait of the emperor Nero, while that of his wife, Julia Severa, also appeared on the smaller coins made for the emperor's mother Agrippina and his wife Poppaea.[43] A rather poignant example is that of Claudia Eugenetoriane at Colossae, whose name appears on her own on coins of the early second century. On one of them, she describes herself as a 'widow', so perhaps she was fulfilling a wish or obligation to make a coin issue, taken on before her husband's death.[44]

Many cities never produced any coinage at all: only twelve of the twenty-eight communities in the Sardis region of the province of Asia ever made any coinage, including a few 'important' cities;[45] of more than 300 cities in the whole province of Asia, fewer than 200 ever produced any coins.[46] Even when there was an 'explosion' of minting in the Peloponnese under Septimius Severus, almost half of the known cities did not contribute.[47] No civic coinage was made in Lycia, except in the reign of Gordian III, and even then by only twenty of its thirty-six towns.[48] These figures are fairly consistent and suggest that only 50–60 per cent of ancient cities ever produced coins in the period of the Roman Empire. New discoveries do sometimes attest new cities, but only extremely rarely.[49]

The cities that did produce coinage did so episodically and in varying quantities. Sometimes their production may have been linked to imperial requirements, such as helping to pay military expenses. It has been suggested that coinage was prompted by the passage of armies or the emperor *en route* to campaign. Definite cases, however, are hard to find. The large production of city coinages in Syria and some cities in Cilicia is probably to be linked to Trajan's Parthian War (113–17),[50] and the flow of coinage from the Peloponnese to Syria in the early 200s has been explained in terms of paying soldiers.[51] Coinage was certainly made at Pergamum and a few other cities to commemorate Caracalla's visit, but the attempt to trace his route across Asia to the Persian War from the incidence of coins in his name has been shown to be misleading.[52]

Generally, however, there seems to have been no link with military requirements or imperial visits, and the causes of production are probably to be found mostly in the unknown internal histories of each city.[53] There is little direct written evidence to help. One of the few ancient texts that gives the motivation for minting comes from Sestus in the late second century BCE, and it refers to

# 124 4 Whose coins?

> **Box 4.3 Coins for Sestus, Thrace**
>
> A long inscription of the second century BCE records an honorary decree of the Council and People of Sestus in favour of Menas, son of Menes, for his services to the city and his generosity in undertaking them. His sponsorships included the production of coinage: 'when the people decided to use its own bronze coinage, so that the city's coin type should be used as a current type and the people should receive the profit resulting from this source of revenue' (τοῦ τε δήμου προελομέγου νομίσματι χαλκίνῳ χρῆσθαι ἰδίωι χάριν τοῦ νομειτεύεσθαι μὲν τὸν τῆς π[όλ]εως χαρακτῆρα, τὸ δὲ λυσιτελὲς τὸ περιγενόμενον ἐκ τῆς τοιαύτης προσόδου λαμβάνειν τὸν δῆμον).[54]

the prestige of the city and to increasing its revenue. A profit would arise because of the premium in face value over the costs of the metal and the coins' manufacture. However, one cannot imagine the profit was very great, since, if it had been a ready and easy source of income, then presumably every city would have minted coinage and on a more regular basis.

The other reasons for producing provincial coins were presumably as manifold as they were for other coinages. Some would have been functional, such as buying food, paying for games, distributions of money, as well as smaller state payments. There may also have been an intention to provide an adequate amount of small change. Certainly there is little sign of a problem of small change in the eastern provincial cities, in contrast to what can be seen in the western Empire (Chapter 5). Other occasions may have been the self-advertisement and financial benefit of the city. Sometimes it may even have been simply to honour the emperor: Apollodotus son of Diodorus recorded on an inscription found at Kavalkar in the reign of Antoninus Pius that he had 'set up [a statue of] the emperor at his own expense . . ., having also struck coins'.[55] This might suggest that making coins with the emperor's portrait was, like setting up a statue, a way of honouring him.[56]

We know little about the denominations of the coins, although it is clear that they were sometimes expressed in Roman denominations and sometimes according to other systems: above all, the Greek drachma and its constituent parts, the obol and the chalkous.[57] Sometimes denominations that seem strange to use were produced, such as those of 5, 7, 9, 10, 11 or 14,[58] which do not seem helpful parts of a denarius divided into sixteen asses (in Greek, *assaria*), or of an obol divided into six or eight chalkoi.

**4.17**   **4.18**

**Figures 4.17–4.18** Coins of Chios with denominations.
The coins of the island of Chios often have inscriptions which name the various denominations in use. At different times, they record the Roman denominations of three assaria (τρία ἀσσάρια: 4.17), two-assaria, one-and-a-half assaria, assarion and half-assarion, as well as the Greek denominations obolos, four-chalkoi, three-chalkoi and two-chalkoi (δίχαλκον: 4.18). At Chios, an obol had eight chalkoi, and was equivalent to two assaria (asses). The coins are not easy to date, but it is clear that by the third century only Roman denominations were used. However, obols and chalkoi survived into the third century at Nicopolis, Seleucia and probably Antioch (Butcher 2004: 207 and 2017), and obols also still seem to have been in use at Coela in Thrace, under Gallienus (*GIC* 754 and 786). (4.18 *RPC III*, 1899)

There are patterns, such as the production of similar denominations in Macedonia in the third century CE, but these are not always cohesive. In general, the coins themselves were produced at what seems to us to be a confusing array of sizes and weights;[59] again, regional patterns can be discerned but there are often exceptions, and the patterns themselves are often inexact. The group of cities in Thrace and Moesia which, in the third century, produced coins marked with values of 2, 3, 4 and 5, did so at varying weight standards, loosely based on a common pattern, but diverging considerably from it and not always producing the same denominations.[60]

Another example is provided by the rare coins of Asia produced in the reign of Trebonianus Gallus and which specify their denomination. They occur at six cities, and each instance implies a unit of a different standard, varying from less than 1½ g to more than 3 g. Diameters too might vary. At two cities, the diameter of an '8' was 29 mm, while the coins of '5' and '6' at two different cities was 32 mm and 30 mm, respectively.[61] We might well agree with a view expressed not long ago by a well-informed scholar, in a slightly different context, that 'for any outsider travelling across northern Asia Minor in the late 230s it must all have been rather bewildering'.[62]

**126**  4 Whose coins?

The bewildered travellers may have had to contend with other problems. The first was what happened when they wanted to exchange a high-value silver coin for some smaller change in bronze. If they had or wanted a denarius, officially tariffed at 16 asses, they would find a different exchange rate in different cities, because of the commission (κόλλυβος) charged by the money-changers: 18 if buying and 17 if selling at Pergamum, and at Ephesus the rate was probably also 18 in the second century, but 21 later.[63]

The Pergamum case is especially interesting, since the information comes from an inscription which tells us that money-changers who departed from these rates 'were acting contrary to justice and the agreement', by which 'they were obliged to take' these rates.[64] The rates were not the result of private speculation, but officially determined by the civic authorities. And they might change.[65]

A second problem may have concerned the validity of the coins of one city in another. Could you use a coin of Ephesus in Pergamum, and vice versa? Here, opinions are divided among modern commentators. Most

---

### Box 4.4 Moneychangers' abuses

An inscription from Pergamum records the resolution of an abuse by moneychangers, who were unreasonably interfering in bulk purchases. The author is unknown, but may have been an emperor or a provincial governor.

> Now the [company of exchange-dealers (i.e., bankers)] were taking it [upon themselves to indulge in actions] which were unjust and contrary to their agreement with the city. For though they were bound to receive 18 asses for a denarius from the tradesmen, small stallholders and fish-sellers, all of whom are accustomed to dealing in small change, and to pay out 17 asses to any who wanted to exchange a denarius, they were not satisfied. They were not satisfied with the exchange of asses, but even when someone bought fish for silver denarii, they exacted an as for every denarius. And so I thought it proper to correct this for the future, so that the buying public should not be taxed by the exchange dealers in kinds of sale in which no authority has in fact been given to them. (*OGIS* 484: Macro 1976, Buttrey 1991; trans. Macro)

assume that a city's coins were valid everywhere, despite the obvious problems which would have arisen from their different sizes and shapes. But there is an alternative view which would see the validity of one city's coinage limited to that city.[66] Other views are also possible: that coins might be accepted in another city only if they fitted the denominational system in use there.[67] Obviously, this cannot always have applied; for example, in those cities which did not make any of their own coinage, where a supply of coinage perhaps had to be purchased.[68] Similarly, in Egypt the single mint of Alexandria supplied the whole province. Elsewhere, however, things may have been different. It has often been observed that the coins excavated from any site are mostly coins minted by the same city,[69] and the other coins found on the site may have been lost by travellers and visitors.[70] A hoard may contain only coins of one city.[71] Moreover, some inscriptions and passages of literature indicate that the coinage of one city was not normally valid in another unless it was so authorised to be valid (δόκιμον or ἔννομον).[72] Similarly, countermarks which were applied by a city to validate coins were normally applied mostly to the coins of the countermarking city.[73]

### Box 4.5 The pattern of coins found in excavations

Excavations show that most of the coins that were lost at any city were coins minted by the same city. For example, in the excavations carried out at Priene and Sardis, a total of 833 and 776 coins, respectively, were recovered, and most of them were minted at the site city (Priene: 564; Sardis: 408) (see Regling 1927 and Buttrey et al. 1981; see also now DeRose Evans 2018). The others were mostly produced for nearby cities: for example, 65 per cent of all the other coins found at Priene were minted by cities located within 50 km, or two days' walk (Knapp & MacIsaac 2005). They presumably reflect the movement of people from those cities to Sardis, enabling a picture of the network of contacts to be established. Johnston 2007, 5–6, note 22, also cites 80 per cent at Troy, 70 per cent at Ephesus, 60 per cent at Aphrodisias and 94 per cent at Athens. Similar patterns can be deduced from countermarks, which tended to be applied by any city to its own coins, reflecting the make-up of the currency in the city (Howgego 1985).

The great complexity of the system was recognised at the time, and simplifying the system to avoid bureaucracy and expense was contemplated, as is clear from the context of a well-known passage of Cassius Dio, written in the third century, but referring to the early years of Augustus:

> None of the cities should be allowed to have its own separate coinage or system of weights and measures; they should all be required to use ours. (Cassius Dio 52.30.9)

An attempt to do just that was tried in the reign of Augustus, as described in Chapter 5, but it was abandoned, presumably because of its inherent difficulties. The status quo resumed, and continued for another 250 years.

All this amounts to a picture whereby a civic coinage was very much the coinage of that city alone, with its production, physical shape, value and appearance all determined by the city, rather than regulated by the Roman emperor or government. It was, however, subject to occasional intervention by the Romans and influenced by long-term cultural, economic and political trends, some regional and some more general. These brought about a number of changes to the character of the coinage, which will be examined in the next chapters.

# 5

# The Revolution of Augustus – and Becoming More Roman in the First Century

The victory of Augustus ushered in the new era of monarchy, and saw changes to almost every aspect of Roman life. The coinage was no exception, and this chapter looks at the new shifts that took place in the provincial coinage and examines how they can enhance our understanding of the process and impact of the change to a new political order.[1]

The greatest change took place on the obverses of the coins. For centuries they had been dominated by the heads of tutelary deities, or the heads of the monarchs who ruled various parts of the Mediterranean world after its transformation by Alexander the Great. From the time of Augustus, portraits of the emperor and his family replaced these civic deities and monarchs. They also started to be accompanied by the emperor's name, whereas earlier coins generally had no inscription on the obverse.

This seems to have been a spontaneous reaction to the new order, and one which took time to occur everywhere. In addition, there was systematic control

**Figure 5.1** *Pax Romana* established.
In 28 BCE, the provincial silver coinage of Asia proclaimed the restoration of peace, following Augustus' defeat of Mark Antony at the Battle of Actium and the end of the civil wars which had shattered the Roman world after the death of Julius Caesar. The reverse shows the figure of PAX (Peace), while the obverse declares that Augustus was the 'deliverer of the liberty of the Roman people'. A related gold coin says that 'he restored the laws and rights of the Roman people'.[2] The restoration of traditional Roman government was, of course, a fiction; Augustus' dominant portrait was the sign of the new order. (*RPC I*, 2203/2)

# 130  5 The Revolution of Augustus

of the images (and texts) on the coinage, and they differed greatly from three dimensional portraits, which followed a limited number of official patterns.[3] Why not?

In the western provinces, coinage started to peter out and finally ended in the middle of the first century. 'Celtic' coinage in Britain and Gaul came to an end at much the same time. Such changes reflect a developing sense of identity in the western half of the Empire, and from the middle of the first century the currency of the western was completely different from that of the eastern part of the Empire. What brought about this difference?

In the east, the production of coins by the cities continued, but changes started to occur. The coinage began to be 'Romanised', in the sense that the coins started to look more like those made at Rome. The coins got bigger, to emulate the asses and sestertii produced at Rome, and Roman monetary units of account began to be used. The Roman 'epigraphic habit' started to pervade the coinage, as the inscriptions grew longer and imperial titles more complex, as well as more abbreviated, in the Roman manner. In these ways, the provincial coins can throw much systematic light on the debate about 'Romanisation'.

As well as the adoption of the imperial portrait, the reverse designs became more numerous and varied, echoing the diversity of designs on the coinage made at Rome. Such new designs might occasionally celebrate an event like Nero's visit to Greece, and they continued to reflect the local identity of the cities which produced them. But the new order brought a new consciousness of Roman values. Themes, like architecture or games, which had rarely appeared on Greek coins started to reflect this new outlook. These changes, at first apparent patchily in the Julio-Claudian period, became more pronounced under Vespasian and especially Domitian. By the end of the first century, the provincial coinage in many areas of the east had a 'Roman' look, although the extent of the change should not be exaggerated. Traditional themes, especially religion, continued to predominate, and some areas, such as the Levant, in particular, retained their earlier non-Roman feel for much longer, despite the adoption of the imperial portrait – itself initially delayed in the Levant, but later pervasive there.

There were also a small number of interventions by the Roman government. They were sometimes on a limited scale, such as the denominations to be used or (apparently) the ending the civic coinage in Greece after Nero. But occasionally they were on a substantial scale, under Augustus, and particularly under Nero. The effectiveness of such interventions, however, was very varied, as will be discussed below.

This chapter has two halves. The first describes ways in which changes took place on the coinage as the result of the changing concerns of the city elites. The second looks at the relatively rare instances of direct Roman intervention. The final section tries to explain how the fundamental difference between the west and the east came about in the middle of the first century, arguing that it reflects a new outlook of the cities rather than the imposition of a new order.

## 5.1 Trends

### 5.1.1 Portraits

Augustus' portrait appeared on the coins of more than 200 cities across the Empire. This was an enormous change. At Rome, the long tradition of 'family types', whereby a moneyer would commemorate on his silver denarii some laudable action of his ancestors, was joined during the civil wars by designs that referred to contemporary events and ultimately some portraits of the leaders of the different factions. The appearance of these portraits in the late first century BCE of the individual leaders was a reflection of the new reality of power. Power came from the leader, so both the leaders and those wishing to recognise them chose to place their features on the coins. As is well known, Caesar placed his portrait on some denarii minted at Rome, but he did so only a few weeks before his assassination in 44 BCE, several years after his dictatorship had begun. 'Non rex sum, sed Caesar' (I am not a king, but Caesar) must have had a hollow ring, since, by being the first Roman to place his portrait on the state coinage, he was indeed behaving like a Hellenistic king, even though he chose a traditional Roman style of portraiture. We can infer, moreover, that he must have recognised that it was a momentous step, since he delayed it for several years, and it appeared only five years after he had crossed the Rubicon and two years after he had declared himself Dictator; and even then it was only one of many different designs on the silver coinage (and never on the gold).

As well as the precious metal coinage of Rome, the bronze coins of the cities of the Empire started to respond to the new realities of power by placing portraits of Roman generals, their family members, and sometimes even their lieutenants, on the obverses of their coins. These replaced the principal deities which had been present for several centuries. The first example may even antedate Caesar at Rome. After his victory over Mithradates VI and his clearance of pirates from the Mediterranean, the Roman general Pompey founded a number of new cities in Asia Minor. One of them, Soli in Cilicia (south-east Turkey), was refounded with the new name Pompeiopolis. Thereafter, it produced a long series of coins portraying its new founder: from the reign of Tiberius, they bear dates from the foundation of the new city. There are a number of undated coins which may perhaps look earlier, but an early date for them is far from certain. A few years later the same thing may have happened at Nysa in Samaria. The city was refounded by one of Pompey's lieutenants, Aulus Gabinius, and took the new name Gabinia. It then started to depict Gabinius (although this is disputed), albeit often rather crudely. These coins are also dated, and the earliest dated issue belongs to 56/5 BCE (Figure 5.2).[4]

With Caesar, however, we are on firmer ground, and the city of Nicaea (north-west Turkey) produced coins with a fine portrait of Caesar on coins dated by the city's era to 47 BCE (Figure 3.31). Shortly afterwards, he was also depicted on coins of the short-lived colony of Lampsacus (Figure 5.3), which he had just founded to settle some of his veteran soldiers.[5] These were, however, isolated examples of a city taking the initiative in recognising the new order, and the great majority of the city coinages still retained their traditional appearance, choosing to depict their principal gods as before.

During the decade of civil war after Caesar's death, both the precious metal coinages of gold and silver, and the bronze coinages of the various cities, saw an increase in the number of the portraits of rulers.[6] Most famously, but to our mind contradictorily, Brutus placed his own portrait on the gold and silver coins which he minted in Greece or Asia to commemorate his re-establishment of liberty (as symbolised by the pileus, the cap placed on a slave's head when he was freed) as the result of his assassination of Caesar (symbolised by two daggers) on the EID MAR ('the Ides of March').[7] The coins show how the

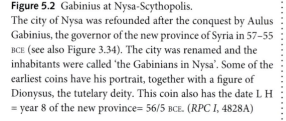

**Figure 5.2** Gabinius at Nysa-Scythopolis.
The city of Nysa was refounded after the conquest by Aulus Gabinius, the governor of the new province of Syria in 57–55 BCE (see also Figure 3.34). The city was renamed and the inhabitants were called 'the Gabinians in Nysa'. Some of the earliest coins have his portrait, together with a figure of Dionysus, the tutelary deity. This coin also has the date L H = year 8 of the new province = 56/5 BCE. (*RPC I*, 4828A)

**Figure 5.3** Julius Caesar at Lampsacus.
Caesar founded a colony for his veterans at Lampsacus in Asia Minor. The colonists honoured him by placing his portrait on the obverse, while the reverse shows the symbolic foundation of a colony. A priest ploughs the 'first furrow' in the ground, marking the extent of the new foundation, just as Romulus was said to have done for Rome, many centuries earlier. See also Figure 3.27 for a smaller denomination. (*RPC I*, 2269/3)

urgent need to establish his own position in the tumultuous context of the years following 44 rapidly set aside any hesitation arising from the monarchical overtones of a coin portrait.

Portraits of all the other principal actors in the Civil Wars appear on the coinage: Octavian, Lepidus, Antony and Sextus Pompey. They appeared principally on the gold and silver but also on some city coinages – a particularly apt choice being made by Ephesus which made some bronze coins with the triple portraits of the 'second' Triumvirate: Octavian, Antony and Lepidus (Figure 5.4). Lepidus, however, was soon forgotten and joint portraits of Antony and Octavian appeared on the so-called 'fleet coinages' of Mark Antony, minted in Greece and Cyprus or Syria (Figure 3.21). These coins also portray Octavian's sister Octavia, reflecting the attempt at dynastic union with her marriage to Antony.

The coinages may reflect Antony's dynastic ambitions. The city of Eumenea had portrayed his first wife Fulvia, when it changed its name to honour her. She was, however, soon set aside for his new wife Octavia, who also appeared with him on the silver cistophori of Asia. In addition, Antony also placed portraits of his younger brother Lucius and later his son, Marcus, on the gold and silver coinage. A number of cities in the Levant honoured his primacy by placing his portrait on their coins (Tripolis, Ptolemais [Figure 5.5], Aradus, Balanea and Marathus), as did other cities, which had been granted to Cleopatra in the 'Donations of Alexandria'. Damascus, Orthosia, Tripolis and Berytus honoured her in the same way, and occasionally they were both honoured together (Ptolemais and Dora; *cf.* also Cyrenaica). More remarkable is the way her portrait sometimes

**Figure 5.4** The triumvirs at Ephesus.
Small bronze coins of Ephesus show the triple portraits of the members of the 'Second Triumvirate'. The portrait of Mark Antony is clearly nearest the viewer, but it is hard to distinguish between Octavian (the later Augustus) and Marcus Lepidus. Normally one would have expected the senior member to appear in the centre, but Ephesus was part of Antony's territory and the engraver decided to give him prominence on the coin by placing his portrait in front of those of his two colleagues. Enlarged × 1.5. (*RPC I*, 2569)

appeared outside her territories, notably at Patras in Greece. Antony also placed her portrait on his silver denarii as 'the queen of kings who are sons of kings': he may have hoped to distract attention by stressing her royal lineage, but the appearance of a 'foreign' queen on the Roman coinage must have seemed a startling innovation.

As well as the principal players, other figures in the civil wars also appeared on the coinage. In Sicily, Sextus Pompey made dynastic gold and silver coins, portraying himself together with his father and brother. Further east, the renegade Labienus made gold and silver coins with his own portrait, while Antony's lieutenant Atratinus was honoured with a portrait on the bronze coinage of Sparta (Figure 5.6).

These cases are all extremely interesting, but one should not exaggerate their impact. They were all very rare, and the city bronze coinages continued largely as before with no change.

It is difficult to assess the true extent of the civic coinage produced during the decade of Antony's domination of the east, since many of the potential coin issues lack a reference to him and have no other way of being dated with any precision. The issues, whether in silver or bronze, which break tradition and adopt his or Cleopatra's portrait are clear enough, but one suspects that many other coins were produced at the time with little or no reference to the new rulers. A clear example is provided by the dated silver coinage of Egypt, which continued largely unchanged during the period, using the traditional designs of the posthumous portrait of Ptolemy I and the eagle. Only the diminutive dating formula has revealed the true dates of these coins in the different years of Cleopatra's reign. At Antioch, the silver

**Map 5.1** Cities making coins with the portrait of Mark Antony

**Figure 5.5** Mark Antony at Ptolemais.
A portrait of Antony in a laurel wreath appears on the city coinage of Ptolemais (also known as Ake). The reverse shows the city's Tyche or personification. (*RPC I*, 4740)

**Figure 5.6** L. Sempronius Atratinus, Sparta, 30s BCE.
Antony's general L. Sempronius Atratinus held various commands, including in Greece, where he was honoured by the city of Sparta, which placed his portrait (labelled ATPATINOC) on its coinage. His name appears on other coins of the time (e.g., Figure 3.28). He deserted Antony before the Battle of Actium and had a successful career under Augustus. (*RPC I*, 1101A)

coinage produced by the Romans, including Antony, in the name of the long dead king Philip continued (Figure 3.34), and the only allusion to Antony's position occurs on a unique small denomination.[8] Once again, it is easy to exaggerate the presence of Antony (and Cleopatra).[9] Their portraits appear on only a few city coinages, hardly any in comparison to what would happen shortly afterwards, after Antony's defeat and the establishment of Augustus' monarchy.

## Box 5.1 The portrait of Augustus

5.7         5.8

**Figures 5.7–5.8** The adoption of the portrait of Augustus.
Augustus' portrait appears at more than 200 cities throughout the empire, from Ebora (= Évira, Portugal: 5.7) in the far west to Amisus (Samsun, Turkey: Figure 5.8) in the far east of the empire, nearly 5,000 km distant. (5.7 *RPC I*, 51; 5.8 *RPC I*, 2148/8)

**Map 5.2** Cities making coins with the portrait of Augustus

# Box 5.1 (cont.)

'We should not minimize the colossal change which had come over the symbolic character of the coinage . . . . What we have is . . . a set of visible and incontrovertible examples of how people construed the world in which they lived' (Millar 1984: 45).

All this changed with Augustus' establishment of sole rule after the Battle of Actium in 31 BCE. Thereafter, the adoption of his portrait becomes standard on provincial coinage, appearing at over 200 cities. It is the most tangible evidence of the change from the Roman Republic to the new monarchy.

If the fact of the almost universal adoption of the imperial portrait by the cities on their bronze coinage is clear, the process and mechanism by which it took place are not.[10] It is difficult to date the first portraits more exactly within in the reign of Augustus. Indeed, it is sometimes not even certain whether a portrait is intended to depict Augustus or one of his successors. As a result, we do not know exactly when Augustus' portrait came into widespread use. In a few cases, it can be determined that portraits were made soon after Actium, but there are few such examples. Nevertheless, in *RPC I* it was concluded that the portrait of Augustus was generally adopted on coinage as soon after the early 20s BCE as coinage was produced.[11]

There were, however, two regional exceptions. In Syria, and especially Phoenicia, the coins often bore dates according to local eras (as they had been before the imperial period), and so they indicate that, although we do have some early portraits (e.g., at Damascus and Gadara), most of the dated portraits are rather later, generally from the last decade BCE.[12] However, the pattern of portraiture on Syrian coins is unusual, as indeed it was for sculptural portraits (which are very few compared with the rest of the Empire). In Cilicia also, then mostly part of the Roman province of Syria, there are almost no portrait coins of Augustus. Tiberius is the first emperor to appear regularly there.[13]

The 'universal adoption' of the portrait of Augustus needs some qualification. The most obvious one is the existence of the so-called 'pseudo-autonomous' coins, which, as discussed in Chapter 4 (Box 4.1), did not use the portrait. Although they are usually regarded as a phenomenon of the eastern Empire, they also occurred in the west. For example, Carteia and Emporion in Spain did not make any coins with portraits of the new

**Figure 5.9** Augustus and the *lituus*.
The portrait of Augustus at provincial cities was often accompanied by the *lituus*, the wand of the augurs, one of the orders of priests (Burnett 2011, 14). Suetonius connects the new name Augustus with the augurate (*Augustus* 7), and its common use on imperial and provincial coins suggests that this was also an official and a popular understanding. It appears at twenty-six provincial cities, many in the eastern Empire, where the Greek speaking population might not have immediately grasped the Latin wordplay augur–Augustus. The frequency of its use suggests that the verbal linkage of *augur* and *Augustus* played an important role in his public image. (*RPC I*, 2894)

emperor, and other Spanish cities similarly made coins without the portrait. The same is true of the 'Celtic' coinage of Gaul made during Augustus' reign: his portrait appears at only a very few places.

Equally surprising, perhaps, is the virtual absence of Agrippa, Augustus' brilliant young admiral and later his 'sort of equal' in power (Dio 54.12.4). Agrippa may have been given great powers – possibly even equal to those of Augustus – but the coinage is a clear witness that the reality of his inferior position was widely recognised.

There were also a few portraits of other people. A number of provincial governors were portrayed, mostly in the first half of the reign of Augustus.[14] Their disappearance is an example of the way that senatorial self-representation gradually fell out of fashion at the same time.[15] The city elites shared the later outlook of Augustus' *Res Gestae*, where there is hardly any mention of Agrippa or the other men on whom Augustus' rule depended.

As well as the portrait of the emperor, the city coinages also started to have portraits of members of the imperial family.[16] Under Augustus, coins portray virtually all of the would-be heirs, who had been chosen in the emperor's ill-fated attempts to name a successor: Marcellus, Agrippa Postumus, Gaius and Lucius Caesars (Figure 5.8) and the ultimately surviving Tiberius.[17]

**Figures 5.10–5.11** Agrippa on provincial coins.
Agrippa's portrait appears in Spain, principally at Gades, where he is styled as *patronus* and *parens*, no doubt reflecting some substantial act of patronage, and at Carthago Nova (*RPC I*, 81). At the colony of Nemausus (COL NEM) in Gaul (5.10), he appears with Augustus: Agrippa is on the left wearing a rostral crown, the sign of naval victory (at the Battle of Actium), and Augustus is on the right, and described by the inscription as Imp divi F P P = Imperator Divi Filius Pater Patriae (the Emperor, son of the God, Father of his Country). A crocodile is shown on the reverse, chained to a palm tree, to which a victory wreath is attached: it is a symbolic representation of the capture of Egypt after the defeat of Antony and Cleopatra. Veterans from the army of conquest may have later been settled at Nemausus. Agrippa is also paired with Octavian at a few other mints in Gaul (Arausio), Africa (Tingi), perhaps Sicily (Agrigentum), Cyrenaica, perhaps Crete (Cnossus) and in Greece (at Sparta and Nicopolis). He was sometimes in a subordinate position (as at Sparta or Nicopolis). He appears only once in the east, at Apamea in Bithynia (5.11). (5.10 *RPC I*, 525; 5.11 *RPC I*, 2008)

Both male and female members of the imperial family often appeared, above all in Asia (Figures 5.13–5.14), where females were sometimes used as denominational markers (on smaller denominations). In this respect, the provincial coinage diverged from the coinage produced at Rome. At Rome, female members were rarely depicted on coins before the reign of Caligula, and they remained infrequent there until the second century.[18] The city elites in Asia had a different conception of the new regime as consisting of a ruling house, rather being the rule of an individual monarch. In this way, they diverged from the main thrust of official iconography, whether on coins or any other medium. This divergence has not, however, been properly investigated, and it is tempting to think that the presence of women on provincial coinages is an instance of the provincial coinage later influencing that of Rome.

The cities, however, shared with official iconography the idea that female portraits would be differentiated, unlike those of the emperor and his male

**Figure 5.12** Caesonia, the wife of Caligula.
The only authentic coin portrait of Caesonia appeared on the coinage of King Agrippa I of Judaea (37–44). It is inscribed ΚΑΙΣΩΝΙΑ ΓΥΝΗ ΣΕΒΑΣΤΟΥ = 'Caesonia, wife of the emperor'. Agrippa had been brought up in Rome, an intimate of the imperial family. He owed his power to the Roman emperor Caligula, and consequently Caligula and his family were featured extensively on Agrippa's coinage. The reverse shows Caligula's daughter Drusilla (ΔΡΟΥΣΙΛΛΑ ΘΥΓΑΤΡΙ ΣΕΒΑΣΤΟΥ = 'to Drusilla, the daughter of the emperor'), also a unique appearance on coinage. In ways such as this, Agrippa's coinage has a greater emphasis on Rome and the imperial family, in contrast to that of the rest of the Levant. (*RPC I*, 4977)

heirs, which tended to be very similar. Female members of the Julio-Claudian (and Flavian) houses tended to have more individualised portraits, particularly as regards their hairstyles, whereas the male portraits were until Nero modelled on that of Augustus. This was true of sculpture as well as coins. It mattered less for women to follow a standard set by Augustus, as they were not trying to draw legitimacy from him. Male rulers, however, modelled their portraits on Augustus to stress their descent from him, and so also emulated his image.

The portrait of the emperor on provincial coins varied greatly between cities, and in this respect it is different from surviving sculptural portraits. More than 200 such sculptures are known and they mainly fall into three or four 'centrally defined' types, the most common remaining unchanged for over forty years.[19] The sculptural portraits show a great uniformity across the Empire, suggesting that they emanate from a central source and that efforts were made to ensure their similarity. On the coins, however, the images are often so different from the standard sculptural image of the emperor that it is sometimes difficult to decide whether they depict Augustus or one of his successors, and sometimes it is even unclear whether a head is supposed to be that of the emperor, as opposed to something else, such as a deity.

This variation is not confined to the provincial coinage, but can also be observed – to a lesser extent – on the centrally minted gold and silver

## Box 5.2 Emperors as gods

During the civil wars of the late Republic, it became a common practice for the leaders to liken themselves to a particular deity, thereby intending to enhance their position. For example, Antony could be compared to the Sun god, and Sextus Pompey to Neptune. The earliest coins of Augustus (or Octavian as he then was) similarly likened him to Jupiter or Apollo. However from 27 BCE, he avoided such divine overtones and presented himself only as a human. The provinces followed suit, and Augustus was only very rarely described as a god (*RPC I*, p. 47). In this respect, his example was followed for Tiberius and Claudius, although there were several exceptions for Caligula and Nero. Divine symbols were, however, used, somewhat more frequently for women on the city coinages (Figures 5.13–5.14), continuing the earlier practice (e.g., Fulvia as the goddess Victory at Eumenea: *RPC I*, 3139–40)

**Figures 5.13–5.14** Female members of the imperial house.
From the reign of Augustus, empresses appeared regularly on the provincial coinage, in contrast to the mint of Rome, where they did not appear until two generations had passed. Also, in marked contrast to male members of the early imperial house, women were sometimes likened to deities. Livia appears as Ἥρα (Hera) at three cities (as on 5.13, with Julia as Aphrodite, from Pergamum) and as θεά (goddess) at another three; Agrippina is θεά at eight cities, while Messalina is described as 'the new Hera' at both Nicaea (as on 5.14) and Nicomedia. The practice was, however, dropped from coin inscriptions in the Flavian period; Titus' daughter was never described in divine terms and Domitian's wife Domitia was called θεά only once, at Smyrna. Figure 5.13 is enlarged × 1.5. (5.13 *RPC I*, 2359; 5.14 *RPC I*, 2038)

**142** 5 The Revolution of Augustus

coins: although they are all recognisable as Augustus, they too vary widely over time and place. The individual coin engravers were free to represent the emperor as they chose. This lack of control can be linked to the way, discussed in Chapter 4, that coins did not generally suffer the *damnatio memoriae* of a hated emperor after his death. Coin portraits were clearly regarded as having less significance than grander portrait sculptures, despite their widespread geographical presence.

The later Julio-Claudians became more individualised, and, in the case of Claudius, characteristics such as his long neck can sometimes be seen in the provincial coins, but on other occasions his portrait may be indistinguishable from that of his predecessors.[20] Only with Nero do portraits become more personalised, and he has three main portrait types. At first he is shown as a young boy, both during the reign of Claudius and also at the beginning of his own reign, often in conjunction with Agrippina. Later, he is shown in a more mature fashion; and then finally, after 63 CE, with his hair shown in a series of 'steps'. This last type of portrait occurs widely, but it was not used exclusively – for example, it occurs only irregularly at the prolific mint of Alexandria. It seems no coincidence that Nero's reign combines a more

**Map 5.3** Cities in the Maeander valley with a common style of portraiture, first century CE

      5.15            5.16

**Figures 5.15–5.16** Coins of Laodicea and Hierapolis with similar portraits.
A meandering engraver. Coin engravers seem to have operated mostly within the city that produced the coinage. Sometimes, however, we do find a common style, such as the very similar portraits which were produced at a large group of eighteen cities in or near the Maeander Valley in Asia Minor for most of the Julio-Claudian period (*RPC I*, pp. 375–6): Orthosia, Cidrama, Apollonia Salbace, Heraclea Salbace, Trapezopolis, Attuda, Laodicea (5.15), Hierapolis (5.16), Hydrela, Tripolis, Apollonoshieron, Blaundus, Dionysopolis, Eumenea, Synnada, Eucarpia, Acmonea and Julia. Their similarity suggests that they were produced by the same engraver, although we do not know how such a system may have worked. This group is, however, exceptional, and most of the portraits seem specific to the city where they were produced. (5.15 *RPC I*, 2917; 5.16 *RPC I*, 2975)

**Figure 5.17** Nero and the freedom of the Greeks.
During Nero's visit to Greece he proclaimed freedom and exemption from taxation for the Greeks, prompting them to hail him as the 'new Sun who shines on the Greeks' and as 'Nero Zeus the Liberator'. The event stimulated many provincial coin issues, such as those of Sicyon and Nicopolis. Here the colony of Patras likens him to Jupiter the Liberator. The coins also implied a divine status for the emperor by showing him with a radiate crown, which, since the deification of Augustus, had become a sign of divinity; similarly Nero is sometimes shown wearing an aegis on his shoulder, another sign of divinity. (*RPC I*, 1279)

realistic form of portraiture with a departure from the Latin form of his name in favour of the simple Νέρων Καῖσαρ (see Section 5.1.2). The dominance of an Augustan portraiture and his name formula was replaced only forty years after his death, when a stronger sense of individual imperial identity emerged.

**144** 5 The Revolution of Augustus

Unsurprisingly, the more traditional Vespasian adopted a traditional type of portraiture, referring back to the period of the Republic, and he was not celebrated with any radiate portraits. They appear again for Domitian, as does the aegis, in much the same way as for Nero. There are a few instances in Greece,[21] but six Bithynian cities once again embraced this divine style of portrayal.[22] A similar pattern recurs for Trajan, continuing this strong regional fashion fifty years later.[23] The similarities between the portraits of Domitian and Trajan are discussed further in the next chapter.

## 5.1.2 Inscriptions

The inscriptions on coins started to change in the imperial period.[24] For a long time, Greek coins had followed a general pattern of having no inscription on the obverse, and on the reverse, either the simple name of the city, in the genitive plural, or the simple name of a king, also in the genitive, preceded by the title ΒΑΣΙΛΕΩΣ ... ('Of King ... '). Sometimes more royal titles might be added, especially in the later Hellenistic period. In Asia Minor, cities started to add the names, more or less abbreviated, of prominent citizens and magistrates, while, in Syria, the cities started to add the civic titles in which they increasingly took pride, such as 'autonomous' or 'inviolate'.

With the establishment of the principate of Augustus, changes started to occur. At first, many provincial coins adopted his portrait, but did not add any inscription, continuing previous practice. However, anonymous portraits started to die out,[25] and the way that they became rare is itself an important shift. It illustrates that, after Augustus, having a name associated with the portrait was a necessary part of imperial identity. This was part of the more general trend in the ancient world, whereby names tended to be inscribed more frequently, as Roman society expanded.[26]

Simple inscriptions started to be added under Augustus, usually in the nominative case. Under Tiberius, Caligula and Claudius, the identity of the emperor looked to the precedent of Augustus and Latin forms of the imperial name, and the Greek version of the Latin formula was most common for them.[27] Under Nero, his new approach to portraiture was matched by a move away from Roman forms of the name, and a simpler Greek-language form (Νέρων Καῖσαρ) became common. Only from his reign did the cities generally try to portray an emperor's individual identity, as just discussed. The Flavians returned to the pattern of inscriptions influenced by Latin forms and portraits derived from Republican models.

The Greek inscriptions on the coins nearly always consist of whole words, but the Latin inscriptions were often abbreviated and they were also accompanied by titles. For example, we find *Aug* (Sicca, Dyme, Macedonia, Parium, Berytus), *Imp Augus* (Calagurris), *Augustus divi f* (many instances), or the more challenging *Imp C d f A p m p p* (Carthage, Lepti).[28] Abbreviation was a feature of Latin names, but rare in Hellenistic Greek.[29] The addition of titles to coin inscriptions is also a feature of Roman practice, as one can see from denarii of the triumviral period. Early Hellenistic royal coins had kept things simpler and fuller, for example ΒΑΣΙΛΕΩΣ ΛΥΣΙΜΑΧΟΥ, although the later kings of Syria had added a number of titles, perhaps providing a model for Roman practice.

The use of the genitive case for Hellenistic royal coin inscriptions contrasts with an overwhelming preference for the nominative for the Roman emperors, including Augustus. The genitive does occur, only a little more often than the accusative or dative, but in all these the use of a case other than the nominative is exceptional. The adoption of the nominative case for Greek inscriptions naming Roman rulers derives from Latin models, which used the nominative rather than the genitive.

As time passed, the inscriptions came to include more elements and more abbreviations, both features of Latin usage and of the coinage produced at Rome (Box 5.3). Similarly, too, Greek cities started to refer to themselves from the Flavian period using the nominative case, in this way also adapting

**Figure 5.18** A long and abbreviated inscription.
The obverse of a coin of Domitian from Nicaea has ΑΥΤ ΔΟΜΙΤΙΑΝΟΣ ΚΑΙΣΑΡ ΣΕΒ ΓΕΡ ('the Emperor Domitian Caesar Augustus Germanicus') and the reverse has ΤΟΝ ΚΤΙΣΤΗ(ν) ΝΕΙΚΑΙΕΙΣ ΠΡΩΤΟΙ ΤΗΣ ΕΠΑΡΧΕΙ(ας) ('Nicaea, first [city] of the province [honours] its founder [the god Dionysus]'. The reverse has an imaginary portrait of Dionysus. (*RPC II*, 637)

# 146 5 The Revolution of Augustus

## Box 5.3 The number of words on the obverses of early imperial provincial coins

The majority (67 per cent) of all Greek legends in the Julio-Claudian period were of two words or less, but by Flavian times the majority (75 per cent) had grown to between two and five words. The increase was not simply a result of the increasing physical size of the coins, since it was perfectly possibly for large coins to have short legends, as was the case with, for example, Hellenistic tetradrachms. Like the increase in size, the increase in the complexity of the legends was a reflection of the growing influence of the practice at Rome. The Greek legends started to look more like Roman ones, both in their complexity and in their use of abbreviations.

| | OBVERSE LEGENDS (% ages) | | | |
| --- | --- | --- | --- | --- |
| | Julio-Claudian period | | Flavian period | |
| Words | Latin | Greek | Latin | Greek |
| 0 | 4 | 15 | – | 3 |
| 1 | 10 | 24 | 1 | 8 |
| 2 | 13 | 28 | 2 | 23 |
| 3 | 16 | 12 | 6 | 13 |
| 4 | 15 | 8 | 23 | 21 |
| 5 | 13 | 6 | 23 | 18 |
| 6 | 12 | 6 | 8 | 1 |
| 7 | 4 | <1 | 9 | 13 |
| 8 | 6 | – | 5 | – |
| 9 | 3 | <1 | 1 | – |
| 10 | 1 | <1 | 10 | – |
| 11 | 1 | <1 | 6 | – |
| 12 | <1 | – | 3 | 1 |
| 13 | – | – | – | – |
| 14 | 1 | – | – | – |
| 15 | – | – | 3 | 1 |
| sample size (n) | 1322 | 2448 | 444 | 1542 |

Latin practice.[30] The occasional date formula for a proconsul used a dative absolute, again importing a Latin form to Greek, rather than using the traditional genitive case.

The reverse inscriptions follow the pattern of the Republican period, and normally have the name of the city in the genitive plural, sometimes accompanied by the name of a local magistrate or prominent citizen. In the west, the personal names are generally accompanied by the name of a magistracy, such as that of *duovir*, one of the two annual chief magistrates of a colony, or that of a more junior aedile. The inscription might often be quite long and abbreviated, as on the obverse.

Apart from Greek and Latin, a few other languages and scripts occurred in small parts of the Roman world, though most of them had disappeared by the reign of Augustus. In Spain, for instance, only Ebusus and Abdera still retained neo-Punic into imperial times.[31] In Africa, a number of cities used neo-Punic in the early first century, often bilingually with Latin, or occasionally with Greek; the language and script are also found on some public inscriptions into the first century CE. With these mixtures of script on the coins, it is always the city name that is in Punic or Greek while the titles of members of the imperial family or Roman governors are in Latin. However, Sabratha and Oea also have the abbreviated names of local *suffetes* (city magistrates) in Punic like *SV=Q ThThE* (the habit of abbreviating in a different language is copied from Latin practice). And, although neo-Punic continued to be used in the Augustan and Tiberian period on the coins of Sabratha and Oea, some of the other cities which had used it replaced it with Latin: in the late Augustan period at Thaena and in the reign of Tiberius at Thapsus and Lepcis. Further east, Phoenician continued in use at Tyre (Figure 6.26), Aradus, Marathus and Sidon, right down to the second century in the case of Tyre, even though by then it was a dead language.[32] It also made an occasional appearance in the third century, even after a colony had been established there. In all these examples, Latin is used for the new imperial power, whereas Punic or Phoenician is used to denote the pride the city took in some aspect of its past.

### 5.1.3 Reverse Designs

The designs on the reverse of provincial bronze coins made during the period of the Republic were fairly static and referred to the issuing city, usually by depicting the deity of one of its principal cults. Later, by the second century CE, a new typology had developed, as discussed in the next chapter, with an intense interest in the real and mythological history of the city. By then, as well as focusing on civic cults, the designs sometimes depicted temples or other structures, and sometimes gave extended, almost narrative, accounts of local myths.

**148** 5 The Revolution of Augustus

Between the simpler approach of the Republican period and the more antiquarian interests of the second century, the first century stands as a period of change. The most significant change is in the increasing diversity of designs (Box 5.4). Individual cities started to produce coins with several different reverse designs for a single emperor, giving the provincial coinage a variety that stands in contrast to its predecessors.

The most likely explanation for this growth in choice and selection is the influence of Roman coins themselves. In the Republican period, the coinage from Rome had been remarkable, indeed unique among ancient coinages, for its multiplicity of designs, and the designs had often referred to the personal histories of the moneyers rather than the Roman state itself. The coinage of the provincial cities is not dissimilar if we think in terms of individual cities rather than the individual moneyers. Both wished to memorialise, respectively, their individual family and their public civic identities. However, although some coins depict provincial cult temples, or on other occasions a Capricorn as a reference to Augustus,[33] nevertheless the character of the majority of the reverse designs remained strongly local.

References to contemporary events are extremely rare in the first century. The Battle of Actium was commemorated only at Pella (Figure 3.36), and the capture of Egypt at Nemausus. Tiberius is shown restoring Magnesia after the terrible earthquake of 17 CE;[35] that this one city alone among the thirteen which received aid and formed a common league is an indication of the normal disregard of contemporary events by the cities when choosing

---

## Box 5.4 The increasing diversity of reverse designs

The increase in the diversity of reverse designs in the provincial coinage[*]

| Period | Designs | Designs per year (approx.) |
| --- | --- | --- |
| 44 BCE–CE 68 | about 4,000* | 40 |
| 69–96 | 2,817 | 100 |
| 96–138 | 6,568 | 160 |
| 138–192 | 15,000 | 300 |
| 218–238 | 9,600 | 480 |
| 249–253 | 2,533 | 700 |

* The table excludes the 1,000 or so entries for the western Empire for the first period; since they do not continue later, they would distort the picture.

## Box 5.5 Buildings on coins

One of the most interesting of the innovations is the depiction of structures, such as temples, arches, bridges or gateways. The presence of structures is a good route to test the changing nature of 'cultural identity' in coin design, since the implicit emphasis on civic space is a Roman characteristic, and contrasts with the Greek predilection for images drawn from the natural world. Buildings appear on Roman but not on Greek coins, while animals or plants predominate as motifs in Greek art, whether on coins, jewellery, or in poetry. Temples start to appear from the reign of Augustus, and then become a standard design in the Julio-Claudian period.[34]

5.19            5.20

**Figures 5.19–5.20** The temple of Augustus at Pergamum.
The first temple to appear on an eastern provincial coin is a crude representation of the temple of Augustus and Rome at Pergamum, on coins signed by the city Secretaries (*grammateis*), Charinos and Kephalion. The coins of Charinos (5.19) show a simple temple façade with six columns; those of Kephalion (5.20) have a façade with two columns enclosing the cult figure of Augustus, but omitting that of Roma. The reality of the temple was, therefore, clear to the city elite at the time. The temple has not yet been discovered, and these coins should not be used as evidence for its exact appearance. The number of columns shown for the same temple often varies and the coins are symbolic rather than photographic representations (Burnett 1999; Elkins 2015). (5.19 *RPC I*, 2358; 5.20 *RPC I*, 2362)

The temples on early imperial provincial coins are often, though not exclusively, associated with the imperial cult, and it may be the case that it was the invention of this new sort of temple that prompted the choice of temple designs. They had never appeared on coinage previously, apart from the coins of Roman Republican moneyers, who used them alongside many other designs as a natural part of the visual language they employed to memorialise the achievements of their families. In this way, some of the provincial coins were 'Romanised' in the sense of becoming more like coins minted at Rome.

**Figure 5.21** Claudius at Mopsus, Cilicia, south-east Turkey.
The rare coins of Mopsus have the head of the city's principal deity, Zeus. The reverse shows the togate figure of the emperor (labelled ΚΛΑΥΔΙΟC ΚΑΙCΑΡ), holding a statuette of Victory. The coin is dated to year 113 of the city = 45/6 CE, and so it is possible that the coin alludes to Claudius' British victory in 43. (*RPC I*, 4054)

coin designs. Claudius' victory in Britain was, perhaps, celebrated at Mopsus alone (Figure 5.21),[36] and there is no obvious reference on the city coinage to Nero's wars in Britain and Armenia.[37] The only exception was late in Nero's reign when several cities in Greece acknowledged his visit there, either with designs which recorded moments from the imperial visit, as at Corinth or Patras (Figure 5.17), or more generally with the adoption of a radiate portrait. Even the great war which broke out in Judaea in 66 made little appearance on the provincial coinage, outside Judaea itself. The city elites were focused on themselves and their cities; events, however momentous, played a lesser role in their consciousness.

### 5.1.4 Physical Properties: Size and Metal

Provincial coins were influenced by the shape and size of those made at Rome, just as they were influenced by Roman coins in the designs they bore. In the Republic and early Empire, bronzes made in the west (except for most of Gaul) tended to be quite large and heavy, a fashion derived from the bronze coinage of Rome, while those in the east were, at first, much smaller, in the general tradition of the regal and civic bronze coinage of the eastern Mediterranean. The physical influences of Roman prototypes were, however, often slow to have an effect, and normally not very strong: even when provincial coins do copy them, they are rarely exactly the same diameter, thickness or weight (for an exception, see Figure 5.25).

Augustus introduced a major reform of the base metal coinage, as discussed in more detail later in this chapter. It saw the replacement of the bronze used in the Republican period, with two new metals, orichalcum (brass) and copper, with a system of new denominations for the coinage minted at Rome.

This new system was followed or adapted by some of the provincial coinages of Spain and Africa.[38] In Spain, two systems emerged (Box 5.6) and the dual scheme was clearly well understood, so that denominational marks were not needed, though even in the same city, more than one system might be used.

5.22

5.23

**Figures 5.22–5.23** Augustan coins from north Africa.
The coinage of Lepti Minus marked its coins with Δ (5.22), B and A, presumably marking them as 4, 2 and 1 asses. The largest coins look like Augustan sestertii from Rome by their size, but they were a little bigger in diameter and somewhat heavier. Hadrumetum (Sousse) even produced massive pieces of about 40 mm diameter and 50–60 g (5.23), which may have been intended to be coins of 8 asses or one quinarius. (5.22 *RPC I*, 784; 5.23 *RPC I*, 777)

### Box 5.6 Augustan coins from Spain

One smaller group of cities in north east Spain followed Roman metrology very closely, using orichalcum as well as bronze or copper and copying Roman weight standards (see Figure 5.33). Elsewhere in Spain and Africa, the Augustan system was adapted, and large denominations were struck in bronze. Both systems were derived from the new Roman system, although in different ways. The graph shows the two systems for making coins of the same value (sestertii) in Spain: the 'old' system of heavy bronze (circles) and the new system of lighter brass (squares).

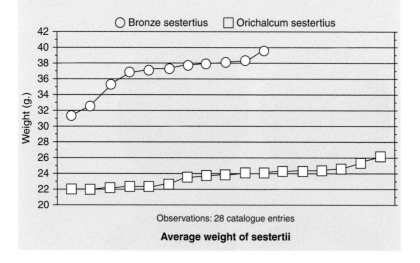

In Gaul, many large bronze coins were minted at Nemausus and, later, Lugdunum, the latter following the Roman metrological system, and they were accompanied by the transportation to Gaul of many bronzes minted in Rome. Little, if any, bronze coinage continued to be produced by local communities in Gaul.[39]

Bronze coinage in the eastern Mediterranean had tended to be small in size, with certain exceptions: Ptolemaic coins were often big during the third and second centuries, and some Syrian coins copied them in the second century BCE. By the first century, such large coins had dropped out of production, although some large pieces were produced in northern Turkey under Mithradates VI, in the early first century BCE.

These Mithradatic coinages had also seen the production of orichalcum or brass coins, as described in Chapter 3, and the new technology was soon transferred to the west. It was used there for military equipment and for the coins minted by the prefect C. Clovius (Figure 5.24) and the praetor Q. Oppius in the mid 40s BCE,[40] and later applied to the reformed base metal coinage of Augustus from Rome, from about 20 BCE and from Lugdunum, from about 7 BCE.[41] It became the standard set of metals for the fractional coinage minted at Rome for the rest of the imperial period: sestertii (4-asses) and dupondii were (2-asses) minted from brass at standards of about 25 g and 12½ g, and asses from copper at about 10½ g. As the diameter of the dupondii and asses was similar, it would have been hard to distinguish them when the coins were not fresh, until from the reign of Nero the radiate crown was adopted for the portrait to denote the dupondius.

Brass was also used, to a limited extent, in Spain: for the coinage of the legate P. Carisius in the 20s BCE, and for some city coinages in the reigns of Tiberius and Caligula. They all followed the pattern used at Rome, of brass sestertii and dupondii, with copper asses. Brass had previously been used in Asia for the reformed 'CA' coinage (Figure 5.30), although the asses were made of bronze.

Brass continued to be used in the eastern half of the Empire, although in some areas, such as Egypt and Syria,[42] coins were never made from it.[43] A series of detailed analyses and qualitative assessments were carried out for *RPC I–II* (Map 5.4), and a longer chronological series for a number of selected mints. They showed that in Greece most of the coins were made from bronze, except for one issue of the colony Corinth, which used brass (*RPC I*, 1133, dated to 17–16 BCE). The Roman system was not generally used in Greece, but, as at Corinth, brass was adopted from time to time. In Macedonia, brass was

**Figure 5.24** The first Roman coins to use brass in the west.
A series of coins was made by a prefect called C. Clovius, referring to Caesar's third dictatorship (46/5 BCE) and celebrating his Victory. (*RPC I*, 601)

not present, and most of the coins were leaded bronzes. From the reign of Claudius, however, pure copper is found at Philippi and Thessalonica, alongside leaded bronze for the smaller denominations.

Brass appeared first in imperial Bithynia at Nicaea, in about 25 BCE (*RPC I*, 2030). This was before the Augustan reform at Rome but probably at the same time as the CA coinage of Asia (see Figure 5.30). From the reign of Claudius it was used extensively in Bithynia, and the two largest denominations were therefore much the same size and weight as sestertii and dupondii from Rome.[44] As with Macedonia, it seems that the choice of metal was a matter of fashion, rather than a reflection of a different denominational structure, since the weight standard was unaffected.

In the province of Asia, the numerous and diverse civic issues of Asia make generalisations difficult. Brass had been used in Republican Asia, as discussed above, and apparently as a means of distinguishing one denomination from another. Its use there set a precedent for the reforms at Rome under Augustus, and also for the enigmatic CA coinage of Asia, minted from the early 20s BCE and perhaps at Ephesus.[45] The CA coinage consisted of large coins made of brass, resembling the later sestertii from Rome, accompanied by smaller denominations made of brass or bronze, and looking as if they were intended to be dupondii, asses and semisses. The civic coins in Asia were similarly made either of brass or bronze.[46] Once again, it seems that the choice of metal was not relevant to the denomination, but was a matter of fashion.

Taking the eastern provinces as a whole, the use of brass in the early imperial period tended to be confined to the same areas that had used it

**Figure 5.25** Tiberius and the deified Augustus, Mytilene.
A remarkable coin of Mytilene shows a togate figure of the emperor Tiberius, and his deified 'father' Augustus, enthroned on an elephant chariot. Very unusually for a civic coin from Asia, it copies the size and metal (brass) used for sestertii from the mint of Rome: an unusually Roman theme was matched by an unusually Roman-looking flan. (*RPC I*, 2343)

## Box 5.7 The quality of brass

It seems no coincidence that brass coins in Asia tend to have been made near the sources of zinc, so their production seems largely the result of a ready supply, rather than any ideological imitation of the coins made at Rome. This is confirmed by the way that, at Rome, the amount of zinc in the brass alloy gradually declined in time, whereas it remained high for the Asian coins. The zinc in the Roman coins became diluted by continuous recycling, whereas the Asian coins were made of freshly produced brass. The Asian coins vary quite considerably from each other, suggesting that the alloy was manufactured locally, perhaps even in each individual city, rather than supplied from some central point (Cowell et al. 2000).

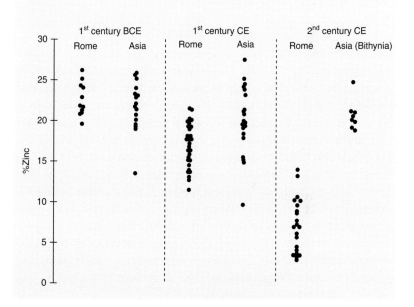

previously, in the first century BCE. Although the influence of Rome coinage can be seen in some instances, with the production of sestertius-sized coins in Bithynia and a few other cities, the choice of brass continued to be a localised fashion, with no general implication for the pattern of denominations, and with no suggestion that the example of the coinage at Rome was very influential.

**Map 5.4** The incidence of brass on provincial city coins in the Julio-Claudian period

Apart from the metals used, there was a very large variation in the sizes and weights used by the cities. However, in early imperial Asia there was a tendency for two typical sizes to be used: one at about 19 mm in diameter and 5–6 g in weight and the smaller at about 15–16 mm and about 3–3½ g, and such coins can be found at some two dozen cities. But many other denominations were made, as is clear from the prolific and well-studied city of Smyrna, which produced coins in five denominations. In *RPC I* an attempt was made to produce a pattern of nine different denominations across the province of Asia in the first century CE, and a similar pattern has been suggested for Asia in the first century BCE.[47] It is difficult to be sure how far such patterns are valid, since they assume that cities would all adhere to a common pattern, to a greater or lesser degree. However, as the individual cities could make their own decisions about their coinage, the imposition of any sort of common framework to cover all of them might seek to find a pattern where none, in fact, existed.

We have seen that in the early Empire there was a tendency for most of the coins to be smaller than 20 mm. By the end of the first century, however, the coins were generally much bigger, as we can see from the large sample from the province of Asia. Box 5.8 part 1 shows the great increase in coins with a diameter of more than 20 mm: it jumps from 13 per cent to 94 per cent.[48] If we look at the number of cities (Box 5.8, part 2), we find the same pattern: a very big increase in the number of them which produced larger coins in the second half of the first century.[49] By the reign of

## Box 5.8 The increasing size of provincial coins of Asia in the first century CE

The first table shows the proportion of larger coins in the province of Asia in relation to the total number of types for the province.

|  | RPC I (Julio–Claudian) | Percentage | RPC II (Flavian) | Percentage |
| --- | --- | --- | --- | --- |
| 30–34 mm | 28 | 2% | 43 | 7% |
| 25–29 mm | 303 | 4% | 303 | 47% |
| 20–24 mm | 84 | 7% | 247 | 40% |
| Total (all sizes) | 1,155 | | 646 | |

The second table shows the number of cities producing larger bronze denominations, in the province of Asia.

| Reign | Number of cities |
| --- | --- |
| Tiberius | 0 |
| Caligula | 2 |
| Claudius | 2 |
| Nero | 11 |
| Vespasian | 12 |
| Domitian | 22 |

Domitian, a number of city coins were being made which were approximately 30–35 mm, the size of Roman sestertii (although their weight standard is generally lighter). Examples can be found from all over the eastern part of the Empire, such as Philippopolis in Thrace, Midaeum and Smyrna in Asia, or Alexandria in Egypt. The increase in size is the result of the same tendency noted above for the inscriptions on the coins; both surely result from a wish to make the city coinage look more like Roman coinage.

## 5.2 Roman Interventions

The trends considered above account for many of the changes that came over the provincial coinage during the first century CE, especially the tendency for the coins to look more like coins minted at Rome. These trends were largely the result of the changing cultural outlooks of the elites in the Empire, rather than interventions by their Roman rulers. The

**158** 5 The Revolution of Augustus

emperors held back from unifying the coinage across the Empire, although this was an explicit possibility in the mind of a later historian. As already mentioned in Chapter 4, Cassius Dio recounted Maecenas' warning to Augustus that cities should not be allowed to have separate coinage, continuing that:

> They should send no embassy to you, unless its business is one that involves a judicial decision; they should rather make what representations they will to their governor and through him bring to your attention such of their petitions as he shall approve. In this way they will be spared expense and be prevented from resorting to crooked practices to gain their object; and the answers they receive will be uncontaminated by their agents and will involve no expense or red tape. (Cassius Dio 52.30.9)

This passage is worth quoting in full, since it shows that even the idea of unifying the coinages of the Empire was not a reflection of any new ideology of a single empire. It was a pragmatic idea, which, if it had been adopted, would have been intended to save bureaucracy and avoid fraud.

The pattern of Roman government was to assimilate the previous practices in the territories which they came to rule, and coinage was no exception. Hence the changes that occurred were mostly the results of general trends, as described above, rather than specific actions. However, some interventions did take place, though not many. They occurred rarely and met with mixed success.

### 5.2.1  Augustus and the Manipulation of Civic Issues

At certain periods, some local coinages were produced in very large quantities, so much so that it is very hard to accept that they were made only to serve the needs of the individual city. The eastern silver coinages made during the Republican period were discussed in Chapter 3. Similarly, under Augustus, the exceptionally large scale of 'six main aes [bronze] coinages' was emphasised many years ago.[50] They were the coinages of Nemausus and Lugdunum (both in Gaul), Rome, Asia (the CA coins and the 'colonist ploughing' coins – now identified as emanating from Alexandria Troas: Figure 5.29)[51], and Syria (the SC coinage of Antioch). Others could be added for Augustus, both in Egypt and Belgic Gaul (Figure 5.26).[52]

These Augustan interventions are usually regarded as intended to supply coinage for military spending, but it seems likely that they were also

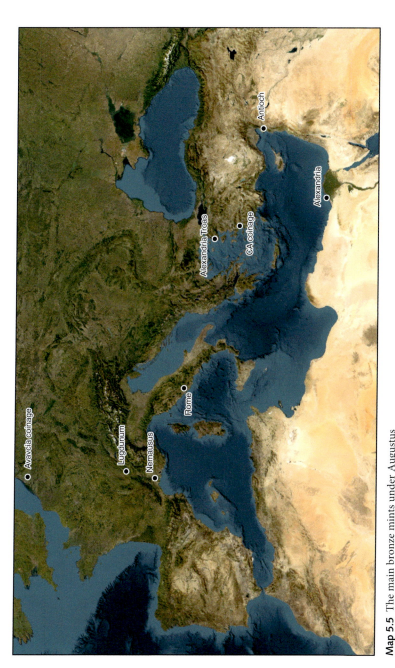

**Map 5.5** The main bronze mints under Augustus
The locations of the mints for the Avavcia and CA coinages are approximate.

**Figures 5.26–5.31** Some regional bronze coinages under Augustus. The small bronze coins enigmatically inscribed AVAVCIA (5.26) are found in large numbers in north-west Gaul and the Rhineland. The mint of Lugdunum made sestertii and other coins for circulation in Gaul and Germany (5.27). Sestertii (5.28) and other base metal coins from the mint of Rome were made with a prominent S C (= Senatus consulto = 'By decree of the Senate), initially with the name of one of the three annual moneyers, here M. Sanquinius. They circulated principally in Italy. The smaller coins with the scene of a foundation of the colony (two men ploughing) of Alexandria Troas (5.29) are found in large numbers in Thrace and north-east Asia Minor. The sestertii and smaller coins with a prominent C A (5.30), perhaps standing for *Caesar Augustus*, were made somewhere in Asia (perhaps Ephesus) and are found at many sites in western Turkey. Antioch made a long-lasting series of bronze coins also inscribed S C (5.31), and they circulated throughout Syria. (5.27 *RIC I*, Augustus 231; 5.28 *RIC I*, Augustus 341; 5.29 *RPC I*, 1656; 5.30 *RPC I*, 2233; 5.31 *RPC I*, 4248)

intended to improve the quality of small change. The state of small change in late Republican Italy was very poor, as discussed in Chapter 3, and the same was true to a lesser degree across the western Empire by the reign of

5.29

5.30

5.31

**Figures 5.26–5.31** (cont.)

Nero. Augustus seems to have tried two tactics. One was the attempted imposition of a uniform set of coins across the Empire, much as was described in the passage from Cassius Dio previously quoted. The brass sestertii and dupondii, together with copper asses, were minted at Rome from about 20 BCE (Figure 5.28). Similar coins were minted in Asia a little earlier, in the early 20s (Figure 5.30), and in Spain at the same time. Some were also produced, perhaps at the same time, in Syria.[53] In Gaul, the mint at Lugdunum made them from 10 BCE or later.[54]

However, this initiative did not work. Only Rome and Lugdunum continued to make these coins, and Lugdunum ceased under Tiberius. A more regional approach to the supply of bronze was also tried, with the production of the coins from Nemausus and Alexandria Troas (Figures 5.10 and 5.29), and the new SC coinage of Antioch, produced

**162  5 The Revolution of Augustus**

at their own weight standards and without any brass (Figure 5.31). They were more successful. In the east, Antioch continued to be a very important regional mint until the third century. A ready supply of small change continued to be produced in other areas, such as in Alexandria Troas[55] and Egypt.[56] However, the problem of small change in the western Empire was not fully solved. No bronze coinage was made at the mint of Rome for almost twenty years under Claudius and Nero, and its lack was exacerbated there by the end of the local city and 'tribal' coinages in the western Empire. In the reign of Claudius, the circulating bronze medium included many crude imitations of coins of Claudius. Claudius' and Nero's response was to set up branch mints to produce coins similar to those minted at Rome. Under Claudius they were probably located in Gaul and Spain,[57] and perhaps Thrace,[58] and under Nero in Gaul and Thrace.

## 5.2.2  Nero and the Silver Coinage of the Empire

A different sort of intervention took place in the reign of Nero, when efforts were made to recover large amounts of silver from the provincial coinages, as described in detail in Chapter 1. The programme of recovery of silver which began under Nero may well have lasted for half a century until the reign of Trajan. The activity of the silver mints was coordinated on a large scale across the Empire. It seems to have contributed to the renewal of provincial silver coinage, and for a time arrested the trend in its decline. However, the system was abandoned in the reign of Hadrian, and provincial silver continued to diminish.

It has been argued that, in general, the administrative reforms of Augustus were intended to remedy the deficiencies of Republican administration by responding to particular situations, rather than reflecting any systematic or global vision for the Empire he had won.[59] The previous discussion, however, may be seen to throw some doubt on that view. There do seem to have been policies to meet the 'problem of small change' and to simplify the coinage system. Their success was, however, limited. More action was needed later, to deal with a continuing shortage of small change, and the attempt to adopt a uniform base metal coinage was abandoned. Nero's reform of the silver was, however, a successful empire-wide policy, although the succeeding system of coordinating silver production was to fail after fifty years. Nevertheless, the gradual change to Roman denominations fits well into the pattern of piecemeal interventions.

### 5.2.3 From Greek to Roman Denominations

There are also signs across the whole empire of a move to introduce Roman denominations in the early imperial period. In Thessaly, a change from local units of reckoning to denarii was made in the reign of Augustus,[60] and the Hadrianic tax law from Palmyra records how, earlier, 'Germanicus Caesar also made clear in his letter to Statilius, to the effect that taxes should be reckoned in Italian asses'.[61] In Gaul, the coinage of Lexovio of 'official semisses' (Figure 3.16) implies the adoption of Roman denominations,[62] as do the value marks that appear on the Augustan coins of Lepti, in Africa (Figure 5.22).[63] The local systems which have been detected at Ebusus, Lepcis and Tauromenium do not seem to have survived into the imperial period. The earliest financial records from Britain use exclusively Roman denominations.[64]

However, the change was not enforced fully, at least not in the eastern Empire. Local denominations survived, the best documented example being in the province of Asia during the second century CE, where a system had evolved whereby the cistophorus, denarius, drachm, obol and as had all been formed into a single system. In Syria, the *chalkous* is attested at Sidon and Antioch in the first century, as are the *drachme* and *didrachmon* at Antioch under Nero, while the obol is also found in Syria into the third century. Roman denominations were never used in Egypt. Lycian cities could pay taxes 'in whatever coin they wanted',[65] but the Koinon had to pay them over to Rome in denarii. There would inevitably be a trend for Roman denominations to dominate, and gradually to extinguish local ones. There was no policy as such to impose Roman denominations. It was only when an issue arose which required a Roman decision that the choice would be in favour of Roman denominations. Otherwise the cities would have been free to choose the system that each wanted.

### 5.2.4 Vespasian and Achaea

'All Greeks living in Achaea and what until now has been known as the Peloponnesus, receive your liberty and freedom from taxation.'[66] This grant of 'freedom', which was made by Nero in 66, was celebrated on the coins of four cities (Corinth, Sicyon, Nicopolis and Patras: Figure 5.17). However, Vespasian withdrew that freedom, alleging civic disturbances.[67]

In revoking the freedom of Achaea, Vespasian also seems to have forbidden the cities to make coinage: not one of the communities of Achaea, including Thessaly with its Koinon, issued coins under Vespasian or Titus (see Box 5.9).

## Box 5.9 The number of cities producing coinage in Achaea in the later first century CE

|                    | Nero | Galba | Vespasian | Titus | Domitian |
|--------------------|------|-------|-----------|-------|----------|
| Corinth            | ×    | ×     | –         | –     | ×        |
| Sicyon             | ×    | –     | –         | –     | –        |
| Patras             | ×    | ×     | –         | –     | ×        |
| Syros              | –    | –     | –         | –     | ×        |
| Thespiae           | –    | –     | –         | –     | ×        |
| Thebes             | –    | ×     | –         | –     | –        |
| Locri              | –    | ×     | –         | –     | –        |
| Chalcis            | ×    | –     | –         | –     | –        |
| Carystus           | ×    | –     | –         | –     | –        |
| Nicopolis          | ×    | –     | –         | –     | –        |
| Buthrotum          | ×    | –     | –         | –     | –        |
| Phoenice           | ×    | –     | –         | –     | –        |
| Magnetes           | ×    | –     | –         | –     | ×        |
| Koinon of Thessaly | ×    | –     | –         | –     | ×        |
| Total              | 10   | 4     | –         | –     | 6        |

The unique coin supposedly of Otho from Thebes does not seem genuine. No coins were minted in the short reign of Vitellius.

Figure 5.32 Domitian and the grant of coinage to Achaea.
The restoration of coinage in Achaea was marked by the issue of some rare and unusual coins by the colony of Patras. The head of Indulgentia is accompanied by the inscription *Indulgentiae Avgvsti moneta inpetrata* ('to the gracious favour of the Emperor for the concession of coinage'). The reverse shows the emperor Domitian in a triumphal chariot. (*RPC II*, 219)

The right to make coinage was explicitly restored under Domitian, as is shown by the inscriptions *Perm Imp* on his coins from Corinth and *Indvlgentiae Avg Moneta Iinpetrata* at Patras.[68]

## 5.2.5 'Roman' Bronze Coinage for the East

Nero had established branch mints for 'Roman' coins at Lugdunum and in Thrace, and they continued into the Flavian period. The Lugdunum mint continued to operate intermittently, and the last issues were made in 77/78. The mint in Thrace produced its last coins in 80–82, and the enigmatic mint in Asia which operated in 77/8, may be related, although its products were produced on a slightly different system, consisting of orichalcum coins (to some extent reminiscent of the Claudian coins from Bithynia). The problem of regional supply to the western Empire and Thrace must have been solved by then, since there was no later occurrence, and the mint of Rome was able to distribute its products throughout the western Empire. Exactly how or when this happened is not clear. It was probably one result of Domitian's coinage reforms of 82, part of which was probably the opening of the new mint building in Rome, located under the modern Church of San Clemente.[69] Its larger size would have enabled the scale of production to be increased, and so would have solved the problem of supply to the western provinces.

A different phenomenon is the intermittent supply of coins minted at Rome and then sent to different parts of the eastern Empire. This supply lasted from Vespasian to Hadrian, roughly the same period that saw the coordination of the production of provincial silver, discussed in Chapter 1. The two phenomena may well be related, but the supply of bronze was on a much more limited scale, and did not have any great impact on the low-value currency in circulation in the eastern provinces.

The following bronze issues can be identified, in chronological order:

1. Vespasian, with Titus and Domitian, Antioch, 74 (*RPC II*, 1982–2005; *RIC II.1*, 756–64, 1564–81, with pp. 47–8);
2. Vespasian, with Titus and Domitian, Cyprus, 75/6 (*RPC II.1*, 1818–26);
3. Agrippa II, Judaea, coins of years 25 and 26, 84–86 (*RPC II.1*, 2265–6, 2269–72) (Figure 5.33);
4. Trajan, Syria, 98–99 (*RPC III*, 3653–3660 = Butcher 2004, 408–9, nos. 13–17);

5. Trajan, quadrantes, with head of Heracles and boar, c. 101 (Butcher 2004, 409–10, no. 18);
6. Trajan, Cyrenaica, c. 110 (*RPC III*, 4–10);
7. Trajan, Cyprus, 114–16 (*RPC III*, 3408–11);
8. Trajan, SC bronzes (in Latin), Syria, 116 (*RPC III*, 3662–83 = Butcher 2004, 410–11, nos. 19–22 and p. 411, no. 24). Many of these coins subsequently travelled to northern Gaul and Britain;
9. Hadrian, orichalcum asses, c. 125 (Figure 5.34). Found in Syria, as well as Greece, the Rhine-Danube and Britain (*RIC II.3*, 750–60; Butcher 2004, 411; *RPC III*, pp. 450, 871);
10. Hadrian, Caesarea, c. 125–7 (*RPC III*, 3158–60 = *RIC II.3*, 136–7, nos. 895–9);
11. Hadrian, Cyrenaica, c. 125–7 (*RPC III*, 11–12 = *RIC II.3*, 893–4).

5.33

5.34

**Figures 5.33–5.34** Base metal coins made in Rome, intended for circulation in the east.
The characteristic style and die axis show that several groups of coins were minted at the mint of Rome and then sent to the eastern provinces, where they are sometimes found. Examples include some rare coins with the portrait of the emperor Domitian made on behalf of the 'client king' Agrippa II of Judaea (5.33), and some orichalcum asses made late in the reign of Hadrian (5.34). The Hadrianic coins often have a countermark of a bucranium, which was applied in Syria, but many of them are also found in the west, showing that they were collected up in Syria and then subsequently transported to another part of the Empire. (5.33 *RPC III*, 2269; 5.34 *RPC III*, 3674)

## Box 5.10 The approximate diameters and average weights for orichalcum coins made in Rome 'for the East'

| | | 25 mm | 23–24 mm | 21 mm | 19–20 mm | 18 mm | 12–13 mm |
|---|---|---|---|---|---|---|---|
| 1 | Vespasian, Antioch | 12.64 | – | 6.15 | 4.21 | 2.89 | – |
| 4 | Trajan, wreath | 12.72 | – | 6.26 | 4.89 | 3.15 | 1.76 |
| 6 | Trajan, SC | – | 8.34 | – | 4.38 | – | 1.11 |
| 9 | Hadrian, Antioch | – | 8.54 | – | 4.28 | – | – |
| 10 | Hadrian, Caesarea | – | – | – | 4.82 | 2.88 | – |
| 11 | Hadrian, Cyrenaica | – | – | – | 2.91 | 2.71 | – |
| | Possible value in Roman denominations | 2 asses | 1½ asses | as | ½ as | ¼ as | ⅛ as |

The Cyrenaican coins for Hadrian might be a single denomination (*RPC III*, p. 11).

The issues of this group have a number of features in common. They all use orichalcum (sometimes accompanied by copper). Some follow the Roman weight standards (nos. 2–3 and 5–7), but the rest adhere to the same idiosyncratic weight standard, although it differs from that in use at Rome. There are also a few hybrids with 'normal' Rome coins (coins which combine a 'normal' Roman die with a die for one of these issues). Most of the coins are also found in more than one area: a region for which the types and inscriptions suggest that they were originally intended, but also elsewhere, in different parts of the Empire.

This pattern could be interpreted in two ways. One could assume that, although the coins were made with a particular destination in mind, there was a change of plan and many of them were sent out from Rome elsewhere. The second is that they were all sent to the target area, but that some mechanism subsequently caused them to move elsewhere. That the second, more complicated, explanation is right is suggested by the presence of several of the coins with a Syrian countermark in Britain and France (Figure 5.34). These coins must have been sent from Rome to Syria, countermarked there, and then removed from circulation in Syria and transferred to Britain and Gaul.[70]

Both groups of coins fit into a more general pattern, which can be observed in the late first and second centuries, of the 'batch' supply of

**168** 5 The Revolution of Augustus

coins from the mint of Rome, whereby blocks of bronze coins went to specific areas. Different blocks of coins of Domitian went to Germany and Britain, while a number have been identified for Britain, in the reigns of Nerva, Hadrian and Antoninus Pius.[71] In that sense, the Trajanic coins of Cyprus and Cyrenaica are not exceptional, apart from their special types, and there is no need to appeal to any special explanation, such as the movement of soldiers. Their production and movement can also be detached from the apparently similar production and transport of silver issues, as discussed in Chapter 1. The two phenomena were linked, literally, by the use of some of the same dies, but otherwise they were distinct: the silver was part of a much wider programme of change to the silver currency, whereas the bronze was part of a pattern of targeted supply.

However, the group with the idiosyncratic metrology (the issues listed in Box 5.10) stands slightly apart, because of the way that some specimens of each issue seem to have travelled from their area of circulation after they had arrived there. This is the exception to the rule that the pool of bronze coins remained in an area once they had arrived there. Troop movements have been invoked,[72] but it is not clear why these specific coin issues were singled out for a secondary movement. The effort of collecting them from circulation must have been considerable, though probably facilitated by the unusual golden appearance (as orichalcum was unusual in the east, as described above). A possible explanation might be that the coins were not popular in the east: neither their metal nor their size and shape accorded well in an area where other standards prevailed, particularly, in the case of Syria, where the prevalent coins were the leaded bronze coins with SC. This might, in turn, explain why the relevant Trajanic coins are always very worn when found in the west (because they circulated longer there). However, this remains speculation, but, if correct, it would represent a failure with some similarities to the failure of Augustus' earlier initiative: in neither case did the attempt to introduce new denominations in the east succeed.

## 5.3 'Two Empires': The End of Local Coinage in the West

Previous chapters have described the pattern of coinage in the western provinces during the late Republican period. Silver was minted in Spain down to the early first century BCE, and in Gaul it continued after the Roman conquest until the reign of Augustus. No silver was minted in the provinces of Sicily or Africa after they were conquered, or in the provinces to the north and east of Italy. Bronze coinage was, however, minted on a large scale in Spain and Gaul; there are also a few civic coins in Sicily and Africa, and a very few in Italy after the Second Punic War. Bronze from Rome came to play an increasing part in the base metal currency of all these areas, and in Sicily many such pieces were countermarked, perhaps at Syracuse.[73]

In the middle of the first century CE, the western bronze coinages came to an end, much as their silver predecessors had. The pattern was similar in Spain, Africa, Italy and Sicily, with all the city coinages ending in the period from Tiberius to Claudius, and the same was probably true of Gaul, although it is harder to establish a chronology there. Little or no coinage was produced in Britain after the conquest of 43 CE. The table in Box 5.11 lists the number of cities producing coinage with an imperial portrait.

It can be seen that the decline in the numbers of cities minting was gradual, and, in the case of Spain, the number was far reduced from the total of over 100 communities which had produced coinages on one occasion or another in the late Republic period. In Italy, only Paestum produced a local coinage under Tiberius, as did Panormus for Sicily, although neither can be dated more precisely within his reign. The latest western coins were produced on the island of Ebusus (Ibiza) (Figure 5.35).

The reason(s) for the ending of local coinages in the west has been much discussed, and there is no consensus about whether political, economic or

## Box 5.11 The end of city coinage in the west

The table lists the number of cities making coins for each emperor. It does not include Gaul, as it is too difficult to date the coins of Gaul precisely, but the modern consensus is that bronze coinage ended there during the reign of Augustus.

The numbers of cities making coins for the first emperors

|  | Augustus | Tiberius | Caligula | Claudius |
|---|---|---|---|---|
| **Spain** | 29–30 | 25 | 8 | 1? |
| **Africa** | 15 | 8 | – | – |
| **Italy** | 1? | 1 | – | – |
| **Sicily** | 7 | 1 | – | – |

**Figure 5.35** The last provincial coins in the west.
The last provincial coins were minted for Claudius I (41–54) from the Spanish island of Ebusus (modern Ibiza). Their date is not certain, since they bear only an imperial portrait. Although it has no obverse inscription, the long neck is characteristic of the emperor Claudius I. The significance of the neo-Punic letter *aleph* on the reverse is not clear. Compare Figure 3.12 for earlier coins of Ebusus. (*RPC I*, 482)

cultural reasons should be preferred. However, there is no particular reason to suppose that western cities were any weaker economically than their eastern counterparts, and the amount of wealth required to produce a bronze coinage would not have been very great. Political intervention too seems unlikely, since a decision to stop would have had an immediate effect, whereas, as we have seen, the coins only gradually peter out over a considerable period of time.

The most likely reason seems to be a cultural one: namely, that the cities started to prefer to use coins minted at Rome, rather than to mint their own. Just as the city elites had spontaneously, but gradually, introduced the imperial portrait under Augustus, so now they preferred to use 'Roman' coins (i.e., those made at Rome) to their own local ones. This would explain the way that coinage stops gradually rather than suddenly.

Some support to this view can be given by looking at the coins made shortly before the cessation. As we have seen in Spain, several cities started to make coins of the same metals and size as those from Rome, and similarly their designs became increasingly similar. Two particularly clear examples come from Caesaraugusta, which made coins for Agrippa exactly like those from Rome, and from Ercavica, which copied both sides of Caligula's coins depicting his portrait and the three standing figures of his sisters. In Africa too, several cities copied the Capricorn holding a globe and rudder from denarii of Augustus,[74] as did other western cities elsewhere.[75] The seated figure of Livia in Spain and Africa was also copied from Rome bronzes of Tiberius.[76] In Gaul, some of the latest coins also copy Roman prototypes.[77]

**Figures 5.36–5.37** Agrippa at Caesaraugusta and Rome.
Coins made at Caesaraugusta (CCA) copy exactly the obverse portrait and inscription (M AGRIPPA L F COS III) from coins minted at Rome in the reign of Agrippa's grandson, the emperor Caligula. (5.36 *RPC I*, 386; 5.37 *RIC I*, Gaius 58)

The preference for Roman coins in the west is also evident from what happened after the city coinage ended there. New coinage seems to have been sent from Rome to provide low-value coinage in the place of the earlier city issues, as is shown by the Pobla de Mafumet hoard, but the new supply was not sufficient.[78] The lack of coinage was, as we have seen, supplemented by the products of branch mints in Gaul and Spain, and, in addition, many unofficial imitations were made to fill the void. The large number of imitations shows that there was an unsatisfied demand for 'Roman' coins. The imitations may have been made officially by the cities or army, or privately, by entrepreneurial individuals; either way, the preference for new non-civic coin is clear, and reflects the different cultural outlook and political aspirations of the west (just as was the case further east in Lycia, as described below). In the west, the focus was on Rome; in the east, it was on competition with other cities.[79] Thus, the eastern provincial coinage would continue for another two centuries, and the changes it underwent are discussed in the next two chapters.

**172  5 The Revolution of Augustus**

## 5.3.1  Lycia and the Western Empire

The dichotomy drawn here between west and east was not without exceptions. One of the most surprising concerns Lycia, in south-western Asia Minor. Lycia also made the same choice not to use locally produced coins, as cities did in the western Empire, and at about the same time.

Before its annexation by Claudius in 43 CE, coinage in silver and bronze had been produced by a number of cities in the Lycian League, and the metrology of the silver has been plausibly connected with that of Roman denarii, quinarii and sestertii.[80] Brutus had made aurei and silver denarii there in the late 40s BCE, some marked L for Lycia,[81] and no doubt made from the gold and silver which he had ordered to be handed over to him (Appian IV.81). Under Augustus, the Lycians made silver 'drachms', with the same weight as contemporary denarii,[82] and at the same time large 'bronzes' were made, looking very much like the CA sestertii and weighing the same.[83] Some rare coins, both silver and bronze, were also produced in the name of Claudius, although it is not clear whether or not they precede the annexation. Their weight standards were reduced, perhaps suggesting the establishment of a closed currency area,[84] possibly linked to the cistophoric system of neighbouring Asia.[85]

Thereafter no coinage was produced for Lycia except for a series of silver 'drachms', minted under Domitian, Nerva and Trajan, and a bronze issue made much later by twenty cities in the reign of Gordian III (238–44). Apart from them, Lycia also used coins from the mint of Rome: there are many finds from the third century, and excavations have also revealed earlier specimens of bronze coins from Rome, from the first and second centuries, even quadrantes.[86]

Both the silver and the bronze coins made for Lycia are of interest. The drachms have a Roman style and were probably made in the mint of Rome. They also share the same fineness as denarii, which explains why they circulated as denarii far afield from Lycia, even in Britain.[87] They were probably regarded in Lycia as denarii, since Lycia seems to have adopted the western monetary system.[88]

The reasons behind the minting of bronze coinage by the twenty cities for only a brief period in the reign of Gordian III now escape us,[89] but its brief and contemporary nature at so many separate cities indicates central direction (presumably from the Koinon). The main denomination was minted at about 30 mm and about 20 g, almost exactly the same as the weight of a sestertius of Gordian from Rome,[90] while the smaller denomination shows the emperor with a radiate crown, as on Roman dupondii. This is surely no accident, and indicates the degree to which the currency system of Lycia was the same as that of the western Empire. Perhaps the minting in Lycia under Gordian was to remedy a perceived local shortage of currency from Rome?

The Neronian customs law for Lycia provides a potential model for understanding the unusual nature of Lycian currency.[91] This law uses only δηνάρια (denarii) and left the collection of Roman taxes entirely in the hands of the Koinon of Lycia, which was required to pay a sum of 100,000 denarii per annum to Rome. The Koinon delegated the collection of import duty entirely to its member cities, which paid the Koinon an annual sum in return; in the Hadrianic period, Myra paid 7,000 denarii and Kaunos probably also 7,000. In all these transactions, payments are expressed in denarii. We can imagine that the greater subsidiary freedom granted to the Koinon and cities might also have applied to other aspects of their currency, including which bronze coins were to be used. It would have been a decision of the Koinon, not the Roman authorities.

Just as in Spain, the last locally-made coins (of Augustus and Claudius) were copied from Roman coins: the silver coins adopted the portrait of Augustus and looked like denarii, while large bronze coins were also made, whose size and designs were copied from the CA coinage of Augustus. In both cases, there is a similar pattern of increasing Romanisation, followed by a decision to abandon their own locally made coins. This Lycian example is significant, since it suggests that the switch could be the result of conscious choice, rather than the product of economic change.

# 6

## Reinforcing Greek Identity in the Golden Age of the Second Century CE

Trajan was the last great conqueror of the Roman Empire. Hadrian brought territorial expansion to an end and proclaimed a Golden Age. The second century can also be seen as the high point of the 'Second Sophistic', a cultural movement which claimed a link with the culture of the distant classical age, and saw many intellectuals ('sophists') flourish with public displays of erudition, intended to recall the great days of ancient Greece.

This new climate of peace and antiquarianism affected the character of many provincial coinages, whose designs often came to represent esoteric moments in a city's past, whether historical or mythological.[1] The coins can provide vivid testimony of this change in taste and self-consciousness, and the way that, like a sophist's speech, they were making the most of their own individual claims as a means of seeking prominence over their neighbours. At the same time they can illustrate other changes in Roman society and its economy: how some areas 'switched' culturally from east to west and vice versa; how the use of Latin was becoming eroded; or how changes to the pattern of denominations can be seen as reflections of the economic changes that were taking place and which were to become more pronounced in the third century. Several such general trends across wide areas will be described in this chapter, but it remains true that the coinage was essentially in the hands of the city elites, as described in Chapter 4. They were free to determine the content of their coins, but they did not do so in isolation, as the extreme example of the coins made for Hadrian's partner Antinous shows. In all these ways, the provincial coinage helps us understand the fabric of life in the provincial cities, and how it was shaped by changing factors, above all the focus of the cities on their own claims to prominence.

**Figure 6.1** Aureus of Hadrian proclaiming a Golden Age. On the reverse, Eternity holds a phoenix, a symbol of rebirth, since, in mythology, it could regenerate from the ashes of its predecessor. Enlarged × 1.5. (*RIC II.3*, Hadrian 297)

## 6.1 Changing Consciousness and the Pattern of Coinage

The second century saw many changes to the provincial coinage. Provincial silver production continued under Trajan and Hadrian, but thereafter was greatly reduced, being confined largely to mints in Syria and Egypt. Even there, production was irregular, as discussed in Chapter 1: Alexandria produced little silver for almost thirty years between 193 and 219, while Antioch made little silver in the second century and none between 219 and 238. The system of coordinated silver production was abandoned after the reign of Trajan. There is no sign during the second century of any of Roman intervention of the sort that had happened to the provincial silver from the time of Nero.

The bronze coinage too developed without any interruptions in the eastern provinces. No emperor repeated the reforms on the scale that Augustus had tried, as was described in Chapter 5. Changes did take place, but were either caused by local initiatives or arose from more general trends.

One such change reflected the shifting concerns of the elites who were responsible for the coinage. The provincial bronze coins stopped using formulae which asked for permission,[2] and their inscriptions stopped mentioning Roman governors: Smyrna had regularly referred to the governors of Asia on its coins in the late first century, but did so only on a single occasion in the second.[3] It may also be the case that there were more 'pseudo-autonomous' coins after the first century, although it is difficult to be sure since they are hard to date with any great accuracy (see Box 4.1). The number of Asian cities celebrating their own Demos and Boule (Figures 4.8–4.9) certainly increased enormously in the second century, while there was a relative decline in the proportion of cities commemorating the Roman Senate.[4] The cities would now express their identities with less reference to the emperor and Rome, and with none at all to the provincial authorities. In a way that may seem surprising to us, the coins show that Rome was coming to play a much lesser role in the minds of the city elites than their own internal affairs and legendary history. The commemoration of these concerns flowered with multiple representations of imaginary scenes from each city's past. The external focus was now on other cities, with whom they might have a competitive rivalry or official friendship. Friendships could be by expressed the 'Homonoia coinages' which proliferated during the period (Figure 6.24). Competition with other cities became so important that, by the third century, it could even be a matter of pride for cities to declare themselves to be the 'sixth' or 'seventh city of Asia' (Figures 4.6–4.7).

An increasing self-consciousness of city elites may also explain why bronze coinage was now produced by more cities than had done so in the first century. It was clearly becoming more fashionable for even small cities to make coins. The increase had started in the Flavian period, and reached a peak in the Severan period.[5]

---

### Box 6.1 The increase in production of provincial coins

The 'index' (bottom row) has been calculated by dividing the number of cities which made coins in each period by the number of years in that period, and rounding the result. The data for *RPC V* are not yet complete. *RPC X* is deemed here to cover only ten years as most cities had stopped minting by early in the sole reign of Gallienus (see Chapter 7 for more details).[6]

## Box 6.1 (cont.)

Average annualised number of coin-issuing authorities in the eastern Empire

| RPC | I | II | III | IV | V | VI | VII | VIII | IX | X |
|---|---|---|---|---|---|---|---|---|---|---|
| Period | 44 BCE–69 CE | 69–96 | 96–138 | 138–192 | 193–218 | 218–238 | 238–244 | 244–249 | 249–253 | 253–end |
| Cyrenaica | 13 | 3 | 3 | 2 | – | – | – | – | – | – |
| Achaea | 25 | 6 | 23 | 27 | c.44 | 2 | 2 | 1 | 1 | 4 |
| Macedonia | 9 | 7 | 11 | 10 | 8 | 9 | 9 | 7 | 2 | 6 |
| Thrace | 7 | 5 | 10 | 20 | 10 | 7 | 8 | 5 | 3 | 6 |
| Moesia | 3 | 2 | 2 | 7 | 3 | 7 | 8 | 5 | 2 | 2 |
| Bithynia-Pontus | 11 | 14 | 18 | 23 | 15 | 14 | 12 | 13 | 8 | 15 |
| Asia | 106 | 93 | 140 | 146 | 169++ | 111 | 74 | 63 | 41 | 91 |
| Lycia-Pamphylia | 19 | 7 | 10 | 12 | 32 | 32 | 49 | 34 | 27 | 22 |
| Galatia-Cappadocia | 17 | 15 | 29 | 39 | 10 | 10 | 8 | 5 | 5 | 7 |
| Cilicia | 18 | 17 | 30 | 37 | 16 | 29 | 15 | 20 | 16 | 26 |
| Cyprus | 2 | 1 | 1 | 1 | 1 | – | – | – | – | – |
| Syria and Judaea | 32 | 18 | 25 | 47 | 37 | 48 | 9 | 15 | 9 | 7 |
| Arabia etc. | – | – | 5 | 3 | 10 | 16 | 5 | 2 | 3 | 1 |
| Egypt | 1 | 1 | 1 | 1 | 1 | 1 | 1 | 1 | 1 | 1 |
| Totals | 263 | 188 | 308 | 375 | c.356++ | 286 | 206 | 181 | 118 | 188 |
| Number of years | 100 | 27 | 42 | 52 | 25++ | 20 | 6 | 5 | 4 | 10 (say) |
| Index by year | 3 | 7 | 7 | 7 | 14++ | 14 | 34 | 36 | 30 | 19 |

Adapted from Heuchert 2005: 32.

## 6.2 A New Mode of Production

The increase in production saw the emergence of a new mode of production, whose nature is much debated today. Its most obvious feature is the way that, in the later second and third centuries, some of the city coinages of Asia Minor, and a smaller number in other regions, were struck with an obverse die which was shared with coins of other cities.

Die-linking between cities is known from earlier in the century, under Trajan, when one pair of neighbouring cities exchanged dies (Colophon and Metropolis), and one or two further pairs did the same under Hadrian (Ilium and Dardanus; Nicaea and Midaeum) some thirty years later.[7] However, these examples were a false dawn, and it was only subsequently that die sharing became more common, especially from the reign of Commodus, and particularly in the third century.[8]

**Figures 6.2–6.3** The first die link between cities.
The first intercity obverse die link recorded by Kraft 1972 occurs for Trajan between coins of Colophon and Metropolis, in about 100 CE. The two cities were very close, only about 15 km apart, suggesting the agency of word of mouth. The coin of Metropolis has been countermarked with the title ΔAKIK = Dacicus, the title taken by Trajan after his victories in Dacia (Romania). (6.2 *RPC III*, 2005; 6.3 *RPC III*, 2010)

In some cases, the die-links may well imply a single mint. For example, dies were shared between a widely dispersed group of cities in Syria in the reign of Philip. The similar shape of their flans, combined with numerous die-links, point towards the likelihood that all the coins were produced in a single mint (Antioch), on behalf of all of the cities.[9]

In Asia, many die-links and many stylistic similarities between the coins of different cities were documented by Kraft in an influential book of 1972.[10] He explained them as possibly representing the products of different 'workshops' – about twelve for the whole of Asia Minor – whose personnel moved from one city to another, taking their dies with them. Since then, even more die-links have been noted,[11] and Kraft's ideas about workshops have been much discussed.[12]

The number of shared dies is now known to have been more than 500, and, although this may seem a lot, it needs to be set in context: for example, the imperial coinage of one city alone (Aphrodisias) was produced from over 300 dies, but only six were shared elsewhere.[13] The total number of dies used on the Asian provincial coinage must have been enormous, so the shared ones can represent only a small fraction of the total. The pattern of die-linking, however, is geographically discontinuous, and it has been suggested that it may only reflect changing fashions.[14] We could make a comparison with modern contrast between 'contracting out' or 'in-house production': overtly to save money, the choice between them often lies in the field of ideology.

It has been argued recently that the sharing of dies and the stylistic similarities between different cities should be seen as separate phenomena, and that the coins were not produced in 'workshops' but in their individual cities, drawing dies from a limited set of engravers. The starting point for this new interpretation is the observation that, while the coins of a group of cities may sometimes exhibit a common style, the dies that are shared between them may have a different style.[15] This suggests that the die-links are, in fact, exceptional. A group of cities might draw its dies from one or more engravers who were working regionally, as they had done in some cases since the first century (Map 5.3, with Figures 5.15–5.16) and occasionally use the same die, engraved by a different engraver, as a means of supplementing their output. That the actual coins – as opposed to the dies – were made in the cities whose names they bear, can also be deduced from their physical properties. A good case is provided by the coins of Perge, which have a fixed 12 o'clock die axis, whereas the coins of other cities which share the same style have a different axis.[16] This is convincing evidence that the coins of Perge were made in Perge and that the stylistically similar coins of other cities were made elsewhere.

**Figures 6.4–6.6** Coins of Julia Domna, the wife of Septimius Severus, struck with the same obverse die.
This die, which belongs to the 'Smyrna workshop' (Kraft 1972, 22–3) struck these three coins from different cities – Smyrna, Clazomenae and Ephesus. The same die was also used for coins of Cyme and Phocaea. Apart from Ephesus, these cities were situated quite close to each other. It seems more likely that the die travelled from city to city, but it is possible that the coins were all struck at a central 'workshop'.

A focus on die-sharing has distracted interest away from the more significant phenomenon of stylistic similarities, which offers the potential for understanding the cultural links between different areas. The geography of Asia Minor, for instance, is usually conceived in terms of the ethnic divisions reported by Strabo and Pliny, in terms of the regions of Ionia,

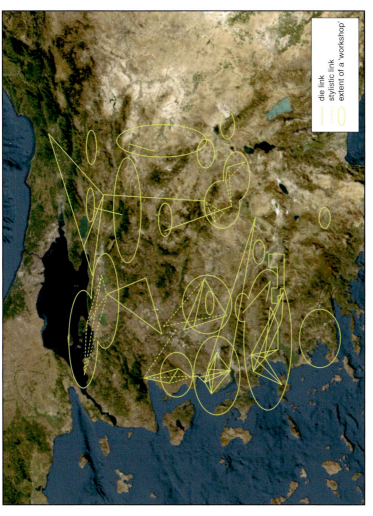

**Map 6.1** Die- and style-links between cities, in the reign of Gordian III (238–44) Adapted from Spoerri 2006b.

**182** 6 Reinforcing Greek Identity in the Second Century

Lydia, Phrygia and so on. But these divisions do not help us to understand the coinage very much, although they do reflect a certain degree of geographical proximity. A recent study of the coinage of Lydia has highlighted the disparate nature of the region and the artificiality of its boundaries.[17] In the valley of the Maeander river, the cities on the right bank were part of Lydia and those on the left part of Caria. The Romans themselves paid no attention to these ethnic divisions, and divided the province of Asia into a number of *conventus*, administrative districts that originally were devised for judicial reasons and whose borders cut across the ethnic divisions. It has been suggested in the past that the *conventus* is the best way of understanding the pattern of coinage, but this view has not proved tenable.

The unity of the cities on both banks of the Maeander valley is a case in point. They shared a similar iconography,[18] and are linked by stylistic similarities (as well as the pattern of die links).[19] A little further to the north, the distribution of finds both within and outside the central part of Lydia, surrounding Sardis and embracing the valleys of the Hermus and Cayster rivers, tends to confirm that this inner part of Lydia had a unity,[20] and they may perhaps also reflect the most common movements of people from one city to another. A similar, predominantly localised unity, can be observed in the analysis of the style of the workshops which produced the dies and application of countermarks to groups of locally produced coins.[21] Later, in the third century, a common style of coin engraving in Pisidia has been found to coincide with a pattern of denominations and, moreover, other aspects of social and cultural outlook, such as names or burial customs.[22]

## 6.3 The End of Small Denominations

During the course of the first three centuries CE, there was a gradual increase in the average size of the coins, and the change is related to the question of the extent of inflation in the Roman world. The size and value of the most commonly used coins gradually increased, while the production of the smallest denominations gradually ceased. Both might be reflections of rising prices, but there are different geographical patterns.

In the western Empire, the most common coin in use changed from the as in the first century to the sestertius in the second century, and at the same time the production of the smallest denominations, the brass semis and the copper quadrans, gradually ceased. The mint of Rome continued to issue them until the middle of the second century, but after the reign of Antoninus Pius (138–61), production stopped and his successors produced no more of these small coins.[23] The circulation of these coins was also uneven in the western Empire. Semisses and quadrantes were little used in northern Gaul and Britain, as site finds show.[24]

We can compare this pattern with the other end of the Empire. First of all, Egypt. There too there was change from smaller denominations to the drachm (equivalent to a sestertius) by the second century, and the smallest denominations also start to disappear. The production of the smallest denominations ended by about 160, much as at Rome, and the production of larger bronze denominations effectively came to an end with the reign of Commodus. The emphasis was then on producing the tetradrachm, equivalent to the denarius. In this respect, the two ends of the Empire were quite similar, although sestertii were made at Rome in large numbers in the second quarter of the third century, a feature not matched in Egypt.

What of the rest of the eastern Empire? Generalisations are much harder to make, and the emergence of more local systems in the third century will be discussed in Chapter 7. The identification of the denominations in use is difficult, as discussed in Chapter 4, but it is clear that more were being made than at Rome. The coinage of Chios named nine denominations, as described in Chapter 4, and although two were equivalent (obol = 2 assaria), it shows that many could be in use at one time or another.

Much the same can be seen from looking at the pattern of a single city such as Smyrna.

Here too, nine different denominations have been identified, although they were never all struck at the same time. The two most common coins minted in Asia during the Julio-Claudian period were (a) about 19 mm in diameter and approximately 5–6 g in weight and (b) about 15–16 mm and approximately 3–3½ g.[25] They are the most common at Smyrna, as Box 6.2

**Figure 6.7** The last small denomination coins from Egypt.
A few examples of the smallest 12 mm denomination were still made in the mid second century at Alexandria in Egypt. Some of the latest were made at the end of the reign of Antoninus Pius, in 160/1 (L KΔ= year 24), as here. (*RPC IV*, temporary number 16083)

**184**  6 Reinforcing Greek Identity in the Second Century

### Box 6.2  Possible denominations at Smyrna

The table (p. 185) shows weights (in g) and hypothetical denominations at Smyrna (data from Klose 1987: 103–9). The values on the left follow Klose's system. He points out that there was a reorganisation in the mid second century.

### Box 6.3  The changing pattern of denominations at Smyrna

The number of specimens recorded for each denomination at Smyrna (data from Klose 1987, 107–9) (p. 186). The median value is in bold. *RPC* periods I–II are the first century; III and IV the second century; and V onwards the third century.

shows, and they have been tentatively identified there as coins equivalent to 1 as and a ½ as. The table shows how new, larger denominations were introduced in the Flavian and Antonine periods, as the coinage came to resemble that minted at Rome (see Chapter 5), and how, over a period of time, the smaller denominations fell out of production, as was also the case at Rome and Alexandria.

Unlike at Rome or Alexandria, however, the 1 and ½ coins remained the most common throughout the second century, as can be seen from Box 6.3. Although some larger denominations were introduced in the second century, there was no change in the most common denomination (the 1). It was only from the Severan period that the larger denominations came to predominate at Smyrna. Even then, smaller coins continued in production long after they had ceased to be made at Rome or Alexandria.

Although the current state of research does not yet allow us to trace developments throughout Asia in any detail, there was a fairly consistent pattern during the second century across the whole of Asia Minor.[26] Very small coins went on being made in appreciable quantities until the third century (Figure 6.8).

There is no obvious reason why smaller denominations should have continued in production and use in Asia but not elsewhere in the Empire, whether in the west or the east. However, it is clear that smaller denominations did not disappear everywhere. It is a counter

**Box 6.2 (cont.)**

Weights and hypothetical denominations at Smyrna

| *RPC* | | I | II | III | IV | V | VI | VII | VIII | IX | Xa | Xb |
|---|---|---|---|---|---|---|---|---|---|---|---|---|
| period | Hellen-istic | 44 BCE–69 CE | 69–96 | 96–138 | 138–192 | 193–218 | 218–238 | 238–244 | 244–249 | 249–253 | 253–60 | 260–8 |
| 6 | – | – | – | 28.00 | 23.72 | 22.42 | 22.65 | 20.97 | 23.73 | – | 16.72 | 8.28 |
| 5 | – | – | – | 19.63 | – | – | – | – | – | – | – | – |
| 4 | – | – | 14.87 | 13.50 | 14.10 | 14.33 | 13.31 | 12.96 | – | – | 11.14 | 6.19 |
| 3 | – | – | – | 10.84 | 9.27 | 8.81 | 8.02 | 6.60 | as VII | – | 5.70 | 4.05 |
| 2 | 12.9 | 8.93 | 7.17 | – | 6.63 | 6.32 | 5.79 | 4.80 | 4.68 | – | 3.63 | – |
| 1½ | – | 5.81 | 6.30 | – | – | – | – | – | – | – | – | – |
| 1 | 6.2 | 5.04 | 4.29 | 5.53 | 5.08 | 3.99 | 3.83 | 3.32 | as VII | | 2.75 | |
| ½ | 3.2 | 3.73 | 3.18 | 3.14 | 3.12 | 2.38 | 1.81 | – | – | – | – | – |
| ¼ | 1.5 | 2.54 | 2.19 | 2.34 | – | – | – | – | – | – | – | – |

## Box 6.3 (cont.)
The number of specimens recorded for each denomination at Smyrna

| RPC | I | II | III | IV | V | VI | VII | VIII | IX | Xa | Xb |
|---|---|---|---|---|---|---|---|---|---|---|---|
| **Period** | **44 BCE–69 CE** | **69–96** | **96–138** | **138–192** | **193–218** | **218–238** | **238–244** | **244–249** | **249–253** | **253–60** | **260–8** |
| **6** | – | – | 18 | 112 | 141 | 32 | 37 | 3 | – | 9 | 99 |
| **5** | – | – | 15 | – | – | – | – | – | – | – | – |
| **4** | – | 29 | 6 | 96 | 170 | 45 | 66 | – | – | 11 | **118** |
| **3** | – | 45 | 66 | 156 | **240** | 29 | **150***| **150*** | – | 24 | 27 |
| **2** | 17 | 99 | – | 42 | 122 | **59** | 110 | 25 | – | **43** | – |
| **1½** | 169 | 70 | – | – | – | – | – | – | – | – | – |
| **1** | **313** | **231** | **52** | **460** | 14 | 68 | 60* | 60* | – | 20 | – |
| **½** | 231 | 103 | 34 | 192 | 46 | 24 | – | – | – | – | – |
| **¼** | 74 | 23 | 31 | – | – | – | – | – | – | – | – |

**Figure 6.8** The last small denominations in Asia Minor.
Small coins (18 mm/3 g) were made at Cyme, in north-west Asia Minor signed by Hermeias, who also signed coins for Valerian and Gallienus. They show the turreted bust of the city personification and Isis holding a sistrum. Similar-sized coins can be found at the same date for other cities, for example Thyatira, Poroselene and Amisus. Even smaller coins of Cyme (14 mm/2 g) probably date to the same period (BMC 124–5, Munich SNG 527–9; others in Berlin), but they also lack the imperial portrait, so the dating is less secure.

example to a picture of hypothetically rising prices eroding the usefulness of smaller coins. If such inflation did take place, it was at a very low level, as will be discussed in the next Chapter, and there was a perceived need for very small denominations in some parts of the Empire right until the middle of the third century. The different pattern is an indication that the monetary economy of the Empire was becoming fragmented. This will be the theme of Chapter 7.

## 6.4 East and West and Latin and Greek

Most provincial coins of the second century have Greek inscriptions, since they were made in the Greek-speaking eastern part of the Empire. Very occasionally, Phoenician appeared, even though it was more or less a dead language by the imperial period. Other languages and scripts were not used. Perhaps the most notable absence is Aramaic, the Semitic language widely spoken and written in the near east.[27] It was not, however, an official language of civic business, and so did not appear on coins. Other languages and scripts, like Palmyrene, Syriac or Hebrew, make no appearance either, for the same reason.[28] In Asia Minor, most of the indigenous languages had anyway died out by the time of the Roman conquest, although Strabo tells us that Lydian was still used in Cibyra, but Carian had not been seen on coins since the fourth century BCE. Latin and Greek were the languages of administration, and only they were used, for example, when the *Res Gestae* of Augustus were set up all over the eastern part of the Roman world.

**188** 6 Reinforcing Greek Identity in the Second Century

The most common language on provincial coins was Greek, and late forms of Greek spelling started to appear on the coinage, becoming more common in the third century. Examples are ΚΣ for Καί (whether as the conjunctive 'and' or part of the title Καίσαρ),[29] ΠΑΣΤΡΣ for πέτραι ('rocks', at Tyre). ΣΙ also occurs for I, as in ΣΙΣΡΟC (ἱερός = 'sacred'),[30] or in the alternate ending for city names (-ΕΙΤΩΝ and – ΙΤΩΝ and even once, ΣΙΟΥΛΙΑ for Julia.[31] The loss of vowel length allowed Ο to replace Ω.[32] On some occasions, the engravers just gave up with the legends and made a series of illiterate marks (for example, Severus at Rhesaena).

Latin occurs on the coins of cities of privileged status, the municipia and colonies. Colonies were of two types, settlements of veterans from the army, and cities which had been rewarded by promotion to a higher status. In the second case, there was no influx of a new population speaking Latin, the language of the army; and, even in the first case, the colonies were often islands in Greek-speaking zones. But not always. Philippi in Macedonia had a strong Latin culture, and most of the inscriptions surviving there are in Latin.[33] The Latin on its coins is correspondingly unexceptionable. Elsewhere, Latin tended to be eroded, and often confused with Greek, as 'the Greek language steadily reasserted itself'.[34] This becomes quite common in the third century,[35] but there are incipient signs in the second century. Coela, on the Hellespont, has IMP CAESAR TRAIAN HADRIANOS (ending –OS rather than –VS) and IMP ADRIAN (missing the initial H) for Hadrian; IMP CAIS ANTONIN[] and IMP CAI MAR AV A (CAIS instead of CAES) for Marcus Aurelius, and AVREL COMMODOS CAES AVG F GERM F for Commodus (again, –OS for VS), during whose reign the engravers also struggled with the city's Latin name: AI(L) MVNI COILA and AEL MONVCI CVILA (its correct Latin name would have been Municipium Aelium Coela). Another municipium, Stobi in Macedonia, where Greek had become dominant by the second century,[36] has IM M AV ANTONINOS for Marcus Aurelius (-OS for –VS). –OS for – VS, the absence of the aspirate H and CAIS(ar) for CAES(ar) all show the influence of Greek spellings (-ΟΣ, Ἀ and ΚΑΙΣ).

The erosion of Latin continued in the third century. The problems can be seen from the coins of colonies, whose supposedly Latin inscriptions might now often include Greek letters or words. One of the most common forms influenced by Greek was the occurrence of GETAS for Geta. Greek letters started to appear in Latin legends, such as IOVLIA MAECA and AY

C M ΑΝΤΩΝΙΟC GORDIANOS (both at Cassandrea). At Antioch in Pisidia, Greek forms had started to appear in the second century (CAISAR); some Severan coins show that the engraver did not understand imperial titulature, names or spelling.[37] Later in the period the quality of engraving at Antioch improved, but mistakes persisted, such as IVLIA AVGASTA or TRANQVILLIANAE, as did Greek spellings (GETAS for Geta or SEOV for Severus Alexander, who is even given the false nominative AΛEXANDRVS; and, later, FILIPPVS for Philip). The legends were, however, reasonably coherent, until the reign of Trebonianus Gallus and Volusian (251–3) when virtually incomprehensible legends appeared, such as IMP C VIR AP CALVSSIANO AVG or IMP C VIMP CALVSSIAVD AV for Volusian.

Not all colonies used Latin. Greek was also used by some of the ones that were founded in the later imperial period in the near east, where Latin was not much in use.[38] Some cities there were rewarded with colonial status by Septimius Severus as a reward for their loyalty in the civil war, and colonial status remained desirable even after the citizenship was universally granted by Caracalla. All the colonies in Phoenicia and Palestine used Latin legends,[39] while Greek was used by the inland colonies in Osrhoene and Mesopotamia, as well as Arabia (Philippopolis), together with Antioch. Laodicea and Heliopolis, on the border between these two areas, used both.[40] The regional differentiation suggests that the choice was a matter of fashion, rather than of any political significance, and the use of Greek shows that many colonies no longer had a strong sense of being 'small

**Figure 6.9** Commodus from Coela in Thrace.
Despite its fine style, the coin mixes Greek and Latin forms (COMMODOS) and makes mistakes: CEΛMΓ at the end of the obverse, presumably a nonsense misunderstanding of GERMA. The reverse has a figure of the city's Genius, but misspells its name (COECANI instead of COELANI, in GENIVS AEL MVNICIPI COELANI). (*RPC IV*, temporary number 10949)

## 190  6 Reinforcing Greek Identity in the Second Century

Romes'. Only Berytus, and to some extent, its offshoot Heliopolis, 'represented a substantial island of Romanisation, of Latin language and culture'.[41] The others were Greek cities with Greek-speaking communities and which had acquired new privileges. This presumably explains the switch at the beginning of the second century from Latin to Greek for the SC bronzes, minted at Antioch.[42] The puzzle is why Antioch bronzes had used Latin in the first century, when the silver tetradrachms minted there and some of the civic and 'archieratic' bronze coins were all in Greek. Perhaps it was the prominence of the Latin SC on the reverse which had prompted the initial choice of Latin for the obverses.

---

### Box 6.4  Latin and Greek at Roman colonies

The language used on coins of the colonies of the Roman near East

| Colony | Foundation | Language |
|---|---|---|
| Berytus | Augustus | Latin |
| Ptolemais | Claudius | Latin |
| Caesarea | Vespasian | Latin |
| Aelia Capitolina | Hadrian | Latin |
| Carrhae | Aurelius | Greek |
| Heliopolis | Severus | mixed |
| Rhesaena | Severus | Greek |
| Laodicea | Severus | mixed |
| Tyre | Severus | Latin[*] |
| Sebaste[†] | Severus | Latin |
| Singara | Severus | Greek |
| Nisibis | Severus | Greek |
| Palmyra | SS/Caracalla? | ? |
| Edessa | Caracalla | mixed |
| Emesa | Caracalla | Greek[‡] |
| Antioch | Elagabalus[43] | Greek |
| Sidon | Elagabalus | Latin[**] |
| Caesarea ad Libanum | Elagabalus | Latin |
| Petra | Elagabalus[44] | Latin |
| Bostra | Sev Alexander | Latin |
| Damascus | Philip | Latin |
| Philippopolis | Philip | Greek |

**Box 6.4 (cont.)**

| Colony | Foundation | Language |
|---|---|---|
| **Neapolis1** | Philip | Latin |
| **Neapolis 2** | Gallus | Latin |
| **Gaza** | ?[††] | no coins |

\* Phoenician is also occasionally present.
† There is no obvious explanation for the bilingual coins of Sebaste during the late first and second centuries, with Latin obverses and Greek reverses.
‡ There are some Latin obverses for Elagabalus.
\*\* The Greek Ἀργοναύτ(αι) appears on some rare coins showing the Argo, much as the Phoenician for Pygmalion was used on the otherwise Latin coins of Tyre.
†† There are Greek coins for Gordian III, but nothing thereafter.

## 6.5 A Liminal Zone: From Moesia to Cyrenaica

The west and the east used different languages, and, as seen in Chapter 5, the western and eastern parts of the Empire had very different patterns of coin production and use from the middle of the first century. The distinction between currencies more or less follows the language division between west and east, and both are aspects of the different outlooks of elites in the different parts of the Empire. In the west, bronze coinage was all supplied from Rome; in the east, it was all supplied from the individual cities, apart from one or two regional coinages (Antioch silver, Alexandria silver and bronze).

This polarisation can, however, be exaggerated, and it disguises a much greater plurality of patterns within each half. In the west, the small semisses and quadrantes are rare in northern Gaul or Britain, though used elsewhere in the western Empire. In Gaul and Britain, too, the supply of sestertii also stopped in the early third century, leaving the silver coins as the principal denomination supplied.[45]

As we saw in Chapter 5, the remarkable case of Lycia (in south-west Asia Minor) in the middle of the first century shows that an area in the east could choose to follow the western model of coinage, even though there is no suggestion that the population dropped Greek in favour of Latin: inscriptions from this region continued to be predominantly in Greek.

## 192  6 Reinforcing Greek Identity in the Second Century

There are also a few other signs of 'switching' coin use from the western to the eastern model, and vice versa.[46] Some other Greek-speaking areas, Cyprus and Cyrenaica-and-Crete, made a similar shift from local to Roman coins a century later. In both provinces, local coinage had continued to be made into the second century, but the presence of Roman coins, especially sestertii, became more pronounced in the late second and third centuries. Cyprus turned to Roman coins in the second century, and, apart from some local coins made in *c.* 210, the bronze currency of the island was dominated by Roman bronze, as can be seen from the excavations at Paphos or Curium.[47] Local coinage was produced for Cyrenaica during the reigns of Augustus and Tiberius, and then again for Trajan and Hadrian. These coins were followed by the last issues (in fact, made in Rome: Figure 6.10), for Marcus Aurelius. Subsequently, the circulating medium was made up of coins from the mint of Rome, although there is not a great deal of evidence.[48]

Cyrenaica was part of the same province as Crete, although the coins of one part do not seem to have circulated in the other.[49] We are not, however,

**Figure 6.10** Marcus Aurelius from Cyrenaica.
The last coins with typically Cyrenaican reverse designs (the god Jupiter Ammon) were made under Marcus Aurelius. Their fine style and die axis show that they were, in fact, made in Rome, and then sent to Cyrenaica. (*RPC IV*, temporary number 6852)

**Figure 6.11** Trajan, from Cydonia, Crete.
The rather crude engraving shows Trajan (*Traianos Kaisar*) and the infant Cydon, the legendary son of Apollo and founder of the city, suckled by a dog. (*RPC III*, 110)

well informed about coin circulation in Roman Crete. Civic minting continued into the second century, and the last city coinage was made by Cydonia under Trajan. Plentiful issues were also made by the Cretan Koinon for Trajan, Hadrian and Antoninus Pius. A survey of single finds produced a clear pattern thereafter of a switch from local to Roman coins in the mid second century.[50]

To the north of the Mediterranean, most parts of the southern Balkan peninsula – Achaea, Macedonia and Thrace – were firmly in the 'eastern half' of the Empire.[51] The number of cities which produced coinage increased from the first and second centuries (as in Asia), the greatest increase being in the inland cities of Thrace, where the production of city coins had been limited in the early Empire.[52] The cities in these areas continued to make coins down to the reign of Valerian and Gallienus, though in decreasing amounts: only a few cities produced coinage after the Severan period (see Chapter 7).

However, the bronze coinage in circulation was a mixture of local and Roman coinages. At Athens, the coin finds show that during the second century Roman coins came to play a more important role.[53] Sestertii were also dominant in the Peloponnese, where finds of Roman sestertii, dupondii and asses may account for 30–50 per cent of coins recovered in excavations, and there are several hoards of the third century which only consist of sestertii. The hoards all seem to date to the third century, so it may be that the change from local to Roman coinage took place then.[54] The circulation of city coinages, in contrast, such as those of Corinth or Sparta, was largely restricted to the city which produced them.[55] The same was true of central Greece and Thessaly, and only in the province of Macedonia did locally produced coins predominate.[56]

Further west and north, there was little city coinage. A small amount had been produced during the first century by cities in Moesia Inferior, and mainly at Tomi. Its coinage was on a small scale, and consisted largely of small denominations, often hard to date, as is also the case at Odessus, Callatis and Istrus. However, the province of Moesia received huge amounts of bronze coins of Augustus from the mint of Rome, together with many Augustan CA pieces, and later Roman coins of Claudius.[57] More local coinage was made in the second century, when the number of mints producing coinage increased. From the reign of Septimius Severus, the coinage produced by the Moesian and Thracian cities was made on a massive scale.

Figure 6.12 Trajan from Tomi. The rare coins depict a trophy, perhaps an allusion to Trajan's victories in nearby Dacia, and a reference to the monument at Adamklissi. (*RPC III*, 779)

The dominance of bronze from Rome, for Augustus and Claudius, and from the CA mint (for Augustus) is clear. Throughout the region, however, there is a notable absence of bronze coins of Nero, which are found in only small numbers at the main sites, such as Novae, Serdica and Aquae Calidae. Coupled with the presence of many earlier imitations, this suggests that the supply of bronze from Rome had largely ceased by the reign of Nero. As a result, a branch mint was set up somewhere in the regions (Perinthus in Thrace has been suggested), which made coins for the family of Claudius, late in his reign, and perhaps for Claudius himself.[58] Subsequently, a Neronian branch mint was also established in the area, making coins which looked very much like the products of Rome or Lugdunum,[59] and it or a similar mint started worked again in 80–82.[60] All these coins, from Claudius to Domitian, follow the pattern of denominations from Rome, and their types are also very similar, including even some 'restored' bronze coins for Titus and Domitian. They are mostly found in southern Thrace, and a mint at Perinthus has been suggested.

The switch from Rome mint coins in Latin to provincial city coins in Greek provides the context for the bilingual coins from Callatis and Philippopolis, right at the moment of transition. When coinage resumed at these two cities, under Hadrian at Philippopolis and Antoninus Pius at Callatis, they used only Greek, reinforcing the switch from one sort of coin and language to the other.[61]

In a similar fashion, the imperial coinage of Cyrenaica had oscillated between Latin (Augustus, Hadrian) and Greek (Tiberius, Trajan, Marcus Aurelius). In Cyprus, coinage was generally in Greek, but in Latin from Augustus to Tiberius, followed by a bilingual issue under Claudius.

In Chapter 5, a change in the cultural outlook of the city elites was put forward to explain the end of local coinage in the west in the mid first century. If that model is correct, then we should look for similar trends in these liminal zones. One can certainly find some parallels, though not as we have seen for Lycia. Bilingual milestones are known from Cyprus,[62] and

**Figure 6.13** Bilingual coin of Domitian from Philippopolis, Thrace (modern Plovdiv).
The Latin obverse is copied from coins minted in Rome (IMP CAES DOMIT AVG GERM COS XIIII cens PER P P), while the Greek reverse (ΦΙΛΙΠΠΟΠΟΛΕΙΤΩΝ) shows the personification of the city standing in front of the reclining river god, Hebrus. (*RPC II*, 351)

**Figure 6.14** Claudius, Koinon of Cyprus.
The coin combines an obverse with a Latin inscription, copied from coins made at Rome (TI CLAVDIVS CAESAR AVG P M TR P IMP), with a reverse which has a Greek inscription (ΚΟΙΝΟΝ ΚΥΠΡΙΩΝ). (*RPC I*, 3928)

most of the inscriptions there which are connected with the emperor were in Latin. Cultural shifts towards Rome were taking place in Cyrenaica.[63] The general linguistic division, the so-called Jireček line, between Latin and Greek is generally thought to have remained stable, with Greek common in the southern part of the Balkan peninsula and Latin in the Danubian provinces,[64] but the pattern of coin use may suggest that this picture should be nuanced.[65] Several areas started to use bronze coins which were inscribed in Latin, in addition to the gold and silver which their populations may have handled, all of which would also have been inscribed in the same language.

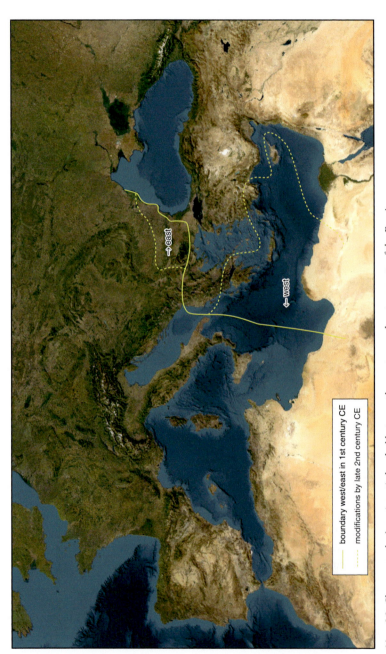

**Map 6.2** Changes to the 'numismatic border' between the western and eastern parts of the Empire

## 6.6 Designs

### 6.6.1 Civic Types

The choice of Latin or Greek more or less distinguishes the western half of the Empire from the east, and, as we have seen, mirrors the fundamental difference in the coins used in the two parts of the Empire. The visual content of the coins was also different in each part. West and East were linked by only one common feature – the general presence of the emperor or a member of his family on the obverse of the coins. However, the reverse designs were completely different. In the west they focused on the emperor, both his qualities and his achievements. In the east the emperor remained more or less absent from the reverses,[66] which focused on the internal concerns of each city.

At first, the civic coinage retained its generally religious character, demonstrating that a city's cults remained the essential part of its identity. Changes started to occur, however, during the Antonine period.[67] A growing number of cults were depicted, showing that city identity was becoming more nuanced, and the ways in which the coins expressed a city's antiquity, qualities or achievements became more varied. These developments are in some ways similar to the change which had come over the Roman Republican coinage in the late second century BCE. Then the choice of – often obscure – designs came to reflect the standing of the individual moneyers. Analogously, the civic coins two centuries later came to use a wider variety of designs, which were at times equally obscure, to illustrate a city's claim to greater prominence.

The increased emphasis on mythology and the real or imaginary histories of cities mirrors the rise of the 'Second Sophistic'. Just as intellectuals and orators (sophists) might address their audiences with elaborate speeches, which might often concern obscure topics, such as the origins of cities,[68] so too the city coinage was, similarly, an epideictic medium, one characterised by display.[69] Most of the mythological writing surviving today was written in the same period, and most of the mythological visual representations come from the city coinages of the second and third centuries. Pausanias' famous description of Greece is similarly a good illustration of the very contemporary interest at the time in the cults and monuments of cities and their past histories and myths. The preoccupation with the local fed into the frenzy of city rivalries and concords, and left almost to one side the relationship of each city to the centre of power in Rome.

The scenes on the coins may often seem obscure to us, but they followed the same trends as occurred to other forms of city decoration, such as on theatres.

For example, the imperial theatre at Nysa in Asia Minor was decorated with the themes of the birth of the god Dionysus, and the 'divine marriage' of Persephone and Hades, god of the underworld. Both stories were supposed to have taken place near Nysa, and both also featured on the city's coinage.[70] Myths were malleable stories that could be adapted to give a focus to individual cities.[71] Multiple foundation stories could be presented without any worry about incompatibility. The following short geographical survey gives a selective view of the designs used and the changes that affected them.[72]

The most inventive of the European mints were the two colonies of Corinth and Patras and the cities of Argos and Nicopolis, all of which produced a wide variety of designs reflecting the myths and cults associated with the city, and with several interesting depictions of buildings and arches. Elis, the city by the site of the Olympic Games made some very fine large coins (Figure 6.15).

The coinage from Asia Minor, and in particular from the province of Asia, was vast and diverse. Yet, a look in detail at the three largest mints in Asia (Ephesus, Pergamum and Smyrna) helps to illustrate the trends described above, even though their characters differ.

Ephesus was the capital of the Roman province, and its coinage was dominated by the cult of Artemis; unsurprisingly so, since it was one of the most important in the ancient world and the Temple was one of the Seven Wonders. The cult might be represented on the coinage in many ways – a depiction of the cult statue; of the temple; of Artemis herself, portrayed in different manners such as that of the huntress; of the stag which she hunted; or by her sacred insect, the bee. The sacred processional car (*hiera apene*) was presumably also part of the cult. Other recurrent designs, such as children playing with astragaloi (knucklebones, used much like modern

**Figure 6.15** The coinage of Hadrian from Elis.
Coins of Hadrian from Elis in Greece were executed in a superb style, and on the reverse they show a head of Zeus, copied from the famous statue of Zeus made by Phidias, from nearby Olympia. (*RPC III*, 308)

dice), are also set in the context of the cult, as they are shown beneath a representation of the cult figure. Such representations account for the major part of the Ephesian coinage, which is unusual in other ways, notably the absence of any 'pseudo-autonomous' coins.

In some cases, there were special reasons for these choices. For example, the emphasis under Elagabalus on ΤΑ ΜΕΓΑΛΑ ΟΙΚΟΥΜΕΝΙΚΑ ('the great world games'), which are also called 'Pythian', 'Olympian' and 'Hadrianic', seems likely to have been a massive celebration prompted by the grant by Elagabalus of a fourth neocorate temple, when the city was awarded, for the fourth time, the honour of having the provincial temple in honour of the emperor.

### Box 6.5  Temples on coins

Temples frequently appear on provincial coins, but we should not regard them as necessarily accurate representations of the relevant structures. Some temples appear on coins which were never, in fact, built. Coin representations may also have varying numbers of columns – the temple of Augustus at Pergamum might be shown with two or six (Figures 5.19–5.20) or other amounts (e.g., eight on Figure 6.16). The facade of the temple is often opened up so that we can see the cult figure in the centre (Figure 6.16), but this is an 'engraver's convention', since it would not have been visible outside the temple. The depictions of temples (and other buildings) on coins were intended to convey the idea of the building, rather than being exact reproductions (Burnett 1999).

**Figure 6.16** The Temple of Artemis at Ephesus – one of the Seven Wonders of the Ancient World.
The great Temple of Artemis at Ephesus was regularly shown on the coinage. On this detailed representation on a coin of Hadrian (who is styled *Olympian*), the temple can be seen with eight columns on a podium with three steps, within which can be seen the cult statue of Artemis Ephesia with supports; the columns are of the Ionic order and the bases of the columns are decorated. The pediment has four statues. Coins such as this have played a part in attempts to reconstruct the original appearance of the temple, and to interpret the surviving remains in the British Museum. (*RPC III*, 2073)

## Box 6.6 The imperial neocorate

From the time of Augustus, provincial cities competed with each other to be allowed to have the provincial temple honouring the emperor (Burrell 2004). This is known as the neocorate, from the Greek word *neokoros*, meaning 'temple-keeper'. Pergamum was awarded the temple for Augustus for the province of Asia, dedicated to 'Roma and Augustus'. Tacitus tells us that eleven cities competed for the honour of this title, and that Smyrna was the winner (Tacitus, *Annals* 4.55–6). Later emperors were honoured in a similar way. Most of our evidence comes from inscriptions and coins from the province of Asia, but other provincial temples are known for other provinces and areas, such as Bithynia, Galatia, Pamphylia, Macedonia, and several others, including Macedonia and Palestine. The importance of the temple can be seen by the choice of the Galatian temple in Ancyra for inscribing the *Res Gestae* of Augustus. Both Pergamum (Figures 5.19–5.20) and Smyrna depicted the temples on their coinage, but the title νεοκόρος (or νεωκόρος: both forms occur) was not commonly used before the middle of the second century. The award of more provincial temples to the same city was a matter of great pride: under Elagabalus, its coins proclaim that it had been awarded to 'Ephesus alone of all cities for the fourth time' (ΕΦΕϹΙΩΝ ΜΟΝΩΝ ΑΠΑϹΩΝ ΤΕΤΡΑΚΙ(ϲ) ΝΕΩΚΟΡΩΝ). The title might also be withdrawn after the death of an unpopular emperor like Elagabalus.

**Figure 6.17** Vows for the imperial cult at Ephesus.
Coins of Macrinus from Ephesus show a temple of the imperial cult enclosing a statue of the emperor. In front of the temple can be seen a row of worshippers about to sacrifice a bull at an altar. The sacrifice would be in fulfilment of the vows (ΒΩΤΑ = *vota*, inscribed in the pediment) which they had made, perhaps for the emperor's safety. Ephesus describes itself as 'first [city] of Asia' (ΠΡΩΤΩΝ ΑϹΙΑϹ).

'Roman' designs are rare – an occasional representation of the wolf and twins or the emperor, and once a reference to Trajan's Parthian War. Certain other themes regularly recur, such as the importance of three local rivers (which starts from the Flavian period), or the foundation myth of Androklos and the boar (from the reign of Trajan). Heraclitus, Ephesus' most famous philosopher, made his first appearance on the coinage of the Antonine period, together with that of the legendary founder, Androklos, a few decades earlier. Both are markers of the renewed interest in civic antiquarian histories at the time. A handful of other poets and intellectuals also appear, at much the same time; Homer, in particular, was claimed by many cities.[73]

**Figure 6.18** The early Greek philosopher Heraclitus celebrated on imperial coins of Ephesus.
The figure of Heraclitus first appears at Ephesus under Antoninus Pius, as here. Labelled ΗΡΑΚΛΕΙΤΟC, he is shown consistently as a standing figure who raises his hand and holds a club. The consistency of the representation suggests that it may be a copy of a statue, but there is no reason for Heraclitus to hold a club, other than the similarity of his name with Heracles. It may perhaps have originally been intended as a citizen's staff (see Muss 2017, 7–9), and shows that his identity was not well understood by the later coin engravers, who may just have thought of him as a distinguished figure from the city's glorious past. (*RPC IV*, temporary number 1125)

The coinage of Pergamum has a similar pattern, though there are substantial differences. It was less focused on the city's principal cult, that of Asclepius. In the Julio-Claudian period, it had been dominated by the award of the province's first neocorate temple, and perhaps because of that, with images of the imperial family. In addition, large numbers of coins were made celebrating the city of Rome and the Roman Senate. The focus on Rome and the imperial family probably arose because of the prestige of having the first neocorate temple. From the reign of Domitian, Pergamum started to use other images, such as the local cults of Athena and Dionysus. Asclepius made his first appearance, as did the personification of the city's eponymous founder, Pergamos, accompanied by Rome and the Senate. The award of a second neocorate temple under Trajan led to a renewed emphasis on Rome, but other cults returned under Hadrian. The

**Figure 6.19** Pergamum under Commodus as Caesar.
An imperial statue of the emperor stands on a column between side views of the two neocorate temples, which had been awarded to Pergamum by the emperors Augustus and Trajan. The inscription reads ΕΠΙ ΝΙΚΟΜΗΔΟΥΣ Β ΝΕΟΚΟΡΩΝ ΠΕΡΓΑΜΗΝΩΝ ('under Nicomedes [the senior magistrate of the city'], Pergamum, neocorate for the second time) A star above each temple signifies the deification of the two emperors. (*RPC IV*, temporary number 3244)

coinage became increasingly complex: one issue had no fewer than twenty different designs,[74] and it started to be dominated by Asclepius and his cult, while designs referring to the city's foundation by Heracles' son, Telephus, also appeared. As at Ephesus, the coinage might be dominated every now and then by a particular event – in Pergamum's case, the visit of Caracalla in the early third century. A variety of scenes record his presence and relationship with the principal cult of the city, Asclepius.

Pergamum also won the honour of being the first city to have a second neocorate temple, under Trajan, but curiously did not proclaim it was ΔΙC ΝΕΩΚΟΡΩΝ until fifty years later, in the reign of Marcus Aurelius. It then started to use extremely long legends as a way of staking its claim to prominence. For example: Η ΠΡΩΤΗ ΤΗC ΑCΙΑC ΚΑΙ ΜΗΤΡΟΠΟΛΙC ΠΡΩΤΗ ΚΑΙ ΤΡΙC ΝΕΩΚΟΡΟC ΠΡΩΤΗ ΤΩΝ CΕΒΑCΤΩΝ ΠΕΡΓΑΜΗΝΩΝ ΠΟΛΙC ('the city of Pergamum, the first city of Asia and first mother city and first temple keeper of the emperors for the third time')!

The rivalry between Pergamum, Ephesus and Smyrna to have more 'neocorate' temples is a constant theme of their coinage. The competition between cities, condemned at the time as 'the follies of the Greeks' by Dio Chrysostom, focused on titles and status, in particular to be the conventus capital or the host of a neocorate temple, or to be a metropolis or the 'first' city.[75]

6.20

6.21

**Figures 6.20–6.21** The great altar of Zeus at Pergamum.
The Great Altar of Zeus at Pergamum, which can today be seen in the Berlin Museum, was shown on some of the coins of the city, here for Septimius Severus and his wife Julia Domna. The coins emphasise the grand staircase and open up the columns so that the altar, which lay behind them, can be seen in the middle. The columns are shown schematically, as is the sculptural decoration.

The coinage of Smyrna was one of the most extensive and most sophisticated of all the provincial coinages. At first, it continued its traditional nature, with the normal addition of the imperial portrait. The award of the imperial temple for Tiberius (with Livia and the Senate) was celebrated on a plentiful issue of coins, which also prompted Pergamum to issue a 'reminder' of its temple at the same time. In the 'year of the four emperors' (68–69 CE) Smyrna hedged its bets by issuing a series of coins which did not recognise any of the contenders, but instead celebrated the imperial temple and city's cults. Corinth had done much the same, apart from a few coins for Galba: the rest were 'safer', dedicated to the Senate and People, or to 'Rome and the Empire'. This tactic may have been followed by other cities, but their coins cannot be dated with sufficient precision to be sure.

From the Flavian period, Smyrna started to produce coins with some of the finest standards of engraving. Much like Pergamum, they started to celebrate the city more generally: its cults, like Zeus or Cybele, and the Hermos river. One or two Nemeses and a figure of an Amazon made their first appearance, referring to stories about the mythical foundation of Smyrna: the city was named after an Amazon called Smyrna, while Alexander the Great had a dream in which the Nemeses ordered him to found a city. Other river personifications appear, such as the Meles and the Kaleon. These themes were developed in the second century: Alexander's dream was visualised, accompanied by other stories. Pelops was, according to another tradition, also a founder of Smyrna, and appears, fresh from his success in the chariot race in which he won the hand of Hippodamia. Fine representations of the Nemeses and the Amazon appear, and superb representations of Semele and her son, the god Dionysus. The poet Homer appears in the Severan period, when there are also a number of representations of the imperial family. During the third century, Smyrna's rivalry with its competitors becomes dominant, with inscriptions declaring the city to be 'the first in Asia to have three neocorates' (CMΥΡΝΑΙΩΝ ΠΡΩΤΩΝ ΑCΙΑC Γ ΝΕ, with the three temples often displayed), and even 'Smyrna the temple keeper of the Emperors for the third time, and the first city of Asia in beauty and size' (CMΥΡΝΑΙΩΝ Γ ΝΕΩΚΟΡΩΝ ΤΩΝ CΕΒΑCΤΟΝ ΠΡΩΤΩΝ ΑCΙΑC ΚΑΛΛΕΙ ΚΑΙ ΜΕΓΕΘΕΙ).

Intercity rivalry is one of the principal themes of the civic coinage in Asia, and was much more important even than stressing links to Rome. 'Rome' does appear, often labelled as such, on many coins like those of Pergamum, but it is treated as if it were some sort of foreign peer, rather than the dominant power. Nicaea and Ephesus can celebrate the Parthian victory of Lucius Verus as the ΡΩΜΑΙΩΝ ΝΙΚΗ, and Nicaea used the same phrase a hundred years later, under Valerian and Gallienus. Carrhae described itself as 'Rome-loving' (*philoromaios*). Sepphoris proclaimed its 'Good faith, friendship and alliance with the Romans'.[76] Sagalassus, Prostanna and Side did much the same, as if they had made an alliance with an independent foreign state.[77]

## 6.6 Designs

**Figure 6.22** The sophist Attalus at Smyrna.
This coin of Marcus Aurelius from Smyrna was signed by the sophist Attalus (ΑΤΤΑΛΟΣ ΣΟΦΙΣΤΗΣ), who was the son of the more famous Polemo (see Figure 4.15). Both father and son came from Laodicea, but lived most of their lives in Smyrna. Hence the coin is also inscribed 'to his home cities Smyrna and Laodicea' (ΤΑΙΣ ΠΑΤΡΙ ΣΜΥΡ ΛΑΟ). The two cities are shown symbolically: Zeus, the principal deity of Laodicea, stands between two figures of Nemesis, cult figures of Smyrna, who had come to Alexander the Great in a dream and instructed him to found the city of Smyrna where he slept. (*RPC IV*, temporary number 2943)

**Figure 6.23** Anazarbus, adorned with Roman trophies.
Coins of Julia Maesa, the grandmother of Elagabalus, from Anazarbus in Cilicia, declare that 'Glorious Anazarbus, the metropolis, was adorned with Roman trophies' (ΑΝΑΖΑΡΒΟΥ ΕΝΔΟΞΟΥ ΜΗΤΡΟΠΟΛΕΩΣ ΡΩΜΑΙΚΟΙΣ ΤΡΟΠΑΙΟΙΣ ΚΕΚΟΣΜΗΜΕΝΗ). The trophies were presumably for Caracalla's campaign against the Parthians in 217, but the language makes it sound as if 'Roman' was some foreign power. The representation of empresses varies from reign to reign. Many appear in the reign of Elagabalus (his grandmother, his mother and each of his three wives); usually the emperor's wife appears, but not always (e.g., under Maximinus, Paulina appears at only three cities). (*RPC VI*, temporary number 7264)

The flipside of rivalry is concord, and it is no accident that the concept was discussed by Dio Chrysostom in the same context as the rivalry between cities.[78] Indeed the Emperor's Concord (ΟΜΟΝΟΙΑ ΣΕΒΑΣΤΗ) occurs on Bithynian coins from the reign of Domitian. It is also used on a wide range of 'Homonoia coins', which celebrated the links between two cities, and are usually characterised by the presence of the word ΟΜΟΝΟΙΑ.[79] The first such coins, however, had not used the word,[80] and under Nero, the *Demoi* (peoples) of Laodicea and Smyrna are accompanied by the word ΟΜΗΡΟΣ, perhaps meaning 'guarantor'.[81] The word ΟΜΟΝΟΙΑ first appears on coins in the Flavian period, but it was not yet universally used, either in the Flavian period or the early second century, and the Concord was still frequently visualised as the *Demoi* of both cities clasping hands.[82] The number of such Concords was still quite small, but they increased greatly in number in the Antonine period.[83] By the later second century, their visual expression became more sophisticated, such as a complicated scene for Cyzicus with Smyrna, where the Demeter of Cyzicus is shown in a processional car drawn by two centaurs, a mode of transport also favoured by the Zeus of Pergamum in Concord with Ephesus. The cities were, by now, typically represented by their mythical founder or their chief deity, rather than a figure of their Demos. These tendencies continued into the third century, and agonistic designs also started to appear, suggesting that the concords were often celebrated with games. Concord and rivalry remained themes on the provincial coinage throughout its later history, and the increasingly learned development of their designs reflects the more general patterns of the time.

**Figure 6.24** 'Concord' between Philadelphia and Ephesus.
A particularly elaborate 'Concord' scene made for the cities of Philadelphia and Ephesus (ΟΜΟΝΟΙΑ, ΦΙΛΑΔΕΛΦΕΩΝ ΝΕΩΚ ΕΦΕCΙΩΝ) under Trajan Decius. It shows Iphigeneia, her brother Orestes, and their companion Pylades, bringing the famous cult-image of Artemis that they took from the Taurians to its new home in Ephesus (Burrell 2005). (*RPC IX*, 722)

As in the first century, the coinage produced in Syria and Phoenicia in the second century is different in many respects from that of Greece and Asia. Both areas retained their more conservative approach, and, as before, this was more emphatic in Phoenicia.

The principal Syrian bronze coinage remained the SC coinage of Antioch (Figure 5.30), which circulated across the region, unlike the civic coinages. As before, the obverses depicted only the emperors, and the female and other members of the imperial family were not portrayed before the reign of Severus Alexander: there were no Faustinas, no Julia Domna and none of the female members of Elagabalus' family, which were so common elsewhere.[84] Thereafter their inclusion became normal, as elsewhere. Women continued also to be rare on the city coinage of northern Syria, appearing only later, and then only occasionally, in the reigns of Severus, Alexander and Philip.[85] They started to appear in southern Syria and Arabia from the second century, but were never as common as in Asia.[86]

The designs on the coins were also much more restricted in number and imagination than the contemporary products of Asia, and were usually dominated by the Tyche (the personification of the city).[87] None of the characteristics of Asia's coinage – mythology, foundation legends, pseudo-autonomous coins, Homonoia issues – were deployed, although the legends did refer to the status of the cities and their titles, such as *metropolis* (mother city), and the descriptions *autonomos* and *hiera kai asylos* (autonomous, holy-and-inviolable).[88] However, they all appeared only intermittently, and it seems that less importance was attached to them than in Asia.

**Figure 6.25** The 'pseudo-autonomous' coinage of Tyre, Phoenicia, 152/3. The 'pseudo-autonomous' coinage of Tyre continued throughout the second century. As before, the principal denominations used a head of the patron deity Heracles-Melqart, and on the reverse the club of Heracles. The city is named in Greek with a monogram of ΤΥΡ at the top of the club and its title metropolis (ΜΗΤΡΟΠΟΛΕΩΣ) is added, together with the date (here ΗΟΣ =279 = 152/3 CE). To the right of the club, the city's name is repeated in Phoenician letters. (*RPC IV.3*, temporary number 2258)

The coinage of Phoenicia had been the most unchanged in the first century, and it remained so for most of the second century. Tyre, for example, continued throughout the period to make coins without the emperor's head, but using the traditional design of Heracles-Melqart, a Tyche, a palm tree and a galley. Much the same is true at Aradus, where the principal reverse designs remained the prancing bull and the figure of Tyche, although there was a slight change on the obverse, with the abandonment after the reign of Trajan of the strange obverse design of a massive head of Tyche dominating a small bust of the emperor, a design that had been current since the reign of Augustus. The coinage produced by most of the other Phoenician cities in the second century remained similarly unchanged, for instance at Tripolis, Ptolemais and Dora. Even at the colony, Berytus, the more Roman types (ploughing scene, standards) and Poseidon continued in much the same manner as before. Phoenicia, however, like southern Syria and Arabia did portray female members of the imperial family from the second century, unlike northern Syria, where they did not appear before the third century, and then only rarely.

However, with the advent of the Severan dynasty, the character of the coinage changed completely. The change was most radical at Tyre, where the foundation of a colony coincided with the end of the traditional 'pseudo-autonomous' types. They were replaced with fine portraits of the imperial family, and a wide range of reverse designs, including elaborate depictions of the cults of the colony. There were also ones that referred to the new military character of the city, the imperial family in various guises, temples and the celebration of games. There are some finely drawn scenes: such as Heracles standing before an altar, holding a club; or images of the 'ambrosial rocks', the two rocks which had stopped their wandering on the sea at the site of the city's foundation. One can also observe the murex shell, from which the famous ancient purple was discovered when the shell was bitten by a dog.

By the third century, the visual content of Phoenician coinage had come to resemble that of Asia and Greece. Syrian coinage, however, retained more of its original character, and did not change to the same extent in the Severan period as that of the Phoenician cities. The changes do match other developments in the culture of the region. There are very few surviving mosaics from the first and second centuries. One of the few from the first century, from Apamea, has a simple geometrical design and a restrained use of colour.[89] In the second century, more colourful mosaics started to appear, with scenes on panels drawn from mythology, and only in the third century did they attain their well-known virtuosity.[90]

**Figure 6.26** Dido and the foundation of Carthage.
Coins of Tyre used Latin script after the foundation of the colony, and in the third century they depicted the figure of the legendary queen Dido, who left Tyre and founded the new city of Carthage in north Africa. On this coin she can be seen supervising the construction of the new city, and she is named in Greek letters as (ΔIΔW) and in Phoenician letters (as Elissa), a remarkable piece of antiquarianism. (*RPC VII.2*, 3565)

**Figure 6.27** The invention of the Greek alphabet by Cadmus.
Cadmus was the son of the King of Tyre in Phoenicia, and Herodotus reported that, when he came to Greece, 'Cadmus brought learning and indeed letters to the Greeks', (*Histories* 5.58), and the Greek alphabet is generally agreed to have its origins in Phoenician script. On some of its coins Tyre proudly referred to this belief, showing Cadmus (ΚΑΔ(μος) presenting a tablet with the alphabet to four Greeks ΕΛΛΗ(νες). As on Figure 6.26, Greek is used to emphasise the pride the city took in its antiquarian past – in this case almost a millennium previously.

### 6.6.2 Imperial and Military Types

Most civic coinages continued with the same range of reverse designs as in the first century, typically honouring one of the cults of each city. In Chapter 5, the increase in the number of designs was regarded as a reflection of practice at Rome, where the mint produced coins with many designs. There were, however, very few allusions to contemporary events among the increasingly numerous designs on provincial coins. Only Domitian's German wars, near the end of the century, prompted some designs.[91] References to them appear prominently on the coinage of Crete, and there are several relevant types among the extensive coinage of Corinth and Patras, though none seems common. Other mints in Bithynia and the province of Asia, as well as, especially, Alexandria, also refer to his victories.[92] A temple for Domitian the Victor was depicted at Laodicea, accompanied by other designs showing Victory and even the wolf and twins (Figure 6.28). But these are few and far between among the totality of the coins made at the time.

Slightly more allusions to contemporary campaigns can be found in the early second century, but they are still rare. Trajan's Dacian wars were mentioned only by a dozen or so cities,[93] including a possible reference to the monument at Adamklissi (Figure 6.12).[94] A temple for Trajan 'the Dacian Victor' was also erected at Silandus, although it did not appear on coins until fifty years later.[95] Trajan's Armenian and Parthian campaigns took place late in his reign and so were mentioned by only a few cities,[96] although they were quite prominent on several types in Alexandria.

The same pattern continued throughout the second century. Ephesus and Aphrodisias alone celebrated the victory of Lucius Verus in Mesopotamia,[97] and Pergamum marked the victories of Marcus Aurelius on the Danube.[98] For Commodus' triumph over the Germans in 180, one Pergamene design shows the emperor in military dress standing and erecting a trophy, in front of which a bound captive is seated; while in the

**Figure 6.28** A Victory temple of Domitian at Loadicea.
The temple of Domitian the Victor (ΕΠΙΝΕΙΚΙΟC is inscribed on the architrave), at Laodicea, Phrygia, shown on a coin portraying Domitian and his wife Domitia on the obverse. The reverse shows two figures; the one on the right wears military uniform and holds a figure of Victory, and is presumably Domitian. The identity of the female figure on the left is not clear, but she is probably the personification of the city. (*RPC II*, 1284)

**Figure 6.29** Temple enclosing the 'Dacian Victor', i.e., Trajan, celebrated on coins of Silandus under Lucius Verus.
The words ΔΑΚΙΚΟC ΕΠΙΝΕΙΚΙΟC are written below the temple, which shows the figure of Trajan in military dress and holding a spear. (*RPC IV*, temporary number 1757)

**Figure 6.30** Coin of Amasea in Pontus, minted for Lucius Verus and showing the emperors Marcus Aurelius and Lucius Verus in civilian dress and clasping hands. The scene symbolises the concord between the two co-emperors. (*RPC IV*, temporary number 1255)

foreground, a man is about to slaughter a sacrificial bull with a double axe.[99] But in both cases, the coins are very rare, and the contemporary coinage refers overwhelmingly to each city's principal cult, Artemis at Ephesus and Asclepius at Pergamum.

A single, partial, exception to this picture stands out, the relatively large number of cities (twenty-four) copying a design from coins minted at Rome of the co-emperors Marcus Aurelius and Lucius Verus clasping hands (Map 6.3). However, even in this case, the number was not so great (only about 15 per cent of cities minting at the time).[100]

**Map 6.3** Cities (24) making coins which portrayed Marcus Aurelius and Lucius Verus standing together and clasping hands

Only in one area, Egypt, did the commemoration of imperial events become a regular feature. Hadrian's own visit to Egypt in 130–1 was marked by a reduction in the number of earlier designs and a concentration on those illustrating his visit, whether the galley used to transport him, his symbolic meeting with the personification of Alexandria, or his performance of ritual sacrifices.[101] Warfare and victory also became a regular theme on the Egyptian coinage: Pius' campaign in Britain, Verus' Parthian victories and Commodus' British campaign are all clear examples, although other campaigns did not appear, such as those in Britain and Judaea under Hadrian.[102]

Alexandria was always more aware, as a mint, of what was happening at Rome, and it is the place in the provinces where one would expect imperial allusions. It had changed its character in the reign of Domitian, when the previous designs, few in number and simple in construction, were replaced with a much more diverse set of images. Some did show the emperor, often in inventive ways: not just on horseback or in a triumphal chariot, but also in chariots drawn by elephants or centaurs. Images from the real and allegorical world were mingled, to celebrate the pre-eminent place of the emperor in interesting ways. The coinage of Domitian set the scene for that of Trajan, which accentuated some of the innovations. A few 'Nome' coins had been made under Domitian, celebrating the different administrative divisions (*nomoi*) of the province, and many more were produced under Trajan. His reign, too, saw a continuation of the various designs depicting the emperor, used as generic references to the emperor, rather than marking specific occasions, and more buildings, temples and arches were shown. Some of them depicted structures at Rome. The coinage was less innovative under Hadrian, though some trends continued, such as an extensive set of Nome coins. They are also found for Antoninus Pius, whose reign was probably the most innovative of any emperor, and several more sets of designs were deployed.[103] As well as nomes and buildings, the most spectacular depicted the labours of Heracles and a complicated group of zodiacal coins, with fine anthropomorphised and animal representations, representing the different constellations set in a zodiacal belt, and reflecting a considerable knowledge of astronomy.

Figure 6.31 Trajan in triumph.
A remarkable coin of Trajan, minted at Alexandria in 113/14, has his nude heroic portrait, with only an aegis on his shoulder and a wreath of laurel leaves and corn ears on the obverse. The unusual wreath, which had also occurred for Domitian, seems to identify the emperor as the guarantor of a good harvest. The reverse shows a triumphal scene, in which the victorious emperor is shown in a four-horse chariot and holding an eagle-tipped sceptre and a laurel branch; behind him stands the small figure of the public slave whose role it was to remind the *triumphator* that he was merely a man (Woytek 2015). In the distance can be seen a column, topped by a statue. This has been interpreted as Trajan's column in Rome, but the statue seems to be a figure of Hercules. (*RPC III*, 4798)

In this respect, the Alexandrian coinage was the most 'Roman' of all provincial coinages, and became as complex and sophisticated as the coinage of Rome, especially under Antoninus Pius and Marcus Aurelius: the set of zodiacal designs or the labours of Heracles under Pius are good examples, and mythological scenes are more prominent than in Asia. In parallel, however, the Alexandrian coinage still retained its predominantly Graeco-Egyptian character – temples might be shown in the Egyptian manner with entrance pylons, and many Egyptian gods are commemorated, both shown as Hellenised personifications and represented by their sacred animals. This dual nature of this coinage makes it stand out from all other provincial coinages, and it is one of the ways in which the Alexandrian coinage was different from other coinages.[104]

The other provincial coinages made even fewer topical allusions, and continued to concentrate on the religious cults of each city. It is curious, for example, how little reference there is to Hadrian's journeys round the Empire. They were celebrated at Alexandria, as we have seen, but otherwise hardly at all. Corinth records the ADV(entus) AVG(usti) by galley. The coinage of Cyzicus copies the galley from Roman coins and translates their accompanying legend (*RPC III*, 1517–18). This, and another type which shows the emperor on horseback and raising his hand (*RPC* 1505), might suggest an imperial visit, but most of the numerous types produced at the

**Figure 6.32** Tutu or sphinx?
Coins of Hadrian from Alexandria in Egypt depicted a wide variety of designs, often of local religious significance. This coin has traditionally been described as having a sphinx, but the correct identification is the Egyptian god Tutu, who would protect people from danger (Matthies 2002). He is shown with the body of a lion and a snake for a tail, and with the head of a crocodile protruding from his chest. Another snake appears below. He has a human head, and wears a feathered headdress. (*RPC III*, 5909)

time continue the city's traditional iconography. Beyond that, new titles mark Hadrian's several city foundations and refoundations,[105] and the well-named Hadrianotherae aptly celebrates his bear-hunting exploits, but there is hardly any mention of his creation of the Panhellenic league of Greek cities.[106] Hadrian's Panhellenion was an idea taken up by only a few cities on their coinage, and not at all by major centres such as Pergamum, Ephesus or Smyrna. In areas such as Phrygia, local non-Greek gods such as Men retained their popularity.

A few of the provincial temples dedicated to the emperor appear, but these neocorate temples do actually feature less than one might have expected, given their importance to the cities that had won the right to have them. Neither the title nor an image appears on the otherwise fiercely competitive coinage of Nicomedia, to which the provincial temple was awarded by Trajan. His Asian temple does appear at Pergamum, as do a few newly awarded ones under Hadrian, and some earlier ones recur.[107] Only in the reign of Marcus Aurelius does the title start to appear regularly at Pergamum.[108] The title 'neocoros' ('temple-keeper': referring to the award of a provincial temple to the emperor at a particular city) appears first on coins of Ephesus under Nero, perhaps for an abortive award; thereafter it did not reappear until the reign of Hadrian, some of whose coins celebrated the second award (ΔIC),[109] which had in fact been made late in the reign of Trajan.[110] Neither the award of the title for the second time nor a temple appear on the coinages of Smyrna and Sardis, even after its award under Hadrian.[111] This 'reluctance' shows how much the cultural outlook of the cities retained their traditional religious focus, and it continued in the Antonine period, when neocorates were celebrated only a little more frequently.[112] The emphasis on neocorates became greater only in the third century.

**Figure 6.33** Hadrian and the bear hunt. The city of Hadrianotherae ('The hunts of Hadrian') was founded by Hadrian in north-west Asia to commemorate his success in hunting. (*RPC III*, 1626)

There are also a few military designs, illustrating a focus on the Roman army and navy, but they are not numerous. The only exception is the depiction of one or more standards, sometimes with a flag (a *vexillum*) naming a legion or a legionary eagle. This is found most commonly on the coinage of colonies, where they refer to the settlement of veterans (sometimes with their original legions being named on the *vexilla*).[113] These designs were, however, used more widely, and appeared on a number of other coinages.

Some of the occurrences on coins of cities which were not colonies can be explained by the presence of military bases. The legionary base of Raphanea, for example, weaves an eagle and the legionary symbol of a bull onto the design of its coins.[114] Several of the other cities were naval bases, indicated by the presence of a galley, and sometimes with the title ΝΑΥΑΡΧΙΣ ('naval command').[115]

One group of military designs that stands out concerns the products of several Bithynian cities in the early third century (Prusa, Nicomedia, Juliopolis, and especially Nicaea). They also have an unusual pattern of circulation, not in Bithynia at all, but large numbers have been found further to the west, especially in Moesia Superior, Pannonia Inferior and Dacia.[116] They are found above all along the Danube, suggesting that they were used, in some sense, in connection with the army, and it seems likely that the designs were chosen with that audience in mind. This is very reminiscent of the practice of matching design to destination, which can be seen on some other occasions (coins of Hadrian and Antoninus Pius depicting Britannia turn up mostly in Britain),[117] but is very unusual for the provincial coinage. It contrasts with the

**Figure 6.34** Veterans at Berytus.
Coins of the colony of Berytus (COL BER) (mod. Beirut) regularly show two legionary eagles, as here on a coin of Hadrian. The eagles refer to the two legions (V Macedonica and III Gallica), whose veterans were settled there by Augustus. (*RPC III*, 3855)

Severan coins which were minted by many (forty-two) cities in the Peloponnese, many of which are found in Syria and as far east as the Euphrates frontier, and which may have been moved there for the use of the army.[118] However, they have 'normal' designs, referring to the cults of the cities that produced them.

An intriguing type that also turns up only at colonies and one municipium is a figure of Marsyas carrying a wine-skin on his shoulder or, in Latin, *cum utriculo*. It occurs from the reign of Domitian,[119] and is distinct from other representations of him, such as Marsyas with the double flute at Apamea in Phrygia, where the myth of his contest with Apollo was situated and where he had an important cult.[120] Marsyas *cum utriculo*, however, is very common at colonies (and one municipium),[121] and is usually associated with the notion of *libertas* and the privileged status of such communities. It seems that the Roman senator Claudius Charax may also have associated it with colonies.[122] Its significance has, however, been much debated and it has never been convincingly explained.[123] Its presence at so many colonies, and one municipium, is exactly the same as the incidence of coins with standards, and suggests it might be connected with the foundation of colonies, and that it was part of the re-creation of the city of Rome, where a famous statue of Marsyas stood in the Forum.[124] Colonies were, famously, like 'little images and copies of Rome'.[125]

**Figure 6.35** Marsyas with a wineskin, depicted at the colony of Laodicea in Syria in the reign of Macrinus.
The obverse spells Macrinus' name with the ending –OS and the reverse inscription is a clumsy attempt at COL LΛVDICIΛE METR IIII PROV = 'the colony of Laodicea, mother city of the four provinces' or divisions into which the imperial cult was divided in Syria. Laodicea had come to play an important role after it was rewarded by Septimius Severus for its loyalty in the civil wars.

## 6.7 Antinous

Hadrian's homosexual relationship with the young Antinous was not celebrated on the coinage minted at Rome, which continued to depict only persons who were formally part of the imperial family. Yet it prompted many provincial cities to make coins which honoured him, illustrating in another way how the provincial coinage was different from that minted at Rome.

Some thirty cities made coins for Antinous.[126] In a sense, this is a small number, since it is only a little more than ten per cent of all the cities which made coins in Hadrian's reign. This suggests that the provincial cities were not sure whether they should honour him on their coins, even though Hadrian himself also 'set up statues, or rather sacred images, of him, practically all over the world' (Dio Cassius 69.11). Perhaps the lack of coins from the mint of Rome made them uncertain, even though it would have been a way to promote their claims for the emperor's attention as they competed with their neighbours for prominence.

The geographical spread of cities making coins for Antinous is odd, as they are largely confined to southern Greece and northern Asia Minor, with a few in Cilicia and Alexandria in Egypt.[127] There was nothing from the central or southern parts of Asia Minor, nor from the Levant.

**Map 6.4** Cities minting coins for Antinous
Amorium and Philadelphia are not included: see note 126.

**Figures 6.36–6.37** The problem of Antinous, Hadrian's lover.
'The Amphictyons', on behalf of Delphi, made coins for 'the hero Antinous, the Defender' (ΑΝΤΙΝΟΟΝ ΗΡΩΑ ΠΡΟΠ). The reverse has a tripod and its inscription records that 'the priest Aristotimos dedicated [the coin]' (Ο ΙΕΡΕΥC ΑΡΙCΤΟΤΙΜΟC ΑΝΕΘΗΚΕ). Many of the coins for Antinous were bigger than any made for the emperor Hadrian at Delphi. Tarsus made large coins depicting Antinous (6.37). He is shown wreathed in ivy, a symbol of the figure of Dionysus who rides a panther on the reverse, to whom he was being likened. He also wears a hem-hem crown, an Egyptian symbol of divinity and the obverse inscription describes him as a 'hero' (ΗΡΩC). (6.36 *RPC III*, 444/1; 6.37 *RPC III*, 3285)

Probably because Antinous' position was so anomalous, the cities which did decide to make coins for him were often unsure about how they should present him. Sometimes he was a god (ΘΕΟΣ), sometimes a hero (ΗΡΩΣ). Many included him in a family group with Hadrian and sometimes Sabina, and often in a minor position, but there were exceptions.[128] More than half of them had unusual features, often using a dedicatory dative and referring to their issuing communities in odd ways,[129] as if they were trying to distance themselves from the coins. Many of them have similar portraits and iconography, just as many Antinous sculptures conformed to a standard model.[130] Sometimes an unexpected private individual adds his name, such as the priests Hostilius Marcellus at Corinth and Aristotimos at Delphi.

The most noticeable feature of many of the coins, from Greece, Bithynia and Asia, is that they are much bigger than the normal denominations that were produced by the relevant cities at the time (Map 6.5), leading to their modern description as 'medallic'.[131] Moreover, many of them were also made of orichalcum (brass),[132] the metal which, as we have seen, was rarely seen outside certain parts of northern and western Asia. However, not enough analyses have been carried out to determine whether Antinous coins were generally made from specially supplied metal, and at the moment the evidence suggests that it is unlikely.[133]

But can the making of 'medallic' pieces just be an accident? It is difficult to accept that the same idea could have occurred spontaneously at so many cities over such a wide area, and it is hard to avoid the conclusion that these issues were in some way connected. The nature of that connection, however, is obscure, but it may be related to the rise in the production of medallions at Rome during the reign of Hadrian, especially the second half.[134] They may

**Map 6.5** Cities making coins for Antinous of medallic size

have prompted an awareness that there could be a different model for making honorary 'coins', one which might sometimes remove it from the mainstream of coinage and hence perhaps seem 'safer'. While most Roman medallions have been found in Rome, there are also many finds from the provinces,[135] and it has even been suggested that the dies for the large Antinous coins, 'large pieces of exceptional beauty', which have a number of stylistic similarities, were made by the engravers from Rome.[136] This may seem a little unlikely, but some explanation is needed for the unusual and similar nature of many of the large pieces, made over such a wide area. There must surely have been contact between the makers, and in a more specific way than is explained by the distribution of his sculptural portrait type.

If the idea of medallic pieces was passed by word of mouth from city to city, then we can calculate the amount of time needed, based on the distances which must have been travelled and the amount of time available. As an example, the minimum distance between all the cities in Asia Minor that made coins for Antinous is 2,641 km.[137]

As for timing, Antinous died in 130, giving a maximum of eight years until Hadrian's death. The coins of Amisus and Aegeae are dated 133/4, and the Alexandrian 134/5 and 136/7. This has prompted the idea that the coinage only began with his festivals to be held every five years in his honour, so from 134. One could also argue that his commemoration is unlikely to have continued after Aelius' promotion in late 136, which would give a minimum period of two years. A maximum of eight and a minimum of two years means that the idea of medallic pieces would have had to travel across Asia at a minimum of 1 km or a maximum of 4 km per day. Both are easily feasible. The same is true even if one allows for transmission to the more distant places, in Greece and Egypt.

A final question arises: did Hadrian know about these coins and, if so, what was his attitude to them? There is no direct evidence for any role played by the emperor in the coins, but one case is intriguing. It concerns the Antinous coins of Smyrna, donated by the famous sophist M. Antonius Polemo (Figure 4.15). Polemo enjoyed the friendship of all the emperors Trajan, Hadrian and Antoninus Pius, and even accompanied Hadrian on his travels round the Empire, famously being chosen to speak in 131 at the inauguration of the great Temple of Olympian Zeus in Athens, in the presence of Hadrian. This was the exact period in which the Antinous coins were made at Smyrna, and it is tempting to think that Hadrian knew about them from Polemo – a man famous for his arrogance, and so unlikely to be reticent.[138]

# 7

## 'From a kingdom of gold to one of iron and rust' in the Third Century CE

Cassius Dio's famous verdict on the decline of the Empire saw the death of Marcus Aurelius in 180 as a turning point in Roman history, and ever since Edward Gibbon published his influential *Decline and Fall* in the late eighteenth century, historians have reflected on the changes that took place after the golden age of the second century. What can provincial coins contribute to the debate?

The third century was a period of momentous political and economic change for the Roman Empire.[1] Citizenship was extended to all male inhabitants of the Empire by Caracalla in 212,[2] and political power was increasingly hard for any emperor to maintain. The period saw more than twenty-five emperors recognised in Rome and numerous usurpers. Most of them reigned for only short periods, and most had been military command-ers. The difficulty of upholding power saw an increasing fragmentation and, after 260, enormous swathes of the Empire fell under separate rulers: the 'Gallic emperors' in Gaul, Spain and Britain, and the Empire of Palmyra in Asia Minor, Syria and Egypt.

Big economic changes also took place. The volume of trade was reduced, as evidenced by the decline in dated shipwrecks; fewer public buildings were constructed; mining activity declined, as shown by evidence from the pollution in ice cores from Greenland; and less meat was consumed, as evidenced by the study of bones from archaeological sites.[3] All such factors suggest a decline in the prosperity of the Empire, and, as discussed below, the economy of the Empire at the same time became more fragmented.

The monetary system also slid from the stability of the early Empire into a never-ending process of debasement and fragmentation, punctuated by occasional reforms. The new silver 'antoninianus' was introduced by Caracalla, and became the staple silver coinage of the Empire from 238. The silver content of the coinage dropped dramatically from the new low of 45 per cent under Septimius Severus and to less than 1 per cent by 275. New mints were established in many new parts of the Empire, presumably because the logistics of central supply had become more difficult.

Some political and monetary stability was re-established by Aurelian (270–5), and later consolidated by Diocletian (284–305). Aurelian reestablished the territorial integrity of the Empire, and introduced reforms that stabilised the coinage, but saw an increase in inflation. Diocletian's division of the Empire into four parts, each with its own principal ruler, and his normalisation of the pattern of mints across the Empire, were both the products of and the solutions to the problems which had beset the Empire for many decades. Like all his successors, however, he failed to stop inflation: his massive Edict of Maximum Prices was issued in 301 and was intended to place a cap on the price of hundreds of materials, goods and services. It was promulgated throughout the Empire, but, despite the threat of the death penalty for a breach, it rapidly failed to achieve its objective.

The provincial coinage can contribute to the history of the third century in several ways, especially for the period after 250. The political changes affected the outlook of the city elites, which placed a greater emphasis on the emperor and military matters on their coinage, while the desire of cities and individuals to claim prominence become more pronounced. We can see how the cities tried to respond to the decline and collapse of the early imperial monetary system, and the changes suggest that the cities were having serious difficulties in their responses even in the 250s, much earlier

**Figure 7.1** Crude engraving in the third century.
The style of engraving became crude and rough on the coins of several cities in the third century. For example, the city of Panemoteichus in inland Pisidia, which had produced coins of a good style in the Severan period, made coins in the reign of Valerian and Gallienus with portraits which look to us like caricatures. This piece depicts the emperor Gallienus and his wife Salonina, with a small bust of their son Valerian II in between. The reverse shows the Tyche or personification of the city; to the left the numeral I denotes 10, the value of the coin.

than is sometimes thought.[4] They also show how the Empire was becoming increasingly fragmented[5] – not just at the macro level of the losses of the Gallic and Palmyrene empires, but even within the provinces and sometimes between individual cities. The final collapse of the monetary system eventually brought all the provincial coinages to an end, and, with their demise, we lose our ability to see the Roman world through the eyes of the city elites.

## 7.1 Political and Security Problems

Each new emperor, and often his family members, would be recorded whenever a city made coinage. The portrait of the emperor would now often have a more military appearance than in the past, although we should not exaggerate this new trend, as the great majority of the designs continued in the traditional mould, with a simple portrait of the emperor.

**Figures 7.2–7.3** Aemilian and Supera.
Even a short-lived emperor like Aemilian, who reigned for about three months in late 253 might appear on the provincial coinage (Watson 2018). He appears at nine cities from Rome to Alexandria (7.2). Coins and papyri place his short reign in late summer and autumn of 253: the Alexandrian coins, for example, are dated to his 'year two' (L B), showing that his reign bracketed the 29th of August (the day on which the year changed in Alexandria). His wife Gaia Cornelia Supera – known only from coins – also appears at three cities. The coins for her from Aegeae (7.3) have the date 299 of the city's era, and the coins from this city have proved that she was the wife of Aemilian (rather than Valerian, as early modern writers thought). (7.2 *RPC IX*, 2332; 7.3 *RPC IX*, 896)

## 7.1 Political and Security Problems

In the first century, the emperor was usually portrayed with a simple head or draped bust, and usually wearing a laurel wreath. This reflected the iconography of the mint of Rome. Depictions became somewhat more inventive in the second century, as at Rome. Trajan might be shown with a nude bust, wearing only a divine aegis, although such heroic or divine representations are common in the provinces only at Alexandria, in the second half of his reign. Here, Trajan was even shown with a wreath incorporating corn ears (Figure 6.31), a depiction almost unprecedented at Rome.

Coin portraits in the provinces became more innovative than those from Rome in the third century. The emperor might often be shown in a military pose, holding a spear and a shield, and wearing armour. He often faces left, rather than the more traditional right, as if to emphasise the special nature of the new designs (Figure 7.4). This type of representation was popular in Thrace and Galatia, and seems to have been invented for Caracalla and his brother Geta, in the period in which they were both Augusti (209–11). It was used increasingly thereafter, especially in northern Asia Minor. In this respect, the provinces set the trend for Rome, as it was only in the reign of Gallienus that similar obverses appeared at Rome and the other silver mints.[6]

A novel version of portrait showed the emperor in the act of raising his hand in salutation, another provincial innovation which was not adopted

**Figure 7.4** Severus Alexander, from Byzantium.
The military obverse is accompanied on the reverse by a depiction of the emperor in a triumphal chariot, being crowned with a laurel wreath by a small figure of Victory – perhaps referring to Alexander's victories against the Persians in the east. The inscription around (ΕΠΙ Μ ΑΥΡ ΦΡΟΝΤΩΝΟΣ ΚΑΙ ΑΙΛ ΦΗΣΤΗ) refers to the city official M. Aurelius Fronto and his wife Aelia Festa (see Chapter 4). (*RPC VI*, temporary number 900)

on the coinage at Rome until much later. Fine examples occur for Elagabalus at Cius, and for Severus Alexander at Cyzicus and Bithynium, all of which show the emperor raising his hand holding a sceptre over his shoulder, while Gordian III was shown raising his hand and holding a globe in Moesia, at Odessus, Tomi (Figure 7.5) and Marcianopolis.[7] Most of these examples are geographically restricted, no doubt reflecting local initiatives; but cumulatively they all demonstrate a new fashion for showing the emperor 'in action'.

Radiate portraits also became more common at the time, presumably reflecting the widespread presence of radiate portraits of the emperor on silver coins after the introduction of the new denomination, the antoninianus. It had first appeared at Rome under Caracalla and then became standard from the reign of Gordian III. In the provinces it was used as a variant of imperial portraiture, generally lacking any specific explanation for its presence, and not being used as a denomination marker, as had long been the case on the bronze coins minted at Rome and also for the new silver coins.

One of the most controversial emperors was the teenage Elagabalus (218–22), whose reign marked a departure from the traditional state religion and a new focus on the worship of the Sun God, which he placed even above Jupiter. We might have expected unusual images for him, but in general his representations do not stand out from the normal run of

**Figure 7.5** The divine ruler as protector of the empire.
At Tomi in Moesia, Gordian III is shown on the obverse in military uniform, and wearing a radiate crown. He raises his right hand, and holds a globe in his left. On the reverse, he is shown riding on a horse and spearing an enemy on the ground, who wears a Persian head-dress, The divine emperor, who holds the world in his hand, raises his hand in greeting, while on the reverse he fulfils his military duties protecting the Empire, in this case in response to the invasion of the Empire by Shapur, the King of Persia. (*RPC VII.2*, 1676)

provincial coin portraiture. There is no sign – even at his birthplace Emesa – of the 'horn' (in reality, a cultic symbol, of a disputed nature),[8] which appears regularly at Rome on coins and medals towards the end of his reign. There are, however, some signs of his religious departure from the Roman norm. The establishment of a festival of the god Sol Elagabal is celebrated on the coins of Sardis, as it was at Rome.[9] The engravers at Sardis looked partly to Roman coins for models for the Sun God, as well as developing their own iconography. The facing chariot of the Sun God with the sacred stone (the symbol of the Sun God) also appears in Syria, at Claudia Leucas, where, for this reign, it replaces the traditional god of the city. The design of a processional chariot with the stone was used at Rome, and was copied at several cities: Prusias ad Hypium, Juliopolis, Ephesus and Hierapolis. Related frontal depictions of the chariot, perhaps also copied from a rare type at Rome, occur further to the south-east, at Anazarbus, Hierapolis-Castabala, Laodicea ad Mare, Neapolis in Samaria, Jerusalem (Aelia Capitolina) and Alexandria. Emesa itself was more restrained: its coinage celebrated the 'Pythian Games of the Sun' (ΗΛΙΑ ΠΥΘΙΑ) with prize crowns, as well as the eagle and sacred stone (the local symbol of the Sun God). The geographical spread of these representations is very wide, showing that Elagabalus' innovations (and a specific knowledge of some of his coins from Rome) were known far and wide, and not restricted to cities he might have visited on his way to Rome. It has also been suggested that they may indicate that the cities in question had also introduced the cult of Elagabal.[10]

Some unusual and rare portraits of Elagabalus' grandmother, Julia Maesa, and his first wife, Julia Paula, show them extending a hand holding a poppy (Figure 7.6).[11] The precise significance of the image is not known, although it suggests a more traditional association with Demeter (compare Figure 5.14), rather than any controversial novelty. Paula usually faces left, and Maesa right, as if to distinguish them. They all occur in a small area of northern Asia Minor, and are all made from a small group of shared dies.[12] At one city (Prusias ad Hypium), the bust is paired with a reverse showing the Emesan stone in a quadriga. At Tium, it is paired with a sacrificial scene of Elagabalus, Maesa and Paula, accompanied by the acclamation ΕΙΣ ΑΙΩΝΑ ΤΟ ΚΡΑΤΟΣ ('Power for ever!'),[13] a record of a celebration of Elagabalus' accession, if not an actual visit.

The designs used in general on the reverses of the coinage also changed during the third century. The person of the emperor becomes more common. A frequent scene shows him on a horse and raising a hand in

**Figure 7.6** Coins of Tium, in north-west Asia Minor, show a portrait of Julia Maesa, the grandmother of Elagabalus (218–22), holding a poppy flower. The poppy is normally a symbol of Demeter or Kore, and the coins of Amastris have been interpreted in this way (Kettenhofen 1979, 149). Much earlier Punic coins had copied coins with Persephone, sometimes with a poppy, to depict Tanit, and, according to Herodian (5.6.4), Elagabalus had the Emesan god marry her equivalent, the Carthaginian Urania. This seems rather far-fetched, however, and the significance of the representation awaits a convincing explanation. The reverse shows the personifications of the Council (*Boule*) and People (*Demos*) of Tium clasping hands.

salutation. This type had first started to appear under Trajan (at Alexandria, where Roman influence was strongest), but it became more common in the third century. Narrative also became a feature of some reverse designs, and a special group consists of those that involve the emperor; a number of scenes might run across several different coins. Exceptional examples of this approach are provided by the coinage of Pergamum and Laodicea, prompted by the presence of the emperor Caracalla in Asia Minor on his way to the Persian war (Figures 7.7–7.9).[14] Caracalla gave Pergamum great honours, in particular the award of a third neocorate temple. The coins of Pergamum show the arrival of the emperor, and how his arrival was greeted by the citizens of the city. He is also shown giving a speech, and visiting the famous temple of Asclepius, before which he is shown sacrificing a bull. He also makes an offering before two military standards.

Caracalla also restored to the city of Laodicea the right to a neocorate temple, which it seems previously to have lost. A series of coins at Laodicea depict the emperor's real arrival in a chariot of horses, and his symbolic arrival like a god in chariots of centaurs, elephants or lions. He is greeted by the city's principal gods, Zeus and Asclepius, and he is shown sacrificing before a temple, with a crowd of people in attendance (Figure 7.9). A related scene is the aerial view of the colonnaded agora of the city (see front cover).

**Figures 7.7–7.8** Caracalla at Pergamum and Laodicea.
The coin of Pergamum shows Caracalla standing before the temple of Asclepius, the principal deity of the city; before him, an attendant is about to sacrifice a bull, perhaps in thanks for Caracalla's recovery from illness. The coin of Laodicea has a most extraordinary expression of the city's adulation: Land (with corn ears) and Sea (with a dolphin) hold up a radiate statue of the emperor above an imperial eagle, which holds a figure of Victory in its talons.[15]

It is lined with the emperor's bodyguard, and the emperor himself stands on the steps of temple – presumably the neocorate temple – while the citizens approach him and raise their hands in acclamation.

As described in Chapter 5, the award of a neocorate temple was celebrated only patchily on the coinage during the first and second centuries. Depictions of neocorate temples were rare in the second century,[16] becoming relatively common only at Cyzicus and even then only long after the title

**Figure 7.9** Caracalla at Laodicea.
The coins of the Asiarch L. Aelius Pigres show Caracalla, veiled in a religious act, holding patera over tripod, and about to make an offering. Two other togate figures stand behind him (perhaps his entourage) and four other figures, perhaps including a woman, are shown to the left, perhaps representing the inhabitants of the city. One of them holds a banner with the word OMONOIA ('Concord'), and another raises an axe to sacrifice a bull. The temple in the background is shown with eight columns, but its deity is uncertain.

had been awarded under Hadrian. This changed in the third century, as perhaps is to be expected. The use of the title became much more common,[17] and it was used as a regular feature on coins of several cities.[18] The award of a third neocorate by Caracalla prompted Nicomedia to start using the title frequently in its coin legends, grandly so ('three times neokoros'), and to depict the three temples on its coinage (Figure 7.10). More were awarded in the third century.[19] The politics of neocorate awards became more complicated with the reign of Elagabalus, as some of his many awards were subsequently withdrawn (Philippopolis, Beroea, Miletus, Ephesus, Sardis, perhaps Hierapolis, Nicomedia), but the honour of a neocorate was a common theme throughout the third century.

As well as depicting a temple, a neocorate legend might often also be accompanied by a design referring to games, although there was only a loose connection between the award of a neocorate temple and the establishment of new games.[20]

Games, which all had a religious character (unlike games today), became an increasingly common theme on the coinage of the third century. Often the name of the games was added, such as the *Kendreiseia Pythia* at

**Figure 7.10** Coins of Elagabalus from Nicomedia celebrate its award of three neocorate temples for Augustus, Septimius Severus and Elagabalus. The temples of Augustus (and Roma) and Septimius are shown to the sides, and the one in the middle has a figure of the goddess Demeter (hence the inscription ΔΗΜΗΤΡΙΑ, referring to the festival in her honour). Demeter was the patron goddess of the city, and it seems that her temple was adapted to house the cult of Elagabalus. It became a temple of Demeter and Elagabalus, just as the first temple was of Augustus and Roma. (*RPC VI*, temporary number 3354)

### Box 7.1 Games on third-century coins

Games came to form a frequent part of the iconography of the coins of the third century, as can be seen from the growing number of cities which deployed a prize crown (on which see Rumscheid 2000) on their coinage for a selection of emperors (not a complete list). The idea of depicting prize crowns originally started in Greece during the second century, before spreading into the province of Asia in the early third century, and later to the cities of southern Asia Minor.

| | |
|---|---|
| Claudius | 1 |
| Trajan | 1 |
| Hadrian | 3 |
| Pius | 5 |
| Aurelius | 2 |
| Commodus | 4 |
| Alexander | 17 |
| Philip | 14 |

**Figure 7.11** Prize crowns at Side.
Coins of Valerian from 'neocorate Side' (CIΔHC NEΩKOPOY) in southern Asia Minor depict two prize crowns on a base. Such crowns might be worn on the head of the victorious athlete. The inscription records the two festivals (the Sacred Pythia and the Sacred Mystery (IEPA ΠΥΘΙΑ, ΙΕΡΟC ΜΥCΤΙΚΟC), both of which were 'worldwide' (ΟΙΚΟΥΜΕΝΙΚΟΙ). In front of the portrait the original number IA = 11 has been altered by countermarking to Ɛ = 5.

Philippopolis. Sometimes a profusion of names may occur. The *Oikoumenika* ('worldwide'), *Chrysanthina* ('golden flowers'), *Aleia Elagabalia* ('of Sol Elagabal'), *Koraia Aktia* ('Actian games for Kore'), are all named on coins of Elagabalus from Sardis, for the principal cults of Kore and (at the time) Sol Elagabal.[21] There are also related 'active' designs, such as the depiction of an athlete, sometimes choosing a lot or crowning himself. Such scenes became more common in the same areas during the third century, and at some cities elaborate series of types referring to games were devised, as at Ancyra under Caracalla or Philippopolis under Elagabalus.

Many of the inscriptions on the coinage retained their traditional aspect, but there was much greater variation, and sometimes they became cluttered with many words and abbreviations (Figure 7.12). The longer legends were almost slogans, rather than just a means of identifying the city, while the personal names and titles of city officials are often set out at great length (Figure 7.13).

The typology of the designs also went in other new directions. The insecurity of the age is reflected in the appearance of an increasing number of defensive structures on the coinage, especially near the Danube frontier, at cities like Marcianopolis or Bizya (Figure 7.14),[22] while further east Caesarea in Cappadocia declared itself as being ΕΝΤΙΧΙΟΝ ('walled') in the reign of Gordian.

## 7.1 Political and Security Problems

**Figure 7.12** Elagabalus, Laodicea (Asia).
The reverse is inscribed ΚΟΜΟΔΟΥ ΚΕ ΑΝΤΩΝΕΙΝΟΥ ΛΑΟΔΙΚΕΩΝ ΝΕΩΚΟΡΩΝ ΔΟΓΜΑΤΙ ϹΥΝΚΛΗΤΟΥ ('Laodicea, neocorate for Commodus and Elagabalus, by decree of the Senate'), referring to the two neocorate temples granted to the city by Commodus and then Elagabalus. It shows the emperor standing in military dress between two seated captives. He holds a small statue of Zeus (the patron deity of Laodicea) and rests on a spear, while being crowned with a wreath by an eagle. (*RPC VI*, temporary number 5498)

**Figure 7.13** Trajan Decius, Philadelphia.
The inscription on the reverse gives the names and title of the city ΦΛ ΦΙΛΑΔΕΛΦΕΩΝ ΝΕΩΚΟΡΩΝ ('Flavian neocorate Philadelphia') and spells out the name and titles of the city magistrate: 'under S. Aur. Rufinus Poll. the younger, son of Caius, first archon for the second time' (ΕΠΙ Ϲ ΑΥΡ ΡΟΥΦΕΙΝΟΥ ΠΩΛΛ Β ΓΑΟΥ ΑΡΧ Α ΤΟ Β, ΦΛ ΦΙΛΑΔΕΛΦΕΩΝ ΝΕΩΚΟΡΩΝ). The reverse probably shows Heracles with the dead Nemean lion. (*RPC IX*, 716)

**Figure 7.14** Coins of Philip from Bizya in Thrace (in European Turkey) give a simplified bird's eye view of the city.
We can see the city wall with ten towers and the city gate. The gate is decorated with a gallery of seven arches containing statues, and is surmounted by Victory in a chariot. At a lower level, to the left of the gate, is a relief of a Thracian rider; on the right is a relief with several standing figures. Inside the city can be seen several buildings and columns. (*RPC VIII*, temporary number 306)

There were some complicated depictions of the emperor (*cf.* Figure 7.8), and the static representations of the past were complemented with a greater use of a narrative approach. The designs sometimes started to tell stories, rather than simply representing frozen references to cult figures or mythology. Spectacular examples can be found at Apamea and Abydus (Figures 7.15–7.17), while Tyre showed various scenes about the mythical Queen Dido: taking ship from her original home city of Tyre, seated on a throne, and supervising the construction of the city walls or the temple of Heracles at the new city of Carthage (Figure 6.26).

There are also signs of the way that the coinage was becoming more 'emotional', in the sense that it might express a direct interaction with the viewer. An example is the instance of the first person pronoun at Neapolis ad Harpasum in the reign of Maximinus: two *grammateis*, Aur. Dionysios and M. Aur Dionysios the younger, both proclaimed how 'I dedicated' the coinage, using the form ΑΝΕΘΗΚΑ, rather than the usual ΑΝΕΘΗΚΕ (he dedicated), which had previously been the norm.

Slightly more common, though still very rare, is the related occurrence of acclamations on the coinage. These start to appear a little earlier, in the later part of the second century, and embody the direct interaction of the citizens

**Figure 7.15** Noah's Ark.
Noah's Ark appears on the coinage of Apamea, in Phrygia, from Septimius Severus to Trebonianus Gallus, reflecting a belief that the presence of a religious community which believed the ark had come to rest nearby after the great flood. Two scenes are combined into one narrative: on the right Noah (ΝΩΕ) and his wife are first seen sailing in the ark, and then standing on dry land after the flood, when the dove had returned with an olive leaf. Mairat 2017 pointed out how the use of Noah's ark represents a fusion of local and of biblical myth, since Kibotos (one of the names of Apamea) is the Greek word also used to denote 'ark'. (*RPC VIII*, temporary number 1630)

of a city with the emperor. In doing so, they import the language of acclamations, otherwise not used on coinage, such as the word κύριος ('lord') to refer to the emperor, or the verb βασιλεύειν ('to be king', i.e., emperor) to refer to his reign. They are rare examples of 'performative speech' on coins, in the sense of the way that the emperor is addressed directly by his subjects (Figure 7.18). Different formulae are used, such as ΙC ΕΩΝΑ ΤΟΥC ΚΥΡΙΟΥC ΕΠ ΑΓΑΘΩ ('the Lords for ever for the good'), or the spectacular CΕΥΟΥΗΡΟΥ ΒΑCΙΛΕΥΟΝΤΟC Ο ΚΟCΜΟC ΕΥΤΥΧΙ ΜΑΚΑΡΙΟΙ ΝΙΚΟΜΗΔΕΙC ΔΙC ΝΕΩΚΟΡΟΙ ('under the rule of Severus, the universe prospers! And blessed (are) the citizens of Nicomedia, twice *neocorate*!').[23]

In all these ways, the character of the provincial coinage had developed away from its predecessors. The coinage became more engaged with the real world of the emperor and the events like temples or games in the cities. The tone of the inscriptions became more strident, as the engravers crammed more words onto their coin dies, in response to a wish by the cities and its elite members to proclaim their prominence more emphatically. As the Empire was beset by invasions and as emperors were replaced more

**Figures 7.16–7.17** Myth and history at Abydus.
Two contemporary coins from Abydus were struck for Septimius Severus, and reflect the way in which history and myth were used to draw attention to a city. One shows the tragic love story of Hero and Leander. Leander would swim each night across the strait of the Hellespont to see her and, in the early morning, swim back to Abydus. To guide him in this dangerous journey, Hero would climb a tower with a lamp. One night, during a bad storm, the lamp was blown out, and Leander drowned having lost his way. Hero committed suicide when she saw the dead body. The other shows Alexander the Great standing on the prow of galley, holding a spear and extending his hand, with two soldiers behind him. Another galley carries a seated figure of Athena, while a herald blows a trumpet from the top of a tower. Thus was Alexander's crossing from Europe to Asia celebrated 500 years after the event.

frequently, a greater sense of insecurity pervaded the cities, and was reflected by the need to make their claims more emphatic. The provincial coins suggest that the 'crisis' of the third century was not just one of the Empire's security and its economy, but also affected the mentality of the elites who governed the cities, and who were also becoming increasingly uncertain in a changing world.

**Figure 7.18** An acclamation for the emperors at Prusias ad Hypium, Bithynia. The reverse shows Caracalla's father, the emperor Septimius Severus, standing between his sons Caracalla and Geta. The inscription reads IC ЄΩNA TOYC KYPIOYC ('Long Life to Our Lords!') The same scene and inscription occurs at far away Tavium in Galatia, and both must presumably reflect a standard imperial iconography.

## 7.2 Economic and Monetary Problems

The changes to the centrally minted gold and silver coinages of the third century were described in Chapter 1. In two generations, silver saw a catastrophic collapse in fineness from 45 per cent pure to less than 1 per cent, and even gold coins became lighter and debased in the 250s. At the same time, smaller bronze denominations fell out of use: no semisses or quadrantes had been made at Rome since the middle of the second century, and by the third century, the principal bronze coin there was the sestertius, rather than the smaller dupondius or as. Sestertii minted by emperors such as Severus Alexander (222–35), Gordian III (238–44) and Philip (244–9) survive in large numbers today, suggesting that they were minted in very large quantities. Did similar changes also take place in the eastern provinces?

The minting of silver in the provinces had declined greatly by the third century. By then, no silver was minted in Greece or the Roman province of Asia. Almost no silver was minted in Egypt for thirty years until 219. Thereafter it continued down to the reign of Diocletian, but its products were made from a very debased alloy of silver and copper. In Syria silver tetradrachms were made in the Severan period, and thereafter episodically at Antioch, but they ceased in 253. The silver mint at Caesarea in Cappadocia stopped for twenty years after Macrinus, and then ceased forever after a brief resumption under Gordian III.

**238**  7 'From a kingdom of gold to one of iron and rust'

A lack of metallurgical data currently makes it difficult to assess the impact of central changes on the provincial silver. The introduction of the antoninianus under Caracalla might be connected with the large amount of Syrian silver minted at the time, and the silver coinage of Caesarea was also reformed, introducing a new set of denominations. But at the moment the details escape us. The reforms of the silver, however, had an effect on the provincial bronze coinage, which underwent a number of changes.

## 7.2.1  The Volume of Provincial Coinage

It was seen in Chapter 6 that the Severan period had seen an increase in the number of cities producing coin (Box 6.1),[24] but it seems to have continued at much the same level until the end of the civic coinage in the early 260s (Box 7.2).

It is worth emphasising that this does not mean that the volume of coinage remained the same, only that the regularity with which individual cities, taken as a whole, decided to issue coinage remained largely the same.

---

**Box 7.2  Calculating the output of provincial coins in the third century CE**

Box 6.1 seemed to imply an increase in the number of cities issuing coinage after the reign of Severus Alexander, but this is statistically misleading. A short period (such as those of *RPC VII, VIII, IX* and *X*) will distort the annualised figure, since a city which produced regularly will 'score' more highly than would be the case if one were to take a longer period (Johnston 1984b: 245). If we aggregate some of the third-century periods and look at the coinage in blocks of approximately 20–25 years, as in the table in this box, then, presented in this way, one can see that there seems no significant change over the period of the first half of the third century. The resulting annual 'index' at the bottom of the table is calculated by dividing the number of cities by the number of years in each period, and rounding the result. The data for *RPC V* are not yet complete (hence ++ in the table). *RPC X* is deemed here to cover only ten years as most cities had stopped minting by early in the sole reign of Gallienus (see Section 7.4.1 for more detail).

## Box 7.2 (cont.)

The number of coin-issuing cities in the eastern Empire during the third century

| RPC | V | VI | VII–X |
|---|---|---|---|
| **Period** | **193–218** | **218–238** | **238–60** |
| Achaea | *c.* 44 | 2 | 4 |
| Macedonia | 8 | 9 | 10 |
| Thrace | 24 | 7 | 12 |
| Moesia | 7 | 7 | 9 |
| Bithynia-Pontus | 8 | 14 | 15 |
| Asia | 169++ | 111 | 122 |
| Lycia-Pamphylia | 32 | 32 | 62 |
| Galatia-Cappadocia | 5 | 10 | 10 |
| Cilicia | 16 | 29 | 28 |
| Cyprus | 1 | – | – |
| Syria and Judaea | 37 | 48 | 26 |
| Arabia etc. | 10 | 16 | 3 |
| Egypt | 1 | 1 | 1 |
| *Totals* | *c.* 362 | 286 | 302 |
| *Number of years* | 25 | 20 | 25 |
| *Index by year* | 14++ | 14 | 12 |

The raw overall figures disguise the great variations in some areas that took place from time to time. There had been a surge in the number of cities in Greece producing coins in the Severan period,[25] and similarly, as discussed in Chapter 5, the group of twenty Lycian cities which issued coins for Gordian III had never done so before, nor were they to do so ever again.

Cities in the province of Asia had predominated in the second century. Some 40 per cent of the cities which produced coins were located there, and this pattern continued until the end of the coinage.[26] However, a smaller proportion of cities in Europe coined in the third century, the number dropping from about 15 per cent to about 10 per cent of the total, and a similar pattern is observable in north-west Asia Minor. Conversely, more cities in southern Asia Minor (the province of Lycia-Pamphylia) made coins, rising from about 10 per cent of the total in the second century to about 20 per cent in the third, and there was a similar, though smaller, increase in Cilicia (from about 10 to about 15 per cent of the total). There is

**240** 7 'From a kingdom of gold to one of iron and rust'

no obvious explanation of this shift to the south of Asia Minor (which did not affect the Levant), which has also been observed in the pattern of die-sharing.[27] For some reason, communities in southern Asia wanted to express their identity through coinage more than those further north.

Was more coinage produced by the cities in the third century, so increasing the amount of money in circulation? Third-century provincial coinage survives in large quantities today, as a glance at any museum collection or auction catalogue demonstrates. However, the coins have more designs and so have been collected in greater numbers by museums, and it is easier to find die identities between them than between earlier coins. These considerations raise the question of whether or not third-century provincial coinage was made in greater quantities than previously. It is, however, a very difficult question to answer.[28]

The obvious place to start is to look at the number of dies in use, although we should remember that the average output of dies might vary considerably. But few relevant die studies have been made. Figures have been used to show a considerable increase in the number of dies used from the first to the third centuries (for Perinthus, Byzantium, Colophon, Magnesia, Sardis and Antioch in Pisidia),[29] and a similar picture has recently been found for a number of Lydian cities. However, there is wide variation in the figures, and the pattern at Smyrna is very different (Box 7.3).

The figures show that, for Smyrna, far more dies are likely to have been used in the first century (well over 300), than in the second (some 150) or third centuries (over 200). The pattern identified for Lydia is different with about 300, about 1,000, and then almost 1,200. The figures for Smyrna suggest a decline over the period, but those for Lydia suggest the exact opposite, with a big increase, especially in the second and third centuries.[30] However, there was a rapid tailing off in Lydia after 235, as indeed one would expect from the pattern, discussed below, of the end of minting in Lydia.

The contradiction in these figures suggests that the volume of coinage varied enormously from one part of the province of Asia to another. There is some plausibility to this picture, since, as we have seen, minting in areas such as Moesia and southern Asia Minor increased greatly in the third century. If that is correct, and, assuming that the figures are credible, then it makes any attempt to measure the overall volume very problematic.

Another attempt could be made by looking at the representation of coins in the principal ('core') collections used in *RPC*, a device intended to provide some sort of index of output, despite the many qualifications which have been made of this approach (Box 7.4).[31]

## Box 7.3

Obverse dies used by Smyrna and in Lydia (based on Klose 1987: 100–2; and Hochard 2020: 544, 548, 581, 616 and 651). The table uses the 'simple' Esty formula

$$e = (n^*d)/(n-d)$$

where $n$ = number of specimens; $d$ = number of dies observed in $n$; and $e$ = the estimated total number of dies originally made.

Obverse dies used by Smyrna and in Lydia

|  | Smyrna | | | Lydia | | |
|---|---|---|---|---|---|---|
| *RPC* | *n* | *d* | *e* | *n* | *d* | *e* |
| *I* | 1031 | 191 | 234 | 847 | 144 | 173 |
| *II* | 520 | 82 | 97 | 429 | 107 | 143 |
| *III* | 308 | 46 | 54 | 842 | 286 | 433 |
| *IV* | 779 | 95 | 108 | 1258 | 392 | 569 |
| *V* | 913 | 50 | 153 | 1544 | 428 | 592 |
| *VI* | 203 | 15 | 16 | 1018 | 277 | 381 |
| *VII* | 584 | 19 | 20 | 311 | 55 | 67 |
| *VIII* | 76 | 4 | 4 | 261 | 54 | 68 |
| *IX* | – | – | – | 197 | 39 | 49 |
| *X* | 547 | 36 | 39 | 324 | 48 | 56 |

The three groups of roughly datable coins listed on Klose 1987: 102 have been arbitrarily assigned to the Antonine, Severan and Valerianic periods. The table also shows that the third-century coinage of Smyrna has survived in much greater quantities than its predecessor, presumably because it circulated for a shorter time. A similar picture could be drawn for Pamphylia, using the figures in Watson (2019a: 568).

## Box 7.4

The numbers of coins for each *RPC* volume from the 'core collections' (a), and divided by the number of years (b) covered by each volume, are used to give a figure for the number of coin per year (c). A problem arises from the increasing diversity of the designs used on the coinage: this means that museums will tend to collect more specimens, to reflect the greater number of designs. However, an allowance can be made by adjusting the annual figure by the number of recorded types (d), to

**242** 7 'From a kingdom of gold to one of iron and rust'

---

## Box 7.4 (cont.)

produce an 'Index' (e: calculated as the average annual figure for the core collections divided by the number of recorded types, and then multiplied by 1,000 to give a whole number). In addition, it can be seen that third-century coins have survived in greater numbers than their predecessors, as can be seen by the ratio of coins to dies.

The numbers of coins for each RPC volume from the 'core collections'

| RPC Vol. | Date | a | b | c | d | e |
|---|---|---|---|---|---|---|
| | | Core specimens | Years | a/b | Types | (c/d)×1000 |
| *I* | 44 BCE–69 CE | n/a | – | – | – | – |
| *II* | 69–96 | 7,075 | 27 | 262 | 2422 | 108 |
| *III* | 96–138 | 19,723 | 42 | 470 | 7595 | 62 |
| *IV.1* | 138–192 | 32,567 | 52 | 626 | 14916 | 42 |
| *V* | 193–218 | n/a | – | – | – | – |
| *VI* | 218–238 | 17,785 | 20 | 889 | 9199 | 97 |
| *VII* | 238–244 | 11,129 | 6 | 1854 | 4971 | 372 |
| *VIII* | 244–249 | 8,806 | 5 | 1761 | 3202 | 550 |
| *IX* | 249–253 | 5,672 | 4 | 1418 | 2399 | 591 |
| *X* | 253–297 | n/a | – | – | – | – |

*RPC I* is not included, because of the difficulty of disaggregating the western city coinages; the data for *RPC V* and *X* are omitted, since their databases are not fully populated.

---

The figures appear once again to show a big increase from the first to the third century. However, caution is clearly needed and the future estimations of volume will depend on the completion of more die studies.[32] No definite conclusion, then, can yet been drawn about the relative volume of coinage minted at different periods, but it seems plausible to think that the output of city coinages was greater in the first half of the third century than it had been previously, and in that respect mirrored the large-scale production of sestertii at Rome. At the same time, however, it contrasts with the decline of private civic benefactions, both in general and for coinage.[33] Some other mechanism must have been behind this increased production, and it is tempting to see it as a reflection of an increase in the amount of coinage in circulation, visible also in the increasing amounts of 'silver' coinage minted and in circulation at the time.

## 7.2.2 Declining Weight Standards and Revaluations

At the same time, the weight standards of the civic bronze coinages declined and the denominations used grew larger. The best evidence comes from the rare cases where a city regularly put value marks on its coinage over a period of time. Four clear cases are provided by Sparta and Argos in Greece, by Tomi in Moesia and Amastris in northern Asia.

Spartan coinage shows a doubling of the weight standard just before 180, followed by a decline of weight, and the introduction of new, higher-value coins, the new 6- and 8-as coins under Gallienus (Box 7.5).

A different pattern can be found at nearby Argos, also in the Peloponnese and less than 70 km away. The denominations appear to be quite stable from the second century to about 230, more or less maintaining their diameters and having gently declining weights. After Alexander, the pattern is harder to determine, as there are not many surviving specimens. However, we can see that there seems to have been some sort of reduction in the standard during the reign of Gordian, when the value marks 4 and 3

7.19

7.20

**Figures 7.19–7.20** Coins of Sparta with value marks.
The coin of Julia Domna, showing a figure of Heracles (7.19), has the value mark Aς Δ = 4 *assaria*, while that of Gallienus, showing the two Dioscuri (7.20), has H A = 8 *assaria*.

## Box 7.5 Value marks on coins of Sparta

The late imperial coinage of Sparta is marked with values expressed in amounts of the AC = *as*.

The late imperial coinage of Sparta

| Value | 1 | 2 | |
|---|---|---|---|
| **Aurelius, unmarked** | 20 mm/5.05 g (22) | 25 mm/9.42 g (28) | |
| **Commodus Caesar, marked AC B** | 25 mm/9.92 g (3) | | |
| **(revaluation)** | 4 | | |
| **Commodus, marked AC Δ** | 25 mm/10.99 g (3) | | |
| **Severus, marked AC Δ** | 25 mm/9.18 g (21) | | |
| | 4 | 6 | 8 |
| **Gallienus, marked AC Δ, ς or H** | 24 mm/*c.* 8 g (41) | 24 mm/*c.* 10 g (22) | 28 mm/*c.* 12 g (52) |

The data are from Grunauer-von Hoerschelmann 1978: 94–6; Johnston 2007: 229 Table 69.

also appeared. It may, in fact, have been a second reduction since the heavier weight for the early specimens of Gordian III seems to imply a change from what had preceded.

After Gordian, no coins were made until the time of Valerian and Gallienus. What happened then is not entirely clear, since not many specimens survive. The numerals attest a strange range of values – 15, 11,[34] 7, 6, 4 and 3. A plausible scheme for the issues has been proposed, although the similar diameters make it hard to be sure exactly where each denomination fits in. Further specimens may clarify the pattern, but it is already clear that there was a rapid fall in size, coupled with a rapid increase in values. The speed of change is shown also by the obverse die-links between different denominations and series, even though they should ostensibly have been made at different diameters.

At Tomi in Moesia, the coins declined in weight from the second to the third century, and then stabilised, before the coinage came to an end under Philip.

Amastris in Paphlagonia marked its coins with the value mark H = 8 for most of the third century. They show a similar decline at first, followed by a steep drop under Gallienus. Other increases also took place in northern Asia Minor in the 260s: for example, coins valued at 8 were then countermarked with 10.[35] The highest values recorded anywhere are the countermarks of 24, 16, 12 and 8 (presumably asses?) applied in Bithynia, at Prusias ad Hypium, probably in the late 250s.[36]

A typical pattern In Asia was for values to be doubled after 260: for instance, at Smyrna coins with a likely value of 2 and 4 in the early third century were countermarked with values of 4 and 6 after 260.[37] The countermark B (GIC 765) on different denominations at Aphrodisias probably means precisely '× 2'.[38]

Further south, in the 'Pamphylian' region, new value marks were introduced under Philip: 5 at Side and 6 at Perge. The reign of Valerian saw the production of coins valued at 6, 8 and 11 at Side and 10 at Perge; the coins of 6 and 8 were soon abandoned, and 12 was adopted at Side after 260.[39] At cities such as Perge and Side, a common pattern can be seen, whereby, at the very beginning of the joint reign of Valerian and Gallienus (253–60), the same denominations and weight standards were in force as had been used previously.[40] This was followed shortly afterwards by the introduction of coins marked with higher value, and then followed by coins of the same higher values but at a lower weight standard.

For Syria, the bronze coinage of Antioch shows a pronounced decline at the beginning of the third century, with the introduction of new, larger

**Figure 7.21** A bronze denarius?
Sinope in northern Asia Minor minted coins for Gallienus in the 330th year of the colony = 260/1, many of which have a 'star' on the reverse. Rather than being a star, it may well be the sign for a denarius (X) (*pace* Johnston 2007, 190). The reverse depicts a figure of Neptune.

## Box 7.6 New values under Valerian in Southern Asia Minor

Although coins marked 5 first appeared in the reign of Philip at Side,[41] all the other higher marks appeared later, from the reign of Valerian:

| Value | Cities |
|---|---|
| 6 | Selge, Perge, Side, Hierapolis, Sagalassus, Carallia, Syedra, Conana, Termessus (?), Colybrassus, Lyrbe, Timbriada, Codrula |
| 7 | Irenopolis |
| 8 | Side, Carallia, Coracesium, Laerte, Syedra, Iotape, Irenopolis, Etenna, Aspendus, Attalea, Lyrbe, Colybrassus, Adada, Selge |
| 9 | Conana, Pednelissus, Termessus, Side |
| 10 | Ariassus, Isinda, Sagalassus, Attalea, Perge, Sillyum, Magydus, Panemoteichus, Pogla, Side |
| 11 | Etenna, Aspendus, Side, Casae, Colybrassus, Coracesium, Laerte, Lyrbe, Syedra, Attalea, Carallia |
| 12 | Adada, Side, Lyrbe, Colybrassus, Selge, Sillyum. |

The data are from Johnston 2007, omitting the uncertain cases she identified.

denominations under Elagabalus. The coinage then remained stable until it ended early in the reign of Valerian (no coins are known for Gallienus).[42]

All these coinages show declines in weight standards and, in many cases, the introduction of new denominations with higher values. Even though the individual patterns are all different, the changes are particularly apparent in the joint reign of Valerian and Gallienus and the sole reign of Gallienus. This shows that by then the city authorities were struggling with the monetary system, and that its previous stability could no longer be relied on. It is no accident that this is the same period as saw the reductions in weight and fineness of the gold coinage. The monetary system of the Empire was not only under strain, but it was now showing visible cracks.

## 7.3 Fragmentation

The third century saw a greater fragmentation of the provincial coinage, in the sense that changes took place over more limited geographical areas.

There are a number of ways of seeing this. For example, die sharing became more localised after 249.[43] Several cities in southern Asia Minor refer to Rome almost as if it were some foreign city with which an alliance could be formed (see Chapter 6, with Figure 6.23), a sign of an increasing mental distance from Rome.

Fragmentation can be seen in a number of other ways – in the different regional patterns for denominations, patterns which were sometimes subject to great local variation; in the localised production of coins of different shapes and sizes; and in problems of the supply of coinage, which led to regional mints being set up in new locations.

## 7.3.1 Regional Variations in Declining Standards

The way that the coins of Sparta, Argos, Tomi and Amastris all showed a decline in standards, but did so in different ways, was mirrored across the whole empire, although we do not have such detailed data about other cases. As the changes took place, they broke up the generally uniform appearance of the earlier city coinages and led to alternative approaches. They were

---

**Box 7.7**

An example of the declining weights of coins of the same denomination (as defined by the consistent use of the same types) is the coinage of Smyrna.

The declining weights of coins

| | Eagle etc | Heracles etc | Nemeseis etc | Amazon etc | Cybele etc |
|---|---|---|---|---|---|
| **Septimius Severus** | 20 mm/ 3–5 g | 22 mm/ 5–9 g | 25 mm/ 6½– 11 g | 30 mm/ 10½– 15½g | 35 mm/17– 27 g |
| **Gordian III** | 19 mm/ 3–4 g | 21 mm/ 4–6½g | 25 mm/5– 8½g | 29 mm/11– 15 g | 34 mm/15– 25 g |
| **Valerian & Gallienus** | 15 mm/ 2½g | 20 mm/ 4 g | 24 mm/ 5½g | 29 mm/10 g | 35 mm/ 17½ g |
| **Gallienus (sole)** | | 19 mm/ 3 g | 21 mm/4 g | 23 mm/6 g | 27 mm/ 8½g |

Adapted from Johnston 2007: 22, Table 3.

broadly defined geographically, and in Asia Minor there were three main approaches:[44]

1. An 'Asian' pattern, whereby the coins retained a similar diameter until the 250s, so that the coins looked the same, but their weights declined. This was the most common pattern in the province of Asia, but it was not confined to Asia.
2. A 'Nicaean' pattern, whereby the diameters and the weights were both reduced, and new denominations were also introduced. This applied to much of northern Asia Minor (especially the province of Bithynia-Pontus). The diameters shrank in the 220s, and by the 240s the coins were half the weight of their Severan predecessors.
3. A 'Pamphylian' pattern, which applied to much of southern Asia Minor, whereby diameter and weight modules were maintained with only small declines. However, new higher denominations were introduced, using the modules previously used for smaller denominations.[45]

7.22

7.23

**Figures 7.22–7.23** Values at Colybrassus.
An issue of coins of the reign of Valerian from Colybrassus in Cilicia have value marks of 11, 8 and 3, a strange set (although 8 + 3 = 11). Here we have coins for Valerian with 11 (showing Athena resting a shield on a column) and for Salonina, the wife of Gallienus, with 3 (showing Hermes).

These three groups were not mutually compatible, as can be seen from some rare instances when coins with marked values travelled from one area to another and were countermarked: some coins of Pisidia and Cilicia struck with value marks of 11, 11 and 8 were subsequently countermarked with values of 3, 4 and 4, respectively, when they went further north into the province of Asia.[46]

## 7.3.2 Local Variations in Declining Standards

It would also be a mistake to over-emphasise the uniformity of these three different areas. Some divergent groups have been identified within Asia:

a. A group of cities using a standard based on 3 (3, 6 and 9), scattered geographically, for example, Aphrodisias, Antioch (Caria), Eumenea and Termessus.[47]
b. A very different standard was used at Ephesus and its hinterland up the Maeander valley after 260, countermarking coins with 1, 2 and 3 (A, B, Γ).[48] The unit of value implied by the countermarks is uncertain but must surely be greater than the *assarion*; alternatives such as obols and sestertii have both been tentatively suggested,[49] and the values might even be expressed in amounts of denarii.[50]

In addition, individual cities within a small region can even show a very different pattern. An example concerns cities in southern Asia Minor in the reigns of Valerian and Gallienus. All added marks of value to their coins, with a rather bewildering range of different denominations (Box 7.8).

Similar local variations took place elsewhere. The examples of Tomi in Moesia and Sparta in the Peloponnese have already been mentioned. Tomi formed part of a group of cities in Thrace and Moesia, which produced coins which look very similar, but were actually made on slightly different standards and in different denominations.[51]

The changes to the monetary system of the third century can, therefore, be seen to have brought about different patterns of response: sometimes there are regional patterns and sometimes a city may have its own system. Each city's freedom to determine its own coinage (see Chapter 4) now brought about inconsistent and – to our minds – very curious results. The decline was common to all areas, but as it gathered pace, it led to a greater fragmentation across the Empire: different regions started to behave in different ways; and even within an area, groups of cities or individual cities might adopt their own, different, strategies.

## Box 7.8
Values present on coins of cities in Pamphylia and Pisidia in the reigns of Valerian and Gallienus

| City | Value | | | | | | | | | | |
|---|---|---|---|---|---|---|---|---|---|---|---|
| | 2 | 3 | 4 | 5 | 6 | 7 | 8 | 9 | 10 | 11 | 12 |
| Aspendus | – | – | – | – | – | – | × | – | × | × | – |
| Attalea | – | × | – | – | – | – | × | – | × | – | – |
| Carallia | – | × | – | – | × | – | × | – | – | × | – |
| Colybrassus 1 | – | × | – | – | – | – | × | – | – | × | – |
| Colybrassus 2 | – | – | – | – | × | – | – | – | – | – | × |
| Coracesium | – | × | – | – | – | – | × | – | – | – | × |
| Isinda 2 | – | × | – | – | – | – | – | – | × | – | – |
| Isinda 3 | – | – | – | – | – | – | – | – | – | × | – |
| Laerte | – | × | – | – | – | – | × | – | – | × | – |
| Lyrbe 1 | – | – | – | – | – | – | × | – | – | × | – |
| Lyrbe 2 | – | – | – | – | – | – | – | – | – | × | – |
| Lyrbe 3 | – | – | – | – | – | – | – | – | – | – | × |
| Magydus 39 | – | × | × | – | – | – | – | – | – | – | – |
| Magydus 40–1 | – | – | – | – | – | – | – | – | × | – | – |
| Perge[*] | – | – | – | – | – | – | – | – | × | – | – |
| Sagalassus[†] | × | – | × | – | × | – | – | – | × | – | – |
| Selge[‡] | – | × | – | – | × | – | – | – | – | – | – |
| Side 2[**] | – | × | – | – | × | – | – | – | – | – | – |
| Side 3–4 | – | – | – | – | – | – | × | – | – | × | – |
| Side 5 | – | – | – | – | – | – | – | – | – | – | × |
| Sillyum[††] | – | – | – | – | – | – | – | – | × | – | – |
| Syedra | – | × | – | – | × | – | × | – | – | × | – |

The data are from Watson 2019a: 17–59, using his periodisation.
* The value 10 continues to Tacitus.
† The values 6 and 10 occur also for Claudius II.
‡ Under Gallienus (sole reign). The mark 12 occurs for Claudius II, and 4, 8 and 12 for Aurelian.
** The mark 10 occurs for Gallienus (sole reign), and 11 for Aurelian.
†† The mark 10 continues for Gallienus (sole reign) and Aurelian.

## 7.3.3 Big and Heavy Coins

One particularly noticeable regional variation, which is a feature of third-century western Asia Minor, is the production of very large and very heavy coins, bigger in both respects than any coins produced at

Rome. There had been some earlier examples, such as the coins for Antinous discussed in Chapter 6 and some other isolated instances (Figure 7.24). It seems quite likely, however, that these examples may have been medallic or commemorative pieces, rather than coins in the sense of currency.

Subsequently more large coins were made. They seem to be high denomination coins rather than just ceremonial, medallic pieces, since they fit well into the denominational structure of the cities that made them. In trying to track this subsequent fashion for big and heavy coins, the somewhat arbitrary criteria have been used of a diameter greater than 35 mm and a weight of several specimens greater than 40 g. Any coins above these limits would be much larger than the largest denomination, the sestertius, produced in the western Empire,[52] and so mark a provincial innovation and departure from the central model.

Under Marcus Aurelius, Nicaea made large and heavy coins, and the habit spread to nearby Prusias ad Hypium. There also was another group, clustering in the central part of western Asia Minor: at Mytilene (again), Pergamum, Acrasus, Thyatira, Phocaea (signed by Attalos), Smyrna (signed by Attalos: the same man?) and Tralles. A very similar group

**Figure 7.24** Large bronze coin minted for Antoninus Pius by Pautalia in Thrace. The very fine portrait on the obverse is accompanied by a scene modelled in high relief on the reverse, showing a standing figure of Heracles. He holds a torch and a club, and is restrained by two small figures of Erotes. In the background can be seen a column surmounted by a statue of Ceres. The scene shows love conquering strength, although its precise origin and significance is unclear. See Thompson 1977 and Grigorova-Gencheva 2011 (who also illustrates a Roman medallion of Pius found in the excavations at Pautalia). (*RPC IV*, temporary number 3925)

produced large coins under Commodus,[53] and five of the nine cities that produced them are linked by the same obverse die (Assus, Mytilene, Pergamum, Thyatira and Silandus).[54] Both the geographical spread and the die links underline how the trend for larger coins was becoming a regional fashion.

The heyday of such large coins was the Severan period, and in the reigns of both Septimius Severus and Caracalla they were made in greater quantities and by a larger number of cities, more than twenty.[55] The distribution of the cities is a little wider, but it still concentrates on the same general area. There are notable absences, such as most of Ionia, Caria and Troas. Subsequent issues became less frequent but remained in the same general area, with a little spread to the south and, from Gordian III, into Thrace.[56]

After the reign of Philip, the number of cases tails off.[57] This is perhaps surprising, given the general increase in the size of denominations that was taking place, but it underlines that the rationale behind the production of these large coins was a fashion, not economic. The restricted geographical zone in which these coins were made is an instance of how the coinage

**Figure 7.25** Gordian III, from Daldis in Lydia.
This enormous coin (diameter 48 mm) has a complex – and rather crude – scene on the reverse. On the right, Perseus is shown walking towards the three Gorgons, who are sleeping under a tree (the small winged figure of Hypnos, the personification of Sleep, is behind them). To the left is a temple of Apollo and a horse. The cult of Apollo is attested for Daldis, so the scene suggests that the city claimed a link with the story of Perseus killing Medusa. (*RPC VII.1*, 200)

## 7.3 Fragmentation 253

began to fragment from the end of the second century, and how different parts started to behave in different ways.

### 7.3.4 Problems of Supply and New Imperial Mints

The supply of coinage in the third century became uneven across the Empire, a reflection of an increasing lack of monetary integration. Very few third-century sestertii and smaller denominations are found in northern Gaul or Britain, while they are plentiful in the Mediterranean provinces. A similar difficulty may have affected Lycia in the reign of Gordian, which prompted the Koinon to organise local minting of bronze (see Chapter 5.3.1).

The same problem seems to have affected Moesia and Dacia, and, as a result, coins were minted in the name of the colony at Viminacium in Moesia (Figure 7.27) and for the Provincia Dacia in the middle of the third century. They supplied a large area of Moesia Superior, Pannonia Superior, Pannonia Inferior and Dacia.[58] The character of these coins was different from that of the city coinages in the east: they were inscribed in Latin, and copied the metrology of Rome. Both coinages were produced in three denominations, probably intended to be sestertii, dupondii and asses.

Although the needs of the cities for bronze coins were still fulfilled by their own local minting, there are signs of problems with silver. The mint of Rome had to help out the local mints of Alexandria and Antioch with special issues of coinage for Severus Alexander and Philip (Figure 7.28).

The supply of silver from the mint of Rome saw a long period of increasing production. The spread of the denarius – and its successor the antoninianus – to Greece, Asia and Syria, was described in Chapter 1. At the same time the proportion of locally produced silver declined, and the resulting increase in the system of supply led to a change in the way that the imperial silver – and eventually gold – was produced, with the monopoly of centralised production in Rome being replaced by a system of more regional supply.

The second half of the third century was marked by the setting up of many new mints for the production of (base) silver radiates (and some gold) (Box 7.9). This is a sign of the increasing fragmentation of the Empire at the time, partly because the frequent periods of warfare made communications more difficult and partly because the production of such debased coins had

**Figures 7.26–7.27** Sestertii from Rome and Viminacium for Gordian III, 239 CE. The first coins of Viminacium looked very similar to those minted at Rome. The mint may have been established by transferring a workshop from Rome to Viminacium, as is suggested by the reduction at Rome at this time from six main reverse types to five. (7.26 *RIC IV.3*, Gordian III 259A; 7.27 *RPC VII.2*, 1)

**Figure 7.28** Syrian tetradrachms minted in Rome.
Silver tetradrachms for Syria were made in 246 at the Mint of Rome (MON VRB at the bottom of the reverse = *Moneta Urbis* = 'Mint of the City [of Rome]'). They were the usual size and shape as coins from Antioch, with the usual Greek inscriptions and designs, but their style shows that their dies were engraved at Rome. (*RPC VIII*, temporary number 2379)

to be on a very large scale, making their transport more challenging. Antioch had made silver denarii (as well as tetradrachms) from time to time in the first and second centuries but from the third century its production became as regular as that of Rome, and it has been shown that it was the sole supplier of silver coinage to the entire province of Syria.[59]

Many of these new mint cities had previously made provincial coins, but, apart from the silver tetradrachms from Antioch, there seems to have been little or no connection between the two coinages, although sometimes the city engravers were re-employed for the new silver coinage.[60] The opening of the new mints matches the closure of the civic mints and the increasing production of debased silver from Rome. From the later third century, the

**Box 7.9**

From the middle of the century, new mints opened every few years, mostly at sites that were well-placed for supplying coinage to the armies defending the frontiers of the Empire (Map 7.1).

New silver mints in the third century

| Rome | already in existence |
|---|---|
| Antioch | already in existence |
| Viminacium | 253 |
| Milan | c. 259 |
| Trier | 260 |
| Siscia | 262 |
| 'SPQR' | c. 266 |
| Cologne | 268 |
| Cyzicus | 268 |
| Lyons | 274 |
| Ticinum | 274 |
| Serdica | 274 |
| Tripolis | 274 |
| (London | 286) |
| Heraclea | c. 293 |
| Alexandria | 295/6 |

The data are from Carson 1990: 250–75, which remains the most helpful summary.

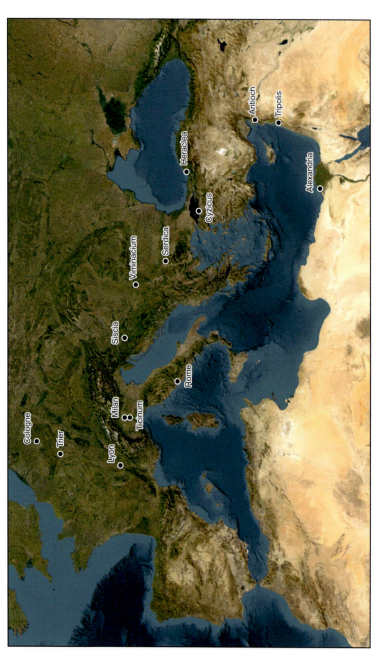

Map 7.1 Silver mints in the late third century CE

## 7.4 The End of Provincial Coinage

### 7.4.1 Survey of Last Issues

At the mint of Rome, bronze coinage petered out and ended in the early 260s.[61] The latest definite date is provided by the coins with VOTIS DECENNALIBVS, which belong in late 262. Some later dates have also been suggested for other types.[62] All such coins, however, were made in small quantities, to judge from their rarity today, far fewer than the big issues of sestertii made in the 240s or the very early 250s.

Sestertii (and double sestertii) were also made in northern Gaul by the usurper Postumus (260–9), and perhaps also by Gallienus in Milan, but in neither case did their production last very long after 260. In Moesia Superior and Dacia, the coinages of Viminacium and Provincia Dacia ended in the joint reign of Valerian and Gallienus, and only small quantities are known for them compared with their predecessors.[63]

The cities in Moesia and of Thrace had mostly stopped before the accession of Valerian, generally ceasing in the reigns of Gordian III and Philip (see Box 7.10). A few cities in the European provinces continued after 253, and the last issues were made sometime in the sole reign of Gallienus at Nicopolis,[64] Dium,[65] Thessalonica,[66] Edessa,[67] Coela, Sestus, Perinthus, and Byzantium.[68] Of these cities, the issues at Perinthus and Coela were not extensive, and those from Thessalonica, Edessa and Sestus are very rare.

In Bithynia and Pontus, most cities seem to have ceased production in the joint reign of Valerian and Gallienus; both Sinope and Nicaea seem to have ceased in 260/1. For the sole reign of Gallienus, coins are very rare for Amastris, Apamea and Prusias ad Hypium, leaving only Heraclea as producing any appreciable amount of coinage in the sole reign, and the limited evidence suggests it did not continue long after 260 (see the table 'The end of coinage in Bithynia-Pontus' on pp. 258–9).

The picture for the province of Asia is less clear, as not all the city coinages have been studied in detail, and so the following discussion will be impressionistic rather than complete. The three biggest mints, Smyrna,[69] Pergamum[70] and Ephesus,[71] all continued into Gallienus'

## The end of coinage in Bithynia-Pontus

| Reign | City | Notes |
| --- | --- | --- |
| **Valerian and Gallienus** | Bithynium-Claudiopolis | Although coins of Gallienus seem somewhat more common than those of Valerian, all the coins of Gallienus look very similar, and their portraits and reverse type match those of Valerian. |
| | Caesarea Germanica | Coins for both Valerian and Gallienus are very rare, and resemble each other closely. |
| | Creteia-Flaviopolis | As previously, coins for both Valerian and Gallienus are very rare, and resemble each other closely. |
| | Tium | Coins for Valerian and Gallienus seem equally common, and resemble each other closely, and can be associated with coins for Saloninus, suggesting a date of 258–60. There are one or two outliers, but both for Valerian and Gallienus. |
| | Cius | Although the coins for Gallienus seem more common than for Valerian, their style seems similar, and the types are shared between them (also with Salonina and Saloninus). The coins of Gallienus generally have a long obverse legend, also suggestive of an early date. |
| | Iuliopolis | The style and reverse types are shared between Valerian and Gallienus, and coins for each occur in similar numbers. |
| | Nicomedia | The coins divide between those celebrating the second neocorate and those the third. The latter group include as many coins for Valerian as for Gallienus, and they are often associated on 'family obverses', some of which included Valerian II (or less, likely, Saloninus).[*] |
| | Prusa ad Olympum | The coins are quite rare, and occur in equal numbers for Valerian and Gallienus. The style seems similar, and most of the reverse types are shared, including one with Valerian II. |

| | | |
|---|---|---|
| **Macrianus** | Heraclea | Includes coins for Macrianus and Quietus (260–61). Coins for Valerian are very rare compared with those for Gallienus, but they all seem to belong together in the joint reign. |
| | Nicaea (260/1) | Includes coins for Macrianus and Quietus (260–61), but otherwise coins for Valerian and Gallienus look similar and share many reverse types.[†] |
| **Gallienus** | Apamea (262) | One die for Gallienus is inscribed COS V = 262. |
| | Amastris | Only three coins recorded, two for Gallienus and one for Salonina. The relatively high-value mark (6) on the coins of Salonina also suggests a late date. |
| | Sinope (to 260/1 CE) | Latest coins recorded are of the year 330 = 260/1, all for Gallienus. |
| | Prusa ad Hypium | Although the coins occur in approximately equal numbers for Valerian and Gallienus, the coins with a gateway and the value mark 8 occur only for Gallienus. They probably belong to the sole reign.[‡] |

[*] Johnston (2007: 132, 137–9) agrees that Nicomedia stopped before 260.
[†] So also, Johnston (2007: 164–5).
[‡] Johnston, however, places them in '?258+' (2007: 148).

**Figure 7.29** The Asian Games at Smyrna.
The latest coins of Smyrna were struck in the sole reign of Gallienus, signed by the *strategos* M. Aur. Sexstos. The elaborate inscription celebrates that Smyrna has three neocorate temples (CMYPNAIΩN Γ NΕΩKOPΩN, around the right-hand side) and that the most important games of the Koinon of Asia were held in Smyrna (ΠΡΩΤΑ ΚΟΙΝΑ ΑϹΙΑϹ ΕΝ ϹΜΥΡΝΗ, in the centre inside the wreath).

sole reign, although it is not clear for how long: only a single magistrate signs the sole reign coins at Smyrna and Pergamum. Sole reign coins of Ephesus are very rare, certainly in comparison with the very abundant issues of the joint reign. Minting, however, was more abundant at Smyrna in the sole reign than it had been in the joint reign, but it had been sparse earlier, under Philip. At Pergamum it seems to have been on about the same scale in both the joint and the sole reigns, to judge from surviving specimens.

Recent studies of the coinage of the region of Lydia, which formed part of the province of Asia, allow a detailed analysis, which shows that coinage continued at a few cities (six, out of a total of thirty-six that minted at any time in the Empire) into the sole reign of Gallienus,[72] but we should not, however, exaggerate the scale of the coinage from Gallienus' sole reign. The coins of two of the cities, Hadrianopolis and Tralles, are very rare today. However, one city in Asia, Cyzicus, continued to produce substantial coinages during and after the sole reign. Five *strategoi* (senior magistrates) signed coins in the sole reign of Gallienus,[73] suggesting a fairly regular production during the eight years of his reign. Cyzicus was also the only city in Asia to produce coins after the reign of Gallienus, in the reign of Claudius II, although coins in his name are rare and all are signed by the same *strategos*, suggesting a short-lived issue.

## 7.4 The End of Provincial Coinage

**Figure 7.30** Perge under Tacitus: The last city coins of the Roman Empire. The very last civic bronze coins were made for the emperor Tacitus (275–6) by the city of Perge. They are very rare today, with fewer than twenty specimens known, and they were struck from only four obverse dies. They may celebrate a visit of the emperor and his grant of the new title of *metropolis* and the grant of a new festival, the *Takitios Metropoleitios*, both of which are celebrated on the coins. The coins all bear the value I = 10. A contemporary inscription acclaims Perge as being 'honoured with silver coinage' (ἡ ἀργυρῷ νομίσματι τετειμημένη) (Rouché 1989), which must surely refer to this exceptional coinage, despite the use of 'silver'. It is perhaps a mistake or an exaggeration (unless ἀργυρωνομίσμα is an elaborate *hapax* just meaning 'coinage'), although other explanations are possible: see Weiss 1991, 379, 383–4.

Apart from Cyzicus (and Alexandria in Egypt), the only cities to make coins after Gallienus were all located in southern Asia Minor. One group, all in the area of inland Pisidia, made coins for Claudius II (268–70): Antioch (Pisidia), Prostanna, Seleucia (Pisidia) and Sagalassus, the last being the most prolific. No city made coins for the short-lived Quintillus (270), but coins were made for Aurelian (270–5) at another group of neighbouring cities, slightly to the south, around Perge:[74] Perge, Side, Sillyum, Cremna and Selge, those of Sillyum and Selge being very rare. The unusual nature of these late issues can be seen from the pattern of the end of city minting in the same area, based on a recent study, which shows that the normal date of cessation was the joint reign of Valerian and Gallienus.[75]

Further east, the productive mint of Caesarea in Cappadocia made its last coins in the reign of Gordian III.[76] A number of cities in Cilicia put dates on their coins according to their city eras, so the last issues can be dated with certainty. All were in the joint reign of Valerian and Gallienus, rather than any later (see the table 'The last city coins of Cilicia' on pp. 262).[77]

## 262 7 'From a kingdom of gold to one of iron and rust'

The last city coins of Cilicia

| City | Era date | CE date |
|---|---|---|
| **Anazarbus** | 272 | 253/4 |
| **Augusta** | 234 | 253/4 |
| **Flaviopolis** | 181 | 253/4 |
| **Epiphanea** | 322 | 254/5 |
| **Anemurium** | 3 | 255/6 |
| **Irenopolis** | 204 | 254/5 |
| **Mopsus** | 323 | 255/6 |
| **Aegeae** | 303 | 256/7 |

As for Syria and Arabia, only a few cities produced coinage after the accession of Valerian, and nearly all seem to have ceased in the joint reign with Gallienus (see the table below, 'The last city coins of Syria and Arabia').

The last city coins of Syria and Arabia

| City | Reign | Notes |
|---|---|---|
| **Antioch** | Valerian (253) | No coins are known for Gallienus, suggesting that the issue was made shortly after Valerian's acclamation as emperor in 253. |
| **Berytus** | Valerian & Gallienus | All the coins of Gallienus have been dated in the joint reign.[*] There are coins for Salonina, perhaps suggesting a date c. 255. |
| **Heliopolis** | Valerian & Gallienus | The coinage has been dated to 256/7 because of an attribution of some coins to Valerian II.[†] However, these are more likely to be coins of Valerian I, thus a date nearer 253 seems more likely. |
| **Damascus** | Valerian & Gallienus | Coins were struck in approximately equal numbers, and they share the same types. There are coins for Salonina, perhaps suggesting a date c. 255. |
| **Tyre** | Valerian & Gallienus | Coins of Valerian seems slightly more common than those of Gallienus, and many of the types are shared. There are coins for Salonina, perhaps suggesting a date c. 255.[‡] |
| **Ptolemais** | Valerian & Gallienus | The coins of Valerian are much more common than those of Gallienus (or Salonina), and most types are shared, and this suggests that coinage did not continue after the death of Valerian.[**] |

## 7.4 The End of Provincial Coinage

(cont.)

| City | Reign | Notes |
| --- | --- | --- |
| **Adraa** | Valerian & Gallienus (256/7) | The very rare coins seem to be in two denominations: the largest for Valerian and the smaller for Gallienus. The coins are dated ANP = year 151 = 256/7 CE. |

\* † By Sawaya 2005.
‡ No opinion was expressed by Rouvier 1904.
\*\* Kadman (1961: 56) says that Ptolemais, as well as Berytus and Tyre, were the only mints to issue coins for Gallienus' sole reign, but he gives no argument.

Alexandria in Egypt continued to make its debased silver coins throughout the later third century, until the reform of Diocletian. The last common 'silver' coins were dated to his year 12 (295/6), and, in the next year, Alexandria started to make the same sort of Latin coins as were made in all the mints of the Empire. This coinage continued as Egypt continued to form a closed currency area until 296, and the 'silver' radiates in use in the rest of the Empire did not circulate there.[78]

Alexandria had minted much bronze coinage, especially in the first and second centuries. Little coinage was minted there in the Severan period, and, thereafter, only a few substantial issues of bronze were

**Figure 7.31** The last provincial coins from Egypt.
The last provincial 'silver' coins were made for Diocletian and his co-emperors in Egypt (Figure 1.31) in 295/6. With the same value as a denarius (by now an obsolete coin, and only a unit of account in the rest of the Empire) they contained no silver, and were minted in a crude style and in very large quantities. This rare piece was made for the Caesar Constantius I in 295, and celebrates imperial victory: an emperor holds a small figure of Victory and stands between a barbarian and a Persian captive, the former perhaps an allusion to his defeat of the rebellious British usurper, Carausius.

**264** 7 'From a kingdom of gold to one of iron and rust'

made (see the table below, 'Issues of bronze coinage from Alexandria in the third century CE').

Issues of bronze coinage from Alexandria in the third century CE

| Reign | Notes |
| --- | --- |
| **Severus Alexander (222–35)** | only year 10 = 230/1 |
| **Philip (244–9)**[*] | years 5–6 = 248 |
| **Gallienus (253–68)** | only year 12 = 264/5 |
| **Claudius II (268–70)** | year uncertain (only 12 specimens known)[†] |

[*] A few rare pieces were minted between Alexander and Philip.
[†] There are also large coins of Aurelian (270–5), from his year 1 = 270/1, which are not so rare, see Bland 2011. It is not clear if they are bronze coins or larger denomination 'silver' coins.

The pattern of bronze at Alexandria is both similar and different as elsewhere. It is similar, inasmuch as the last big issue for Gallienus and the trickle for Claudius fit well enough with what we have seen elsewhere, but the virtual absence of any minting for the previous seventy years seems exceptional among the larger mints of the Empire.

## 7.4.2 Explanations

The foregoing analysis shows that bronze coinage had largely ceased in the joint reign of Valerian and Gallienus or the early part of Gallienus' sole reign. At that time, some 160 cities were still producing coinage, but the number decreased dramatically thereafter.

This sudden drop came, however, after a long period of decline from the Severan period. Many cities had stopped their coin production before the joint reign of Valerian and Gallienus. In Lydia, two thirds of the cities had already ceased,[79] and the same pattern can be observed more generally. Almost as many cities (125) stopped minting in the fifteen years before the accession of Valerian (Box 7.9) as went on to coin for him and Gallienus.

There have been several attempts to provide a general explanation for the end of the provincial coinage. One such recent explanation sees the end as the result of four main factors:[80]

1   increase in prices: bronze coinage became obsolete;
2.  the cost of production was too high, for cities or benefactors;
3.  a lack of metal: too much had disappeared in hoards or had been requisitioned by imperial mints;

## 7.4 The End of Provincial Coinage 265

### Box 7.10 The number of cities whose coinage ceased, by reign, before Valerian

| Reign | Number | Notes |
| --- | --- | --- |
| **Gordian III** | 57 | Hadrianopolis (Thrace), Anchialus, Nicopolis, Odessus, Dionysopolis, Istrus, Calchedon, Siphnus, Dioshieron, Acrasus, Stratonicea, Tabala, Tiberiopolis, Trajanopolis, Halicarnassus, Bargylia, Harpasa, Hydisus, Hyllarima, Accilaeum, Alia, Bruzus, Hyrgaleis, Lysias, Ococleia, Sebaste, Tripolis, Docimeum, Nacolea, Sibidunda, Caesarea (Cappadocia), Singara, Claudia Leucas, Aradus, Nysa Scythopolis, Gaza, Gadara, plus the 20 Lycian cities which minted only for Gordian III. |
| **Philip** | 42 | Cassandrea, Beroea, Pella, Sestus, Bizya, Deultum, Mesambria, Marcianopolis, Callatis, Tomi, Iuliopolis, Poemanenum, Eresus, Hadriani ad Olympum, Miletopolis, Apollonia ad Rhyndacum, Perperene, Hyrcanis, Chios, Briula (only one coin known), Synaus, Cos, Stectorium, Appia, Verbe, Apollonia Mordiaeum, Adada, Amblada, Trapezus, Dalisandus, Barata, Ilistra, Cidyessus, Laranda, Diocaesarea, Zeugma, Samosata, Nicopolis, Cyrrhus, Hierapolis (Syria), Raphia, Philippopolis. |
| **Decius** | 14 | Elaea, Teos, Anineta, Maeonia, Apollonoshieron, Metropolis (Phrygia), Colbasa, Tityassus, Selinus, Celenderis, Rhesaena, Paltus, Aelia Capitolina, Bostra. |
| **Gallus** | 13 | Maronea, Peltae, Cadi, Philomelium, Themisonium (only one coin known), Hadrianopolis, Baris, Olbasa, Etenna, Ionopolis, Pompeiopolis, Caesarea Maritima, Neapolis. |

4. the market was swamped by too much low-value coinage in circulation.

Other factors have also been cited in the past:[81]

5. a degree of economic disruption, political instability, and military crisis;
6. the changing cultural preferences of the elite, in how they devoted their energies and deployed their surplus wealth.[82]

It seems clear that the changes to the imperial monetary system at the time, with the continuing debasement of the coinage, were the major factor. In Chapter 6, the disappearance of smaller denominations in Rome and Egypt was discussed. Although it was observed that the same pattern did not occur in Asia, there is no doubt that, by the later part of the third century, most of the small denominations had disappeared. At the same time, the face value of many coinages had increased, and smaller denominations had been superseded with higher ones (e.g., at Sparta, from 4 asses to 8 asses). Earlier coins were countermarked with higher values.

What brought about this need for coins of higher value? A natural explanation would be to think of inflation: just as in the modern world rising prices dispense with the need for coins of low value. Yet most scholars are agreed that there seems to have been little inflation of prices between the second century and the late third century, to judge from the best set of prices available, that of wheat from Egypt. As a result, there has always seemed to be a problem with our understanding of contemporary inflation and its relationship with the changes in common coin denominations. However, it may be that wheat prices were unusual,[83] and, if so, a link between a gradual increase in prices and a gradual disappearance of smaller denominations could be re-established. The final falling off of minting by about 260–5, and the sudden jump in face value, matches well with the severe debasements of the silver coinage in the sole reign of Gallienus. As a result of the debasements and the increased volume of production of the 'silver' radiates, their purchasing power would have fallen so much that their fractional pieces, the bronze coinage, could provide no useful role, and so their production came to an end.

**Figure 7.32** Countermarking to revalue coins.
Earlier coins, such as this coin of Elagabalus from Tium, were countermarked several decades later to increase their value. Here the new value H = 8 has been stamped on the obverse, probably in about 260 (*GIC* 827). (*RPC VI*, temporary number 3569)

However, the pattern of minting in the third century, as described above, shows that there was a gradual cessation of the minting of provincial bronzes, and that this was occurring long before the effective end of bronze coinage at Rome and elsewhere in the 260s. How are we to account for this more gradual change? One way would be to compare it with the end of western city coinage two hundred years earlier. It was argued in Chapter 5 that a shift in the concept of Roman identity led to a preference by the cities to adopt Roman rather than local institutions, including coinage, and one could similarly posit a shift by the elite of the use of their (declining) resources. A similar mechanism was suggested in Chapter 6 for the switching in liminal areas from civic to Roman coins.

It seems quite possible to argue the same in relation to the last eastern city coinages, but there are differences. There are only a few signs of a tendency to make the city coins more like Roman ones, as was observed earlier in areas such as the west Empire and in Cyprus, although the coins produced in the third century by Viminacium, Dacia and Antioch in Pisidia could easily be mistaken for Roman sestertii, which they greatly resemble. But such similarities are exceptional.[84] One could also point to the increasing presence on the coinage of the emperor, and a greater role for imperial officials, who may have stimulated coinages in some areas, such as for the last coinages in Pisidia.[85]

However, the most emphatic cause was surely the increasing supremacy of the silver coinage from Rome and the new mints for it located in the provinces: as we have seen, most of the provincial silver petered out in the course of the Empire, to be replaced by Roman denarii and later radiates, and the production of radiates spread from a monopoly at Rome to many mints, including a number in the east.

### 7.4.3   The Reforms of Aurelian and Diocletian

In early 274, Aurelian introduced a fundamental reform of the silver coin. It was now marked with the letters XXI denoting that it consisted of 5 per cent silver (twenty parts of bronze to one part of silver), and the new coins may have been worth four denarii, rather than two (the likely value of the antoninianus, though this is disputed). It is likely that the value of gold started to float against the 'denarius' (by now a unit of account), a change which ushered in the increasing money inflation of the later third and fourth centuries (see Chapter 1).

This reform found an echo in the last remaining provincial 'silver' coinage, that of Alexandria in Egypt. At about the same time, the weight of the Alexandrian tetradrachm was reduced by about 20 per cent.[86] The changes seem to have prompted some subsequent overstriking of coins and affected the pattern of hoarding, but the precise relationship with the main change to the reformed silver of the rest of the Empire is unclear. A reduction in weight suggests a debasement or reduction of some sort.

As we have seen, bronze coins were made at only a very few cities for Aurelian: only the small group in southern Asia Minor, consisting of Perge, Side, Sillyum, Cremna and Selge.[87] There is no way of telling if they were made before or after Aurelian's reform of the silver. Perge went on to make coins for his successor, Tacitus (275–6), and, although marked with the same value (I = 10) (Figure 7.30), they are – unexpectedly – somewhat bigger and heavier than those made for Aurelian. This might perhaps suggest some sort of recalibration, but it is, however, hard to see any direct explanation: if Aurelian's new coins were now worth four denarii rather than the previous two, one would expect the face value of a bigger bronze coin greater than ten asses, but the same value persisted.[88] Perhaps, as has been suggested, it was a matter of fashion.

The idea that there might be a connection between the reform and the countermarking at Side of coins marked H, IA and IB to a new value of E (Figure 7.11) might seem more promising,[89] although it is hard to see that a doubling of the value of the silver coin would lead to the halving of the value of the bronze coin. However, although an upward valuation would surely seem more likely, a change from 10 and 12 asses (say) to 5 denarii (say) would have been a huge revaluation ($\times$ 7 or $\times$ 8), and does not seem intuitively plausible. Moreover, there is no evidence to date the countermark later than the reign of Gallienus, and it was not applied to the coins of Gallienus marked with I. The puzzling change seems to have arisen from some local set of revaluations at Side, and Side alone, and at some time before Aurelian's reform.

A related question is that of how long the provincial coins remained in circulation after minting had ceased. There is no good evidence. On the one hand, it is reasonable to suppose that they continued in circulation until at least late in the reign of Gallienus, since minting went on in many places until that date. One could probably extend that argument by another ten years to the reigns of Aurelian and Tacitus. On the other hand, they would certainly have ceased to circulate when Diocletian introduced his comprehensive coin reform in the 290s. However, there is no convincing evidence between these rather obvious points. There are very few hoards of mixed silver and bronze which might help. A small hoard from Onogur in Bulgaria contained nine *antoniniani* to Claudius II, and twenty-nine provincial bronzes from Macrinus to Philip.[90] Another, slightly larger, Bulgarian hoard from Debelt (Deultum) consisted of seventy-one Rome bronzes from Domitian to Commodus, three third-century bronzes from Deultum and two coins of Diocletian and Maximian, but, despite being found in a ceramic vessel, it looks more like an accumulation of coins from different sources than a 'currency hoard'.[91]

The reforms of Diocletian introduced a single monetary system across the Empire for the first time, and finally abolished the closed currency system of Egypt. Coins were now intended to look the same in whatever part of the Empire they were minted, from London to Alexandria. In theory, it might have been possible for the cities to produce coinage, but they did not do so. The nearest thing to a city coinage was the curious set of coins produced by Maximinus Daza in 312 at Nicomedia, Antioch and Alexandria.[92] They all had legends and designs that referred to the cities and their cults, but coordination of the coins from the different mints shows that the initiative to produce them came not from the cities, but from the emperor in whose territory the

**Figure 7.33** The coming of Christianity.
The Roman Empire became officially Christian only after the conversion of Constantine in the fourth century, but there were many Christians earlier. Christian symbols were not officially placed on the earlier provincial coinage, but there are occasional signs of provincial coins in the possession of Christians. Several third-century provincial coins were excavated from the catacomb of San Panfilo in Rome, from Pergamum (Caracalla), Thyatira (Elagabalus), Poroselene (Severus Alexander) and Gordian III (Tarsus and Perinthus), mostly pressed into the plaster of the walls as ornaments or souvenirs (Serafini 1937, Hostein 2019). This coin of the city of Cyzicus from the reign of Caracalla (211–17) was later engraved with the Christian symbols chi-rho (XP – behind the emperor's neck – being the beginning of 'Christ' in Greek) and A ⱷ (alpha and omega), as well as the Latin word PAX (peace), written backwards in front of his chin.

**Figure 7.34** Diocletian, mint of Ticinum (modern Pavia).
Small coin inscribed *utilitas publica* ('public benefit'). (*RIC VI*, Ticinum 27a)

mints were located. The small *vota publica* coins depicting Egyptian deities, intended for distribution at Rome on 3 January during the fourth century, are similarly local, but they were in no sense civic coins, since they, too, were produced under imperial authority.[93]

City coinage had no place in the new empire of Diocletian, where different ideologies of imperial control and uniformity across the Empire prevailed, whether of prices, government, coinage or imperial images. The provision of fractional coinage was no longer an obligation of the cities, but was now recognised as the responsibility of the imperial administration, to provide what was needed for the *Utilitas publica*.[94]

# Guide to Further Reading

The standard account of the provincial coinage during the Republican period can be found in Crawford 1985, together with subsequent surveys in Burnett & Crawford (eds.) 1987. The coinage of Italy during the third century BCE is listed in Rutter (ed.) 2001, and those of the territories around the Aegean Sea have been recently analysed in Ashton & Badoud (eds.) 2021.

For the imperial period, good introductions have been provided by Jones 1963, Howgego 1985 and Butcher 1988. Many topics are well covered in the essays in Howgego, Heuchert & Burnett 2005. Several of the contributions in Metcalf 2012 cover the topic, especially Amandry 2012, Yarrow 2012, Johnston 2012 and Geissen 2012. Yarrow 2021 also included many provincial coins in her book on the Republican coinage. The relationship of the various early imperial silver coinages is explored in Butcher & Ponting 2015. A general account of the third century was given by Harl 1987. A brief overview can also be found at https://rpc.ashmus.ox.ac.uk/introduction.

More general accounts of ancient or Roman coinage, often incorporating aspects of the provincial coinages, are Burnett 1987b, Howgego 1995 and Amandry (ed.) 2017.

The *Roman Provincial Coinage Online* website (https://rpc.ashmus.ox.ac.uk) has a catalogue of the relevant material, and is nearly complete – at the time of writing only one part remains to be completed, for the Severan period (*RPC V*). Publication on the website is followed by printed volumes, which add the introductory material and interpretation. So far vols. I–III, VII.1, VII.2 and IX have been published, and IV.2, IV.4 and VIII will appear soon. After a volume has been published, the catalogue is kept up to date on the website, as new material is always appearing.

Surveys of research are published every few years in connection with every International Numismatic Conference. The most recent are Heuchert 2003; Kremydi 2009; Spoerri Butcher & Calomino 2015 and Callegarin et al. 2015; and Geneviève et al. 2022 and Stroobants 2022. They are available online at https://inc-cin.org/home/publications/survey/.

# Bibliography

Aarts, Joris, & Nico Roymans. 2009. 'Tribal emission or imperial coinage? Ideas about the production and circulation of the so-called AVAVCIA coinages in the Rhineland', in *Coinage in the Iron Age: Essays in honour of Simone Scheers*, eds. Johan Van Heesch & Inge Heeren, 1–17. London: Spink.

Abdy, Richard, with Peter Mittag. 2019. *The Roman Imperial Coinage, Vol. II.3: From AD 117–138. Hadrian (RIC II.3)*. London: Spink.

Abela, Giovanni Francesco, 1647. *Della Descrittione di Malta isola nel Mare Siciliano: con le sue antichità, ed altre notizie*. Malta: Paolo Bonacota.

Adams, J. N. 2003. *Bilingualism and the Latin Language*. Cambridge: Cambridge University Press.

Albarède, Francis, Janne Blichert-Toft, Marion Rivoal & Philippe Telouk. 2016. 'A glimpse into the Roman finances of the Second Punic War through silver isotopes'. *Geochemical Perspective Letters* 2, 127–37.

Alexandropoulos, Jacques. 2007. *Les monnaies de l'Afrique antique: 400 av. J.-C. – 40 ap. J.-C.* Toulouse: Presses universitaires du Mirail.

Alföldi, Andreas. 1937. *A Festival of Isis in Rome*. Budapest: Institute of Numismatics and Archaeology of the Pázmány University.

Amandry, Michel. 2012. 'The coinage of the Roman provinces through Hadrian', in *The Oxford Handbook of Greek and Roman Coinage*, ed. William Metcalf, 391–404. Oxford: Oxford University Press.

(ed.) 2017. *La Monnaie Antique*. Paris: Ellipses.

Amandry, Michel. 2018. 'Un nouvel atelier imperial de Claude Ier? *Bulletin de la Société Nationale des Antiquaires de France*, 2012: 89–92.

2020. 'Antinoüs *RPC III* 2408 (Sardes) et 2667 (Amorium): deux cas de regravure d'époque moderne', in *Detur dignissimo. Studies in honour of Johan van Heesch*, eds. Fran Stroobants & Christian Lauwers, 309–13. Brussels: Cercle d'études, Travaux du Cercle d'études numismatiques 21.

2021. 'Rome et les monnayages de Grèce centrale, Attique, Peloponnèse et Crète', in *Graecia capta? Rome et les monnayages du monde égéen (IIe–Ier s. av. J.-C.)*, eds. Richard Ashton & Nathan Badoud, 101–10. Basel: Schwabe Verlag, *Aegeum* 1.

Amandry, Michel, & Andrew Burnett. 2015. *Roman Provincial Coinage, Vol. III: Nerva, Trajan and Hadrian (AD 96–138). (RPC III)* London: British Museum, and Paris: Bibliothèque nationale de France.

Anderson, Graham. 1993. *The Second Sophistic*. London and New York: Routledge.

Arena, Valentina. 2020. 'The god Liber and Republican notions of *Libertas* in the late Roman Republic', in *Libertas and Res Publica in the Roman Republic: Ideas of Freedom and Roman Politics*, ed. Cataline Balmaceda, 55–82. Leiden: Brill.

Ashton, Richard, & Nathan Badoud (eds.) 2021. *Graecia capta? Rome et les monnayages du monde égéen (IIe–Ier s. av. J.-C.).* Basel: Schwabe Verlag, *Aegeum* 1.

Asolati, Michele, & Cristina Crisafulli. 2018. *Cirene e la Cirenaica in età greca e romana. Le monete. I. I ripostigli.* Rome: Bretschneider, Monografie di Archeologia Libica 47.

Asolati, Michel, & Giovanni Gorini (eds.). 2006. *I ritrovamenti monetali e la legge di Gresham: atti del III Congresso internazionale di numismatica e di storia monetaria, Padova, 28–29 ottobre 2005.* Padova: Esedra.

Barbato, Marta. 2015. 'The Coins of Clovius and Oppius (*RRC* 476/1 and 550/1–3): New evidence from find-spots'. *Numismatic Chronicle* **175**, 103–116.

2022. 'Interruption in the production of bronze coinage during the Late Roman Republic: Pattern of circulation of official and 'unofficial' bronze in the finds from Rome'. *Revue Belge de Numismatique* **168**, 15–28

Barja De Quiroga, Pedro López. 2018. 'The *Quinquatrus* of June, Marsyas and *libertas* in the late Roman Republic'. *Classical Quarterly* **68** (1), 143–59.

Balty, Janine. 1977. *Mosaïques antiques de Syrie.* Brussels: Centre belge de recherches archéologiques à Apamée de Syrie.

1995. *Mosaïques antiques du Proche-Orient.* Paris: Belles Lettres.

Bell, Harold W. 1916. *Sardis XI: Coins. Pt. 1: 1910–1914.* Leiden: Brill.

Bellinger, Alfred. 1961. *Troy: The Coins.* Princeton, NJ: Princeton University Press.

Bennett, Robert. 2014. *Local Elites and Local Coinage. Elite Self-Representation on the Provincial Coinage of Asia, 31 BCE to CE 275.* London: Royal Numismatic Society.

2017. 'Ann Johnston and the so-called 'Pseudo-Autonomous' coins thirty years on'. *Numismatic Chronicle* **177**, 183–200.

Bernard, Seth. 2017. 'The Quadrigatus and Rome's monetary economy in the third century'. *Numismatic Chronicle* **177**, 501–13.

2018. 'The social history of early Roman coinage'. *Journal of Roman Studies* **108**, 1–26.

Besombes, Paul-André, & Jean-Noël Barrandon. 2000. 'Nouvelles propositions de classement des monnaies de «bronze» de Claude I$^{er}$'. *Revue Numismatique* **155**, 161–88.

Blanco-Pérez, Aitor. 2018. '*EPINIKIA*: celebrating Roman Victory in the Eastern Provinces of the Empire'. *Tyche* **33**, 9–42.

Bland, Roger. 1996. 'The Roman coinage of Alexandria, 30 BCE–CE 296: Interplay between Roman and Local Designs', in *Archaeological Research in Roman Egypt: The Proceedings of the Seventeenth Classical Colloquium of the*

*Department of Greek and Roman Antiquities, British Museum*, ed. Donald M. Bailey, 113–27. Ann Arbor, MI: Journal of Roman Archaeology, Suppl. Series 19.

2011. 'The Coinage of Vabalathus and Zenobia from Antioch and Alexandria', *Numismatic Chronicle* **171** (2011), 133–86.

2013. 'What happened to gold coinage in the 3rd *c.* A.D.?' *Journal of Roman Archaeology* **26**, 263–80.

2014. 'The gold coinage of Philip I and family.' *Revue numismatique* **171**, 93–149.

2017. 'An imperial visit to Antioch in AD 239. The numismatic evidence', in *Rome et les Provinces. Monnayage et Histoire. Mélanges offerts à Michel Amandry*, eds. Laurent Bricault, Andrew Burnett, Vincent Drost & Arnaud Suspène, 351–65. Bordeaux: Ausonius, Numismatica Antiqua 7.

2023. *The Coinage of Gordian III from the Mints of Antioch and Caesarea*. London: Royal Numismatic Society.

Bland, Roger, & Loriot, Xavier. 2010. *Roman and Early Byzantine Gold Coins found in Britain and Ireland*. London: Royal Numismatic Society.

Blouin, Katherine, & Andrew Burnett. 2020. 'From kings to emperors: the development and integration of the Egyptian monetary system into the Roman Empire', in *Money Rules! The Monetary Economy of Egypt, from Persians until the Beginning of Islam*, ed. Thomas Faucher, 233–87. Cairo: Institut Français d'Archéologie Orientale Bibliothèque d'Étude 176.

Bouchon, Richard. 2008. 'L'ère auguste: ébauche d'une histoire politique de la Thessalie sous Auguste'. *Bulletin de Correspondance Hellénique* **132**, 427–71.

Boschung, Dietrich. 1993. *Die Bildnisse des Augustus*. Berlin: Mann.

Bransbourg, Gilles. 2013. '*Fides et Pecunia Numerata*. Part II: the Currencies of the Roman Republic'. *American Journal of Numismatics* **25**, 179–242.

2022. 'The Roman coinage under the Antonines: An economy of silver, not gold'. Paper given at the International Numismatic Conference, Warsaw, 11–16 September.

Brenot, Claude. 1973. *Les fouilles de Mariana (Corse), 4. Les monnaies romaines*. Bastia: Fédération d'associations et groupements pour les études corses.

Bricault, Laurent. 2008. *Sylloge Nummorum Religionis Isiacae et Sarapiacae* Paris: Académie des inscriptions et belles lettres.

2017. 'Sarapis au droit des monnaies provinciales romaines d'Asie Mineure et de Thrace'. *Numismatic Chronicle* **177**, 213–44.

Bricault, Laurent, Andrew Burnett, Vincent Drost & Arnaud Suspène (eds.). 2017. *Rome et les Provinces. Monnayage et Histoire. Mélanges offerts à Michel Amandry*. Bordeaux: Ausonius, Numismatica Antiqua 7.

Brixhe, Claude. 1987. *Essai sur le grec anatolien au début de notre ère*. Nancy: Presses universitaires de Nancy.

Bulut, Süleyman, & Mehmet Şengül. 2014. '2009-2012 Yılları Andriake Kazı Sikkeleri ve Yerleşim Tarihine Katkıları', in *First International Congress of the Anatolian Monetary History and Numismatics, 25–28 February 2013, Antalya. Proceedings*, eds. Kayhan Dörtlük, Oğuz Tekin & Remziye Boyraz Seyhan, 79–110. Antalya: İstanbul: Suna & İnan Kıraç Research Institute on Mediterranean Civilizations.

Burnett, Andrew. 1982. 'The currency of Italy from the Hannibalic War to the reign of Augustus'. *Annali dell'Istituto Italiano di Numismatica* **29**, 125–37.

1986. 'The iconography of the Roman coinage of the third century BC'. *Numismatic Chronicle* **146**, 67–75

1987a. 'Africa', in *The Coinage of the Roman World in the Late Republic*, eds. Andrew Burnett & Michael Crawford, 175–85. Oxford: British Archaeological Reports International Series 326.

1987b. *Coinage in the Roman World*. London: Seaby.

1989. 'The beginnings of Roman coinage'. *Annali dell'Istituto Italiano di Numismatica* **33**, 33–64.

1991. 'The coinage of Roman Alexandria in the Roman world'. *NNF–NYTT. Norsk Numismatisk Tidsskrift*, **1991**, 9–33.

1999. 'Buildings and Monuments on Roman Coins,' in *Roman Coins and Public Life under the Empire*, eds. George Paul & Michael Ierardi, 137–64. Ann Arbor, MI: University of Michigan Press.

2002a. 'Latin on coins of the western empire', in *Becoming Roman, Writing Latin?* ed. Alison Cooley, *Journal of Roman Archaeology, Supplementary Series* **48**, 33–40.

2002b. 'Syrian coinage and romanisation from Pompey to Domitian,' in *Les monnayages syriens: quel apport pour l'histoire du Proche-Orient hellénistique et romain? Actes de la table ronde Damas, 10–12 novembre 1999*, eds. Christian Augé & Frédérique Duyrat, 115–22. Beirut, Damascus, Amman: Institut Français d'Archéologie du Proche-Orient.

2005. 'The Roman West and the Roman East', in *Coinage and Identity in the Roman Provinces*, eds. Christopher Howgego, Volker Heuchert & Andrew Burnett, 173–80. Oxford: Oxford University Press.

2011. 'The Augustan Revolution seen from the mints of the provinces'. *Journal of Roman Studies* **101**, 1–30.

2016a. 'Trajan's campaigns in Armenia and Parthia (CE 113–117)', in *Armenian Numismatic First International Conference dedicated to the Memory of Kh. Moushegian (Erevan, 3–4 June 2015)*, 103–35. Venice: Mechitarian Editing House.

2016b. 'Rome's first silver fraction,' in *Suadente nummo vetere. Studi in onore di Giovanni Gorini*, eds. Michele Asolati, Bruno Callegher & Andrea Saccocci, 143–8. Padua: Esedra.

2016c. 'Zela, Acclamations, Caracalla – and Parthia?' *Bulletin of the Institute of Classical Studies* **59** (1), 72–110.

## 276 Bibliography

2021a. 'Overview and some methodological points', in *Graecia capta? Rome et les monnayages du monde égéen (IIe–Ier s. av. J.-C.)*, eds. Richard Ashton & Nathan Badoud, 17–33. Basel: Schwabe Verlag, *Aegeum* 1.

2021b. Review, *Numismatic Chronicle* **181**, 534–42.

in press a. 'Two emperors who reformed the coinage: Augustus and Nero', in *The Julio-Claudian Principate: Tradition and Transition*, ed. Christina Kuhn, Stuttgart.

in press b. 'Female signatories on provincial coins', in *Scritti in onore di Maria Caltabiano per i suoi 50 anni di studi numismatici*, eds. Benedetto Carroccio, Daniele Castrizio, Katia Mannino, Mariangela Puglisi & Grazia Salamone, Messina.

Burnett, Andrew, Michel Amandry & Pere Pau Ripollès. 1992. *Roman Provincial Coinage, Vol. I: From the Death of Caesar to the Death of Vitellius (44 BC – AD 69)*. (*RPC I*). London: British Museum, and Paris: Bibliothèque nationale de France.

Burnett, Andrew, Michel Amandry & Ian Carradice, *Roman Provincial Coinage, Vol. II: From Vespasian to Domitian (AD 69–96)*. (*RPC II*) London: British Museum, and Paris: Bibliothèque nationale de France.

Burnett, Andrew, & Michael Crawford. 1987. (eds.) *The Coinage of the Roman World in the Late Republic*. Oxford: British Archaeological Reports International Series 326.

2014. 'Coinage, money and mid-Republican Rome. Reflections on a recent book by Filippo Coarelli'. *Annali dell'Istituto Italiano di Numismatica* **60**, 231–65.

Burnett, Andrew, & Duncan Hook. 1989. 'The fineness of silver coins in Italy and Rome in the late fourth and third centuries BC'. *Quaderni Ticinesi* **18**, 151–67.

Burnett, Andrew, & Katharina Martin. 2018. 'An early Imperial Coinage from Alexandria Troas?', in *Second International Congress on the History of Money and Numismatics in the Mediterranean World, 5–8 January 2018*, eds. Oğuz Tekin & Remziye Boyraz Seyhan, 245–252. Antalya: AKMED, Koç University, Suna & İnan Kıraç Research Center for Mediterranean Civilization.

Burnett, Andrew, & Andrew McCabe. 2016. 'An early Roman struck bronze with a helmeted goddess and an eagle,' in *Nomismata, Studi di numismatica antica offerti ad Aldina Cutroni Tusa per il suo novantatreesimo compleanno*, eds. Lavinia Sole & Sebastiano Tusa, 238–74. Ragusa: Edizioni di storia e studi sociali.

Burnett, Andrew, & Maria Cristina Molinari. 2015. 'The Capitoline hoard and the circulation of silver coins in central and northern Italy in the third century BC,' in *FIDES. Contributions to Numismatics in Honor of Richard B. Witschonke*, eds. Peter van Alfen, Michel Amandry & Gilles Bransbourg, 21–126. New York: American Numismatic Society.

Burrell, Barbara. 2004. *Neokoroi: Greek Cities and Roman Emperors.* Leiden and Boston: Brill, Cincinnati Classical Studies IX.

2005. 'Iphigeneia in Philadelphia'. *Classical Antiquity* **24** (2), 223–6.

Butcher, Kevin. 1988. *Roman Provincial Coins: An Introduction to the Greek imperials.* London: Seaby.

Butcher, Kevin. 1989. 'Two notes on Syrian silver of the third century AD'. *Numismatic Chronicle* **149**, 169–72.

2002. 'Circulation of bronze coinage in the Orontes Valley in the late Hellenistic and early Roman periods', in *Les monnayages syriens: Quel apport pour l'histoire du Proche-Orient hellénistique et romain? Actes de la table ronde Damas, 10–12 novembre 1999,* eds. Christian Augé & Frédérique Duyrat, 145–52. Beirut, Damascus, Amman: Institut Français d'Archéologie du Proche-Orient.

2004. *Coinage in Roman Syria: Northern Syria, 64 BC – AD 253.* London: Royal Numismatic Society.

2014. 'Lycian drachms and the monetary system of the Roman Empire', in *First International Congress of the Anatolian Monetary History and Numismatics, 25–28 February 2013, Antalya. Proceedings,* eds. Kayhan Dörtlük, Oğuz Tekin & Remziye Boyraz Seyhan, 111–16. Antalya: İstanbul: Suna & İnan Kıraç Research Institute on Mediterranean Civilizations.

2017. 'Arbitrary standards? On the so-called four-and-a-half assaria coins from Tomis, and value marks on coins of Moesia and Thrace', in *Ex Nummis Lux: Studies in Ancient Numismatics in Honour of Dimitar Draganov,* ed. Dilyana Boteva, 273–90. Sofia: Bobokov Bros. Foundation.

2019. '"This extravagant trade of false money": Commercial speculation and coin distribution', in *Money Matters: Coin finds and ancient coin use,* eds. Stefan Krmnicek & Jérémie Chameroy, 45–54. Bonn: Habelt.

2021. 'Eastern Imitations and the Beginning of the Antiochene SC Coinage', in *Studies on Items, Ideas and History Dedicated to Professor Aleksander Bursche on the Occasion of his 65th Birthday,* eds. Renata Ciołek & Roksana Chowaniec, 45–49. Wiesbaden: Harrassowitz Verlag.

Butcher, Kevin, & Matthew Ponting. 2015. *The Metallurgy of Roman Silver Coinage: From the reform of Nero to the reform of Trajan.* Cambridge: Cambridge University Press.

Buttrey, Theodore V. 1972. 'A hoard of sestertii from Bordeaux and the problem of bronze circulation in the third century CE.' *American Numismatic Society Museum Notes* **18**, 33–58.

1991. 'The president's address'. *Numismatic Chronicle* **151**, i–xii.

Buttrey, Theodore V., & Kenan Erim, Thomas Groves & R. Ross Holloway. 1989. *Morgantina Studies Vol. II. The Coins.* Princeton, NJ: Princeton University Press.

## 278 Bibliography

Buttrey, Theodore V., Ann Johnston, Kenneth M. MacKenzie, & Michael L. Bates. 1981. *Greek, Roman, and Islamic Coins from Sardis*. Archaeological Exploration of Sardis Monograph 7. Cambridge, MA: Harvard University Press.

Cadwallader, Alan, & James Harrison. 2019. 'Perspectives on the Lycus Valley: An inscriptional, archaeological, numismatic and iconographic approach,' in *The First Urban Churches 5: Colossae, Hierapolis and Laodicea*, eds. James Harrison & Larry Welborn, 3–72. Atlanta: SBL Press.

Cagnat, René (ed.) 1906–28. *Inscriptiones Graecae ad res romanas pertinentes.* (*IGRR*). Paris: Librairie Ernest Leroux.

Callegarin, Laurent, Suzanne Frey-Kupper & Vincent Geneviève. 2015. 'Les monnayages provinciaux: les provinces occidentaux', in *A Survey of Numismatic Research 2008–2013*, eds. Carmen Arnold-Biucchi & Maria Caccamo Caltabiano, 220–27. Taormina: International Numismatic Commission and International Association of Professional Numismatists.

Calomino, Dario. 2011. *Nicopolis d'Epiro. Nuovi studi sulla zecca e sulla produzione monetale.* Oxford: British Archaeological Reports.

2012. 'Die-sharing in Moesia Inferior under Gordian III'. *Numismatic Chronicle* **173**, 105–26.

2014. 'Bilingual Coins of Severus Alexander in the Eastern Provinces'. *American Journal of Numismatics* **26**, 199–222.

2016. *Defacing the Past – Damnation and Desecration in Imperial Rome.* London: Spink.

2019. 'Supplies for the army: Bithynian coins in the Balkans in the 3rd century CE'. *Chiron* **49**, 131–60.

2020. 'Caracalla and the divine: emperor worship and representation in the visual culture of Roman Asia Minor'. *Anatolian Studies* **70**, 153–179.

Caltabiano, Maria Caccamo, Benedetto Carroccio & Emilia Oteri. 1997. *Siracusa ellenistica. Le monete 'regali' di Ierone II, della sua famiglia e dei Siracusani.* Messina: Dipartimento di Scienze dell'Antichitè dell'Università degli Studi di Messina, *Pelorias* 16.

Campo, Marta, Jean-Claude Richard & Hans-Markus von Kaenel, 1981. *El tesoro de La Pobla de Mafumet (Tarragona): Sextercios y dupondios de Claudio I.* Barcelona: Asociacion Numismatica Español and Instituto Antonio Agustin De Numismatica Del Consejo Superior De Investigaciones Cientificas.

Carbone, Lucia. 2014. 'Money and power: The disappearance of autonomous silver issues in the Roman province of Asia'. *Omni* **8**, 10–32.

2020. 'Mark Antony and the bronze revolution', in *Coins of the Roman Revolution*, eds. Anton Powell & Andrew Burnett, 43–78. Swansea: Classical Press of Wales.

2021. 'The introduction of Roman coinages in Asia (133 BC – 1st century AD)', in *Graecia capta? Rome et les monnayages du monde égéen (IIe–Ier s. av. J.-C.)*, eds. Richard Ashton & Nathan Badoud, 233–93. Basel: Schwabe Verlag, *Aegeum* 1.

in press. *Coinage in the Roman Provinces before RPC. A Catalogue of the Richard B. Witschonke Collection at the American Numismatic Society*. New York: American Numismatic Society.

Carradice, Ian, & Theodore V. Buttrey. 2007. *The Roman Imperial Coinage, Vol. II: From AD 69-96. Vespasian to Domitian. (RIC II.1)* London: Spink.

Carrié, Jean-Michel. 2003. 'Aspects concrets de la vie monétaire en Province'. *Revue numismatique* **159**, 175–203.

Carroccio, Benedetto. 2004. *Dal basileus Agatocle a Roma. Le monetazioni siciliane d'età ellenistica*. Messina: Dipartimento di Scienze dell'Antichitè dell'Università degli Studi di Messina, *Pelorias* 10.

Carson, Robert A. G. 1990. *Coins of the Roman Empire*. London: Methuen.

Cavagna, Alessandro. 2012. *Provincia Dacia: i conî*. Milan: Società italiana numismatica, Collana di Numismatica e Scienze Affini 7.

Çelikbaş, Ersin, & Kasim Oyarçin. 2012. 'Roman Provincial Coins of Paphlagonian Hadrianopolis'. *Numismatic Chronicle* **182**, 179–87.

Chambers, Mortimer, Walter Cockle, John Shelton & Eric Turner. 1981. *Oxyrhynchus Papyri 48 (Graeco-Roman Memorial)*. Graeco-Roman Memoirs 67. London: Egypt Exploration Society.

Chaves Tristán, Francisca. 1991–93. 'Consideraciones sobre los tesorillos de monedas de bronce en Hispania. República e inicios del Imperio Romano. II', *Acta Numismàtica* **21–23**, 267–84.

Chevrollier, François. 2016. 'From Cyrene to Gortyn. Notes on the relationship between Crete and Cyrenaica under Roman domination (1st century BCE–4th century CE)', in *Roman Crete. New Perspectives*, eds. Jane Francis & Anna Kouremenos, 11–26. Oxford: Oxbow Books.

CHRR Online. Coin Hoards of the Roman Republic Online. http://numismatics.org/chrr/.

Claes, Liesbeth. 2014. 'A note on the coin type selection by the *a rationibus*'. *Latomus* **73**, 164–73.

Cluett, Ronald. 2002. 'The End of the Greek Imperials: Old problems and new interpretations', in *Actes du Ier Congrès International sur Antioch de Pisidie*, eds. Thomas Drew-Bear, Mehmet Taşlıalan & Christine M. Thomas, 385–91. Paris: De Boccard, Collection Archéologie et Histoire de l'Antiquité 5.

Coles, Amanda. 2020. 'Roman colonies in Republic and Empire'. *Brill Research Perspectives in Ancient History* **3** (1), 1–119.

Cope, Lawrence, Cathy E. King, Peter Northover & Theresa Clay. 1997. *Metal Analyses of Roman Coins Minted Under the Empire*. London: British Museum Occasional Paper 120.

## 280 Bibliography

Cottier, Michel, Michael Crawford, Charles Crowther, Jean-Luis Ferrary, Barbara Levick, Mireille Corbier, Stephen Mitchell, Olli Salomies & Michael Wörrle. 2008. *The Customs Law of Asia*. Oxford: Oxford University Press.

Cowell, Michael, Paul Craddock, Alistair Pike & Andew Burnett. 2000. 'An analytical survey of Roman provincial copper-alloy coins and the continuity of brass manufacture in Asia', in *XII. Internationaler Numismatischer Kongress Berlin 1997. Akten – Proceedings – Actes*, eds. Bernd Kluge & Bernhard Weisser, 670–77. Berlin: Staatliche Museen zu Berlin Preussischer Kulturbesitz.

Cox, Dorothy. 1959. *Coins from the excavations at Curium, 1932–1953*. New York: American Numismatic Society, Numismatic notes and monographs 145.

Craddock, Paul, Andrew Burnett & Keith Preston. 1980. 'Hellenistic copper-base coinage and the origin of brass', in *Scientific studies in numismatics*, ed. W. Andrew Oddy, 53–63. London: British Museum, British Museum Occasional Paper No 18.

Crawford, Michael H. 1969. *Roman Republican Coin Hoards*. (*RRCH*). London: Royal Numismatic Society.

1974. *Roman Republican Coinage*. (*RRC*). Cambridge: Cambridge University Press.

1982. 'Unofficial imitations and small change under the Roman Republic'. *Annali dell'Istituto Italiano di Numismatica* **29**, 139–163.

1985. *Coinage and Money under the Roman Republic*. London: Methuen.

2002. 'The oval series of aes grave'. *Coin Hoards* **IX**, 269–70.

Cribb, Joe. 1992. *A Catalogue of Sycee in the British Museum: Chinese silver currency ingots c. 1750–1933*. London: British Museum Press.

Dalaison, Julie. 2017. 'Les monnayages sans portrait impérial du nord de l'Asie Mineure (Bithynie, Paphlagonie, Pont et Arménie mineure)'. *Numismatic Chronicle* **177**, 261–306.

2021. 'Le monnayage des cités de Bithynie au 1er s. av. J.-C.,' in *Graecia capta? Rome et les monnayages du monde égéen (IIe–Ier s. av. J.-C.)*, eds. Richard Ashton & Nathan Badoud, 295–339. Basel: Schwabe Verlag, *Aegeum* 1.

De Callataÿ, François. 1997. *L'Histoire des Guerres Mithradatiques vue par les Monnaies*. Louvain: Département d'archéologie et d'histoire de l'art, séminaire de numismatique Marcel Hoc.

2011. 'More then it seems. The Use of Coinage by the Romans in Late Hellenistic Asia Minor (133–63 BC)'. *American Journal of Numismatics* **23**, 55–86.

2015. 'The late Hellenistic didrachms of Leukas: Another case of Greek coinage for the Roman Army', in *Fides: Contributions to numismatics in honor of Richard B. Witschonke*, eds. Peter van Alfen, Gilles Bransbourg & Michel Amandry, 239–70. New York: American Numismatic Society.

2016. 'The coinages struck for the Romans in Hellenistic Greece: A quantified overview (mid 2nd -mid 1st C. BCE)', in *Neue Forschungen zur Münzprägung der römischen Republik*, eds. Florian Haymann, Wilhelm Hollstein & Martin Jehne, 315–38. Bonn: Habelt, *Nomismata* 8.

2021. 'Le financement des armées romaines en Méditerranée orientale au moyen de frappes pseudo-civiques locales: aux racines perses du modèle', in *Graecia capta? Rome et les monnayages du monde égéen (IIe–Ier s. av. J.-C.)*, eds. Richard Ashton & Nathan Badoud, 35–61. Basel: Schwabe Verlag, *Aegeum* 1.

De Hoz, María-Paz. 2016. 'The Goddess of Sardis: Artemis, Demeter or Kore?' in *Between Tarhuntas and Zeus Polieus: Cultural crossroads in the temples and cults of Graeco-Roman Anatolia*, eds. María Paz de Hoz, Juan Pablo Sánchez Hernández & Carlos Molina Valero, 185–224. Leuven: Peeters.

De Romanis, Federico. 2020. *Indo-Roman Trade and the Muziris Papyrus*, Oxford and New York: Oxford University Press.

Debernardi, Pierluigi. 2021. 'The M-hoard of Roman Republican denarii and a new chronology for the later anonymous silver series'. *Numismatic Chronicle* **181**, 39–52.

Debernardi, Pierluigi, & Olivier Legrand. 2015. 'Roman Republican silver coins of the quadrigatus period struck in Spain'. *Revue Belge de Numismatique* **161**, 273–92.

Delrieux, Fabrice. 2021. 'Rome et les monnayages grecs de Carie aux IIe et 1er s. av. J.-C.', in *Graecia capta? Rome et les monnayages du monde égéen (IIe–Ier s. av. J.-C.)*, eds. Richard Ashton & Nathan Badoud, 187–232. Basel: Schwabe Verlag, *Aegeum* 1.

DeRose Evans, Jane. 2018. *Coins from the Excavations at Sardis: Their archaeological and economic contexts: Coins from the 1973 to 2013 excavations*. Cambridge, MA and London: Harvard University Press. Archaeological Exploration of Sardis Monograph 13.

Devoto, Claudia, & Barbara Spigola. 2020. 'Scipio and Cato in 47–46 BC: Ideals and expectations seen through coins', in *Coins of the Roman Revolution*, eds. Anton Powell & Andrew Burnett, 79–96. Swansea: Classical Press of Wales.

Dittenberger, W. 1903. *Orientis Graeci inscriptiones selectae.* (*OGIS*). Leipzig: S. Hirzel.

Drinkwater, John. 2019. *Nero: Emperor and court*. Cambridge: Cambridge University Press.

Duncan-Jones, Richard. 1994. *Money and Government in the Roman Empire*. Cambridge: Cambridge University Press.

Dyck, Andrew. 2012. *Speeches on behalf of Marcus Fonteius and Marcus Aemilius Scaurus*. Oxford: Oxford University Press.

Eck, Werner. 1984. 'Senatorial self-representation: developments in the Augustan period', in *Caesar Augustus: Seven aspects*, eds. Fergus Millar & Erich Segal, 129–68. Oxford: Oxford University Press.

## 282 Bibliography

Eck, Werner, & Claus Nader. 2009. 'The administrative reforms of Augustus: Pragmatism or systematic planning?' in *Augustus*, ed. John Edmondson, 229–49. Edinburgh: Edinburgh University Press.

Eckstein, Arthur M. 2012. *Rome Enters the Greek East: From anarchy to hierarchy in the Hellenistic Mediterranean, 230–170 BC.* Malden, MA, Oxford and Chichester: Wiley-Blackwell.

Elkins, Nathan. 2015. *Monuments in Miniature: Architecture on Roman coinage.* New York: American Numismatic Society.

Elliott, Colin. 2014. 'The acceptance and value of Roman silver coinage in the second and third centuries A.D.' *Numismatic Chronicle* **174**, 129–52.

Fajfar, Helena, Zdravko Rupnik & Žiga Šmit. 2015. 'Analysis of metals with luster: Roman brass and silver'. *Nuclear Instruments and Methods in Physics Research* **B 362**, 194–201.

Filges, Axel. 2015. *Münzbild und Gemeinschaft: Die Prägungen der Römischen Kolonien in Kleinasien.* Bonn: Habelt. Frankfurter archäologische Schriften 29.

Fischer-Bossert, Wolfgang. 2014. 'Kleinfunde und Fundmünzen', in *Karatepe-Aslantaş, Azatiwataya*, ed. Halet Çambel, Vol. 2, 155–76. Mainz am Rhein: Philipp von Zabern.

Flament, Christophe & Patrick Marchetti. 2011. *Le monnayage argien d'époque romaine* Athens: Ecole français d'Athènes.

Flower, Harriet. 2006. *The Art of Forgetting: Disgrace and oblivion in Roman political culture.* Chapel Hill, NC: University of North Carolina Press.

Franke, Peter, & Marguerite Nollé. 1997. *Die Homonoia-Münzen Kleinasiens und der thrakischen Randgebiete I.* Saarbrücken: Saarbrücker Druckerei und Verlag.

Frey-Kupper, Suzanne. 2013. *Die antiken Fundmünzen vom Monte Iato 1971–1990: Ein Beitrag zur Geldgeschichte Westsiziliens.* Studia Ietina X. Prahins: Éditions du Zèbre.

   2014. 'Coins and their use in the Punic Mediterranean. Case studies from Carthage to Italy (fourth to first century BC)', in *The Punic Mediterranean Identities and Identification from Phoenician Settlement to Roman Rule*, eds. Josephine Quinn & Nicholas Vella, 76–108. Cambridge: Cambridge University Press.

Frey-Kupper, Suzanne, & Clive Stannard. 2018. 'Evidence for the importation and monetary use of blocks of foreign and obsolete coins in the ancient world', in *Infrastructure and Distribution in Ancient Economies*, ed. Bernhard Woytek, 283–345. Vienna: Verlag der Österreichischen Akademie der Wissenschaften.

Fröhlich, Pierre. 2004. *Les cités grecques et le contrôle des magistrats (IVe–Ier siècle avant J.-C.).* Geneva and Paris: Droz. Hautes études du monde gréco-romain 33.

Fujii, Takashi. 2013. *Imperial Cult and Imperial Representation in Roman Cyprus*. Stuttgart: Steiner Verlag.

Galani, Georgia. 2022. 'Imprints of Roman Imperium: Bronze coinages in the Republican Eastern Provinces'. Doctoral thesis in Archaeology and Classical Studies at Stockholm University.

García-Bellido, Maria Paz. 2011. 'New coins of pre- and denarial system minted outside Italy', in *Proceedings of the XIVth International Numismatic Congress, Glasgow 2009*, ed. Nicholas Holmes, 678–85. Glasgow: International Numismatic Commission.

García-Bellido, Maria Paz. 2013. Los sistemas ponderales en el mundo púnico de Iberia e Ibiza, in *La moneda y su papel en las sociedades fenicio-púnicas, 68*, eds. Benjamí Costa & Jordi H. Fernández, 35–60. Ibiza: Museu Arqueològic d'Eivissa i Formentera.

Gautier, Georges. 2017. 'Vtilitas Pvblica. Essai de synthèse: sur les monnaies divisionnaires de la réforme de Dioclétien', in *Rome et les Provinces. Monnayage et Histoire. Mélanges offerts à Michel Amandry*, eds. Laurent Bricault, Andrew Burnett, Vincent Drost & Arnaud Suspène, 437–50. Bordeaux: Ausonius. Numismatica Antiqua 7.

Gebhardt, Axel. 2002. *Imperiale Politik und provinziale Entwicklung: Untersuchungen zum Verhältnis von Kaiser, Heer und Städten im Syrien der vorseverischen Zeit*. Berlin: Akademie.

Geissen, Angelo. 2012. 'The coinage of Roman Egypt', in *The Oxford Handbook of Greek and Roman Coinage*, ed. William Metcalf, 561–83. Oxford: Oxford University Press.

Geneviève, Vincent, Laurent Callegarin & Suzanne Frey-Kupper. 2022. 'Les monnayages Provinciaux: Les provinces Occidentales', in *A Survey of Numismatic Research 2014–2022*, eds. Michael Alram, Jarosław Bodzek & Aleksander Bursche, 509–22. Warsaw, Krakow, Winterthur: International Numismatic Council.

Gerov, Boris. 1980. 'Die lateinisch-griechische Sprachgrenze auf der Balkanhalbinsel', in *Die Sprachen im Römischen Reich der Kaiserzeit*, eds. Günter Neumann & Jürgen Untermann, 147–165. Bonn: Bonner Jahrbücher Beiheft 40.

Glenn, Simon. 2022. 'A third-century hoard of sestertii from Paros', *Numismatic Chronicle* **182**, 375–94.

Göbl, Robert. 2000. *Moneta Imperii Romani 36, 43, 44 Die Münzprägung der Kaiser Valerianus I / Gallienus / Saloninus (253–268), Regalianus (260) und Macrianus / Quietus (260/262)*. Vienna: Verlag der Österreichischen Akademie der Wissenschaften.

Gorecki, Joachim. 2007. 'Wozu Fundnumismatik in Limyra? Eine Zwischenbilanz', in *Studien in Lykien. Jürgen Borchhardt zum 70. Geburtstag am 25. Februar 2006 gewidmet*, eds. Martin Seyer, 83–91. Vienna: Ergänzungshefte zu den Jahresheften des Österreichischen Archäologischen Institutes 8.

## 284 Bibliography

Gorini, Giovanni. 2015. 'A new hoard of Romano-Campanian coins from Nora (Sardinia)', in *Studies in ancient coinage in honour of Andrew Burnett*, eds. Roger Bland & Dario Calomino, 31–40. London: Spink.

Grandjean, Catherine. 2003. *Les Messéniens de 370/369 au 1er siècle de notre ère. Monnayages et histoire*. Athens: École française d'Athènes and Paris: de Boccard. *Bulletin de correspondance hellénique Supplément* 44.

Grant, Michael. 1953. *The Six Main Aes Coinages of Augustus: Controversial studies*. Edinburgh: Edinburgh University Press.

Grigorova-Gencheva, Valentina. 2011. 'Deux médaillons d'Antonin le Pieux du territoire de Pautalia (Thrace)', in *Proceedings of the XIVth International Numismatic Congress, Glasgow 2009*, eds. Nicholas Holmes, 709–14. Glasgow: International Numismatic Commission.

Gruen, Eric S. 2010. *Rethinking the Other in Antiquity*. Princeton, NJ: Princeton University Press.

Grunauer-von Hoerschelmann, Susanne. 1978. *Die Münzprägung der Lakedaimonier*. Berlin: De Gruyter.

Habicht, Christian. 1975. 'New evidence on the Province of Asia'. *Journal of Roman Studies* **65**, 64–91.

Haklai-Rotenberg, Merav. 2011. 'Aurelian's monetary reform: Between debasement and public trust'. *Chiron* **41**, 1–40.

Hallmannsecker, Martin. 2020. 'The Ionian Koinon and the Koinon of the 13 cities at Sardis'. *Chiron* **50**, 1–27.

Harl, Kenneth. 1987. *Civic Coins and Civic Politics in the Roman East, A.D. 180–275*. Berkeley and Los Angeles: University of California Press. *The Transformation of the Classical Heritage* 12.

Harris, William V. 2008. 'The nature of Roman money', in *The Monetary Systems of the Greeks and Romans*, eds. William Harris. Oxford: Oxford University Press.

Harris, William V. 2019. 'Credit-money in the Roman economy.' *Klio* **101** (1), 158–189.

Harvey, Tracene. 2019. *Julia Augusta: images of Rome's first empress on the coins of the Roman Empire*. London and New York: Routledge.

Haymann, Florian, Wilhelm Hollstein & Martin Jehne. 2016. (eds.). *Neue Forschungen zur Münzprägung der römischen Republik*, Bonn: Habelt. *Nomismata* 8.

Hekster, Olivier. 2008. *Rome and its Empire, AD 193–284*. Edinburgh: Edinburgh University Press.

Heller, Anna. 2006. *'Les bêtises des Grecs': Conflits et rivalités entre cités d'Asie et de Bithynie à l'époque romaine: 129 a.C.–235 p.C.* Bordeaux: Ausonius.

Helly, Bruno. 1997. 'Le diorthôma d'Auguste fixant la conversion des statères thessaliens en deniers: une situation de "passage à la monnaie unique"'. *Topoi* **7** (1), 63–91.

Heuchert, Volker. 2003. 'Roman provincial coinage', in *A Survey of Numismatic Research 1996–2001*, eds. Carmen Alfaro & Andrew Burnett, 313–43. Madrid: International Numismatic Commission and International Association of Professional Numismatists.

— 2005. 'The chronological development of Roman provincial coin iconography', in *Coinage and Identity in the Roman Provinces*, eds. Christopher Howgego, Volker Heuchert & Andrew Burnett, 29–56. Oxford: Oxford University Press.

Heymans, Elon. 2021. *The Origins of Money in the Iron Age Mediterranean World*. Cambridge: Cambridge University Press.

Hobbs, Richard. 2013. *Currency & Exchange in Ancient Pompeii: Coins from the AAPP excavations at Regio VI, Insula 1*, London: Institute of Classical Studies, Supplement 116.

Hochard, Pierre-Olivier. 2020. *Lydie, terre d'empire(s): Études de numismatique et d'histoire (228 a.C.–268 p.C)*. Bordeaux: Ausonius.

Holleran, Claire. 2012. *Shopping in Ancient Rome: The retail trade in the late Republic and the Principate*. Oxford: Oxford University Press.

Hollstein, Wilhelm. 2016. 'The Aureus of Casca Longus (*RRC* 507/1)'. *Numismatic Chronicle* **176**, 155–70.

Holmes, Nicholas (ed.). 2011. *Proceedings of the XIVth International Numismatic Congress, Glasgow 2009*. Glasgow: International Numismatic Commission.

— 2020. 'Some unusual coin issues of the Valerianic dynasty (AD 253–68)'. *Numismatic Chronicle* **180**, 181–206.

— 2022. 'The gold coins of Valerian I and Gallienus attributed to the mint of Samosata'. *Bulletin du Cercle d'études numismatiques* **59** (1), 26–30.

Hopkins, Keith. 1980. 'Taxes and trade in the Roman Empire (200 B.C. – A.D. 400)'. *Journal of Roman Studies* **70**, 101–25.

Hopkins, Keith. 2002. 'Rome, Taxes, Rents and Trade', in *The Ancient Economy*, eds. Walter Scheidel & Sitta von Reden, 190–230. Edinburgh: Edinburgh University Press.

Horster, Marietta. 2013. 'Coinage and images of the imperial family: Local identity and Roman rule'. *Journal of Roman Archaeology* **26**, 243–61.

Hostein, Antony. 2013. 'La visite de Caracalla à Pergame et à Laodicée du Lykos: l'apport des monnaies', in *Les voyages des empereurs romains dans l'Orient romain: Époques antonine et sévérienne*, eds. Antony Hostein & Sophie Lalanne, 205–27. Paris: Errance.

— 2017. 'Les grands mutations du IIIe siècle', in *La Monnaie Antique*, ed. Michel Amandry, 219–62. Paris: Ellipses.

— 2019. 'Des médaillons pour les morts. Observations sur les monnaies de la catacombe de Saint Pamphyle un siècle après leur découverte.' *Journal of Archaeological Numismatics*, **9**, 241–260.

# 286 Bibliography

Hostein, Antony, & Jerome Mairat. 2016. *Roman Provincial Coinage, Vol. IX: From Trajan Decius to Uranius Antoninus (AD 249-254). (RPC IX).* London: British Museum, and Paris: Bibliothèque nationale de France.

Howgego, Christopher. 1985. *Greek Imperial Countermarks: Studies in the provincial coinage of the Roman Empire. (GIC).* London: Royal Numismatic Society.

  1989. 'After the colt has bolted: a review of Amandry on Roman Corinth'. *Numismatic Chronicle* **149**, 199-208.

  1990. 'Why did ancient states strike coins?' *Numismatic Chronicle* **150**, 1-25.

  1994. 'Coin circulation and the integration of the Roman economy'. *Journal of Roman Archaeology* 7, 5-21.

  1995. *Ancient History from Coins.* London: Routledge.

  2005. 'Coinage and identity in the Roman provinces', in *Coinage and Identity in the Roman Provinces*, eds. Christopher Howgego, Volker Heuchert & Andrew Burnett, 1-17. Oxford: Oxford University Press.

  2014. 'Questions of coin circulation in the Roman world', in *First International Congress of the Anatolian Monetary History and Numismatics, 25-28 February 2013, Antalya. Proceedings*, eds. Kayhan Dörtlük, Oğuz Tekin & Remziye Boyraz Seyhan, 307-18. Antalya: İstanbul: Suna & İnan Kıraç Research Institute on Mediterranean Civilizations.

Howgego, Christopher. 2023. *Roman Provincial Coinage, Vol. IV.4: From Antoninus Pius to Commodus (AD 138-192): Egypt.* (RPC IV.4). London: British Museum, and Paris: Bibliothèque nationale de France.

Howgego, Christopher, Volker Heuchert & Andrew Burnett (eds.). 2005. *Coinage and Identity in the Roman Provinces.* Oxford: Oxford University Press.

Ialongo, Nicola, & Giancarlo Lago. 2021. 'A small change revolution. Weight systems and the emergence of the first Pan-European money'. *Journal of Archaeological Science* **129**, Article 105379. https://doi.org/10.1016/j.jas.2021.105379.

Isaac, Benjamin. 2017. 'Latin in Cities of the Roman Near East Empire and Ideology in the Graeco-Roman World', in id., *Empire and Ideology in the Graeco-Roman World. Selected Papers*, 257-84. Cambridge: Cambridge University Press.

Jackson, Anne. 1973. 'The coins', in *Knossos: The sanctuary of Demeter*, ed. Nicholas Coldstream, 99-11. Athens: British School at Athens, Supplementary Volume 8.

Jaworski, Piotr. 2009. 'A hoard of Roman coins from Ptolemais', in *Archeologia a Tolemaide: Giornate di studio in occasione del primo anniversario della morte di Tomasz Mikocki, 27-28 maggio 2008*, eds. Elżbieta Jastrzębowska & Monika Niewójt, 146-56. Rome: Accademia Polacca delle Scienze.

  2012. 'Roman Republican coins found in Ptolemais', in *Ptolemais in Cyrenaica: Studies in memory of Tomasz Mikocki*, ed. Jerzy Żelazowski, 285-91. Warsaw: University of Warsaw, Institute of Archaeology. Ptolemais 1.

2016. 'Some remarks on the coins in circulation in Ptolemais', in *Le monete di Cirene e della Cirenaica nel Mediterraneo. Problemi e prospettive: Atti del V Congresso Internazionale di Numismatica e di Storia Monetaria, Padova 17-19 marzo 2016*, ed. Michele Asolati, 293–303. Padua: Esedra.

Jehasse, Jean, & Laurence Jehasse. 1962. 'Les monnaies puniques d'Aleria'. *Corse Historique* **8**, 27–48.

——— 1973. *La nécropole préromaine d'Aléria*. Paris: Centre National de la Recherche Scientifique.

Jehasse, Marie-Juliette, 1987–88. 'Une monnaie romaine d'époque républicaine découverte à Porto-Vecchio'. *Archeologica Corsa* **12–13**, 44–45.

——— 1989. 'La circulation monetaire à Aleria (Corse) de la Republique à la fin de l'empire romain'. PhD thesis, Lyon Lumière.

——— 1991–92. 'Nouvelles monnaies puniques d'Aléria'. *Archeologia Corsa* **16/17**, 24–34.

Jenkins, G. Kenneth. 1973. 'North Africa', in *An Inventory of Greek Coin Hoards (IGCH)* eds. Margaret Thompson, Otto Mørkholm & Colin Kraay, 343–4. New York: American Numismatic Society.

——— 1978. 'Coins of Punic Sicily Part 4'. *Schweizerische Numismatische Rundschau* **57**, 5–68.

——— 1987. 'Hellenistic gold coins of Ephesus', in *Festschrift Akurgal*, ed. Cevdet Bayburtluoğlu, *Anadolu XXI, 1978-1980*, 183–88. Ankara.

Jenkins, G. Kenneth, & Richard Lewis. 1963. *Carthaginian Gold and Electrum Coins*. London: Royal Numismatic Society. Special Publication No. 2.

Johnston, Ann. 1982–83. 'Die sharing in Asia Minor: The view from Sardis'. *Israel Numismatic Journal* **6–7**, 59–78.

——— 1983. 'Caracalla's path: The numismatic evidence'. *Historia* **32** (1), 58–76.

——— 1984a. 'New problems for old: Konrad Kraft on die-sharing in Asia Minor'. *Numismatic Chronicle* **144**, 203–7.

——— 1984b. 'Greek imperial statistics: A commentary'. *Revue Numismatique* **26**, 240–57.

——— 1985. 'The so called "pseudo-autonomous" Greek imperial coinage'. *American Numismatic Society. Museum Notes* **30**, 89–92.

——— 2007. *Greek Imperial Denominations, ca. 200–275: A study of the Roman provincial bronze coinages of Asia Minor*. London: Royal Numismatic Society.

——— 2012. 'The provinces after Commodus', in *The Oxford Handbook of Greek and Roman Coinage*, ed. William Metcalf, 453–67. Oxford: Oxford University Press.

Jones, Tom. 1963. 'A numismatic riddle: The so-called Greek imperials'. *Proceedings of the American Philosophical Society* **107** (4), 308–47.

Kadman, Leo. 1961. *Corpus Nummorum Palestinensium IV: The coins of Akko Ptolemais*. Jerusalem: Israel Numismatic Society.

## 288 Bibliography

Kagan, Jonathan, & Aneurin Ellis-Evans. 2022. 'Bimetallism, coinage, and empire in Persian Anatolia'. *Phoenix* **76**, 178–227.

Katsari, Constantina. 2003. 'Opramoas and the importation of bronze coins in Roman Lycia'. *Epigraphica Anatolica* **35**, 141–5.

2011. *The Roman Monetary System*. Cambridge: Cambridge University Press.

Katsari, Constantina, & Stephen Mitchell. 2008. 'The Roman colonies of Greece and Asia Minor: Questions of state and civic identity.' *Athenaeum* **95** (1), 219–47.

Kay, Philip. 2014. *Rome's Economic Revolution*. Oxford: Oxford University Press.

Kelly, P. V. 2021. Third-century price inflation reassessed. *Theoretical Roman Archaeology Journal* **4** (1): 5. DOI: https://doi.org/10.16995/traj.4338

Kettenhofen, Erich. 1979. *Die syrischen Augustae in der historischen Überlieferung*. Bonn: Habelt.

Kinns, Philip. 1987. 'Asia Minor', in *The Coinage of the Roman World in the Late Republic*, eds. Andrew Burnett & Michael Crawford, 109–19. Oxford: British Archaeological Reports International Series 326.

Klaver, Sanne. 2019. Women in Roman Syria: The cases of Dura-Europos, Palmyra, and Seleucia on the Euphrates. University of Amsterdam, PhD thesis.

Kleiner, Fred. 1978. 'Hoard evidence and the late cistophori of Pergamum'. *Museum Notes* **23**, 77–105.

2020. 'Julia Augusta: images of Rome's first empress on the coins of the Roman Empire'. *Bryn Mawr Classical Review* **2020** (07), 27.

Klose, Dietrich. 1987. *Die Münzprägung von Smyrna in der Römischen Kaiserzeit*, Berlin: De Gruyter.

Knapp, Robert C., & John D. MacIsaac. 2005. *Excavations at Nemea III: The Coins*. Berkeley, CA: University of California Press.

Kourempanas, Theodoros. 2011a. 'The chronology of the Hellenistic coins of Thessaloniki, Pella and Amphipolis', in *Proceedings of the XIVth International Numismatic Congress, Glasgow 2009*, ed. Nicholas Holmes, 251–55. Glasgow: International Numismatic Commission.

2011b. 'Three parallel issues of Thessaloniki, Pella and Amphipolis at the end of the 2nd century BC'. *Nomismatika Khronika* **29**, 25–33.

Kraft, Konrad. 1972. *Das System der kaiserzeitlichen Münzprägung in Kleinasien: Materialien und Entwürfe*. Berlin: Mann.

Kremmydas, Christos. 2021. 'The Rhetoric of Homonoia in Dio Chrysostom's Civic Orations', in *The Rhetoric of Unity and Division in Ancient Literature*, ed. Andreas Michalopoulos, Andreas Serafim, Flaminia Beneventano della Corte & Alessandro Vatri, 293–316. Berlin: de Gruyter.

Kremydi-Sicilianou, Sophia. 1996. Η Νομισματοκοπια της Ρωμαικης Αποικιας του Διου. Athens: Greek Numismatic Society.

2005. '"Belonging" to Rome, "remaining" Greek: Coinage and identity in Roman Macedonia', in *Coinage and Identity in the Roman Provinces*, eds.

Christopher Howgego, Volker Heuchert & Andrew Burnett, 95–106. Oxford: Oxford University Press.

Kremydi, Sophia. 2009. 'Roman provincial coinage', in *A Survey of Numismatic Research 2002-2007*, ed. Donal Bateson & Michel Amandry, 182–95. Glasgow: International Numismatic Commission and International Association of Professional Numismatists.

2021. 'From the Antigonids to the Romans: Macedonia and Thessaly in the 2nd and 1st Centuries BC', in *Graecia capta? Rome et les monnayages du monde égéen (IIe–Ier s. av. J.-C.)*, eds. Richard Ashton & Nathan Badoud, 81–99. Basel: Schwabe Verlag, *Aegeum* 1.

Kremydi, Sophia, & Joel Ward. 2017. 'The Severan issues of the Peloponnese: Minting authorities and dating', in *Rome et les Provinces. Monnayage et Histoire. Mélanges offerts à Michel Amandry*, eds. Laurent Bricault, Andrew Burnett, Vincent Drost & Arnaud Suspène, 303–12. Bordeaux: Ausonius, Numismatica Antiqua 7.

Kroll, Jack. 1993. *The Athenian Agora, Vol. XXVI: The Greek coins*. Princeton, NJ: Princeton University Press.

Kuhn, Christina. 2011. 'M. Antonius Polemon und die Dionysia: Zur Bedeutung des Prora-Motivs auf kaiserzeitlichen Münzen Smyrnas'. *Athenaeum* **99**, 145–53.

Kurke, Leslie. 1999. *Coins, Bodies, Games and Gold: The politics of meaning in ancient Greece*. Princeton, NJ: Princeton University Press.

Laronde, André. 2004. 'Les rivalités entre les cités de la Cyrenaique à l'époque impériale', in *L'Hellenisme d'époque Romaine Paris. Actes du colloque international à la mémoire de Louis Robert, Paris, 7–8 juillet 2000*, ed. Simone Follet, 187–93. Paris: De Boccard.

Le Blanc, Robyn. 2021. 'The Marsyas of the forum motif on coins from Roman Mesopotamia and Osrhoene'. *Numismatic Chronicle* **191**, 157–79.

Lemercier, Christophe. 2021. 'Le monnayage d'argent de Stratonicée en Carie sous Antonin le Pieux'. *Bulletin de la Société Française de Numismatique* **76** (4), 150–7.

Leschhorn, Wolfgang. 1985. 'Die kaiserzeitlichen Münzen Kleinasiens: Zu den Möglichkeiten und Schwierigkeiten ihrer statistischen Erfassung'. *Revue Numismatique* **27**, 200–16.

Levick, Barbara. 1967. *Roman Colonies in Southern Asia Minor*. Oxford: Oxford University Press.

Levy, Brooks. 1987. 'Indulgentiae Avgvsti moneta inpetrata: A Flavian episode', in *Mélanges de Numismatique offerts à P. Bastien à l'occasion de son 75ᵉ anniversaire*, eds. Hélène Huvelin, Michel Christol & Georges Gautier, 39–49. Wetteren: Éditions NR.

Libero Mangieri, Giuseppe. 2012. 'Taranto 1883: Il medagliere prima del museo'. *Eos. Collana did Studi Numismatici* **4**, 11–216.

**290** Bibliography

Lindner, Ruth. 1994. *Mythos und Identität: Studien zur Selbstdarstellung kleinasiatischer Städte in der römischen Kaiserzeit.* Stuttgart: Steiner.

Lo Cascio, Elio. 2016. 'Why did the issuing authority discontinue the production of bronze coins after Sulla?' in *Neue Forschungen zur Münzprägung der römischen Republik*, eds. Florian Haymann, Wilhelm Hollstein & Martin Jehne, 339–46. Bonn: Habelt, *Nomismata* 8.

Lozano, Ferdinando. 2017. 'Emperor Worship and Greek Leagues: The organization of supra-civic imperial cult in the Roman East', in *Religious Change in Greek Cities under Roman Rule*, ed. Elena Muñiz Grijalvo, Juan Manuel Cortés Copete & Fernando Lozano Gomez, 149–76. Leiden: Brill.

MacDonald, David. 1992. *The Coinage of Aphrodisias*. London: Royal Numismatic Society.

Macro, Anthony D. 1976. 'Imperial provisions for Pergamum: *OGIS* 484'. *Greek, Roman and Byzantine Studies* **17**, 169–79.

Mairat, Jerome. 2007. 'L'ouverture de l'atelier impérial de Cyzique sous le règne de Claude II le Gothique'. *Revue Numismatique* **163**, 175–96.

2017. 'Le monnayage d'Apamée de Phrygie de Septime Sévère à Élagabal', in *Rome et les Provinces. Monnayage et Histoire: Mélanges offerts à Michel Amandry*, eds. Laurent Bricault, Andrew Burnett, Vincent Drost & Arnaud Suspène, 313–25. Bordeaux: Ausonius. Numismatica Antiqua 7.

Mairat, Jerome, & Marguerite Spoerri Butcher. 2022. *Roman Provincial Coinage, Vol. VII.2: From Gordian I to Gordian III (AD 238–244)*. (*RPC VII 2*) London: British Museum, and Paris: Bibliothèque nationale de France.

Manfredi, Lorenza Ilia. 1999. 'Note storiche e archeometriche sulle monete puniche da Tharros', in *Tharros nomen*, eds. Enrico Acquaro, M. T. Francisi, Tatiana Kirova & Alessandra Melucco Vaccaro, 181–6. La Spezia: Agora.

Manganaro, Giuseppe. 2005. 'Contramarche su chalkos siciliota e su aes augusteo in Sicilia'. *Mediterraneo Antico Economie, Società, Culture* **VIII** (1), 265–81.

2012. *Pace e guerra nella Sicilia tardo-ellenistica e romana (215 a.C.–14 d.C.): Ricerche storiche e numismatiche*. Bonn: Habelt.

Martin, Katharina. 2013. *Demos – Boule – Gerousia: Personifikationen städtischer Institutionen auf kaiserzeitlichen Münzen aus Kleinasien*. Bonn: Habelt. Euros. Münstersche Beiträge zu Numismatik und Ikonographie 3.

Martin, Stéphane. 2015. *Du statère au sesterce. Monnaie et romanisation dans la Gaule du Nord et de l'Est (III^e s. a.C./I^{er} s. p.C.)*. Bordeaux: Ausonius. Scripta Antiqua 78.

Martini, Rodolfo. 2009. 'Monetazione bronzea orientale di Augustus tra emissioni imperiali, coniazioni provinciali e produzioni locali: I 'sesterzi' della Lycia ed i 'dupondi' (?) della serie AVGV/STVS (Asia Minor) alla luce di nuove analisi metallografiche,' in *Ancient History, Numismatics, and Epigraphy in the Mediterranean World: Studies in memory of Clemens E. Bosch and Sabahat*

*Atlan, and in honour of Nezahat Baydur*, ed. Oğuz Tekin, 231–46. Istanbul: Ege Yayinlari.

2017. 'Countermarks with "God standing" and "spiked helmet" types struck in Sicily on Rome-minted Augustan sesterces from Moesia-Thrace region: New evidence of legionary movements in Julio-Claudian times', in *Ex Nummis Lux: Studies in ancient numismatics in honour of Dimitar Draganov*, ed. Dilyana Boteva, 235–59. Sofia: Bobokov Bros. Foundation.

Martini, Rodolfo, & Evgeni Paunov. 2004. 'Early Roman imperial countermarked coins from Moesia: First critical observations (typology, frequency, chronology and analysis of distribution)', *Numismatic and Sphragistic Contributions to History of the Western Black Sea Coast: International Conference Varna, 12–15 September 2001*, 159–74. Varna: Zograf, Acta Musaei Varnaensis 2.

Matthews, John. 1984. 'The tax law of Palmyra: Evidence for economic history in a city of the Roman East.' *Journal of Roman Studies* **74**, 157–80.

Matthies, Sandra. 2002. 'Sphinx oder Tutu?' *Eos* **2002**, 15–17.

Mattingly, H. B., E. A. Sydenham & C. H. V. Sutherland. 1949. *The Roman Imperial Coinage, Vol. IV Part III. (RIC IV.3)*. London: Spink.

McConnell, Joseph, Andrew Wilson, Andreas Stohl, Monica Arienzo, Nathan Chellman, Sabine Eckhardt, Elisabeth Thompson, Mark Pollard & Jørgen Peder Steffensen. 2018. 'Lead pollution recorded in Greenland ice indicates European emissions tracked plagues, wars, and imperial expansion during antiquity'. *Proceedings of the National Academy of Sciences* **115** (22), 5726–31.

McIntosh, Frances, & Sam Moorhead. 2011. 'Roman quadrantes found in Britain, in light of recent discoveries recorded with the Portable Antiquities Scheme.' *British Numismatic Journal* **81**, 223–30.

Meadows, Andrew. 2013. The closed currency system of the Attalid Kingdom, in *Attalid Asia Minor: Money, international relations, and the state*, ed. Peter Thonemann, 149–205. Oxford: Oxford University Press.

2019. *Between Greece and Rome: Coinage in the imperium of Mark Antony*. Athens: Kipke. Memoranda Numismatica Atheniensia 4.

2021. 'The penetration of the denarius and quinarius standards into Asia Minor in the 1st century BC', in *Graecia capta? Rome et les monnayages du monde égéen (IIe–Ier s. av. J.-C.)*, eds. Richard Ashton & Nathan Badoud, 127–85. Basel: Schwabe Verlag. Aegeum 1.

Melville Jones, John. 2015. 'The Location of the Trajanic Mint at Rome'. *Numismatic Chronicle* **175**, 137–45.

Meta, Albana. 2021. 'L'arrivée des Romains en Illyrie méridionale et son effet sur la production et la circulation des monnaies', in *Graecia capta? Rome et les monnayages du monde égéen (IIe–Ier s. av. J.-C.)*, eds. Richard Ashton & Nathan Badoud, 63–79. Basel: Schwabe Verlag. Aegeum 1.

## 292 Bibliography

Metcalf, William. 1998. 'Aurelian's reform at Alexandria', in *Studies in Greek Coinage in Memory of Martin Jessop Price*, eds. Richard Ashton & Silvia Hurter, 269–76. London: Spink.

Metcalf, William (ed.). 2012. *The Oxford Handbook of Greek and Roman Coinage*. Oxford: Oxford University Press.

Migeotte, Léopold. 2014. 'Les grands livres de Tauroménion en Sicile', *Comptabilités: Revue d'histoire des comptabilités* **6**. http://journals.openedition.org/comptabilites/1483.

Millar, Fergus. 1984. 'The impact of monarchy', in *Caesar Augustus: Seven aspects*, eds. Fergus Millar & Erich Segal, 37–60. Oxford: Oxford University Press.

   1990. 'The Roman coloniae of the Near East: A study of cultural relations', in *Roman Eastern Policy and Other Studies in Roman History*, eds. Heikki Solin & Mika Kajava, 7–58. Helsinki: Societas Scientiarum Fennica. Also reprinted as Millar 2006a.

   1993. *The Roman Near East: 31 BC – AD 337*. Cambridge, MA and London: Harvard University Press.

   1995. 'Latin in the epigraphy of the Roman Near East,' in *Acta Colloquii Epigraphici Latini. Helsinki 3–6 Sept. 1991*, ed. Heikki Solin, Olli Salomies & Uta-Maria Liertz, 403–19. Helsinki: Societas Scientiarum Fennica. Also reprinted as Millar 2006b.

   2006a. 'The Roman coloniae of the Near East: A study of cultural relations', in *Rome, the Greek World, and the East, Vol. 3: The Greek World, the Jews, and the East*, eds. Fergus Millar, Hannah M. Cotton & Guy M. Rogers, 164–222. Chapel Hill, NC: University of North Carolina Press.

   2006b. 'Latin in the epigraphy of the Roman Near East', in *Rome, the Greek World, and the East, Vol. 3: The Greek World, the Jews, and the East*, eds. Fergus Millar, Hannah M. Cotton & Guy M. Rogers, 2006, 223–42. Chapel Hill, NC: University of North Carolina Press.

Mitford, Timothy. 1939. 'Milestones in Western Cyprus'. *Journal of Roman Studies* **29**, 184–98.

Molinari, Maria Cristina. 2003. 'Gli aurei a nome di Giulio Cesare e Aulo Irzio'. *Rivista Italiana di Numismatica* **104**, 165–210.

Molinari, Maria Cristina. 2011. 'A hoard of bronze coins of the 3rd century BC found at Pratica di mare (Rome)', in *Proceedings of the XIVth International Numismatic Congress, Glasgow 2009*, ed. Nicholas Holmes, 828–38. Glasgow: International Numismatic Commission.

Moorhead, Sam. 2015. 'Coins of British Association', after David Walker and David Shotter, with additions by Sam Moorhead'. https://bit.ly/3upw6gP

Morrison, Cécile, Claude Brenot, Jean-Pierre Callu, Jean-Noël Barrandon, Jacques Poirier & Robert Halleux. 1985. *L'or monnayé, I: purification et altérations de Rome à Byzance*. Paris: Éditions du Centre National de la Recherche Scientifique. Cahiers Ernest-Babelon 2.

Mosch, Hans-Christoph, & Laura-Antonia Klostermeyer. 2015. 'Ein Stempelschneider auf Reisen: Die Antinoosmedaillons des Hostilios Markellos und Hadrians Reise im Jahr 131/2 n. Chr.', in *ΚΑΙΡΟΣ: Contributions to numismatics in honor of Basil Demetriadi*, eds. Ute Wartenberg & Michel Amandry, 285–325. New York: American Numismatic Society.

Muss, Ulrike. 2017. 'Ephesos und Heraklit', in *Heraklit im Kontext*, eds. Enrica Fantino, Ulrike Muss, Charlotte Schubert & Kurt Sier, 7–48. Berlin: De Gruyter.

Naimann, Matthew G., & Marleen Termeer. 2020. 'Roman and Campanian bronze coinage in Etruria in the 3rd C. BC'. *Annali dell'Istituto Italiano di Numismatica* **66**, 211–66.

Neumann, Kristina. 2021. *Antioch in Syria: A history from coins (300 BCE–450 CE)*. Cambridge: Cambridge University Press.

Nicolaou, Ino. 1990. *Paphos II: The coins from the house of Dionysos*. Nicosia: Cyprus Department of Antiquities.

Nieto, Sylvia. 2004. 'Monnaies arvernes (Vercingétorix, Cas) en orichalque'. *Revue numismatique* **6**, 5–25.

Niniou-Kindeli, Vanna, & Nikos Chatzidakis. 2016. 'The Roman theatre at Aptera: A preliminary report', in *Roman Crete: New perspectives*, eds. Jane Francis, Anna Kouremenos, 127–53. Oxford: Oxbow Books.

Noguera Guillén, Jaume. 2008. 'Los inicios de la conquista romana de Iberia: Los campamentos de campaña del curso inferior del río Ebro'. *Archivo Español de Arqueología* **81**, 31–48.

— 2009. 'Los campamentos romanos en el curso inferior del río Ebro durante la Segunda Guerra Púnica', in *LIMES XX: XX Congreso Internacional de Estudios sobre la Frontera Romana. XXth International Congress of Roman Frontier Studies León (España), Septiembre, 2006*, eds. Ángel Morillo Cerdán, Norbert Hanel & Esperanza Martín Hernández, 329–38. Madrid: Anejos de Gladius 13.

Noguera, Jaume, & Nuria Tarradell-Font. 2009. 'Noticia sobre las monedas del campamento romano de la Segunda Guerra Púnica de la Palma (l'Aldea, Tarragona)', in *Actas XIII Congreso Nacional de Numismática 'Moneda y Arqueología', Cádiz, 22–24 de octubre de 2007*, ed. Alicia Arévalo González, I, 119–42. Madrid: Museo Casa de la Moneda, and Cádiz: Universidad de Cádiz.

Nurpetlian, Jack. 2017. 'A survey of Roman provincial pseudo-autonomous coins of the Levant'. *Numismatic Chronicle* **177**, 307–11.

— 2020. *Coinage in late Hellenistic and Roman Syria: The Orontes Valley (1st century BCE–3rd century CE)*. London: Royal Numismatic Society.

## 294  Bibliography

Olivier, Julien, & Charles Parisot-Sillon. 2013. 'Les monnayages aux types de Cléopâtre et Antoine: Premiers résultats et perspectives'. *Bulletin de la Société Française de Numismatique* **68** (9), 256–68.

Olivier, Julien, & Héloïse Aumaître. 2017. 'Antoine, Cléopâtre et le Levant: Le témoignage des monnaies', in *Rome et les Provinces: Monnayage et Histoire: Mélanges offerts à Michel Amandry*, eds. Laurent Bricault, Andrew Burnett, Vincent Drost & Arnaud Suspène, 105–22. Bordeaux: Ausonius. Numismatica Antiqua 7.

Östenberg, Ida. 2018. '*Damnatio memoriae* inscribed: The materiality of cultural repression,' in *The Materiality of Text – Placement, perception, and presence of inscribed texts in classical antiquity*, eds. Andrej Petrovic, Ivana Petrovic, & Edmund Thomas, 324–47. Leiden: Brill.

Özüdoğru, Şükrü. 2002. Patara sikke basımları ve Patara kazılarından (1989–2001) ele geçen sikkeler. Akdeniz University, MA thesis.

Parisot-Sillon, Charles. 2018. 'Soldats, vétérans et monnaies romaines: Le cas du victoriat au I$^e$ siècle av. n. è.' *Revue Numismatique* **175**, 241–83.

Parisot-Sillon, Charles, & Guillaume Sarah. 2018. 'Production monétaire et stratégies d'approvisionnement de l'argent en Occident nord-méditerranéen (II$^e$-I$^{er}$ siècle av. n. è.)', in *Los metales preciosos: De la extracción a la acuñación (Antigüedad – Edad Media)*, eds. Christian Rico & Almudena Orejas, 137–63. Madrid: Dossier des Mélanges de la Casa de Velázquez. Nouvelle série 48.1.

Parks, Danielle. 2002. 'Epitaphs and tombstones of Hellenistic and Roman Cyprus', in *Ancient Journeys: A Festschrift in honor of Eugene Numa Lane*, ed. Cathy Callaway, 1–32. The Stoa: A Consortium for Electronic Publication in the Humanities. www.stoa.org/lane.

Paunov, Evgeni. 2014. 'Early Roman coins from Novae. Patterns and observations'. *Novensia* **25**, 145–76.

2015. 'The coin assemblage from the sacred spring of Aquae Calidae in Thrace: main problems, patterns and conclusions', in *Studia in memoriam Tsonyae Drajeva*, 245–55. Burgas: Regional Museum of History.

2020. 'Sestertii of Britannicus Caesar and Agrippina Minor from Moesia and Thrace', in *From Zalmoxis to Quetzalcoatl: Studies in honor of Stefan Yordanov*, 461–4. Veliko Tărnovo: Leviathan. Studiorum socii et potestatis scripta 3.

2021. 'Thrace and Both Moesiae', in *Graecia capta? Rome et les monnayages du monde égéen (IIe–Ier s. av. J.-C.)*, eds. Richard Ashton & Nathan Badoud, 111–25. Basel: Schwabe Verlag. Aegeum 1.

Perassi, Claudia, 2007. '"Le medaglie, fedeli historie e veridici documenti di bronzo": Considerazioni numismatiche nella *Descrittione di Malta isola nel mare Siciliano* di Francesco Giovanni Abela (1647)', *Quaderni Ticinesi di Numismatica e Antichità Classiche* **36**, 367–402.

2018. *Produzione e uso della moneta sull'arcipelago maltese in età antica*. Milan: Educatt Università Cattolica del Sacro Cuore.

Pesce, Gennaro. 1955–57. 'Il primo scavo di Tharros (anno 1956)'. *Studi Sardi* **14–15**, 307–72.

1961. 'Il tempio punico monumentale di Tharros'. *Monumenti Antichi della Accademia Nazionale dei Lincei* **45**, 333–439.

Pera, Rossella. 1984. *Homonoia sulle monete da Augusto agli Antonini: Studio storico-tipologico*. Genoa: Melangolo.

Peter, Ulrike. 2017. 'Die "pseudo-autonomen" Münzen von Moesia Inferior – ein erster ikonographischer Überblick'. *Numismatic Chronicle* **177**, 244–59.

Petzl, Georg. 2017. *Sardis: Greek and Latin Inscriptions. II: Finds from 1958 to 2017*. Cambridge, MA and London: Harvard University Press.

Piacentin, Sofia. 2022. *Financial Penalties in the Roman Republic: A study of confiscations of individual property, public sales, and fines (509–58 BC)*. Leiden: Brill.

Polosa, Annalisa. 2006. 'Appunti sulla circolazione monetaria in Sardegna fino all'età augustea'. *Annali dell'Istituto Italiano di Numismatica* **52**, 119–64.

Powell, Anton, & Andrew Burnett (eds.). 2020. *Coins of the Roman Revolution 49 BC –AD 14: Evidence without hindsight*. Swansea: Classical Press of Wales.

Price, Simon. 2005. 'Local mythologies in the Greek East', in *Coinage and Identity in the Roman Provinces*, eds. Christopher Howgego, Volker Heuchert & Andrew Burnett, 115–24. Oxford: Oxford University Press.

Prins, Jelle, & Marleen Termeer. 2021. 'Coins and aes rude as votive gifts: The coins and aes rude from the Hellenistic votive deposit at Satricum and the first coinage in Latium'. *Ancient Numismatics* **2**, 43–91.

Psoma, Selene. 2009. 'Monetary terminology in pre-Roman Asia Minor'. *Epigraphica Anatolica* **42**, 170–80.

Puglisi, Mariangela. 2009. *La Sicilia da Dionisio I a Sesto Pompeio: Circolazione e funzione della moneta*. Messina: Dipartimento di Scienze dell'Antichitè dell'Università degli Studi di Messina. Pelorias 16.

Rebuffat, François. 1997. *Les enseignes sur les monnaies d'Asie Mineure: Des origines à Sévère Alexandre*. Athens: Bulletin de Correspondance Hellenique. Supplement 31.

Reece, Richard. 1982. 'A collection of coins from the centre of Rome'. *Papers of the British School at Rome* **50**, 116–45.

Regling, Kurt. 1927. *Die Münzen von Priene*. Berlin: H. Schoetz.

1930–32. 'Ein Kistophorenschatz aus der Provinz Brussa'. *Frankfurter Münzzeitung* **3**, 506–10.

Reynolds, Joyce. 2000. 'Cyrenaica', in *The Cambridge Ancient History XI: The High Empire, CE 70–92*, eds. Alan Bowman, Peter Garnsey & Dominic Rathbone, 547–58. Cambridge: Cambridge University Press.

## 296 Bibliography

Richter, Daniel, & William Johnson. 2017. *The Oxford Handbook of the Second Sophistic*. Oxford and New York: Oxford University Press.

Ripollès Alegre, Pere Pau. 2012. 'The ancient coinages of the Iberian peninsula', in *The Oxford Handbook of Greek and Roman Coinage*, ed. William Metcalf, 356–74. Oxford: Oxford University Press.

2017. 'The Iberian Coinages, 6th–1st Centuries BC'. *Numismatic Chronicle* 177, 1–8.

Ripollès Alegre, Pere Pau, & Manuel Gozalbes. *Moneda Ibérica (MIB)*, Valencia. https://monedaiberica.org

Ripollès Alegre, Pere Pau, & Manuel Gozalbes. 2017. 'The Unofficial Roman Republican Asses produced in Spain', in *XV International Numismatic Congress, Taormina 2015: Proceedings, Vol. I*, eds. Maria Caccamo Caltabiano, Benedetto Carroccio, Daniele Castrizio, Mariangela Puglisi, Grazia Salamone, 691–5. Rome: Arbor Sapientiae editore.

Ripollès Alegre, Pere Pau, & Richard Witschonke. 2015. 'The unofficial semisses struck in Spain', in *Studies in Ancient Coinage in Honour of Andrew Burnett*, eds. Roger Bland & Dario Calomino, 51–108. London: Spink.

Rizakis, Athanasios. 1995. 'Le grec face au latin. Le paysage linguistique dans la péninsule balkanique sous l'Empire', in *Acta Colloquii Epigraphici Latini, Helsinki 3–6 September*, eds. Heikki Solin, Olli Salomies & Uta-Maria Liertz, 373–91. Helsinki: Societas Scientarium Fennica. Commentationes Humanarum Litterarum 104.

Robert, Louis. 1977. 'La titulature de Nicée et de Nicomédie: la gloire et la haine'. *Harvard Studies in Classical Philology* 81, 1–39.

Robinson, E. Stanley G. 1944. 'Greek coins found in the Cyrenaica'. *Numismatic Chronicle*, 4 (1/4), 105–13.

Roueché, Charlotte. 1989. 'Floreat Perge', in *Images of Authority: Papers presented to Joyce Reynolds on the occasion of her 70th birthday*, eds. Charlotte Roueché & Mary Mackenzie, 206–28. Cambridge: Cambridge Philological Society.

Rouvier, Jules. 1904. 'Numismatique des Villes de la Phénicie. Tyr'. *Journal International d'Archéologie Numismatique* 7, 65–108.

Rowan, Clare. 2012. *Under Divine Auspices: Divine ideology and the visualisation of imperial power in the Severan period*. Cambridge and New York: Cambridge University Press.

2016a. 'Ambiguity, iconology and entangled objects on coinage of the Republican world'. *Journal of Roman Studies* 106, 1–37.

2016b. 'Imagining empire in the Roman Republic', in *Neue Forschungen zur Münzprägung der römischen Republik*, eds. Florian Haymann, Wilhelm Hollstein & Martin Jehne, 279–92. Bonn: Habelt, *Nomismata* 8.

2019. *From Caesar to Augustus (c. 49 BC–AD 14): Using coins as sources*. Cambridge: Cambridge University Press.

Rumscheid, Jutta. 2000. *Kranz und Krone: zu Insignien, Siegespreisen und Ehrenzeichen der römischen Kaiserzeit*. Tübingen: Wasmuth.

Rutter, N. Keith. 2001. *Historia Numorum: Italy*. (*HN*). London: British Museum Press.

Sánchez, Pierre. 2021. 'Une émission monétaire inédite d'Amisos, *ciuitas libera et foederata* sous le Principat'. *Revue Numismatique* **178**, 115–36.

Sartre, Maurice. 2005. *The Middle East under Rome*. Cambridge, MA and London: Harvard University Press.

Sawaya, Ziad. 2005. *Histoire de Bérytos et d'Héliopolis d'après leurs monnaies, Ier siècle av. J.-C.–IIIe siècle apr. J.-C.* Beirut: Institut Français du Proche Orient.

Schaick, R. Palistrant. 2021. 'The "Marsyas of the Forum" image on Roman city coins of the Southern Levant'. *Scripta Classica Israelica* **40**, 169–202.

Scheidel, Walter. 2009. 'The Monetary Systems of the Han and Roman Empires', in *Rome and China, Comparative Perspectives on Ancient World Empires*, ed. Walter Scheidel, 127–208. Oxford: Oxford University Press.

Schönert-Geiss, Edith. 1972. *Die Münzprägung von Byzantion*. Berlin: Akademie.

Seaford, Richard. 2002. 'Reading Money: Leslie Kurke on the politics of meaning in archaic Greece'. *Arion* **9** (3), 145–65.

Seaford, Richard. 2004. *Money and the Early Greek Mind: Homer, philosophy, tragedy*. Cambridge: Cambridge University Press.

Seltman, Charles. 1948. 'Greek sculpture and some festival coins'. *Hesperia* **17** (2), 71–85.

Serafini, Camillo. 1937. 'Saggio intorno alle monete e medaglioni antichi ritrovati nelle catacombe di Panfilo sulla via Salaria Vetus in Roma', in *Scritti in onore di Bartolomeo Nogara raccolti in occasione del suo LXX anno*, ed. R. Paribeni, 421–43. Vatican City: Bartolomeo Nogara.

Sideropoulos, Kleanthis. 2004. 'Νομισματική ιστορία της ρωμαϊκής και προτοβυζαντινής Κρήτης (67 π.Χ –827 μ. Χ): Testimonia et desiderata', in *Creta romana e protobizantina: Atti del Congresso internazionale (Iraklion 23–30 settembre 2000)*, eds. Monica Livadiotti & Ilaria Simiakaki, 193–225. Padua: Bottega d'Erasmo.

Smekalova, Tatiana. 2009. 'The earliest application of brass and "pure" copper in the Hellenistic coinages of Asia Minor and the northern Black Sea coast', in *Mithridates VI and the Pontic Kingdom*, ed. Jakob M. Højte, 233–48. Aarhus: Aarhus University Press.

Smith, Christopher, & Liv Mariah Yarrow (eds.). 2012. *Imperialism, Cultural Politics, and Polybius*. Oxford: Oxford University Press.

Smith, R. R. R. 1996. 'Typology and diversity in the portraits of Augustus', *Journal of Roman Archaeology* **9**, 30–47.

Spoerri, Marguerite. 2006a. *Roman Provincial Coinage, Vol. VII.1: De Gordian Ier à Gordian III (238–244 après J.-C.). Asia*. (*RPC VII 1*) London: British Museum, and Paris: Bibliothèque nationale de France.

## 298 Bibliography

2006b. 'L'organisation de la production monétaire au sein de la province d'Asie à l'époque de Gordien III (238–244)'. *Revue Suisse de Numismatique* **85**, 97–128.

Spoerri Butcher, Marguerite, & Dario Calomino. 2015. 'Provincial coinages: Eastern provinces', in *A Survey of Numismatic Research 2008–2013*, eds. Carmen Arnold-Biucchi & Maria Caccamo Caltabiano, 228–43. Taormina: International Numismatic Commission and International Association of Professional Numismatists.

Stannard, Clive. 2018. 'The crisis of small change in Central Italy of the second and first centuries BC, and the function of overstriking'. *Revue belge de numismatique* **164**, 97–170.

Stannard, Clive, & Alejandro Sinner. 2014. 'A central Italian coin with Dionysus/ panther types, and contacts between central Italy and Spain, in the 2nd and 1st centuries BC'. *Saguntum: Papeles del Laboratorio de Arqueología de Valencia* **46**, 59–180.

Starr, Chester G. 1967. 'Naval activity in Greek imperial issues'. *Schweizerische Numismatische Rundschau* **46**, 51–7. Also reprinted as Starr 1979.

Starr, Chester G. 1979. Naval activity in Greek imperial issues. In *Essays on Ancient History*, eds. Arther Ferrill & Thomas Kelly, 278–85. Leiden: Brill.

Stella, Andrea. 2021. 'Le monete', in *Scavi di Nora, X. Nora: Il Tempio Romano 2008–2014, Vol. II.2: I materiali Romani e gli altri reperti*, eds. Jacopo Bonnetto, Valentina Mantovani & Arturo Zara, 505–24. Rome: Edizioni Quasar.

Strasser, Jean-Yves. 2020. 'Le mariage éphémère d'Hélios et de Koré à Sardes'. *Revue Numismatique* **177**, 127–64.

Stroobants, Fran. 2022. 'Roman provincial coinages: Eastern provinces', in *A Survey of Numismatic Research 2014–2022*, eds. Michael Alram, Jarosław Bodzek & Aleksander Bursche, 523–53. Warsaw, Krakow, Winterthur: International Numismatic Council.

Suspène, Arnaud, Jérémy Artru, Sylvia Nieto-Pelletier, Julien Olivier & Benjamin Gehres. 2023. 'The sources of the first Roman gold coins (3rd century BC)', in *AVREVS. The Power of Gold – Le Pouvoir de l'or. Proceedings of the International Conference*, eds. Arnaud Suspène, Maryse Blet-Lemarquand, Frédérique Duyrat & Sylvia Nieto-Pelletier. Bordeaux: Ausonius.

Suspène, Arnaud, Maryse Blet-Lemarquand, Sylvia Nieto-Pelletier, Benjamin Gehres, & Julien Flament. 2023. 'Gold for a revolution: The sources of Caesar's gold coinage', in *AVREVS. The Power of Gold – Le Pouvoir de l'or. Proceedings of the International Conference*, eds. Arnaud Suspène, Maryse Blet-Lemarquand, Frédérique Duyrat & Sylvia Nieto-Pelletier. Bordeaux: Ausonius.

Sutherland, C. H. V. 1967. *The Roman Imperial Coinage, Vol. VI: From Diocletian's reform (A.D. 294) to the death of Maxentius (A.D. 313). (RIC VI)*. London: Spink.

Sutherland, C. H. V. 1984. *The Roman Imperial Coinage, Vol. I: From 31 BC to AD 69 (RIC I)*. London: Spink.

Sweetman, Rebecca. 2013. *The Mosaics of Roman Crete*. Cambridge: Cambridge University Press.

Sydenham, Edward. 1919. 'The Roman Monetary System: part II'. *Numismatic Chronicle* **19**, 114–71.

Takmer, Burak. 2007. 'Lex Portorii Provinciae Lyciae: Ein Vorbericht über die Zollinschrift aus Andriake aus neronischer Zeit'. *Gephyra* **4**, 165–88.

Taliercio, Marina. 1986. 'Il bronzo di Neapolis', in *La monetazione di Neapolis nella Campania antica, Atti Convegno VII del CISN, Napoli 2024 aprile 1980*, 219–373. Rome: Istituto Italiano di Numismatica.

Taeuber, Hans. 2016. 'Graffiti und Inschriften', in *Hanghaus 2 in Ephesos. Wohneinheit 7*, ed. Elizabeth Rathmayr, 233–58. Vienna: Österreichische Akademie der Wissenschaften.

Tek, Tolga. 2005. 'The coins of Gordianus III found at Arykanda: Evidence for an earthquake relief fund in Lycia?' in *XIII Congreso internacional de numismática, Madrid 2003, Actas-Proceedings-Actes*, eds. Carmen Alfaro, Carmen Marcos & Paloma Otero, 945–57. Madrid: Ministerio de Cultura.

Termeer, Marleen. 2019. 'Minting Apart Together: Bronze Coinage Production in Campania and beyond in the Third Century BC', in *Processes of Cultural Change and Integration in the Roman World*, ed. Saskia Roselaar, 58–76. Leiden: Brill.

Terrenato, Nicola. 2019. *The early Roman expansion into Italy: Elite negotiation and family agendas*. Cambridge: Cambridge University Press.

Thompson, Margaret. 1954. *The Athenian Agora, II: Coins from the Roman through the Venetian period*. Princeton, NJ: Princeton University Press.

1977. 'A Greek imperial medallion from Pautalia'. *American Numismatic Society Museum Notes* **22**, 29–36.

Thompson, Margaret, Otto Mørkholm & Colin Kraay (eds.). 1973. *An Inventory of Greek Coin Hoards. (IGCH)*. New York: American Numismatic Society.

Thonemann, Peter. 2011. *The Maeander Valley: A historical geography from antiquity to Byzantium*. Cambridge: Cambridge University Press.

2015. *The Hellenistic World: Using coins as sources*. Cambridge: Cambridge University Press.

Tomlin, Roger. 2016. *Roman London's First Voices: Writing tablets from the Bloomberg excavations 2010–2014*. London: Museum of London Archaeology. Monograph 72.

300 Bibliography

Touratsoglou, Iannis. 1987. 'Macedonia', in *The Coinage of the Roman World in the Late Republic*, eds. Andrew Burnett & Michael Crawford, 53–78. Oxford: Archaeopress. British Archaeological Reports International Series 326.

1988. *Die Münzstätte von Thessaloniki in der römischen Kaiserzeit*. Berlin: De Gruyter.

2006. *Greece and the Balkans before the End of Antiquity*. Athens: Hellenic Numismatic Society.

2010. 'Coin production and coin circulation in the Roman Peloponnese', in *Roman Peloponnese III: Society, economy and culture under the Roman Empire: Continuity and innovation*, eds. Athanasiso Rizakis & Claudia Lepenioti, 235–51. Athens: National Hellenic research Foundation, and Paris: De Boccard.

Toynbee, Jocelyn. 1934. *The Hadrianic School: A Chapter in the history of Greek Art*, Cambridge: The University Press.

Toynbee, Jocelyn. 1944. 'Greek Imperial Medallions'. *Journal of Roman Studies* **34**, 65–73.

Troxell, Hyla. 1982. *The Coinage of the Lycian League*, New York: American Numismatic Society.

Van Heesch, Johan. 1979. 'Studie over de Semis en de Quadrans van Domitianus tot en met Antoninus Pius'. University of Ghent, PhD thesis.

1993a. 'Proposition d'une nouvelle datation des monnaies en bronze à l'autel de Lyon frappées sous Auguste'. *Bulletin de la Société française de Numismatique* **48** (4), 535–8.

1993b. 'The last civic coinages and the religious policy of Maximinus Daza (AD 312)'. *Numismatic Chronicle* **153**, 65–75.

2005. 'Les Romains et la monnaie gauloise: Laisser-faire, laisser-aller?' in *Les Celtes et Rome, nouvelles études numismatiques*, eds. Jeannot Metzler & David Wigg-Wolf, 229–45. Mainz: von Zabern. Studien zur Fundmünzen der Antike 19.

2009. 'Providing markets with small change in the early Roman empire: Italy and Gaul'. *Revue Belge de Numismatique* **155**: 125–41.

Veyne, Paul. 1961. 'Le Marsyas colonial et l'indépendance des cités'. *Revue de philologie* **35**, 86–98.

Visonà, Paolo. 1992. 'Carthaginian Bronze coinage in Sardinia', in *Numismatique et histoire économique phéniciennes et puniques: Actes du Colloque tenu à Louvain-la-Neuve, 15–16 Mai 1987*, eds. Tony Hackens & Ghislaine Moucharte, 121–132. Leuven: Séminaire de numismatique Marcel Hoc, Université Catholique de Louvain. Studia Phoenicia 9.

Vitale, Rosa. 1998. 'Catalogo dei rinvenimenti sporadici, in stipe, in ripostigli', in *La monetazione romano-campana (Atti del X Convegno del Centro Internazionale di Studi Numismatici, Napoli 18–19 Giugno 1993)*. Rome: Istituto Italiano di Numismatica.

## Bibliography  **301**

Von Aulock, Hans. 1975. *Die Münzprägung des Gordian III und der Tranquillina in Lykien.* Tübingen: Wasmuth.

Von Glahn, Richard. 1996. *Fountain of Fortune: Money and monetary policy in China 1000–1700.* Berkeley, CA and London: University of California Press. 2016. *The Economic History of China. From antiquity to the nineteenth century.* Cambridge: Cambridge University Press.

Von Kaenel, Hans-Markus. 1984. 'Britannicus, Agrippina minor und Nero in Thrakien'. *Schweizerische numismatische Rundschau* **63**, 127–50.

Von Reden, Sitta. 1995. *Exchange in Ancient Greece.* London: Duckworth.

Von Reden, Sitta. 1997. Money, law and exchange: Coinage in the Greek Polis. *Journal of Hellenic Studies* **117**, 154–76.

Vout, Caroline. 2005. 'Antinous, archaeology and history.' *Journal of Roman Studies* **95**, 80–96.

Walker, David R. 1988. 'The Roman coins', in *The Temple of Sulis Minerva at Bath II: The finds from the sacred spring*, ed. B. Cunliffe, 281–358. Oxford: Oxford University Committee for Archaeology. Monograph 16.

Wankel, H. 1979. *Die Inschriften von Ephesos: Band I.* Bonn: Habelt.

Watson, George. 2017. 'Die-sharing and the 'pseudo-autonomous' coinages'. *Numismatic Chronicle* **177**, 201–11.

2018. 'The provincial coinage of Aemilian: A study in imperial communication'. *Numismatic Chronicle* **178**, 185–212.

2019a. *Connections, Communities and Coinage: The system of coin production in southern Asia Minor, AD 218–276.* New York: American Numismatic Society.

2019b. 'Fear and loathing in Roman Asia Minor? Inter-polis relations in the light of the numismatic evidence', in *Kontinuität und Diskontinuität, Prozesse der Romanisierung: Fallstudien zwischen Iberischer Halbinsel und Vorderem Orient*, eds. Thomas Schattner, Dieter Vieweger & David Wigg-Wolf, 105–19. Rahden: Marie Leidorf.

2020. 'Kraft in the 21st century: A new listing of shared dies in the Roman provincial coinage'. *American Journal of Numismatics* **32**, 219–72.

2021. 'The development and spread of die sharing in the Roman provincial coinage of Asia Minor'. *American Journal of Archaeology* **125** (1), 123–42.

Webb, Percy H. 1927. *The Roman Imperial Coinage, Vol. V Part 1.* (*RIC V.1*). London: Spink.

Weiss, Peter. 1991. 'Auxe Perge: Beobachtungen zu einem bemerkenswerten städtischen Dokument des späten 3. Jahrhunderts n. Chr.' *Chiron* **21**, 353–93.

1992. 'Zur Münzprägung mit den Formeln ΑΙΤΗΣΑΜΕΝΟΥ und ΕΙΣΑΝΓΕΙΛΑΝΤΟΣ', in *Studien zum antiken Kleinasien II*, ed. Elmar Schwertheim, 167–80. Bonn: Habelt. Asia Minor Studien 8.

## 302 Bibliography

2000. 'Euergesie oder römische Prägegenehmigung? Αἰτησαμένου-Formular auf Städtemünzen der Provinz Asia, Roman Provincial Coinage (RPC) II und persönliche Aufwendungen im Münzwesen'. *Chiron* **30**, 235–54.

2004. 'Städtische Münzprägung und zweite Sophistik,' in *Paideia: The World of the Second Sophistic*, ed., Barbara Borg, 179–200. Berlin: de Gruyter.

2005. 'The cities and their money', in *Coinage and Identity in the Roman Provinces*, eds. Christopher Howgego, Volker Heuchert & Andrew Burnett, 57–68. Oxford: Oxford University Press.

Weisser, Bernhard. 2005. 'Pergamum as paradigm', in *Coinage and Identity in the Roman Provinces*, eds. Christopher Howgego, Volker Heuchert & Andrew Burnett, 135–42. Oxford: Oxford University Press.

Westner, Katrin, Thomas Birch, Fleur Kemmers, Sabine Klein, Heidi Höfer & Hans-Michael Seitz. 2020. 'Rome's rise to power: Geochemical analysis of silver coinage from the Western Mediterranean (fourth to second centuries BCE).' *Archaeometry* **62** (3), 577–92.

Wilkes, John. 2000. 'The Danube provinces', in *The Cambridge Ancient History XI: The High Empire, CE 70–92*, eds. Alan Bowman, Peter Garnsey & Dominic Rathbone, 577–603. Cambridge: Cambridge University Press.

Williams, Daniela. 2011. 'Note sulla circolazione monetaria in Etruria meridionale nel III secolo a.C.', in *Proceedings of the XIVth International Numismatic Congress, Glasgow 2009*, ed. Nicholas Holmes, 1103–14. Glasgow: International Numismatic Commission.

Williams, Jonathan, & Andrew Burnett. 1998. 'Alexander the Great and the coinages of western Greece', in *Studies in Greek Coinage in Memory of Martin Jessop Price*, eds. Richard Ashton & Silvia Hurter (eds.), 379–93. London: Spink.

Wilson, Andrew. 2012. 'Neo-Punic and Latin inscriptions in Roman North Africa: Function and display', in Alex Mullen and Patrick James (eds.), *Multilingualism in the Graeco-Roman Worlds*. Cambridge: Cambridge University Press, 265–315.

Woolf, Greg. 1996. 'Monumental writing and the expansion of Roman society in the early Empire'. *Journal of Roman Studies* **86**, 22–39.

Woytek, Bernhard. 2004. 'Die Metalla-Prägungen des Kaisers Traian und seiner Nachfolger'. *Numismatische Zeitschrift* **111/12**, 35–68.

2011a. 'The coinage of Apamea Myrlea under Trajan and the problem of double communities in the Roman East'. *Numismatic Chronicle* **171**, 121–32.

2011b. 'Die bilinguen Münzen Traians: Eine Fallstudie zu numismatischen Erscheinungsformen des Bilingualismus im römischen Reich.' *Chiron* **41**, 417–59.

2015. '"Hominem te memento!" Der mahnende Sklave im römischen Triumph und seine Ikonographie'. *Tyche* **30**, 193–209.

2016. 'The denarii RRC 445/3, signed by the consuls Lentulus and Marcellus: A die study', in *Neue Forschungen zur Münzprägung der römischen Republik*, eds. Florian Haymann, Wilhelm Hollstein & Martin Jehne, 173–214. Bonn: Habelt. Nomismata 8.

2019a. 'Inschriften und Legenden auf Münzen des Augustus im Kontext: Eine numismatisch-epigraphische Studie.' *Chiron* **49**, 383–440.

2019b. 'Elagabalus and the *Aedes Dei Invicti Solis Elagabali*'. *Numismatic Chronicle* **179**, 205–24.

Yaraş, Ahmet, & Dinçer Savaş Lenger. 2013. 'Un ripostiglio di metá terzo secolo d.c. rinvenuto as Allianoi in Mysia'. *Annali dell'Istituto di Numismatica* **59**, 271–89.

Yarrow, Liv Mariah. 2012. 'Antonine coinage', in *The Oxford Handbook of Greek and Roman Coinage*, ed. William Metcalf, 423–52. Oxford: Oxford University Press.

2021. *The Roman Republic to 49 BCE: Using coins as sources*. Cambridge: Cambridge University Press.

Yonge, David. 1979. 'The so-called Interregnum coinage'. *Numismatic Chronicle* **139**, 47–60.

Zanker, Paul. 1988. *The Power of Images in the Age of Augustus*. Ann Arbor, MI: University of Michigan Press.

Zelnick-Abramowitz, Rachel. 2013. *Taxing Freedom in Thessalian Manumission Inscriptions*. Leiden: Brill.

Zuiderhoek, Arjan. 2009. *The Politics of Munificence in the Roman Empire: Citizens, elites and benefactors in Asia Minor*. Cambridge: Cambridge University Press.

APPENDICES

# 1. Numismatic Glossary

(by Andrew Meadows, updated and revised by the author)

**asiarch**   Chief priest of the provincial cult of the emperor in Asia.

**authority**   The formal guarantor of the value of a coin. For civic coinages, the authority is generally presumed to be the government of the city itself. Within kingdoms and empires, the authority may the supreme ruler (e.g., king or emperor), or an appointee (e.g., provincial governor).

**axis**   See **die-axis**.

**bronze**   A term used loosely to refer to any copper alloy coin. Pure bronze is an alloy of copper and tin; brass is an alloy of copper and zinc. Some lead might be added to either alloy. It is impossible to determine which alloy was used for a particular coin, and scientific analyses are fairly few and far between.

**cast**   Extremely large bronze coins were made by casting. A mould was prepared with the required designs and molten metal was then poured in. This method was unusual for coinage and was used mainly because the technical difficulties of making a large coin by **striking** were too great.

**circulation**   The movement of coinage once it has been issued. The circulation of ancient coinage can be studied through the evidence of **hoards** and **single finds**, as well as from documentary sources.

**circulation wear**   The wear, or deterioration in condition visible on a coin due to the time it has spent in **circulation**.

**control-mark**   A mark engraved, generally into the **reverse die**, apparently to indicate some aspect of the administration of the production of the coin.

**copper alloy**   See **bronze**.

**countermark**   A mark in the form of letter(s), a symbol, a **monogram**, or a combination of these punched into a coin. The reason for the application of such marks is not always certain, and probably varied from case to case. Some served to reauthorise a coin for **circulation** in new areas. Others perhaps assigned new **denominations** to old coins.

**denarius** The name of the standard Roman silver coin, originally worth 10 asses (hence denarius = 'tenner'), but later, in the second century BCE, retariffed at 16 asses. See Appendix 2: Denominational Systems.

**denomination** The value of an ancient coin. These values are generally expressed in a standard set of units, subdivisions and multiples thereof. See Appendix 2: Denominational Systems.

**didrachm** The name of a coin denomination, meaning 'two drachms'. The name of the standard silver coin in Italy during the third century BCE. See **drachma**.

**die** A piece of metal engraved with a design and then used to **strike** coins. Two dies were required to strike the two faces of a coin: the **obverse die** and the **reverse die**.

**die-axis** The relative orientation of **obverse** and **reverse** images on a coin.

**die-engraver** The artist responsible for the engraving of the design onto **dies**. They are generally anonymous on ancient coinage.

**die-link** The use of the same die for two different coins.

**die-study** A technical numismatic study of a coinage that involves the identification of the **dies** used to **strike** a coinage. Such studies allow for the establishment of the relative chronology of a coinage. They also permit quantification of a coinage by identifying the number of dies used to produce a given coinage.

**die-wear** The wear, or damage experienced by a **die** in the course of its use to **strike** coins. This may take the form of gradual deterioration or sudden breaks. It can be used by numismatists as part of a **die-study** to determine the relative chronology of production.

**distater** The name of a coin denomination, meaning two staters. See **stater**.

**drachma** or **drachm.** The name of a coin denomination, common in the Greek world. See Appendix 2: Denominational Systems.

**electrum** An alloy of gold and silver.

**emergency hoard** A **hoard** of coins, and perhaps other precious objects, secreted together in antiquity at a time of emergency. Such deposits tend to consist of a cross-section of coins in **circulation** at the time of deposit. They may thus serve as evidence for the nature of the coin supply at a given time.

**ethnic** A **legend** indicating the identity of the people (e.g., the citizens of a city) acting as the **authority** behind a coinage.

**exergue** The area on a coin below the ground-line of a design.

**fiat** See **fiduciary**.

**306** Appendices

**fiduciary**   Coinage that takes its value not from the content of the metal that it contains, but from the *fiat* (order or decree) of the **authority** behind it. See also **over-valuation**. Nearly all bronze coins had a value higher than at of the metal they contained, and in that sense they were fiduciary.

**field**   An empty area of a coin design wherein subsidiary symbols such as **mint-marks**, **control-marks**, or **legends** may be placed.

**flan**   The metal blank from which a coin is struck.

**hoard**   A group of coins deposited together in antiquity, and thus forming a single archaeological context for multiple objects. The reasons for deposit are likely to have been varied, and are rarely recoverable with certainty from the archaeological deposits. Categories of hoard include but are perhaps not limited to **savings hoards**, **emergency hoards** and **ritual deposits**.

**imitation**   A coin that, more or less slavishly, copies the types of a model coinage, but is not a product of the same **authority** as its model.

**intrinsic**   Coinage that takes its value from the quantity (weight) of metal that it contains.

**issue**   Either the process of officially placing a coin into circulation; or a specific subsection of a period of coin production, identifiable by specific **control-marks** or **mint-magistrate**'s signatures.

**issuer**   The person administratively responsible for the production of a coin. The identity and indeed status of the issuer of an ancient coin is often unclear. The terms **moneyer** and **mint-magistrate** are often used to refer to officials known or assumed to have been responsible for the production of coin within a state.

**legend**   The inscription(s) that appear on a coin.

**magistrate**   See **mint-magistrate**.

**mint**   A place where coins are produced. In the vast majority of ancient cases, no evidence exists for the nature of physical locations of mints, and many may not have consisted of permanent facilities. The term is therefore rather loosely used for the ancient world to indicate place and facility of production.

**mint-magistrate**   The official, whether elected or appointed, responsible for oversight of the production of coins within the **mint**. The names of many private individuals that appear on ancient coins are assumed to be those of mint-magistrates. See also **moneyer**.

**mint-mark**   A mark engraved, generally into the **reverse die**, to indicate the mint in which a coin was produced. Such marks may consist of letters, symbols or monograms. Such marks may appear in association with **control marks**.

**moneyer**   The official, whether elected or appointed, responsible for oversight of the production of coins within the **mint**. The term is most commonly used in ancient numismatics to refer to the **mint magistrates** of the Roman Republican mint.

**monogram**   An identifying mark made up of a number of letters overlaid and/or ligatured. These are often found on coins as **mint-marks** or **control marks**, or in **countermarks**.

**neocorate**   The term 'neocoros' means 'temple-keeper' and was used to denote the award to an individual city of a provincial temple in honour of an emperor. The title might be repeated for the second, third or even fourth such temple ('four times neocorate').

**obverse**   The 'heads' side of a coin, produced by the **obverse die**. It is most often the side of the coin on which a portrait or other form of head is depicted, sometimes thereby providing an indication of who the **authority** behind the coin was. See also **reverse**.

**obverse die**   The **die** used to **strike** the **obverse** side of a coin.

**overstrike**   A coin produced by **striking** an existing coin with a new pair of **dies**. Overstrikes tend to be imperfect, and thus allow identification of the designs of both the original coin and those struck over it.

**over-valuation**   Precious metal coins (gold and silver) often had a value greater than that of the intrinsic value of the metal they contained. This greater value is known as the 'over-valuation'.

**posthumous coinage**   A coinage produced in the name of a ruler after their death.

**quinarius**   The name of a Roman silver coin, originally worth 5 asses (hence quinarius = 'fiver'), but later, in the second century BCE, retariffed at 8 asses. Quinarii were made in small numbers at Rome in the late Republic and imperial period; confusingly they were then called **victoriati**. The term is also applied to silver coins made in Gaul during the first century BCE, which were made to approximately the same standard.

**reverse**   The 'tails' side of the coin, produced by the **reverse die**. It is often the side of the coin bearing the **legend**, and thus provides a clear indication of where the coin was produced. See also **obverse**.

**reverse die**   The **die** used to strike the **reverse** side of a coin.

**ritual deposit**   A group of coins deposited together, not for purposes of saving, but for religious purposes such as offerings to gods. Unlike

**many** hoards, such deposits were arguably not intended to be recovered.

**romanisation** A much disputed term, which is used in this book in a limited sense to denote the process whereby coins minted at places other than Rome came to resemble those minted at Rome.

**savings hoard** A group of coins gathered together in a single deposit over a period of time by means of, or for the purposes of, saving.

**sestertius** The name of a Roman coin denomination, originally a silver coin worth 2½ asses (hence sestertius = semis tertius = (literally) 'and half the third'), but later, in the second century BCE, retariffed at 4 asses. A few silver sestertii continued to be made in the first century BCE, but in the imperial period the sestertius was a large bronze coin, made of orichalcum.

**single-find** A coin found in isolation either by accident or by deliberate means such as metal-detecting. This may occur within a controlled archaeological survey or excavation environment, or not.

**stater** The name of a coin denomination, usually in gold or silver.

**strike/striking** The process by which the majority of ancient coins were produced. This consisted of placing a blank of metal (**flan**) on the **obverse die**, positioning the **reverse die** on top of the blank, and then applying force in the form of hammer blows (striking) in imprint the designs of the two **dies** onto the piece of metal. See also **cast**.

**test-cut** A cut made into an **intrinsic** value coin to make sure that it is made of solid metal, and not plated.

**tetradrachm** The name of a coin denomination, common in the Greek world, meaning four drachms. See Appendix 2: Denominational Systems.

**type** The numismatic term for the design that appears on a coin; this may thus be subdivided into **obverse**- and **reverse**-types.

**victoriate** A Roman silver coin, made only about 200 BCE, named after the figure of Victory on the reverse. The coins were debased and contained about the same amount of silver as the purer silver quinarii, which is probably why quinarii later came to be called victoriati (see also **quinarius**).

**weight standard** The official system of weights in use in an ancient state. In an **intrinsic** value coinage, value depended on weight. Weight standards thus become a means of unifying or dividing **circulation** of coinage, depending on decisions taken about adoption or rejection of specific weight standards.

## 2. Denominational Systems

(by Andrew Meadows, updated and revised by the author)

### (a) The Greek World before the Romans

The Roman world was not unified by a single monetary system before the fourth century CE. In the Greek world, before the Roman conquests and annexations, archaic and classical periods, the basic unit was the drachma ('handful'), which was subdivided into six obols ('spits'); in turn the obol might be divided into a varying number of 'chalkoi' ('bronzes'). Small denominations are often described today as 'fractions'.

### (b) Rome

The Roman monetary system before the Second Punic War (218–201 BCE) was complex and unstable. The earliest silver coinage of the late fourth/early third century BCE was essentially based on the Greek drachma system, as used in southern Italy, on a variety of different standards. From the start this coinage was accompanied by bronze money in a variety of forms. The basic Roman bronze unit was the as, originally weighing one Roman pound of 12 ounces (approx. 324 g). At the end of the third century the weight of the as dropped to 2 ounces (approx. 56 g). Around 212 BCE, the Roman state introduced a new silver denomination known as the denarius (a 10-as piece). This would remain the basic Roman silver coin until the third century CE. In about 141 BCE the denarius was re-tariffed at 16 asses, and remained at this value for centuries. The full range of denominations issued in silver and bronze under the Republic can be set out as follows:

**Silver**
1 denarius = 16 asses
1 quinarius = half denarius = 8 asses
1 sestertius = quarter denarius = 4 asses

**Bronze**
1 as (= 1/16 denarius)
1 semis = half as
1 triens = third as
1 quadrans = quarter as

1 sextans = sixth as
1 uncia = twelfth as

Under Augustus the bronze coinage was reformed to produce the following denominations:

Sestertius (4 asses or ¼ denarius)
Dupondius (2 asses or half sestertius)
As (quarter sestertius)
Semis (half as)
Quadrans (quarter as)

In addition the gold aureus, which had started to be produced in serious quantities by Julius Caesar, was standardised at a value of 25 denarii.

## (c)  Roman Provinces

As the Romans took over new territories they inherited different systems. In the western part of their empire (west of the Adriatic) any local denominations quickly disappeared and were replaced by Roman ones.

The picture in the eastern part of the Empire was more complicated. The two systems were both in use, although gradually the Roman system prevailed. For the Roman province of Asia, inscriptions show that a system was developed to accommodate both systems, whereby:

1 drachm = ¾ of a denarius = 12 asses
1 obol = 2 asses

In the east the 'as' was called the 'assarion' in Greek. However, the sestertius and the dupondius were not used in the east.

The position in other provinces is less clear, but a few coin inscriptions show that obols continued, at least at some cities, until the third century CE. The process of transition cannot be documented at all precisely, and so we are usually in the dark about the denominations used for the bronze coins of the cities in the Empire.

In the third century CE a new silver coin was introduced, known today as the antoninianus (after the emperor whom we call Caracalla, but whose real name was Antoninus, during whose reign it was first produced) or the radiate, from the radiate crown worn by the emperor, to distinguish it from the denarius. Its precise relationship to the denarius is, however, not known, and values of both 2 denarii and 1½ denarii have their supporters.

## 3. The Production of Ancient Coinage

(by Andrew Meadows)

Ancient coinage was hand made, in two senses. First the actual process of striking the coins was carried out by hand. A coin was produced by placing a blank piece of metal on a die set within an anvil, or similar anchoring device. This is known to numismatists as the 'obverse die', or sometimes the 'anvil die'. A second die on the end of a punch (the 'reverse die') was then placed on top of the blank and hit forcefully with a hammer, probably several times. The result was a flat, roundish piece of metal with, potentially, designs or 'types' on both sides.

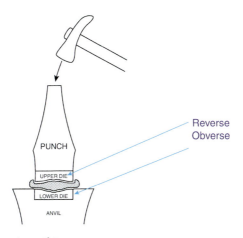

The coin striking process.

The second hand-crafted element of coin production was the engraving of the designs that appeared on ancient coins. Unlike modern coin dies, which are all mechanically copied from a single master engraving, each ancient die was individually engraved and thus different from every other. These two elements of hand-production produce an interesting mixture of results. On the one hand, there is an individuality of design of dies, which allows us to trace the products of an ancient mint in a way that is impossible for modern coins. It also allows us to count the number of dies used to produce a particular coinage, and thus to quantify it. On the other, hand striking, although not nearly so fast as modern machine production, allows for the production of thousands of identical or closely similar objects within a very

## 312 Appendices

short space of time. Coins in this sense are one of the very rare examples from the pre-modern world of mass production.

The substance of ancient coinage was also profoundly different from that of today's coins. In origin, coinage was a monetary instrument of intrinsic value. The earliest coins, produced in Asia Minor from the mid-seventh to mid-sixth centuries BCE were made of carefully controlled amounts of electrum, the alloy of gold and silver. Subsequently, most probably under the influence of the prevailing monetary tradition of the Near East, coinage was throughout the latter part of the sixth century through to the first century CE largely produced in high-quality silver, with gold being produced when circumstances of supply or demand particularly prompted it. The fact that these precious metal coins took their value from their weight often made it possible for them to circulate over wide areas, and beyond the borders of the political authorities that had produced them. Nevertheless, there were constraining factors. The novelty of coinage, in contrast to the earlier Near Eastern practice of making payments with weighed amounts of silver bullion, lay both in the carefully regulated weights (denominations) at which coins were produced, which added facility of use, and in the designs that were struck on them, which provided clear statement of origin, and thus guaranteed their metal quality (value). While both developments added convenience and functionality, they also served potentially to constrain monetary behaviour. The localised system of weight standards of the ancient world according to which ancient coins were denominated could fragment as well as unify monetary behaviour. Similarly, a mark of guarantee could only function where it was recognised. This was particularly the case when the phenomenon of bronze coinage arose in the latter part of the fifth century BCE. Such coinages were, on the whole, produced as fiduciary instruments, whose value lay not so much in their metal content, which was far less tightly controlled than in precious metal coinage, but in the guaranteed system in which they circulated. Such fiduciary coinages depended for their value essentially on the confidence of the recipients of the coin in their ability to reuse it later.

# Notes

## Preface

1. The approach is chronological, except for Chapter 1, which deals with coins in gold and silver (for the most part very different in nature from the city coins which form the main focus of the book); and Chapter 4, which sets out a general model for the way that city coinage behaved in the imperial period.
2. At https://rpc.ashmus.ox.ac.uk/map/create.

## 1 Precious Metal Coinages at Rome and in the Provinces

1. For most of the period the city coinages were mainly in bronze and their development will be traced in the remaining chapters of the book.
2. Harris 2008, 2019.
3. Heymans 2021 is the most recent discussion. I omit here the strange phenomenon of the early electrum coinage (an alloy of gold and silver) that was the 'beginning' of coinage in the Greek and Persian worlds.
4. For Bronze Age antecedents, see Ialongo & Lago 2021, especially pp. 3–4 (the presence of scales and their Fig. 4 map).
5. Although, for most of the Julio-Claudian period, the principal mint for gold and silver was located at Lugdunum (Lyons) in southern France.
6. The Broads hoard from Norfolk, consisting of ten (so far) aurei of Augustus, mostly of the Caius and Lucius type: see https://finds.org.uk/database/artefacts/record/id/866028
7. A similar approach could be taken for silver. Examples are the way that many silver denarii of the Republican period found their way to Armenia. Many of Augustus and Tiberius went to India, presumably as objects of trade. There are many third-century hoards of Roman denarii from free Germany; the majority show a preference for denarii minted before the Severan debasement. However, space precludes a discussion in this book.
8. For a discussion of the methodological clash between the archaeological and literary evidence on the Roman use of silver coinage, see Burnett & Crawford 2014.
9. Westner *et al.* 2020. The analyses reported in Burnett & Hook 1989 show that the first Roman coins were very similar to contemporary coins of Neapolis, suggesting that they may have been made there.

**314** Notes to Pages 6–26

10. Burnett & Molinari 2015.
11. Albarède *et al.* 2016.
12. Burnett & Hook 1989: 154.
13. The chronology of the later third-century Italian coinage is not very secure, as there is not much evidence to go on. It has been suggested that the coinage of Tarentum continues until the Second Punic War by Libero Mangieri 2012.
14. There are no silver hoards from Sicily dateable to 240–220, but one early Roman coin has been reported from near Enna (Vitale 1998: 297).There are also five pieces in the Palermo Museum and one in the Syracuse Museum (Vitale 1998: 298; 351), all likely enough to be local finds.
15. The analyses reported by Westner *et al.* 2020 suggest that most of the bullion used by Rome for its coinage before the denarius came from Greece, from sources around the Aegean, just as was used by the south Italian cities for their coinage.
16. See Chapter 2 for a discussion of Roman motives.
17. Yarrow 2021: 35–7.
18. Parisot-Sillon 2018 is the latest discussion.
19. Meadows 2013.
20. Debernardi 2021.
21. Crawford 1985: 145–6.
22. For an earlier debasement, at the time of the Social War, see Parisot-Sillon & Sarah 2018.
23. Ripollès 2017.
24. Gorini 2015.
25. Van Heesch 2005.
26. De Callataÿ 2011, 2015 and 2021.
27. Burnett 2021a.
28. Helly 1997.
29. *OGIS* 629, with Matthews 1984.
30. Lemercier 2021 makes a good case for associating the small silver coinage of Stratonicea (known from only four specimens) with an imperial gift of 250,000 denarii to help reconstruction after an earthquake.
31. Blouin & Burnett 2020: 240.
32. The interpretation given here is set out more fully in Burnett in press a.
33. Butcher & Ponting 2015.
34. Butcher & Ponting 2015.
35. Hopkins 1980 and 2002, with the critique of Buttrey 1991.
36. McConnell *et al.* 2018.
37. However, Drinkwater (2019: 56–80) has argued that Nero's inner circle looked after the administration of the empire, while he indulged in his aesthetic and athletic interests.

Notes to Pages 26–38 **315**

38. Butcher 2004: 81–92. For details of the coins, see *RPC II*, p. 11, and *RPC III*, pp. 797–8 (with table on 800).
39. Many – perhaps all – of the cistophori of Hadrian were struck on earlier cistophori, of Antony, Augustus and Claudius, and so they should be considered in the same light as the Egyptian tetradrachms of Nero. In this case, once again, the purpose seems to have been to save silver.
40. See Chapter 7.
41. The use of many mints in reminiscent of the recoinage of cistophori in Asia under Hadrian.
42. Butcher 1989.
43. Butcher & Ponting 2015.
44. Burnett 2005.
45. This rule, named after the Elizabethan financier Thomas Gresham (1519–79), holds that people remove fine coins out of circulation and add them to their own savings or melt them down, leaving only the more debased coins in circulation. For an application to the ancient world, see, e.g., Asolati & Gorini 2006.
46. Blouin & Burnett 2020: 275–8, where also the overvaluation of the tetradrachm against the denarius is set out.
47. 439 denarii and 216 cistophori, found in a jug, as reported in the Turkish press in January 2021. The last coins seem to date from the middle years of Augustus' reign. An account of the hoard was given to the American Numismatic Society on 5 November 2021 by Hüseyin Köker (Suleyman Demirel University).
48. *AE* 2009, 1428.
49. Cottier *et al.* 2008: 61.
50. Cribb 1992: 13 (gold ingots as 'the normal medium for large-scale monetary transactions'; silver rare until the Tang period); Scheidel 2009; Von Glahn 1996: 29–39 (gold as an important form of currency in China, with jade and pearls and with spade and knife 'coins'; and later with copper coins, but suggesting a reduced role in the Qin and Han periods); Von Glahn (1996: 99–100) is sceptical about the extended use of gold in Qin China; *cf.* 154.
51. Kagan & Ellis 2022.
52. Kagan & Ellis 2022.
53. Yarrow 2021: 143.
54. Jenkins 1987.
55. Kay 2014: 245–51.
56. Suspène, Blet-Lemarquand, Nieto-Pelletier *et al.* 2023.
57. Molinari 2003: 202–3.
58. See the graph in Elliott 2014: 134.
59. See note 46.
60. But see note 5, for the production of imperial gold at Lugdunum in the Julio-Claudian period.

**316** Notes to Pages 40–53

61. Bland 2017: 358–9 (Gordian), Bland 2014: 108–9 (Philip).
62. For Samosata, see Holmes 2022.
63. De Romanis 2020.
64. For Diocletian's edict of 301, which set the maximum price for many commodities and services, see further in Chapter 7.
65. Morrison *et al.* 1985.
66. Bland 2013.
67. A good example is the papyrus published by Chambers *et al.* 1981 no. 3401 (mid fourth century): 'To Sir my brother Papnouthis, Dorotheus sends greetings. You did well to write to me about the solidi: suddenly, I started looking for and I found the required quantity from the Alexandrian, at the rate of 135[0] myriads of denarii. Also, take care to send me some common coin tomorrow common, because rumour has it about raising the recruiting gold, and everyone seeks to procure solidi, and the price of it rises day by day. But quickly send common coins for us to finalise the purchase (of solidi).' (Translation after Carrié 2003: 187).

## 2    The Beginnings of an Empire in Italy and the Western Mediterranean (300–200 BCE)

1. For an analysis of Roman expansion at this time, see now Terrenato 2019.
2. 'Aes signatum', derived from Pliny's remark that 'Servius Tullius primus signavit aes' (*Natural History* 33.43), translates as 'struck bronze', but these ingots were cast, not struck.
3. See Williams & Burnett 1998. Two main explanations have been invoked to explain this increase. The first is spending on warfare, and especially the hiring of mercenaries and mercenary kings by the various Greek cities in Italy. This took place in their struggle with the inland and indigenous communities and subsequently with the growing power of Rome. A second, and complementary, explanation is made in terms of the new fashion of displaying wealth that came in during the fourth century with the spectacular victories of the Macedonians in the east.
4. See the relevant entries in Rutter 2001.
5. Burnett 2016b.
6. Heraclides of Pontus fr. 122 = Plutarch, *Camillus* 22. See also Strabo V.3.5, 232, on the supposed embassies from Alexander the Great and Demetrius to Rome, which referred to Rome's 'kinship with the Greeks'.
7. Bernard 2017 and 2018.
8. Horace, *Epistle* II, 156–7: Graecia capta ferum victorem cepit.
9. Burnett & Molinari 2015.

Notes to Pages 53–62 **317**

10. The term *aes rude* is derived from Pliny's report that before the adoption of coinage the Romans used uncoined bronze in Rome ('antea rudi usos Romae': *Natural History* 33.42; *cf.* Livy 26.11 on 'rudera').

11. Apart from the small issues of Tarentum and Metapontum of the Second Punic War, struck for Hannibal at a Punic weight standard.

12. Taliercio 1986. See also Termeer 2019.

13. There seem to be only two later silver hoards of the early denarius period from the region: Pisa *RRCH* 102 (all victoriati) and Tarquinia *RRCH* 108 (12 denarii).

14. The series from Etruria: Volaterrae, Tarquinii and the wheel series; from Umbria: Iguvium, Tuder and the oval series (on which, see Crawford 2002).

15. Williams 2011. The main exception to this pattern is Cosa, where earlier Roman coins, both struck and *aes grave* were found. It was, of course, the site of a Roman colony founded in 273 BCE, which may perhaps explain its exceptional nature. See now Naimann & Termeer 2020.

16. For this paragraph, see Burnett & Molinari 2015: 33–7, 41–7 and 90–1.

17. Jehasse 1987–88 and 1989. P. Visonà has confirmed (*in litt.*) that this is the case.

18. Jehasse & Jehasse 1962, and Jehasse 1991–92.

19. Jehasse & Jehasse 1973: 117, 235 no. 594 (*RRC* 190/4); Jehasse 1987–88 (a bronze semilibral uncia, as *RRC* 38/6, and 'à Aléria le monnayage romain le plus ancien consiste en monnaies d'argent, des *victoriats* frappés en 211'); Jehasse 1989 (details of 115 pieces, including these pieces, adding a further twenty-three victoriates, as well as a more normal run of bronzes and later silver); Jehasse 1991–92: 33 ('26 monnaies républicaines: 13 victoriats, 6 as, 1 semis, 2 triens, 4 quadrans'). Brenot 1973 also catalogued twelve Roman Republican coins from Mariana.

20. Finds of the Punic coins found at Tharros have been published by Manfredi 1999 and in other articles by the same author. For the Roman period, see Polosa 2006. See also Pesce 1955–57 and 1961.

21. *RRCH* 32. Another quadrigatus has been recorded from Bingias de Susu (Guspini, environs).

22. Gorini 2015 and Stella 2021, with earlier references.

23. The earliest hoard dates to the 190s BCE: Polosa 2006: 145.

24. See the summary by Jenkins 1973: 343–4.

25. Visonà 1992.

26. Puglisi 2009; Manganaro 2012; Buttrey *et al.* 1989 (Morgantina); Frey-Kupper 2013 (Monte Iato); Frey-Kupper 2014.

27. *IGCH* 2231 = *RRCH* 62.

28. Caltabiano *et al.* 1997, esp. 49–60. This dating is not accepted by Manganaro 2012: 27, whose own dating is not clear, but he dated the burial of the hoards to 215–201 BCE (p. 31). Carroccio (2004: 83–5) sees a gap in silver production from 263 to 217 BCE.

**318** Notes to Pages 62–9

29. Jenkins & Lewis 1963: 35–42, Jenkins 1978: 36–42. The hoards: Puglisi 2009, H159, H250, H308, H375 and *Coin Hoards* VIII.296.

30. There is some tenuous evidence for Roman silver of the period from Sicily: the plated core of Mars/horse's head ROMANO didrachm from Monte Marzo (Vitale 1998: 297). Some support for the view could be derived from the presence of some early Roman silver coins (ones minted before the quadrigati) in Sicilian museums. There is one in Syracuse and five in Palermo, listed by Vitale, presumably on the supposition that they may all be local Sicilian finds (Vitale 1998: 298 and 351). Two of the five pieces in Palermo are specimens of the Mars/horse head ROMANO silver, like the one from Monte Marzo. Intriguingly, Abela 1647: 205–6 (with Perassi 2007: 383 and Perassi 2018: 136), illustrates a silver didrachm (as *RRC* 25/1) found in Malta.

31. The two possible earlier ('semilibral') hoards, which are not well documented, are *Coin Hoards* VII.198 = Manganaro 2012 IX = (probably) XLIII, and Vitale 1998: 297. The later ('post-semilibral') hoards are Puglisi 2009 H26, H30, H31, H60, H94, H95 and Vitale 1998: 298.

32. Puglisi 2009, H18 = *RRCH* 17.

33. *RRC* 23. See Burnett & McCabe 2016. Another specimen was recovered in the excavations at Morgantina in 2016.

34. Frey-Kupper 2013: 180–2. The same is true at Morgantina, although the finds have not been fully analysed in this way.

35. Burnett & Crawford 2014: 246–7 (with earlier references).

36. Ripollès 2012 and 2017.

37. La Escuera, the 'Turiel hoard' and one from Torre de Doña Blanca.

38. Noguera Guillén 2008 and 2009; Noguera & Tarradell-Font 2009. The date is derived from the coin finds, *contra* García-Bellido 2011: 677–8.

39. Granada, Los Villares, Cádiz, and Cerro Colorado. The Cerro Colorado hoard also contained half of a Roma/Victory ROMANO didrachm. The quadrigati remained in circulation for the early years of the denarius system.

40. Debernardi & Legrand 2015.

41. Chaves Tristán 1991–93.

42. Burnett & Molinari 2015.

43. See the calculations in Burnett 1989: 47–8.

44. Kay 2014.

45. Ialongo & Lago 2021.

46. On these and other votive deposits, see Prins & Termeer 2021.

47. Piacentin 2022: 36–59 (Rome) and 60–76 (Italy).

48. Prins & Termeer 2021.

49. Reece 1982.

50. Burnett & Crawford 2014: 251–2.

51. Holleran 2012: 106–7.

52. Kay 2014.

Notes to Pages 69–84 **319**

53. Von Reden 1995 and 1997; Kurke 1999; Seaford 2002 and 2004.
54. *HN* 210–11 and 654–5.
55. Gruen 2010: 115–40.
56. This was rejected by Crawford 1985: 35, although he seems to have accepted it in the later case of Syracuse (p. 113).
57. Crawford 1985: 113.
58. Terrenato 2019: 269.

# 3 The Growth of an Empire during the Late Republic (200–31 BCE)

1. There are several general accounts: Crawford 1985; Burnett & Crawford 1987. See also Thonemann 2015: 169–90 (for the eastern empire). There are also now two good modern accounts: Galani 2022 and Carbone in press.
2. Burnett & Molinari 2015.
3. Burnett 1982. For details, see *HN* 733–4 (Barium), 743–52 (Brundisium), 1220–58 (Paestum), 1337–40 (Velia), 1448 (Heraclea), 1935–9 (Copia), 2262–8 (Vibo Valentia), Perhaps also Caelia (*HN* 762–72) and Graxa (*HN* 779–82).
4. Crawford 1974: 596.
5. *RRC* no. 368. See Lo Cascio 2016.
6. Crawford 1982; Stannard 2018: 138.
7. Hobbs 2013. For some general reflections about such movements, see Frey-Kupper & Stannard 2018 and Butcher 2019.
8. Stannard & Sinner 2014, Frey-Kupper & Stannard 2018 (Ebusus and Cos), Barbato 2022.
9. Cicero, *de Officiis* III. 80: iactabatur enim temporibus illis nummus sic, ut nemo posset scire, quid haberet.
10. Bransbourg 2013: 218–19; but see Lo Cascio 2016: 342. For the debasement at the time of the Social War, see Parisot & Sarah 2018.
11. See Buttrey *et al.* 1989 and Frey-Kupper 2013. Three cities made a much larger production than the others, but even so their circulation tended to be regional: Panormus (Palermo) in western Sicily and Syracuse and especially Catana (Catania) in the eastern part of the island.
12. Frey-Kupper 2013: 208–71: especially the distribution map on p. 260.
13. At Centuripae, we find •••, •• and IX; Catana has XII and II.
14. Migeotte 2014. See also the inscriptions ISic001247–55 and 002985–86 at the I.Sicily project compiled by Jonathan Prag, http://sicily.classics.ox.ac.uk/insc riptions/.
15. The best source for ancient Spanish coins of the Republican period is the growing website https://monedaiberica.org. There are general summaries in Ripollès 2012 and 2017.

**320** Notes to Pages 84–95

16. See CHRR Online.
17. Chaves 1991–93: 268.
18. Ripollès & Witschonke 2015; Ripollès & Gozalbes 2017.
19. Crawford 1985: 133–42, Burnett 1987a: 179; Alexandropoulos 2007: 125 ('au moins jusqu'à l'epoque augustéenne').
20. Bogud: *RPC I*, 856 (25 mm, 10.73 g); Bocchus: *RPC I*, 873 (29 mm, 14.57 g).
21. Jaworski 2012 summarises earlier reports: a plated denarius from Cyrene; ½ *as* from Apollonia; 4 denarii from Cyrene. The Polish finds from Ptolemais included 3 Republican denarii and 1 worn Republican *as. cf.* Jaworski 2016. Robinson 1944 included only Greek coins, particularly Ptolemaic ones, and quite a lot of Roman provincial, including silver. But the title of his article suggests that presumably he did not include such Roman coins as there may have been in the list. Both Robinson and Jaworski list a number of the provincial coins of Cyrenaica (and Crete).
22. *RPC I*, pp. 226–7; see now Galani 2022: 124–35.
23. Martin 2015.
24. Van Heesch 2005: 240. The semis was half an *as* in the Roman system.
25. *Pro Fonteio* 5.1: nemo Gallorum sine cive Romano quicquam negoti gerit, nummus in Gallia nullus sine civium Romanorum tabulis commovetur. As Dyck 2012 comments, 'Cicero's assertions about the centrality of Roman citizens to the economic life of Gaul are no doubt rhetorically exaggerated but must at least have been plausible to the jury'. Elsewhere (*pro Fonteio* 9), he attests taxes in Gaul tariffed in denarii and victoriati (= quinarii).
26. However, the use of orichalcum, otherwise unknown in the west, for coins, including those of Vercingetorix, may suggest the influence of the eastern Mediterranean, surprising though this may seem: Nieto 2004, who, however, stresses the exceptional nature of the coins.
27. Lugdunum: *RPC I*, 514 (31 mm, 21.17 g), and 515 (31 mm, 18.19 g); Vienna *RPC I*, 517 (30 mm, 19.07 g); Narbo: *RPC I*, 518 (29 mm, 16.30 g); and Arausio or Tolosa: *RPC I*, 533 (28 mm, 17.45 g).
28. Meta 2021.
29. Kremydi 2021, Amandry 2021 and Paunov 2021.
30. See now Galani 2022: 33–90.
31. De Callataÿ 2011, 2016 and 2021.
32. Appian, *Mithridatic Wars,* 5.30, with De Callataÿ 2016: 322.
33. De Callataÿ 2016: 317; Kremydi 2021.
34. Polybius 2.15.6: ἡμιασσαρίου· τοῦτο δ᾽ ἔστι τέταρτον μέρος ὀβολοῦ.
35. *IG* V, 1, 1433. Grandjean (2003: 252–4) discussed the dating and suggested 50–25 BCE.
36. See also Kremydi 2021: 94.
37. On these and related Macedonian coins, see Touratsoglou 1987 and Kourempanas 2011a, 2011b. That the I and the S (for semis) on related coins

## Notes to Pages 96–108 **321**

are marks of value was rejected by Touratsoglou (1987: 65–66), who regarded the S as a misinterpreted dolphin.

38. Grunauer-von Hoerschelmann 1978: 162, Group XXIII; *RPC I*, no. 1551.
39. For the coinage of the Roman period, see Kinns 1987.
40. On the name, see Psoma 2009.
41. Butcher & Ponting 2015: 466, were unable to substantiate Walker's results for the Republican cistophori, due to a lack of material. But Walker's results are sufficient to indicate that the cistophorus of the first century BCE was less fine than contemporary denarii, even though we cannot be sure of the degree.
42. Carbone 2014 and 2021; Meadows 2021; Delrieux 2021: 221; Kinns 1987: 110–11and 113. For the small amounts of gold, see Chapter 1.
43. *IGCH* 1459, of 99/8 BCE, had more than five times as many coins of Pergamum than Ephesus; *IGCH* 1356, of 77/6 BCE, had over six times as many; and *IGCH* 1464, of 55/4 BCE, had three times as many.
44. The hoard is *IGCH* 1358 = Regling 1930–32. The dating suggested by Kleiner 1978 gives: 98–95 BCE: none; 95–92: 2; 92–88: 16; 88–85: 18; 85–76: 59; 76: 15. The hoard closed in 76.
45. See Chapter 1. A few denarii are mentioned in the Delian inventories from 154 BCE, but in insignificantly small numbers: De Callataÿ 2011: 57–8.
46. *RRC* 445/3, with Woytek 2016.
47. Meadows 2021; Delrieux 2021; Carbone 2020 and 2021; see also now Galani 2022.
48. The coins of Lampsacus (*RPC I*, 2272–3):16mm/4 grams; Atratinus (*RPC I*, 2226): 23mm/14grams.
49. Cottier *et al.* 2008, line 12: 5 denarii as the maximum tax per head on slaves; *cf.* lines 97–99.
50. Lines 78–9: a tax of *assaria tessara* per 100 pounds of minerals exported from Asia to Rome.
51. *RPC I*, 2272–3.
52. *RPC I*, 2226.
53. Craddock *et al.* 1980; Cowell *et al.* 2000; Smekalova 2009; Fajfar *et al.* 2015.
54. Dalaison 2021.
55. Kinns 1987: 111; Galani 2022: 136–50.
56. Neumann 2021: 118–19 accepts the case that has been made for some silver before Gabinius. Even if correct, they are very rare, and can have been minted in only small quantities.
57. The attribution is regarded as 'possible, though heavily debated' by Neumann 2021: 123. See also Olivier & Parisot-Sillon 2013, and Olivier & Aumaître 2017.
58. Burnett 2021a.
59. Eckstein 2012: 4–5. See also the critique in Smith & Yarrow 2012. Terrenato (2019: 24–30) summarises modern approaches to Roman 'imperialism'.
60. Thonemann 2015: 13–21.

**322** Notes to Pages 108–11

61. But see Galani 2022: 179–87, for the view that there were 'some major transformations in both iconographical and metrological terms'. At the same time, she points out that she does not want 'to impress the reader with a misleading image of a huge Roman impact on the provincial coin iconography'.
62. Rowan 2016a and 2016b.

# 4    Whose Coins? A Model for City Coinage in Imperial Times

1. Claes 2014 has also argued for his influence on coin designs. A role beyond Italy has not been considered, and it is not necessarily excluded by the poetic use of 'Ausoniae . . . Monetae' ('Italy's mint'), which was just one of the responsibilities of the father of Claudius Etruscus when he was *a rationibus* (Statius, *Silvae* 3.3.105).
2. Burnett 2005: 173–4. For χρήματα τῆς ἀρχῆς in an inscription recording a decision of Hadrian, dating to 128/9 CE, from between Magnesia on Maeander and Priene, see *AE* 2009, 1428. The customs law of Asia (Cottier *et al.* 2008, line 60) has the phrase ὑπέρ τε χαλκοῦ καὶ ἀργύρου κεχαραγμένου, νομίσματός τε ἠριθμημένου implicitly among 'the public affairs of the Roman people', echoing the 'pecunia . . . signata forma p(ublica) p(opulei) R(omanei)' of the *Lex de Gallia Cisalpina* XXI–II.
3. See Bennett 2014: 22, for other examples. For *exetastai* in general, see Fröhlich 2004: 117–67.
4. Very occasionally, parallel coinages were minted at the same time for different communities within the same place, where a colony had been founded alongside an earlier Greek community. Both Myrlea and the colony of Apamea made coins under Claudius (Woytek 2011a, with references to the doubts of historians regarding a double community there), as did the Greek community of Claudiconium and the new colony of Iconium under Vespasian and Hadrian.
5. There were still some city coinages in silver, all on a small scale, but they became fewer and fewer: Lepcis in Africa (Augustus); Crete (Tiberius to Nero); Nicopolis in Greece (Antoninus Pius); Byzantium (Tiberius); Amisus (Hadrian, Pius); Chios (Augustus); Rhodes (Domitian, Nerva); Stratonicea (Augustus? Claudius? Pius); Mylasa (Augustus); Tabae (Augustus?); Aegeae, Cilicia (Hadrian); Elaeusa (Aurelius); Seleucia, Cilicia (Hadrian, Pius, Aurelius); Mopsus (Hadrian, Pius); Tarsus (Domitian, Trajan, Caracalla, Macrinus); Apamea, Syria (Claudius); Laodicea ad Mare (Hadrian); Sidon (Augustus to Claudius); Tyre (Augustus to Nero). See also Chapter 1.
6. Other examples are discussed in Chapter 5.

Notes to Pages 112–8 **323**

7. Howgego 1985: 17–20. He pointed out that, in the East, there were two phases: under Nero and under Lucius Verus.
8. Lozano 2017.
9. *RPC II*, p. 3. See also Chapter 3.
10. Howgego 1989: 199–200, calculated that the entire output of Corinth, one of the most prolific provincial mints, over a century would have been insufficient to pay a Roman legion for half a year.
11. See Johnston 1985; Martin 2013; Bennett 2017; Watson 2017; Bricault 2017; Peter 2017; Dalaison 2017 and Nurpetlian 2017. The coins are often and inevitably very hard to date. See also Horster 2013, who emphasises the phenomenon as a feature of civic identity, but she exaggerates their importance, even within the province of Asia.
12. For what follows, see the various studies by Weiss 1992, 2000 and 2005.
13. Harl 1987, 140 cites as other examples: Iconium under Vespasian; Ninica under Hadrian; and Tyre under Elagabalus. However, the first example is a case of a double community (see Chapter 4 note 4), while the other two are examples of a colony losing its status (but continuing to produce coinage).
14. Calomino 2016. On 'memory sanctions' more generally, and some exceptions, see Flower 2006 and Östenberg 2018 (although they do not discuss coins very much). Östenberg notes that bronze inscriptions, whether public or on *diplomata*, were not erased, perhaps giving at least a partial parallel to the coinage. Dio tells us that the senate decreed that 'all the bronze coinage which had Caligula's likeness stamped upon it should be melted down (60.22.3), but the evidence that this happened is at best ambiguous, and it certainly cannot have been fully effective.
15. Howgego 1985: 3–4. The only exceptions are the military countermarks discussed above.
16. Cercina (Augustus: of proconsul), Thaena (Augustus: of proconsul), Paterna (Tiberius: of proconsul x 3). Similarly, at the colony of Berytus in Syria, one finds *permissu Silani* (*RPC I*, 4541, 4544).
17. Emerita (Augustus, Tiberius), Ebora (Augustus), Italica (Augustus; Tiberius: of Divus Augustus), Romula (Tiberius: of Divus Augustus), Iulia Traducta (Augustus), Patricia (Augustus).
18. Carteia (Augustus), Osca (Tiberius), Turris Libisonis (late first century), Segesta (late first century), Utica (Tiberius), Carthage (Augustus), Paterna (Augustus, Tiberius), Cnossus (Augustus), Dyme (Caesar), Buthrotum (Augustus, Claudius), Dium (Tiberius to Philip), Apamea in Bithynia (Augustus, Vespasian to Gallienus), Sinope (Augustus to Claudius), Parium (late first century, Trajan), Uncertain colony of Galatia (late first century), Alexandria in Troas (Vespasian). Other phrases for payment are S(ua) P(ecunia) D(ono) D(edit) ('gave from his own money') and D(e) S(ua) P(ecunia) ('from his own money').

**324** Notes to Pages 118–21

19. As in the cases of Simon Maccabaeus asking the King of Syria for permission (I Maccabees 15.6), and Alexander of Abonoteichos similarly asking the emperor (Lucian, *Alexander* 58), discussed above. For its use in asking the emperor for his permission for a market, see *RPC II*, p. 2.
20. αἰτησαμένου or variants occurs at Ancyra (Nero), Appia (Trajan), Alia (Trajan), Stratonicea (Hadrian), Eucarpia (Hadrian) and Stectorium (Aurelius).
21. Mylasa (Domitian: also with ἀνέθηκεν), Stratonicea (early second century).
22. Eumenea (Domitian).
23. Only at Mylasa (Augustus, Titus). An example (the only one?) of an imperial gift (in some sense) of coinage is provided by Sepphoris, whose coins proclaim that ΤΡΑΙΑΝΟΣ ΑΥΤΟΚΡΑΤΩΡ ΕΔΩΚΕΝ ('the emperor Trajan gave'): *RPC III*, 3936–9. On similar verbs, see Bennett 2014.
24. Only at Neapolis in Caria (Maximinus).
25. Zuiderhoek 2009: 18, 154–9.
26. ἐπιμελητής, ἐπιηελημθέντος or some variety: Mastaura (Tiberius) Chalcis (Nero), Philadelphia (Vespasian: two people together; Domitian), Cotiaeum (Domitian, Antonine), Antioch ad Maeandrum (Domitian), Aphrodisias (Flavian), Miletopolis (Trajan x3; Hadrian), Grimenothyrae (Trajan), Aezani (Hadrian), Hadriani ad Olympum (Hadrian), Eucarpia (Hadrian, Antoninus Pius, Septimius Severus), Apamea (Antoninus Pius), Attuda (Marcus Aurelius, Septimius Severus), Hieropolis (Marcus Aurelius), Stratonicea (Septimius Severus), Apamea (Septimius Severus), Mastaura (Maximinus).
27. *RPC II*, p. 4.
28. *RPC III*, 2587–90.
29. See Zuiderhoek 2009, on the decline of recorded benefactions in the third century.
30. Bennett 2014. Bennett preferred the term 'eponym', for which he followed the wide interpretation of the term; but it is rather confusing, and only one role was regarded as the 'principal eponym' of a city in a given year. So the term is not used here except in that more strict sense of 'principal eponym'.
31. The language of the inscription about Moschion at Magnesia in Ionia shows that there was no special office, but that it was a function added to the roles of each individual: Moschion son of Moschion at Magnesia in Ionia recorded how he was 'appointed over the striking of small bronze' (*OGIS* 485: κατασταθεὶς δὲ καὶ ἐπὶ τῆς χαράξεως τοῦ λεπτοῦ χαλκοῦ). No coins are known at Magnesia signed by Moschion, but many of the coins bear no name.
32. There is one case, however, where such an involvement seems possible. It cannot be an accident that the coins with the name of the early Flavian proconsul Clodius Marcellus from Hierapolis, Laodicea and Sardis all lack the emperor's portrait (*RPC II*, p. 3). Marcellus was a man of great influence, and perhaps he thought that the new regime, with its Republican pretensions, would

Notes to Pages 121–3  **325**

revert to the days, a hundred years previously, when city coinages did not have ruler portraits.

33. *RPC II*, p. 5; *RPC III*, p, 864; Bennett 2014: 8.
34. Po. Ail. Tryphon at Apamea under Severus Alexander (*RPC VI* temporary number 5710); Aur. Aineias at Magnesia under Philip (*RPC VIII* temporary number 1061); and M. Aur. Philetos under Valerian and Gallienus (Klose 1987, number LXXIV.6).
35. Hochard 2020, number 2156 (reign of Valerian and Gallienus).
36. Hochard 2020, number 544 (reign of Valerian and Gallienus): ΠΠΠΙΚΟΥ ϹΥΝΓ ϹΥΝΚΛΗ.
37. Bennett 2014: 25. Other examples occur at Ephesus under Augustus, or Adramyteum (the *strategoi* περί . . . under Hadrian).
38. Bennett 2014: 26–8.
39. Antandrus (Titus), Tabae (Domitian), Laodicea (Domitian), Attuda (Domitian, Trajan, Hadrian, Marcus Aurelius – alternatively ἐπιμεληθέντος in one case – Severus), Apollonia in Caria (Trajan), Cidrama (Hadrian, Antoninus Pius) and Trapezopolis (Hadrian, Antoninus Pius × 3: one is a benefactor from Attuda). Apart from the outlier Antandrus (in the Troad) the others are all close to each other. For cases of the apparent interchangeability of διά and ἐπιμεληθέντος, see *RPC II*, p. 4.
40. Ceretapa (Commodus), Apamea (Commodus, Decius, Valerian and Gallienus), Siblia (Severus) and Metropolis in Phrygia (Decius).
41. See Bennett 2014: 29, for the inscriptions referring to a Moschion at Magnesia in Ionia, where the production of coinage is included amongst a list of city benefactions. Moschion does not appear on Magnesia's coinage, but for the case of Apollodotus at Hyrgaleis (with the formula ἐπί), see Chapter 4 note 43.
42. Burnett, in press b.
43. See also the Republican coins of Paestum in Italy with the name and portrait of Mineia M.f., known from inscriptions as a benefactress.
44. For another widow (Mineia at Paestum) see Figure 3.4.
45. The communities are listed in Wankel 1979, no. 13. Pliny *Natural History*, 5.111 names the more important cities and refers to the others as 'alii ignobiles'. Burnett 1987b: 60–1.
46. The figure of 300+ cities is an estimated guess by Habicht 1975: 67. The *RPC* database currently includes 187 cities from the province of Asia, https://rpc.as hmus.ox.ac.uk.
47. See also Kremydi & Ward 2017: only 42 of the 77 cities listed by Pausanias made coins.
48. Pliny *Natural History*, 5.28. See also Chapter 6, for a discussion of whether such coins were actually produced at the cities whose names they bear or on their behalf by a much more restricted number of production centres acting on their behalf.

**326** Notes to Pages 123–6

49. A very recent example is Timbrium (TIMBPIANΩN), a city in Phrygia, for which two coins are now known: one was discovered in 2017, and the other in 2020. See also, now, Çelikbaş & Oyarçin. 2012 for a new mint: Hadrianopolis in Paphlagonia. Enigmatic coins of Commodus inscribed with LEG XV and a griffin (the legion's badge) have also been discovered, and some provenance information suggests that they were made at the legionary fortress of Satala, for which coinage is not otherwise known (and they perhaps also imply that a colony had been founded there).

50. *RPC III*, pp. 868–70, and Burnett 2016a.

51. However, other explanations are possible, in terms of the movement of blocks of coinage – see Frey-Kupper & Stannard 2018.

52. Johnston 1983. See also Chapter 7 for a similar problem with the attempt to trace Elagabalus' journey from the east to Rome.

53. Howgego 1990.

54. *OGIS* 339 = *IK* Sestos 1, ll. 43–9 (trans. Austin).

55. *IGRR* 4.769: κόψας καὶ [νομ]ίσματα. The inscription is usually associated with the Apollodotus who signed coins of this period for the Hyrgaleis, as by Howgego 1985: 87; Bennett 2014: 29; and Thonemann 2011: 121–2.

56. It might, alternatively, just mean that paying for an issue of coins was the sort of benefaction expected from a member of the elite, like setting up a statue of the emperor.

57. Other systems also existed in the west. Ebusus (Ibiza) made coins inscribed '20–20–10': see Figure 3.12, with García-Bellido 2013: 56–7. An inscription from Lepcis in Africa refers to a sum of 133 *dn'ry'*, comprising two other sums of 80 *dn'ry'* 9 *kndrm* and 52 *dr'ry'*[]. *Dn'ry'* seems clearly to be 'denarii', but *kndrm* perhaps refers to some local system for smaller denominations (Wilson 2012: 293–6, 313).

58. For examples, see Johnston 2007: 104–26.

59. Sometimes it is virtually impossible to determine even the relative denominations, since the diameters and weights varied so enormously: Edessa in Mesopotamia and Tripolis in Phoenicia are examples, both in the third century.

60. Butcher 2017. The cities are: Marcianopolis, Odessus, Dionysopolis, Anchialus, Callatis, Istrus and Tomi. Tomi even produced pieces of 1½ and 4½. See also Chapter 7.

61. *RPC IX*, p. 38: the cities are Nicomedia (Γ), Amastris (H), Ionopolis (H), Side (E) and Pompeiopolis (ς).

62. Johnston 2007: 162–3.

63. *OGIS* 484 (Pergamum); the Salutaris inscriptions from Ephesus (early second century), for which see Johnston 2007: 17, and graffito GR 370 at Ephesus (third century), for which see Taeuber 2016.

# Notes to Pages 126–32 **327**

64. *OGIS* 484 ll. 7–8, 10: παρὰ τὸ δίκαιον καὶ παρὰ τὴν συναλλαγὴν [πράττειν]. . . . λαμβάνειν ὀφείλοντες.
65. As is envisaged in the Salutaris inscriptions from Ephesus (Johnston 2007: 17, citing l. 251: [ἐὰν δὲ μείζων ἦ ὁ γεν]όμενος κόλλυβος), and the change from 18 in the second century to 21 in the third.
66. Butcher 2004: 144; Butcher 2002; Burnett 2005: 175; Howgego 2014: 308–10. There are other possibilities on the spectrum: Howgego 1985: 39, suggested that countermarks and a hoard imply that coins of Heraclea Pontica and Tium were used in both cities; in a similar way, Troy seems to have used coins of both Troy and Alexandria Troas, both of which supplied the great majority of coins found there, as catalogued by Bellinger 1961: 51 coins of Ilium and 61 of Alexandria (including the ploughing type, on which see Burnett & Martin 2018).
67. Watson 2019a: 150. See also note 68.
68. Butcher 2004: 144–5; Katsari 2003.
69. Johnston 2007: 5–6, note 22. The figure for imperial provincial coins from the Sardis excavations (Bell 1916; Buttrey *et al.* 1981) is 60%. Johnston drew the opposite conclusion from that suggested here (though she accepted it for Syria).
70. The best example is the coins lost at the stadium of Nemea, where the pattern of lost coins shows clusters of coins from Corinth, Sicyon, Argos, Phlius and Cleonae, which seem to indicate where people from those cities sat as spectators: Knapp & MacIsaac 2005: 22–30.
71. The third-century hoard from Allianoi (near Pergamum) consisted of 11 imperial silver coins and 62 bronze coins, all of Pergamum: Yaraş & Lenger 2013.
72. Especially Plato, *Laws* 742: ὧν ἕνεκά φαμεν τὸ νόμισμα κτητέον αὐτοῖς μὲν ἔντιμον, τοῖς δὲ ἄλλοις ἀνθρώποις ἀδόκιμον; Xenophon *Poroi* III.2: ἀλλὰ μὴν καὶ τοῖς ἐμπόροις ἐν μὲν ταῖς πλείσταις τῶν πόλεων ἀντιφορτίζεσθαί τι ἀνάγκη· νομίσμασι γὰρ οὐ χρησίμοις ἔξω χρῶνται; *ISmyrn* 573 = *OGIS* 229, ll. 54–55 (Magnesia): δεχέσθωσαν δὲ καὶ ἐμ Μαγνησίαι τὸ νόμισμα τὸ τῆς πόλεως [ἔνν]ομον.
73. Howgego 1985: 32.

# 5  The Revolution of Augustus – and Becoming More Roman in the First Century

1. Amandry 2012.
2. www.britishmuseum.org/collection/object/C_1995-0401-1
3. Zanker 1988; Boschung 1993.
4. See Hendin in Carbone, in press.
5. Corinth also produced fine portraits of Caesar, but probably after his death.
6. See *RPC I*, pp. 38–39; Meadows 2019: 17–23; and Carbone 2020: 44–55.

**328** Notes to Pages 132–47

7. Rowan 2019, Figure 3.20.
8. *RPC I*, 4135. Is it just a coincidence that, in Egypt, Cleopatra's portrait also occurs only on the rare silver drachms, and not the staple tetradrachms?
9. Even on the gold and silver coinage, where claims to loyalty were made more frequently by such portraits, they were in a minority.
10. Burnett 2011: 21–4.
11. *RPC I*, p. 40.
12. See the table in *RPC I*, pp. 584–5.
13. Mallus does seem to have made coins with Augustus' portrait (*RPC I* 4015), and Tarsus made some rare silver coins with his portrait (*RPC I*, 4004). The first portraits at Pompeiopolis, Aegeae, Mopsus, Anazarbus, Hierapolis-Castabala, Epiphanea and Rhosus are of Tiberius.
14. For a list, see Burnett 2011: 22.
15. Eck 1984: 138–9. The case of Cibyra is exceptional as such portraits seem to have continued there until the Flavian period (T. Clodius Eprius Marcellus).
16. Horster 2013.
17. Rowan 2019: 160–7.
18. Horster 2013: 253–5, states the phenomenon, without offering an explanation, although she says (258) that it may have been to demonstrate 'their alleged close relationship, and a more personalised expression of that relationship, to the ruling Romans'. See also the review by Kleiner 2020 of Harvey 2019.
19. Smith 1996, Zanker 1988, Boschung 1993.
20. Burnett 2011: 23–4.
21. Corinth, Thespiae and, further north, Philippopolis.
22. Cius, Nicaea, Nicomedia, Bithynium, Tium and Amastris. So also Nacolea in the province of Asia, but near to the province of Pontus and Bithynia. There were again some outliers: Rhodes and Alexandria again, and also Samos and Caesarea Maritima.
23. Trajan is radiate at Cyrenaica, Phoenice, Thessalonica, Perinthus, Calchedon, Byzantium, the Koinon of Bithynia, Tium, Amastris, Sinope, Parium, Nacolea, the Koina of Galatia and Cappadocia, Sidon and Alexandria, The senatorial Nerva was never shown radiate.
24. Burnett 2011; Woytek 2019a: 411–16. For bilingual issues, see Chapter 6.
25. Burnett 2011: 13.
26. Woolf 1996. Similarly, inscriptions become quite common on Gallic coinage in the second half of the first century BCE.
27. Burnett 2011: 11.
28. Imperator Caesar Divi Filius Augustus Pontifex Maximus Pater Patriae (the Emperor Caesar Augustus, son of the God, Chief Priest, Father of his Country).
29. Adams 2003: 45, for abbreviations.
30. *RPC II*, 33–34.
31. Burnett 2002a, Adams 2003: 207–9; *cf.* 223.

Notes to Pages 147–58 **329**

32. Millar 1993: 289: 'The coinage of Tyre did not of course serve to symbolize revolt, or even any real freedom. But it did, in a wholly distinctive way, express the continued attachment of Tyre to its identity as a Phoenician city with a long and glorious history.

33. *RPC I*, p. 46; Rowan 2019: 157–8.

34. There are a few early examples from Africa, probably all dating to the late Republican period: Juba I (Alexandropoulos 2007: 402, no. 34 = *RPC I*, 717); Sabratha (Alexandropoulos 2007: 445–6, nos. 38–9: 'vers 60–50 av. J.-C.?'); Cirta (Alexandropoulos 2007: 467, no. 127: 'vers 46 av. J.-C.').

35. *RPC I*, 2451.

36. *RPC I*, 4054. The British victory is also celebrated on the silver coinage of Caesarea (*RPC I*, 3625), an imperial coinage.

37. *RPC I*, pp. 45–6. Some rare coins made by Sinope in 57/8 showing the emperor in a triumphal quadriga are paired with an obverse for Divus Augustus (*RPC I*, 2136), and are anyway too early in date for Nero's victories.

38. For Spain, see the discussion by Ripollès in *RPC I*, pp. 65–6.

39. Apart from some rare and enigmatic coins which follow the Roman system: *RPC I*, 537–8 and 5431. A provenance from near Trier suggests they were produced far in the north, and, if so, they show the degree to which the local outlook had changed. 'TA' temptingly invites Treverorum Augusta, but there is no reason why the parts of the city's name should have been reversed from the standard Augusta Treverorum.

40. *RRC* 476 and 550, with Barbato 2015: especially 108–9. She inclines towards the idea that both issues were minted in Rome.

41. For the Lugdunum date, see Van Heesch 1993a.

42. Butcher 2004: 205–6: SC coins from Antioch were made of pure bronze, about 90% copper and 10% tin; but civic coinage was generally made of leaded bonze, even at Antioch. As time passed, the amount of lead increased, while tin decreased.

43. Some 'Syrian' coins of Trajan were made of brass, but they were minted in Rome, and then sent to Syria: Butcher 2004: 35.

44. The Bithynian 'sestertii' are slightly lighter, at about 20–22 g, rather than 25 g.

45. *RPC I*, p. 380. A few of the coins seem also to have been made and circulated in Cyprus and Syria: see now Butcher 2004: 321.

46. See *RPC I*, pp. 371–2.

47. See also Carbone 2020 and 2021.

48. Data from *RPC* database.

49. Source: *RPC I*, p. 375; II, p. 124.

50. Grant 1953; Burnett in press a.

51. Burnett & Martin 2018. They circulated widely in north west Asia and Thrace.

52. The small bronze coins, probably to be attributed to the Tungri people: Aarts & Roymans 2009.

# 330 Notes to Pages 161–70

53. Butcher 2021.
54. Van Heesch 1993a, for the later date.
55. For the importance of Alexandria Troas in the third century, see *RPC IX*.
56. There was a concentration of minting small denominations in Egypt under Hadrian.
57. Besombes & Barrandon 2000.
58. Amandry 2018.
59. Eck & Nader 2009.
60. See Chapter 3.
61. *OGIS* II 629, 182–3, with Matthews 1984: 179 (translation). Germanicus was there in 17–19 CE.
62. See also, more generally, Martin 2015. Perhaps the 'floral ornament' on *RPC I*, 507 might also be an attempt at an S.
63. *RPC I*, 784–91.
64. Tomlin 2016.
65. ἐν ᾧ ἂν βούληται νομίσματι τῶγ ἐν Λυκίᾳ [πρ]οχωρούντων. Takmer 2007, translates 'mit Münzen, die in Lykien vorher im Umlauf waren'.
66. *IG* VII, 2713, ll. 14–15. See also next note.
67. Philostratus, *Life of Apollonius* 5.41: Νέρων ἐλευθέραν ἀφῆκε τὴν Ἑλλάδα ... Οὐεσπασιανὸς δὲ ἀφικόμενος ἀφείλετο αὐτὴν τοῦτο στάσεις προβαλλόμενος καὶ ἄλλα οὔπω τῆς ἐπὶ τοσόνδε ὀργῆς [Nero set Greece free ... Vespasian, however, came and took this away, alleging civil disturbances and other things not at all deserving of such anger]. Suetonius, *Vespasian* 8. 4: Achaiam ... libertate adempta.
68. Levy 1987. See also Chapter 4.
69. Melville Jones 2015, with earlier literature (especially Coarelli and Woytek).
70. For general reflections on such movements, see Frey-Kupper & Stannard 2018 and Butcher 2019.
71. Moorhead 2015, for the British finds; Walker 1988, esp. 286–8, for the regional distribution of Domitian's bronze coinage.
72. *GIC*, p. 28.
73. Manganaro 2005; Martini 2017.
74. Thapsus, Sabratha, Lepcis Magna, Iol.
75. Italica in Spain; Forum Iulii and Matavo in Gaul; and Panormus (just the Capricorn) in Sicily.
76. Caesaraugusta in Spain; Hippo Regius, Utica, Carthage, Paterna, Thapsus and Lepcis Magna in Africa; Panormus in Sicily; and Paestum in Italy.
77. The coins signed by Carina and Hirtius copy denarii of Julius Caesar (*RPC I*, 501–2); the butting bull on coins of Germanus is copied from aurei or denarii of Augustus (*RPC I*, 506; *cf. RPC I*, 507 and 509).

Notes to Pages 171–3  **331**

78. Campo *et al.* 1981.The sestertii and dupondii were all uncirculated and with many die links. They had been transported in rolls. These features all imply a batch of coinage sent from the mint at Rome.

79. Burnett 2005: 176–9.

80. Troxell 1982: 121. Some were analysed in the 1970s, and found to be a little less fine; but the results are not now regarded as reliable, and the coins have not yet been re-examined (Butcher & Ponting 2015: 490–2).

81. *RRC* 507, with Hollstein 2016.

82. However, one specimen from Masicytes was analysed by Martini 2009, and found to be a leaded bronze (83% Cu, 9% Sn and 7% Pb).

83. *RPC I*, 3317a–e.

84. *RPC I*, pp. 526–7; Katsari 2011: 236–7. No Lycian silver of Claudius was analysed by Butcher and Ponting, but they emphasised the low weight and cast doubt on the earlier analyses of Walker (Butcher & Ponting 2015: 491–2).

85. *cf.* Butcher & Ponting 2015: 492, which is sceptical.

86. Andriake: Bulut & Şengül 2014 (including 5 sestertii, 1 as and 1 semis). Arykanda: Tek 2005: 956 table 2 (Roman coins throughout the imperial period); Limyra: Gorecki 2007: 91 (38 Roman bronze coins). Patara: Özüdoğru 2002 (coins which were found during the excavations of 1989–2001: first century: a sestertius, 2 asses and a quadrans; second century: 4 sestertii, 2 dupondii and a quadrans; third century: 9 sestertii and 4 dupondii). See also Johnston 2007: 9–10 note. 44.

87. Butcher & Ponting 2015: 493–5; see also Butcher 2014.

88. This might help to explain the well-known inscription from Cibyra, which states that a denarius was worth 16 asses, and a Rhodian drachm worth 10 (*IGRR* 4.915.6). The remote city of Cibyra oscillated between the provinces of Asia and Lycia, and might well have adopted the Lycian system. If so, accepting the denarius at 16 asses makes perfect sense, while the Rhodian drachma (= the cistophoric drachma), which one would expect to be worth 12 asses (as in Asia), might well have been discounted to 10, to keep it in Asia and out of Lycia.

89. Von Aulock 1975; Katsari 2003; Tek 2005; and see now *RPC VII.2*, pp. 393–4.

90. Sydenham 1919: 169 gave an average weight of 325.5 grains = 21.09g. The denominations were discussed by Johnston 2007: 193–4, concluding that 'we can only guess that the two principal denominations were 2- and 4-assaria', but she did not take Roman sestertii into consideration.

91. *Supplementum Epigraphicum Graecum* 57, 1666 = 62, 1471, from Andriake = ancient Myra. See Takmer 2007. The inscription awaits definitive publication.

## 332 Notes to Pages 174–82

# 6 Reinforcing Greek Identity in the Golden Age of the Second Century CE

1. The division between Chapter 5 and Chapter 6 could have been made earlier, in the Flavian period, when many of the characteristics of the second century coinage start to appear. There are also other possibilities, such as after the reign of Trajan, when the co-operation between silver mints stops, or the reign of Commodus, when the 'workshop system' (see Section 6.2) becomes more visible. Any division is arbitrary, as the development of the coinage was a continuum and geographically diverse. See Yarrow 2012 for the Antonine period (a rare attempt to integrate the imperial and provincial coinages).

2. There are no examples under Antoninus Pius, and only a single one under Marcus Aurelius (at Stectorium). Even if there were other instances, there was no wish to record it on the coins.

3. At Smyrna, the latest was under Antoninus Pius, and none had been mentioned previously after 98/99. The latest example of a proconsul's name to appear on any provincial coin was at Laodicea, under Marcus Aurelius.

4. This remark is based on an analysis of the data in the *RPC* website.

5. So also, *RPC III*, p. 817, for Asia.

6. See also Johnston 1984b.

7. As the relatively lengthy obverse legends include the title *Germanicus*, but not *Dacicus*, the coins can be dated more closely to 98–102. That they were definitely minted before Trajan became *Dacicus* is shown by the way some of the relevant Metropolis coins were later countermarked ΔAK. The Hadrianic coinage of Ilium was probably produced in the last ten years of his reign: *RPC III*, p. 189. For the link between Midaeum and the coins probably made by the Koinon of Bithynia, see *RPC III*, 1156 and 2646.

8. Watson 2021: 125–7.

9. Butcher 2004: 47, 396. The cities are Antioch, Cyrrhus. Hierapolis, Zeugma, Samosata and Philippopolis. The coins of Syrian Laodicea may also have been made at Antioch.

10. Kraft 1972.

11. Watson 2020.

12. Johnston 1982–83 and 1984a; Spoerri 2006b; Watson 2019b.

13. MacDonald 1992.

14. Watson 2021: 139.

15. Watson 2019a and 2021; *cf.* Watson 2017.

16. Watson 2019a: 118–19.

17. Hochard 2020, II: 695–746.

18. Thonemann 2011: 33–48, for the Maeander pattern on coins; see also Chapter 5 about similar obverse styles.

19. For the die links, see the map in Watson 2021: 132, fig. 6.3.

20. Hochard 2020.
21. Howgego 1985: 43–4.
22. Watson 2019a: 173.
23. Van Heesch 1979; Woytek 2004, for the 'mine coins': finds show that they circulated in Italy and other parts of the empire, as well as the mining areas in the Danubian provinces which they name; Abdy in Abdy & Mittag 2019: 2, 48.
24. Van Heesch 2009: 130–1; McIntosh & Moorhead 2011: 34 examples were known, a tiny proportion of the thousands of coins registered in the database. They included 1 Caligula, 24 Claudius, 1 Domitian, 2 Trajan and 4 anonymous. A few more have since been recorded on the PAS database, including one of Antoninus Pius (misdescribed as a quadrans, but actually a semis; the database does not distinguish accurately between quadrantes and semisses).
25. *RPC I*, p. 372.
26. Johnston 2007: 29: 'it appears that most cities in Asia Minor were striking coins on roughly the same standard ca 200'; *cf.* p. 43.
27. It was very occasionally used for a countermark, as was Edessan: *GIC* 694–6 (Aramaic and Edessan).
28. Hebrew, of course, had appeared on the coins of the First and Second Jewish Wars, in the late first and early second centuries. It was chosen deliberately to stand apart from Latin and Rome.
29. The earliest examples were for Nerva (Cyme) and Marcus Aurelius (Perperene, Epiphanea, Laodicea ad Mare); otherwise, most examples fall in the third century. Switching between E, EI and AI had occurred throughout the imperial period at Thessalonica (both in the ethnic, and occasionally in other words, such as ΚΕ(Ι)ΣΑΡ, ΔΟΜΕΤΙΑΝΟΣ).
30. Ancyra, Caracalla; Side, Valerian; Perge, Gallienus. *cf.* the spelling of the name Hierokles at Tralles, Severus Alexander. *cf.* ΕΙΕΡΟϹ ΔΗΜΟϹ at Cadi.
31. Julia Mamaea, Edessa, and Julia Maesa, Dionysopolis. Other examples include ΠΙΑΙΡΙΑϹ for ΠΙΕΡΙΑϹ at Seleucia, and the title ϹΑΙΒΑϹΤΗ for Tranquillina at Trapezus. One could go on.
32. See more fully Brixhe 1987.
33. Katsari & Mitchell 2008: 226.
34. Millar 1990 = Millar 2006a.
35. Levick 1967: chapters 11–12; Howgego 2005: 12–14; Katsari & Mitchell 2008; *RPC IX*, pp. 12–13.
36. Kremydi-Sicilianou 2005: 104.
37. IMP C SEP SEV PER X, omitting the IMP before X, *cf.* L SEPT SEV PERT AG IM, omitting the V from AG; PLAVTILIA for Plautilla; and P SEPTIMIOS OETA for P. Septimius Geta.
38. Millar 1995 = Millar 2006b; Isaac 2017. In addition, further west, Greek was used at Thessalonica after it acquired the status of a colony.

# 334 Notes to Pages 189–93

39. Tyre also occasionally employed Phoenician, in a deliberately archaising way, to name the legendary Phoenician figures of Dido (Elissa) and Pygmalion, and, in a similar way, Greek for the scenes of Greeks being given the alphabet by Cadmus (ΕΛΛΗ ΚΑΔΜΟC), sometimes of ΔΙΔΩ, and of the Ambrosial rocks (ΑΜΒΡΟCΙΩΝ ΠΕΤΡΩΝ). See also below, for Greek at Sidon.
40. As also Emesa, for Elagabalus. There are also some bilingual coins of Elagabalus at Byblus, which was not a colony, but they too may be explained by the location of Byblus near the Greek/Latin border.
41. Millar 1990: 7–8 (= Millar 2006a: 165). At Heliopolis 131/306 surviving inscriptions are in Latin, neatly reflecting the coins: Isaac 2017: 264.
42. Burnett 2002b: 119–20.
43. Butcher 2004: 44, 223 for Elagabalus rather than Caracalla.
44. Millar 1990: 51 (= Millar 2006a: 214).
45. Buttrey 1972.
46. On linguistic 'code switching', see Adams 2003: 18–29, 297.
47. Cox 1959; Nicolaou 1990.
48. Two large hoards, deposited in the third century, have been reported containing many coins of the second century, and isolated pieces have also been recorded (Jaworski 2009, Asolati & Crisafulli 2018: 145–48, 205–25). Sestertii and other bronze from Rome had already started to circulate at the beginning of the second century, and made up a large proportion (426 of 1043) of the Cyrene Agora hoard of c. 113.
49. Chevrollier 2016: 18: 'This scarcity of coin circulation between the two parts of the double province can be extended to the whole period of the Principate'. Laronde 2004: 177, referring to the museum of Shahat.
50. Sideropoulos 2004: 209. See also Jackson 1973 (two coins each for Hadrian and Antoninus Pius); Niniou-Kindeli & Chatzidakis 2016: 44 (a sestertius of Septimius Severus from Aptera); and Sweetman 2013: 158 (a sestertius of Faustina II from the Villa Dionysus at Cnossos).
51. The Thracian kingdom of Rhoemetacles I and his successors continued until the reign of Claudius. Its coinage was produced in large quantities, as shown by the finds from Aquae Calidae.
52. The maps in Heuchert 2005: 34–35, illustrate the increase in cities in Thrace and Moesia Inferior between the Julio-Claudian and Antonine periods.
53. Thompson 1954: 2: 'during the second century after Christ the Athenian Imperial coinage begins to be supplemented to a noticeable extent by the silver and bronze coinage of Trajan, Hadrian and the Antonines'.
54. Glenn 2022 for a large hoard of sestertii from Paros, to early Valerian and Gallienus.
55. Touratsoglou 2010: 243–5.
56. Touratsoglou 2006, 2010: 243–5.

Notes to Pages 193–7 **335**

57. Paunov 2015, for Aquae Calidae; Paunov 2014, for the legionary camp at Novae, near Svishtov, Bulgaria on the Danube frontier. Many of the Augustan pieces had been previously countermarked in Sicily, indicating a large transfer of coinage from there to Moesia: Martini & Paunov 2004; Martini 2017.

58. Family coins: Von Kaenel 1984; Paunov 2020: 461–4, for a Britannicus found in Sofia (Serdica). Claudius: Amandry 2018.

59. *RPC I*, 1758–62.

60. *RPC II*, 501–43.

61. *RPC I*, 1802 (Nero, Callatis); *RPC II*, 351–4 (Domitian, Philippopolis), and *RPC III*, 744–5 (Trajan, Philippopolis). On bilingual coins, see Woytek 2011b; Calomino 2014. Many of them are just aberrant dies, perhaps brought about by the tendency that 'within Greek communities who adopted Latin on coins, Greek tended to re-emerge almost as a form of resistance to the non-local idiom' (Calomino 2014: 215), but the case of Abydus, in the area under consideration here, seems more systematic: IMP CI M VIP SEV ALEXANDRO AVG and IVLIA MAMЄA AVG. Bilingual coins are also known from Sestos, in the same general area, from the reign of Gallienus.

62. Mitford 1939. However, Greek remained dominant in Cyprus. Parks 2002 has only 1% of epitaphs from Cyprus in Latin; Fujii 2013 has 90 inscriptions, all but three in Greek.

63. Reynolds 2000: 550: 'People of lesser status too were assimilating elements from Roman culture; thus Latin names were increasingly taken into their onomastic repertoire, and, more significantly, a change in funerary custom, which began in the later first century BCE, was gaining strength. By the beginning of the second century the busts of the nameless and faceless goddess which traditionally marked Cyrenaean tombs had been replaced for current burials by stelae and/or funerary portraits on the Roman model'. The known inscriptions from Cyrenaica are split almost equally between Greek and Latin.

64. Gerov 1980; Wilkes 2000: 602: 'The Latin language was dominant throughout the frontier provinces of the Danube. Greek remained confined to the southern Balkans and did not spread significantly beyond the limits of Hellenistic Macedonia and Thrace. As most recently defined from the evidence of inscriptions, the linguistic frontier in Roman Europe followed more or less the southern boundaries of Latin Dalmatia, Moesia Superior and Moesia Inferior; and this demarcation altered hardly at all during the Roman era'.

65. *cf.* Rizakis 1995: 373–91.

66. Some exceptions are mentioned by Heuchert 2005: 53–4, such as the Capricorn on coins of Augustus.

67. Heuchert 2005: 48–55.

**336** Notes to Pages 197–04

68. Anderson 1993: esp. 101–32. See in general, Richter & Johnson 2017. From the middle of the second Sophistic, some of the sophists even described themselves as such on the coins of Smyrna which they signed: Cl. Proclus, Attalus and Cl. Rufinus.

69. Weiss 2004: 181, calls the civic coinage 'ein epideiktisches Medium'.

70. Lindner 1994.

71. Price 2005: 115–24, discusses scenes on coins of Acmonea, Hierapolis and Nysa, all in central Asia Minor, which are all appropriate versions of myths, made local, and which can be compared with other sources for city self-presentation. See also Lindner 1994.

72. Necessarily, such an approach means omitting some fine designs, such as the judgement of Paris at Tarsus under Maximinus (*RPC VI* Online temporary no. 7109): Paris sits in judgement before a warlike Athena, a seated Hera and a nude Aphrodite. Similar designs had occurred at Ilium, Scepsis and Alexandria.

73. *Poets.* Anacreon: Teos (Severan-Gallienus); Arion: Chalcis (Severus); Homer: Amastris (second to third century), Nicaea (Commodus to Gallienus), Tium (Antonine), Chios (late first century and second century: even with the book of the IΛIAC), Smyrna (second to third century), Colophon (third century), Ios (Antonine), Cyme (second century), Temnus (third century), perhaps Apollonia Mordiaeum (third century); Sappho: Eresus, Mytilene (first century? Antonine). *Philosophers.* Bias: Priene (Augustus, Flavian, Hadrian, Antonine); Chrysippus and Aratus: Soli-Pompeiopolis (second-third century); Eukleides: Megara (Hadrian); Pythagoras: Samos (Trajan to Gallienus). *Astronomer.* Hipparchus: Nicaea (Pius to Gallienus). *Authors*: Herodotus: Halicarnassus (Trajan to Pius; Gordian); Theophanes: Mytilene (third century). Homer had appeared before imperial times at Smyrna and Colophon, as had Bias at Priene. See Heuchert 2005: 52, and https://ancient coinage.org/poets-philosophers-astronomers-etc.html.

74. Weisser 2005: 135–42. The suggestion made there that some of the designs reflect the personal career of one of Pergamum's most distinguished sons, Aulus Julius Quadratus, now seems less plausible: the Dionysus design had already been used for Domitian, as a new discovery shows (*RPC II*, 920A).

75. Robert 1977; Heller 2006; and Watson 2019b: 105–19.

76. ΠΙC(τις) ΦΙΛ(ια) CΥΜΜΑΧΙ(ια) ΡΩΜΑΙ(ων).

77. Sagalassus has clasped hands with the inscription CΑΓΑΛΑCCΕΩΝ ΡΩΜΑΙΩΝ, sometimes accompanied by ΦΙΛΗC ΚΑΙ CΥΝΜΑΧΟΥ ('Sagalassus, friend and ally of Rome'. Aspendus has ΑCΠΕΝΔΟC CΥΜΜΑΧΟC ΡΩΜΕΩΝ (Gallienus); Side has ΠΙCΤΙC ΦΙΛΗC CΥΜΜΑΧΟΥ ΡΩΜΑΙΩΝ ΜΥCΤΙΔΟC CΙΔΗC (Salonina); Prostanna has ΦΙΛΗC CΥΝΜΑΧΟΥ ΡΩΜΕΩΝ ΠΡΟCΤΑΝΝΕΝΩ (Gallienus). The letters S R at Antioch are nowadays usually interpreted as standing for 'socii

Romanorum' (see *RPC IX*); but, slightly bizarrely, they also occur on the coins of Iconium, a colony.

78. Dio Chrysostom 34.48–9, with Kremmydas 2021.
79. Franke & Nollé 1997. Their book now needs updating, and more information can be found in the various parts of *RPC*. In Latin it was CONCORD(IA), as shown by the joint coinage of Corinth and Patras under Hadrian (*RPC III*, 163).
80. The alliances of Sardis and Pergamum under Augustus (*RPC I*, 2362 and 2988), and Sardis and (probably) Hypaepa under Augustus and Tiberius (*RPC I*, 2528A and 2538E, formerly listed as 5445 and 5446), and definitely Sardis and Hypaepa (*RPC I*, 2538C–D).
81. *RPC I*, 2928; *cf.* 2912. If 'guarantor', then between some sort of boundary dispute, for example. This interpretation is accepted by Martin 2013: 206, note 269. On the meaning of the word and the legend, see also Pera 1984: 26; Cadwallader & Harrison 2019: 40–1.
82. *RPC II*, pp. 6–7, 34–5; III, p.839. To the list in *RPC II* can be added Sardis and Smyrna under Titus (1315A–B); to that in *RPC III* can be added the alliance of Thyatira and Pergamum (1821A).
83. The reign of Pius saw the only late concord with Rome, significantly by Alexandria in Egypt (Nilus and Tiber at Alexandria: *RPC IV.4*, temporary nos. 15272, 17057). Alexandria's coinage enjoyed many close links with the capital, as discussed above. Apart from Alexandria and Corinth, as mentioned above, the practice was largely confined to Asia. The other exceptions are: Thessalian League and Rome (*RPC I*, 1553); Amisus and Rome (*RPC I*, 2143); and Ephesus and Alexandria (*RPC VII.1*, 400–20).
84. With the strange exception of some very small and very rare coins made in the name of Lucilla, some dated to 177/8: Butcher 2004: 378–9 nos. 449–449a. Compare Klaver 2019: 237: most of the 70 representations of women at Seleucia date to the second and third centuries. On the representation of Antonine women, see Yarrow 2012: 433–7, and, more generally, Horster 2013.
85. Not at all at Rhosus, Chalcis, Beroea, Samosata, Doliche or Germanicia; at Seleucia and Nicopolis only during the Severan period; Hierapolis only under Severus and Alexander; Cyrrhus and Zeugma only under Philip.
86. The earliest is an isolated appearance of Sabina at Gaba; only from the Antonine period did women become more frequent.
87. *cf.* Klaver 2019: 213, 216–8, on houses becoming more 'Roman' from the late second century.
88. Butcher 2004: 220–2; Sartre 2005: 183–5.
89. Balty 1995: 60 and pl. I.1.
90. Balty 1995: 30; *cf.* Balty 1977: 5–6.
91. See the discussion by Blanco-Pérez 2018: esp. 10–14.
92. *RPC II*, pp. 35–6.

**338** Notes to Pages 210–5

93. *RPC III*, pp. 858–9: Amphipolis, Tomi, Crete, Bithynia, Germe, Stratonicea Hadrianopolis, Samos, Clazomenae, Bargylia, Halicarnassus, Sardis, Trajanopolis, Tripolis (Lydia), Appia, Nacolea, Neoclaudiopolis and Caesarea Maritima. However, some of the types may not be specific, e.g., the emperor on a horse had occurred earlier at Amphipolis, and Victory at Stratonicea Hadrianopolis, Bargylia, Trajanopolis and Caesarea may just be generic.

94. At Tomi: *RPC III*, 780–2.

95. *RPC IV* temporary number 2989. For the context, see Burnett 2021b: 538–9.

96. *RPC III*, p. 860: only Crete, Bithynia, Ephesus (add a reference to *RPC* 2053–6) and Nicopolis ad Lycum.

97. The coins show Victory inscribing a shield, but the inscription has not yet been fully legible: see Burnett 2016c: 102.

98. *RPC IV* temporary number 9254 and 3222 (= BMC 289).

99. *RPC IV* temporary number 3255.

100. A few of the coins are dated: Alexandria, years 1–3 = 161/2–163/4; Mopsus year 230 = 162/3; and Amasea years 164–5 (161/2–162/3). These suggest a fairly fast transmission. See also Section 6.7, on Antinous.

101. *RPC III*, pp. 661–2, 860.

102. See *RPC III*, pp. 658–9, for the view that the Victory types at Alexandria under Hadrian have no specific reference, and are just a celebration of the emperor in general.

103. For the notion of 'sets', see Howgego 2023: 61–5.

104. Burnett 1991; Bland 1996.

105. *RPC III*, p. 858.

106. *RPC III*, pp. 858–9. See also Price 2005: 122, for the 'patchiness' of the Panhellenion in Greece and Asia.

107. *RPC III*, p. 861–2.

108. *cf.* Burrell 2004: 29: 'It was also during the joint reign of Marcus Aurelius and Lucius Verus that the title 'neocoros' first began to appear regularly on coins of Pergamum, which state a simple 'twice neocoros' without much fanfare'.

109. The reading NEΩ on the Trajanic coins for Augustus (*RPC III*, 1703 = I, 2357) remains uncertain, and now seems unlikely since the first letter seems indubitably to be a K. Even if it were a reference to a neocorate, its extremely diminutive presence on the coinage would only emphasise how little importance was attached to the title.

110. In the reign of Pius, when a few coins of Ephesus show three temples, some do not even mention the title.

111. Burrell dated the second neocorate at Sardis to the reign of Antoninus Pius, but see Petzl 2017: 8 (a reference I owe to M. Hallmannsecker).

112. A. Pius: Nicomedia, Cyzicus, Ephesus (ΔIC); M. Aurelius: Nicomedia, Cyzicus, Pergamum (ΔIC), Ephesus (ΔIC), Amasea; Commodus: Nicomedia (ΔIC),

Cyzicus, Pergamum (ΔΙC), Ephesus (ΔΙC), Amasea, Neocaesarea (Pontus), Tarsus (ΔΙC).

113. Rebuffat 1997: and, more generally, Filges 2015.
114. Nurpetlian 2020: 6, 27–8.
115. The term is used only on coins of Cilicia and Phoenicia. At Dora and Tripolis (both ΝΑΥΑΡΧΙΣ) the city Tyche holds a standard, and at both cities a galley also appears on the coinage (quite rare at Dora, but common at Tripoli); at Corycus (ΝΑΥΑΡΧΙΣ) the city Tyche holds an aplustre and rests her foot on a prow; the coins of Elaeusa-Sebaste (ΝΑΥΑΡΧΙΣ) sometimes depict a (military?) eagle; and a galley with a standard appears at Aegeae (ΝΑΥΑΡΧΙΣ). For its significance, see Gebhardt 2002: 164–96. The interpretation as indicating naval detachments was rejected by Starr 1967: 54 = Starr 1979: 281. A galley with a standard also appears at Corcyra, Cyzicus, Apamea and Ephesus, while at Ephesus and Side a prow (and, at Side, a standard) may appear with the city Tyche. Gadara also has a galley with a standard, and was presumably the naval base on the Sea of Galilee.
116. Calomino 2019. The connection between the opening of the mint of Viminacium and the end of the transfer of Bithynian coins is convincing.
117. See also Chapter 4.
118. Kremydi & Ward 2017; Butcher 2004: 179. However, other explanations are possible: see Frey-Kupper & Stannard 2018.
119. The earliest occurrence seems to be on a new coin from Sinope for Domitian: *RPC II*, 723A Online.
120. Mairat 2017: 313.
121. At 25 colonies: Deultum, Thessalonica, Sinope, Apamea Bithynia, Alexandria Troas, Parium, Antioch Pisidia, Cremna, Iconium, Parlais, Lystra, Ninica, Mallus, Berytus, Heliopolis, Laodicea ad Mare, Caesarea ad Libanum, Damascus, Tyre, Sidon, Ptolemais, Neapolis, Bostra and Edessa. The municipium is Coela; other municipia with Marsyas (not on coins) are listed by Veyne 1961 (see next note). Le Blanc 2021 suggests that the small figure identified as Marsyas on coins of Carrhae and Rhesaena is in fact Aquarius.
122. Cited and discussed by Veyne 1961: 89–90: Ἐσπούδαζον δὲ καὶ ἃς ᾤκουν πόλεις οἱ Ἰταλοὶ τιμὴν ταύταις παρέχειν, ἀνιστάντες δαίμονά τινα ὡς πρεσβύτην ὅμοιον Σειληνῷ, ἵνα καὶ τῇ κοινωνίᾳ τῶν ἱερῶν συγκραθῶσιν. Αἱ δὲ πέδαι περιτιθέμεναι δηλοῦσι τὸ ὑπήκοον, τῷ συνδεδέσθαι αὐτοῖς τὰς πόλεις τὰς ἐχούσας τὰ τοιαῦτα ἀγάλματα. Ταῦτα εἴρηται Χάρακι ἱστοριογράφῳ [They also took care to honour the cities inhabited by the Italians, by erecting the statue of a supernatural being, a sort of old man similar to Silenus, so that the community of worship was one more link. As for the fetters that have been placed on it, they symbolise the state of subjection, the cities which have statues of this type being chained to them. According to historiographer Charax].

## 340 Notes to Pages 217–21

123. Filges 2015: 238–42 (with a summary of earlier views); Barja De Quiroga 2018; and Arena 2020: 69–71, denying the link between Marsyas and liberty. The most recent discussion is Schaick 2021, who suggests that it also indicates the wealth and prosperity of the city.

124. Millar 1990: 15 = Millar 2006a: 172 (on Berytus).

125. Aulus Gellius, *Noctes Atticae* 16.13: 'quasi effigies parvae simulacraque'. There is much discussion of the extent to which this may or may not have been true of their physical reality: Coles 2020: 79–84.

126. *RPC III*, pp. 851–7. Some of the coins are very rare and there is a suspicion that some may be modern forgeries. The unique coin of Amorium and one of the varieties at Sardis have already been rejected, the latter now seen to be an altered specimen of *RPC* 2408A: see Amandry 2020. The unique coin from Philadelphia can now also be seen also to be a likely forgery (see the comments on *RPC III*, 2386 and 2386A Online). Significant doubts also attach to the unique coins from Bithynia (*RPC* 1025) and Sinope (*RPC* 1228). The coin of 'Antinous' tentatively attributed to Prusa in Triton VI, 14 Jan. 2003, lot 564, is a misread coin of Antioch in Pisidia, with Hermes/cock. One specimen of Sardis was recovered from the Sardis excavations (*RPC III*, 2407/11).

127. *RPC III*, p. 855.

128. At Pergamum and Tmolus he comes between Hadrian and Sabina; at Hadrianopolis he is on the largest denomination.

129. 'The Arcadians' or 'The Amphictyons'.

130. Vout 2005.

131. See also *RPC III*, pp. 815, 817.

132. *RPC III*, pp. 829–33.

133. Many of them are made from high Zn orichalcum, which is a feature of coins made in Asia Minor, and not Rome, where 'diluted' orichalcum is the norm in the second century.

134. For the new, intensified production of medallions under Hadrian, see Mittag in Abdy & Mittag 2019: 60–2. For what it is worth, a mount like that on some medallions occurs on two of the large Antinous coins from Nicomedia (*RPC III*, 1093/5 and 7), but one of them (at least) seems to be cast.

135. For Asia Minor, a medallion of Marcus Aurelius is known from Ceretapa in Phrygia: Fischer-Bossert 2014: 162, 167, no. 23. Fischer-Bossert mentions a similar piece from Dura-Europos.

136. Toynbee 1944; Seltman 1948: 77–85, attributed the ones from Greece to an 'Alpheios master', whose works he thought that he could identify among the Rome medallions of Hadrian. See also, more recently, Mosch & Klostermeyer 2015.

137. Many thanks to G. Watson for discussion and advice. The distribution is not unlike that for the image of Aurelius and Verus clasping hands (above,

Map 6.3), where the limited chronological data suggests a similarly fast transmission.

138. Kuhn 2011 sees them as intended to gain more favours for Smyrna from Hadrian.

# 7 'From a kingdom of gold to one of iron and rust' in the Third Century CE

1. Hekster 2008; Johnston 2012; Harl 1987.
2. Traces of Caracalla's introduction of universal citizenship are difficult to detect, although the way in which several city magistrates describe themselves as being of equestrian rank may reflect the greater access of civic elites to that order: Hochard 2020: 899 (although Hermolodas is a misreading). There are several other cases outside Lydia. A good example is Aur. Ail. Attianos at Saitta whose name appears on coins of the reign of Elagabalus (*RPC VI* temporary number 4434), and then his son (presumably) appears later under Gordian III, describing himself as 'son of an Asiarch of equestrian rank' (ΥΟΥ III ACI: *RPC VII*, 219). Presumably the father had been appointed Asiarch and had acquired equestrian status in the intervening twenty years.
3. See Zuiderhoek 2009: 20–21, with references, especially to De Callataÿ.
4. Haklai-Rotenberg 2011, for example, regards the period up to Aurelian as essentially stable.
5. Though see Howgego 1994 for the point that the high empire was never fully integrated from the monetary point of view.
6. Some rare provincial coins of Gallienus show him wearing a helmet. They were made in a small area, occurring only at Tralles, Antioch in Caria and Aphrodisias.
7. Calomino 2012: 112–13.
8. See the references gathered by Woytek 2019b: 207 note 19.
9. Strasser 2020.
10. Rowan 2012: 178–87, noting, however, that the dated issues are too late.
11. Paula: Prusias ad Hypium (with sacred stone quadriga), Tium, Creteia-Flaviopolis and Bithynium; Maesa: Tium, Amastris, Creteia-Faviopolis, Bithynium and Ionopolis. In fact, the earliest use of this design is known from a coin of Julia Domna from Pessinus in Galatia (Classical Numismatic Group EA 272, 2012, lot 246). The coin is inscribed ΙΟΥΛΙΑ ΑΥΤΟΥCTA, and it might be tempting to think that it also depicts Maesa; but Pessinus produced no coinage after the reign of Septimius Severus, and the same legend occurs for some other coins of Domna. Maesa was Domna's sister, but it is not clear if this can explain the link; and Pessinus was a long way away.

**342** Notes to Pages 227–40

12. *cf.* Kraft 1972: 72 and Taf. 101, without any comment. For the linked cities, see also his Karte 16 (for Maximinus).
13. Classical Numismatic Group 55, 13 September, 2000, lot 950.
14. Hostein 2013 and Calomino 2020.
15. Adapted from the similar coins of Pergamum for Commodus and also Caracalla. But at Pergamum, the figure is nude and holds a thunderbolt, so presumably is Zeus. At Laodicea, he wears a military uniform and is radiate – clearly the emperor himself.
16. Trajan: Nicomedia, Pergamum; Hadrian: Ephesus, Tarsus; Antoninus Pius: Cyzicus, Ephesus; Marcus Aurelius: Nicomedia, Cyzicus, Pergamum, Ephesus, Ancyra; Commodus: Nicomedia, Cyzicus, Tarsus. The most notable absence is Smyrna. The coin of Neocaesarea for Trajan (Burrell 2004: 206) is, in fact, altered from a coin of Trajan from Alexandria, Egypt.
17. Burrell 2004: 373: 'under the Severi it [the use of the title] burgeoned'.
18. For example, under Severus Alexander: at Perinthus, Nicomedia, Cyzicus, Pergamum, Ephesus, Sardis, Philadelphia, Caesarea and Aegeae. However, it still remained in only occasional use at Caesarea in Cappadocia.
19. The coin apparently attesting a neocorate for Antandrus under Caracalla (Burrell 2004: 133) is an altered coin of Sardis (as SNG Cop 533).
20. Burrell 2004: 335. On the other hand, the association is implicit on a rare coin of Elagabalus from Philippopolis which show the emperor presenting a temple to the city's patron deity Apollo Kendreisos; below the temple is a depiction of a table surmounted by an agonistic crown (RPC VI, temporary number 498). The apples show that it refers to the Kendreiseia Pythia. Blanco-Pérez 2018: 15–17.
21. Strasser 2020; De Hoz 2016 has suggested that the *Chrysanthina* were in honour of Artemis.
22. Examples can be found at Augusta Traiana (Marcus Aurelius), Anchialus (Commodus, Septimius Severus, Maximinus, Gordian III), Nicaea (Septimius Severus), Isaura (Septimius Severus), Nicopolis ad Istrum (Elagabalus, Gordian III), Sardis (Elagabalus), Sidon (Elagabalus), Tomi (Maximinus), Marcianopolis (Gordian III), Hadrianopolis (Gordian III), Bizya (Philip), Parium (Gallienus), Aegeae (Aemilian), Prusias ad Hypium (Gallienus), and Side (Valerian, Gallienus).
23. Burnett 2016c.
24. So also Johnston 1984b: 242, with earlier references.
25. Kremydi & Ward 2017.
26. By then, Phrygia-Caria had been split off from Asia as a separate province, so the figures have been added to make a proper comparison.
27. Watson 2021: 137.
28. Johnston 1984b: 253. For a response, Leschhorn 1985.
29. Johnston 1984b: 254–5.

Notes to Pages 240–9 **343**

30. The calculation is, of course, crude, and it could be argued that the later coins are generally bigger than the earlier ones and so represent relatively greater amounts of money.
31. See *RPC I*, 35–7.
32. Die studies of Thessalonica (Touratsoglou 1988), Aphrodisias (MacDonald 1992) and Dium (Kremydi-Sicilianou 1996) confirm the picture of an increasing number of dies from the first to the third centuries.
33. Zuiderhoek 2009: 154–9, for the decline in euergetism, especially after 200; see also Chapter 4 above for the disappearance of the ἀνέθηκε formula for coinage in the third century.
34. Flament & Marchetti 2011 regard I A as indicating 10 Asses, but 11 would be the natural interpretation.
35. Johnston 2007: 30, 139–47.
36. Johnston 2007: 14, 150–2, 175, with *GIC* 837.
37. On the very last issues: Johnston 2007: 21, 30, 44.
38. Johnston 2007: 44. See also *GIC* 765 (the countermark B).
39. Johnston 2007: 31.
40. Watson 2019a: 44–5, 54–55. The same pattern can be observed elsewhere in his area of study.
41. The letters Aς at Pompeiopolis, which first occurred in the reign of Severus Alexander, are not, in my view, value marks.
42. The largest denomination is sometimes marked with H, the next occasionally with Δ, and the two smallest sometimes with B and A, thus indicating that the denominations of the third century are 8, 4, 2 and 1 units.
43. Watson 2021: 137.
44. Johnston 2007: 29–31.
45. See also Johnston 2007: 46–62.
46. Johnston 2007: 48.
47. Johnston 2007: 80–2.
48. Johnston 2007: 82–90. The cities, mostly from the Ephesus workshop, include Samos, Colophon, Priene, Magnesia, Nysa, Tralles, Metropolis and Hypaepa.
49. See Johnston 2007.
50. This would explain the 'star' = a denarius symbol, which occurs on some of the countermarks, those with B and Γ. (By this date, values could have been high; there is even a countermark KΔ = 24 (asses) = 1½ denarii at Prusias ad Hypium, together with 12 and 16; there is also a possible bronze denarius at Sinope. See Section 7.2.1.)
51. Butcher 2017: 273–90. Butcher tentatively suggested that the units may have been the drachm or the obol, rather than the *assarion*. Some of the cities (Odessus, Marcianopolis and Tomi) are also linked by the production of large coins ('medallions') under Gordian III, all struck from a single obverse die; see Calomino 2012.

## 344 Notes to Pages 251–7

52. Until *c*. 250–65, with the rare double sestertii for Trajan Decius, Gallienus and Postumus, on which see Section 7.4.

53. Cyzicus, Assus = Mytilene = Pergamum = Thyatira = Silandus, Elaea, Saitta and Tralles. Here, the sign = denotes the use of the same obverse die.

54. Kraft 1972, die 261 = pl. 88.14 for Assus, Mytilene and Pergamum. For them and the other two cities, see *RPC IV* Online no. 2457, for the links.

55. Septimius Severus: Hadrianotherae, Germe, Mytilene, Thyatira, Attalea, Pergamum, Elaea, Hypaepa, Synaus, Acrasus, Bagis, Daldis, Maeonia, Saitta, Sardis, Silandus, Mylasa, Stratonicea, Attuda, Dionysopolis, Sebaste, Cremna, Adana; Caracalla: Cyzicus, Hadrianotherae, Mytilene, Thyatira, Pergamum, Clazomenae, Smyrna, Nicaea Cilbianorum, Bagis, Blaundus, Philadelphia, Sardis and Laodicea.

56. Macrinus: Cibyra; Elagabalus: Germe, Mytilene, Pergamum, Thyatira, Saitta, Stratonicea (Lydia), Iulia Gordus, Laodicea, Dionysopolis, Perge; Severus Alexander: Cyzicus, Germe, Mytilene, Apollonis, Hierocaesarea, Acrasus, Aegae, Magnesia (Lydia), Thyatira, Silandus, Apollonia, Tarsus; Maximinus: Pergamum, Elaea, Stratonicea, Nysa, Thyatira, Cremna; Gordian III: Perinthus, Anchialus, Cyzicus, Hadrianeia, Miletopolis, Elaea, Germe, Pergamum, Thyatira, Daldis, Sardis, Ephesus, Acmonea, Apamea, Dorylaeum; Philip: Bizya, Miletopolis, Hadrianeia, Perperene, Phocaea, Thyatira, Blaundus, Tralles, Sardis, Daldis, Iulia Gordus, Ancyra (Phrygia), Apamea, Temenothyrae, Laodicea, Isinda.

57. Trajan Decius: Pergamum, Aegae; Trebonianus Gallus: Blaundus; Valerian & Gallienus: Ilium, Mytilene, Pergamum, Thyatira, Sardis, Temenothyrae, Sillyum; Gallienus (sole): none; Claudius II: Cyzicus.

58. Cavagna 2012: 128, has suggested that the Provincia Dacia coins were also made at Viminacium, as there are die links between the two coinages.

59. Bland 2023.

60. Mairat 2007 for Cyzicus.

61. Many double sestertii were made in the reign of Trebonianus Gallus. Some sestertii (and very rare double sestertii: See Göbl 2000, nos. 435 and 454; see also Classical Numismatic Group EA 442, lots 175–176) were minted for Gallienus after the death of Valerian, as indicated by the use in the reverse legends of AVG, rather than the previous AVGG.

62. Holmes 2020 has dated the coins with GALLIENVM P R and GALLIENVM AVG SENATVS to 264–5. The curious pieces with GENIVS P R and INT VRB, some of which are radiate (doubles) were made in spring 268, according to Yonge 1979.

63. Viminacium a little to year 16 = 254/5; Provincia Dacia a little to year 10 = 255/6.

64. Calomino 2011: 284–6.

Notes to Pages 257–67 **345**

65. Kremydi-Sicilianou 1996: no coins known for Valerian, but Gallienus and Salonina are well attested.
66. Touratsoglou 1988: 81.
67. A unique coin, formerly attributed to Tranquillina, is probably of Salonina; and a coin has recently been discovered for Gallienus. Their style suggests the sole reign.
68. Schönert-Geiss 1972, II: 16–17.
69. The magistrate M. Aur. Sexstos is known only on the common coins of Gallienus and Salonina: see Klose 1987: 316–27. Klose also assigned some coins without a magistrate's name to the sole reign.
70. The magistrate Sex. Kl. Seilianos is known only for Gallienus and Salonina.
71. Johnston 2007: 85 (with earlier references).
72. Burnett 2021b.
73. Paulos, Asclepiades, Hermolaos, Severos and Basileus. A sixth name (Stellos) is based on a misreading of a coin of Hermolaos.
74. Watson (2019a: 47, note) points out that the supposed coin for Aurelian at Sagalassus is a misread coin of Claudius II.
75. Watson 2019a: 17–59.
76. The supposed coin of Gallienus has been altered in modern times from one of Neocaesarea.
77. The only possible exception is Antioch ad Cragum, whose coins of Gallienus have a very different style from those of Valerian, suggesting that they may belong to the sole reign.
78. The very rare tetradrachms and reformed coins of Maximian dated to his year 12 (296/7) suggest that the reform took place in late 296, although the last substantial issues took place in the preceding Egyptian year. The coinage of Domitius Domitianus subsequently embraced both systems.
79. Burnett 2021b.
80. Hostein 2017.
81. Howgego 2005: 16 *cf.* Howgego 1995: 138–40.
82. Howgego 1995 continues: 'The demise of local coinage needs to be viewed in the context of the decline of civic euergetism, of civic building, and of monumental inscriptions, and a marked increase in the 'privatisation' of display'. *cf.* Howgego (1995, 98–99) on the 'declining position of the decurial class'; Zuiderjoek (2009: 18 and 154–9) on the steep decline in civic benefactions in the third century: but this contrasts with the apparent increase in the amount of civic coinage produced at the time.
83. Kelly 2021.
84. The last issues of Patras under Caracalla 'are of such good style that they might be products of the Rome mint': Johnston 2012: 463.
85. Howgego 1995: 140.

## 346 Notes to Pages 267–70

86. Metcalf 1998. A few analyses were published by Cope *et al.* (1997: 6–7 and 34–5), which seem to show that the coins continued to contain as much silver as under Claudius II (about 2%), but that from late in the reign of Probus there was none, or at least <1%.

87. It remains something of a mystery why coinage continued in this small area of southern Asia Minor, though its geographical isolation or perhaps just fashion seem the most likely reasons (see Watson 2019a: 158, contra Cluett 2002).

88. See Johnston (2007: 60–1, with Table 18); on 63, she regards this change as being made 'rather surprisingly', and suggests that they were reusing old flans (so also her 124).

89. Johnston 2007: 67–70, has a full discussion. The countermark is *GIC* no. 805.

90. Coin Hoards of the Roman Empire: https://chre.ashmus.ox.ac.uk/hoard/10457.

91. Coin Hoards of the Roman Empire: https://chre.ashmus.ox.ac.uk/hoard/12322.

92. Van Heesch 1993b.

93. Alföldi 1937; Bricault 2008: 198–201.

94. Gautier 2017.

# Index

*a rationibus*, 110
Abakainon, 63
abbreviation, xxxiii, xxxv, 61, 82, 118, 130, 144, 145, 146
Abdera, Spain, 147
Abonoteichus-Ionopolis, Paphlagonia, 116, 324, 326, 341, 342
Abydus, Troas, 234, 335
Accilaeum, Phrygia, 115, 342
acclamation, 227, 229, 234
accusative case, 145
Achaean League, 93
Acilius, Manius, 82
Acmonea, Phrygia, 123, 143, 336, 344
Acrasus, Lydia, 251, 342, 344
Actium, Battle of, 108, 129, 135, 137, 148
Adada, Pisidia, 246, 342
Adana, Cilicia, 344
Adraa, Arabia, 263
Adramyteum, Mysia, 325
Adranon, 63
Aegae, Aeolis, 344
Aegeae, Cilicia, 19, 224, 262, 322, 328, 339, 342
    Antinous, 221
Aelia Capitolina. *See* Jerusalem
Aemilian, 224
Aenianes, 93
aes grave, 48, 53, 57, 63, 68
    Etruscan, 56
    oval series, 317
aes rude, 45, 53, 68
Aesernia, 55
Aesillas, 93, 109
Aezani hoard, 32, 99
Aezani, Phrygia, 324
Africa
    coinage in the second and first centuries BCE, 89
    third century BCE coinage, 65–6

Agathocles, king of Syracuse, 61
agonistic designs, 206, 342 *See* also games
Agrigentum, 8, 63, 139
Agrippa I, King of Judaea, 140
Agrippa II, King of Judaea, 26, 165
Agrippa Postumus, 138
Agrippa, M., 138, 139, 170
Agrippina, wife of Claudius, 141
Agyrion, 63
Aineias, Aur., 325
aitesamenos, 118, 123
Aitna, 63
Akrai, 63
Akunniadad, 55
Alaisa, 63
Alba, 8
Aleia Elagabalia, 232
Aléria, 16, 59
Alexander the Great, 32, 33, 34, 50, 108, 109, 236
    dream, 204, 205
    iconography, 48, 70, 72
Alexander, prophet, 116
Alexandria, Egypt, 2, 23, 25, 26, 42, 127, 157, 175, 183, 191, 210, 212, 218, 227, 228, 237, 255, 261, 263, 267, 269, 328, 337
    contemporary events, 212
    mint building, 121
Alexandria, Troas, xxxvi, 111, 158, 160, 161, 323, 327, 336, 339
Alia, Phrygia, 324, 342
Allianoi hoard, 327
Allifae, 8, 51
Alontion, 63
Alpheios master, 340
Amasea, Pontus, xxxiii, 338
Amastris, Paphlagonia, 243, 245, 247, 257, 326, 328, 336, 341
Amblada, Pisidia, 342

## 348 Index

Ambrosial rocks, 334
Ameselon, 63
Amestratus, 63
Amisus, Pontus, 101, 137, 187, 322, 337
 Antinous, 221
Amorium, Phrygia, 340
Amphictyons
 Antinous, 219
Amphipolis, Macedonia, 92, 95, 338
Anacreon, 336
Anazarbus, Cilicia, 205, 227, 262, 328
Anchialus, Thrace, 326, 342, 344
Ancyra, Galatia, 232, 333, 342
 neocorate temple, 200
Ancyra, Phrygia, 118, 324, 344
Andriake, 331
Androklos, 201
Anemurium, Cilicia, 262
anetheke, 118, 234, 343
Anineta, Lydia, 342
Antandrus, Troas, 325, 342
Antinous, 119, 174, 218–21, 251
Antioch
 SC coinage, 207
Antioch, Caria, 249, 324, 341
Antioch, Pisidia, 189, 240, 261, 267, 339
Antioch, Syria, 2, 23, 25, 26, 40, 103, 111, 125,
 134, 160, 189, 190, 191, 207, 237, 255,
 262, 269, 332
 SC coinage, 158, 161, 168, 190, 329
Antiochus IV, king of Commagene, 102
antoninianus, 4, 28, 32, 111, 226, 253, 263,
 266, 267, 268, 310
 debasement, 41, 222, 237
 introduction, 41, 222, 238
Antoninus Pius, 251, 342
 British war, 212
 last small denominations, 182
Antony. See Mark Antony
Apamea, Bithynia, 101, 257, 322, 323, 339
Apamea, Phrygia, 100, 234, 324, 325, 344
Apamea, Syria, 19, 322
Aphrodisias, Caria, 115, 179, 210, 249, 324,
 341
Apollo Kendreisos, 342
Apollodotus, son of Diodotus, 124

Apollonia Mordiaeum, Pisidia, 336, 342
Apollonia, Caria, 143, 325, 344
Apollonia, Cyrenaica, 320
Apollonia, Illyria, 91, 93
Apollonia, Mysia, 342
Apollonis, Lydia, 344
Apollonoshieron, Lydia, 143, 342
Apollotodotus, 325
Appia, Phrygia, 324, 338, 342
Aquae Calidae, 194
aquila. See eagle
Aquinum, 55
Aradus, Phoenicia, 103, 133, 147, 342
aramaic, 187, 333
Aratus, 336
Arausio, 139
Arcadians
 Antinous, 340
archon, 121, 122, 233
Argos, Greece, 198, 243, 247
Ariassus, Pisidia, 246
Arion, 336
Aristotimos, 220
Arpi, 8, 51, 55
Arsaos, Spain, 85
Arse, 84 See also Saguntum
Arykanda, 331
Asia Minor
 coinage in the imperial period, 206
 coinage in the second and first centuries
 BCE, 101
asiarch, 113, 121, 230, 304, 341
Aspendus, Pamphylia, 246, 250
assaria, 124, 125, 173, 183, 243, 249, 310, 321,
 331, 343
Assus, Troad, 252, 344
Atella, 55
Ateula, 91
Athens, 17, 18, 32, 93, 111, 115
 mint site, 120
athlete, 232
Atratinus, 99, 134, 135
Attalea, Lydia, 344
Attalea, Pamphylia, 246, 250
Attalid Kingdom, 11, 18, 31, 88
Attalos, 251

# Index 349

Attalus, 205, 336
Attianos, Aur. Ail., 341
Attuda, Caria, 143, 324, 325, 344
Augusta Traiana, Thrace, 342
Augusta, Cilicia, 262
Augustus, xxxvii, 2, 25, 77, 80, 81, 95, 129
   capricorn, 21, 148, 170, 330, 335
   coinage reform, 151, 161, 175
   lituus, 138
   Parthian standards, 103
   portrait, 109, 131
Aurelian, xxxi, 223, 341
   city coinage, 261
   coinage reform, 41, 267
Ausculum, 55, 70
Avavcia, 159

Bagis, Lydia, 344
Balanea. *See* Leucas, Syria
bankers, 1, 126
   early Roman, 68
Barata, Lycaonia, 342
Bargylia, Caria, 338, 342
Baris, Pisidia, 342
Basillos, Tiberius, 118
Beneventum, 55
Beroea, Macedonia, 230, 337, 342
Berytus, Phoenicia, 133, 145, 190, 208, 216, 262, 323, 339
Bias, 336
Bibulus, L. Calpurnius, 95
bilingual coins, 147, 194, 334, 335
bilingual milestones, 194
Bithynia
   coinage of the first century BCE, 101–2
Bithynium, Bithynia, 101, 226, 328, 341
Bizya, Thrace, 232, 234, 342, 344
Black Sea, 33
Blaundus, Lydia, 143, 344
board of magistrates, 122
Bocchus II, 89
Bogud, 89
Bolscan. *See* Osca
booty, 6, 10, 35, 37, 62, 68
Bostra, Arabia, 190, 339, 342
Boule, 115, 176, 228

brass, 99, 151, 152, 153, 155, 162, 165, 166, 167, 220, 320, *See* orichalcum
Bredgar hoard, 40
Brescello hoard, 38
Brettii, 7
Britain
   financial records, 163
   Lycian drachms, 172
   Roman conquest, 169
Briula, Lydia, 342
Broads hoard, Norfolk, 313
Brundisium, 55, 80
Brutus, 172
   portrait, 132
Bruzus, Phrygia, 342
buildings on coins, 149, *See* also temple
Buthrotum, Epirus, 164, 323
Butuntum, 55
Byblus, Phoenicia, 334
Byzantium, Thrace, 121, 122, 225, 240, 257, 322, 328

CA coinage, 153, 154, 158, 159, 160, 172, 173, 193, 194
Cáceres el Viejo, 85
Cadi, Phrygia, 342
Cadmus, 209, 334
Caelia, 8, 55
Caesaraugusta, Spain, 170, 330
Caesarea ad Libanum, Phoenicia, 190, 339
Caesarea, Cappadocia, 2, 27, 28, 29, 166, 232, 237, 261, 342
Caesarea, Samaria, 190, 328, 338, 342
Caesonia, 140
Cagliari hoard, Sardinia, 16, 60
Caiatia, 55
Caiazzo hoard, 38
Calagurris, 145
Calchedon, Thrace, 328, 342
Cales, Italy, 7, 55
Caligula, 140, 170
Callatis, Moesia, 193, 194, 326, 342
Cannae, Battle of, 54
Canusium, 8, 55
Capito, L. Servenius, 123
Capua, 8, 55

**350** Index

Caracalla, 41, 123, 222, 225, 226, 228, 232, 237, 252, 344, 345
   Parthian War, 205
   Pergamum, 202
Carallia, Cilicia, 246, 250
Carbo, C. Papirius, 101
Carina, 330
Carisius, P., 153
Carrhae, Mesopotamia, 190, 204, 339
Carteia, 137, 323
Carthage, 145, 234, 323, 330
   find of quinarii, 66
Carthaginian coinage, 7, 9, 13, 33, 34, 36, 59, 62, 66, 79, 84, 117
Carthago Nova, 139
Carystus, Greece, 164
Casae, Cilicia, 246
Cassandrea, Macedonia, 189, 342
Cassius Dio, xxxiv, 128, 158, 161
catacombs, Rome, 269
Cato, M. Porcius, 89
Celenderis, Cilicia, 342
Celtiberian script, 14, 87
Cercina, Africa, 323
Ceretapa-Diocaesarea, Phrygia, 325, 340, 342
Chalcis, Greece, 164, 324, 336
Chalcis, Syria, 337
chalkos, 83, 94, 124, 125, 163, 309
Charinos, 149
Chios, 19, 98, 115, 125, 183, 322, 336, 342
Christianity, 269
Chrysanthina, 232
Chrysippus, 336
Cibyra, Phrygia, 187, 344
   inscription, 29, 331
Cicero, 12, 18, 19, 24, 29, 84, 90, 97
Cidrama, Caria, 143, 325
Cilicia
   coinage in the first century BCE, 102
circulation, 127
Cirta, Africa, 149
Cisalpine Gaul, 16
cistophori, 18, 19, 21, 27, 28, 29, 30, 31, 97, 101, 133
cistophoric drachm, 30
city magistracies, 111, 260

city view
   Amasea, xxxiii
   Bizya, 234
   Laodicea, 228
Cius, Bithynia, 226, 328
Claudiconium Lycaonia, 322
Claudius, 31, 40, 142
   annexation of Lycia, 172
   branch mints, 162, 194
   British victory, 150
   Ebusus, 170
Claudius II, 260, 344
   city coinage, 261
Clazomenae, Ionia, 180, 338, 344
Cleopatra, 17, 21, 77, 103, 105
   portrait, 133
closed currency system, xxxvi, 29, 31, 97, 126, 172, 263, 269
Clovius, C., 153
Cnossus, 139, 323, 334
Codrula, Pisidia, 246
Coela, Thrace, 125, 188, 189, 257, 339
coining scene, 80
Colbasa, Pisidia, 342
Cologne, 255
colony, xxxvi, 7, 57, 70, 80, 91, 99, 108, 109, 118, 132, 139, 143, 147, 153, 164, 198, 208, 216, 245, 253
   definition, 188
   foundation scene, 158, 160
   Greek, 5, 13, 61
   Latin, 188, 190
   Marsyas, 217
Colophon, Ionia, 178, 240, 336, 343
Colossae, Phrygia, 123
Colybrassus, Cilicia, 246, 248, 250
Commodus, 178, 183, 233, 252, 342
   British war, 212
   German war, 210
competition between cities, 114, 176, 202
Compulteria, 55
Conana, Pisidia, 246
Constantine, xxxi
contemporary events, 148
conventus, 182
cooperation of silver mints, 26, 162, 175, 253

Copia, 80
copper, 167
Cora, 8, 51
Coracesium, Cilicia, 246, 250
Corcyra, 339
Cordova hoard, 85
core collections, 240
Corinth, Greece, 116, 153, 164, 193, 198, 204, 210, 323, 328, 337
Cornutus, C. Caecilius, 101
Corsica, 16, 58–9
Corycus, Cilicia, 339
Cos, 342
Cosa, Etruria, 56, 70, 317
Cotiaeum, Phrygia, 324
countermarks, 59, 112, 117, 127, 166, 167, 169, 178, 182, 232, 245, 249, 266, 268, 323, 327, 333, 335, 343
Crassus Mucianus, C. Licinius, 112
Cremna, Pisidia, 261, 268, 339, 344
Crete, 23, 25, 192, 210, 338
Creteia-Flaviopolis, Bithynia, 341
crisis of the third century CE, xxxi, xxxvii, 222–3, 236
Croton, 7, 50, 55
crown
  agonistic. See prize crown
  hem-hem, 219
Curium, 192
currency bar, 46
Cydonia, Crete, 192
Cyme, Aeolis, 187, 333, 336
Cyprus, 166, 192, 194, 195
Cyrenaica, 133, 139, 166, 192, 194, 328
  coinage in the second and first centuries BCE, 90
Cyrene, Cyrenaica, 90, 320
  Agora hoard, 334
Cyrrhus, Syria, 332, 337, 342
Cyzicus, Mysia, xxviii, 206, 214, 226, 229, 255, 260, 261, 269, 338, 339, 342, 344

Daldis, Lydia, 252, 344
Dalisandus, Lycaonia, 342
Damascus, Syria, 133, 190, 262, 339
damnatio memoriae, 117, 142, 323

Dardanus, Troas, 178
dative case, 145, 146, 219
debasement, 4, 12, 23, 26, 40, 266, 266, 319
Debelt, Bulgaria hoard, 269
decurions, xxxvi, 118, 345
Delos accounts, 94
Delphi, Greece, 219
Demeter, 231
demonetisation, 10, 16, 23, 55, 67, 75, 80, 89, 106
Demos, 115, 176, 206, 228
denarius, 309
  bronze at Sinope, 245
  countermark, 343
  early, 9, 10, 11, 78
  retariffing at 16 asses, 12
denominations, 99, 106, 124–5, 151, 163, 223, 243–6, 309–10, 343
  small, 86, 182–7, 237, 253, 266, 324
designs
  civic, 197–208
  imperial, 209–18
  military, xxxv, 209–18, 232
Deultum, Thrace, 339, 342
dia, 122
Dido, 209, 234, 334
didrachm, 163
die counts, 33, 38, 68, 81, 92, 103, 105, 240, 261
  third century BCE, 50
die links between cities, 178–82, 240, 247, 252
Dio Chrysostom, 202
Diocaesarea. See Ceretapa-Diocaesarea
Diocletian, xxxi, xxxvi, 223, 237, 263
  Alexandrian coinage, 42
  coinage reform, 263, 269
  price edict, 41, 223
Dionysios, Aur., 234
Dionysios, M. Aur. the younger, 234
Dionysopolis, Moesia, 326, 342
Dionysopolis, Phrygia, 143, 333, 344
Dioshieron, Lydia, 342
Dium, Macedonia, 257, 323
Docimeum, Phrygia, 342
Doliche, Syria, 337
Domitia, 141

**352** Index

Domitian, 145
  coinage reform, 26, 165
  distribution of bronze coinage, 168
  German wars, 210
  and Greece, 116, 165
Domitius Domitianus, 345
Dora, Phoenicia, 133, 208, 339
Dorylaeum, Phrygia, 344
double communities, 322
drachm, 343
drachma, 124, 163, 172, 183, 309
Drusilla, daughter of Caligula, 140
Duilius, C., 35, 72
duovir, 80, 147
Dura-Europos, 340
Dyme, Greece, 145, 323
Dyrrhachium, 93

eagle, legionary, 216
Ebora, 137, 323
Ebusus, 13, 86, 147, 163, 169, 170,
  326
  imitations, 81
Edessa, Macedonia, 257
Edessa, Mesopotamia, 190, 326, 333, 339
Egypt. *See* also Alexandria, Egypt
  gold coinage, 38
El Saucejo hoard, 85
Elaea, Aeolis, 342, 344
Elaeusa-Sebaste, Cilicia, 322, 339
Elagabalus, 40, 226, 232, 233, 246, 266, 326,
  341, 342, 344
electrum, 34
electrum coinage, 7, 13, 16, 59, 61, 62, 313
Elis, Greece, 198
Emerita, 323
Emesa, Syria, 190, 227, 334
emotional, 234
emperor
  on horse, saluting, 227
emperors as gods, 141
Emporion, 84, 137
Emporion imitations, 66
Enna, 64
Enna hoard, 314
Entella, 64

Ephesus, Ionia, 180, 198, 204, 206, 210, 230,
  257, 325, 337, 338, 339, 342, 344
  cistophoric mint, 98
  customs law, 32, 99, 322
  exchange rate, 126
  first city in Asia, 114, 200
  gold coinage, 36
  graffiti, 326
  neocorate temples, 200, 215
  portraits of triumvirs, 133, 134
  sacred stone of Elagabal, 227
  Salutaris inscriptions, 30, 326, 327
epi, 122
epimeletes, 119, 123
Epiphanea, Cilicia, 262, 328, 333
equestrian rank, 121, 341
Ercavica, Spain, 170
Eresus, Lesbos, 336, 342
Erythrae, Ionia, 111, 120
Eryx, 64
Etenna, Pisidia, 246, 342
Etruria, third-century coinage, 57
Etruscan script, 57
Etruscus, Claudius, 322
Eucarpia, Phrygia, 115, 122, 143, 324
Eugenetoriane, Claudia, 123
Eukleides, 336
Eumenea, Phrygia, 133, 141, 143, 249,
  324
exetastai, 111, 120

Festa, Aelia, 225
fetial ceremony, 111
fines, 69
Fistelia, 8, 51
Flaccus, M. Fulvius, 56
Flamininus, 35, 107
Flaviopolis, Cilicia, 262
fleet coinage, 95, 133
forgery, 340
Forum Iulii, 330
Frentani, 55
Fronto, M. Aurelius, 225
Fronto, M. Claudius, 113
Fulcinnius, L., 111
Fulvia, 133, 141

Gaba, Syria, 337
Gabinius, Aulus, 103, 104
portrait, 132
Gadara, Galilee, 339
Gadara, Syria, 342
Gades, 13, 66, 84
Gadir. *See* Gades
Gaius and Lucius Caesars, 138
Galba, 38, 112
Gallia Narbonensis, 16
Gallic emperors, 222
Gallienus, 42, 223, 243, 244, 245, 246, 257, 341, 342, 344
games, 96, 124, 130, 198, 199, 206, 208, 227, 230–2, 235, 260
religious character, 230
Gaul
coinage in the second and first centuries BCE, 91
Gaza, Judaea, 191, 342
Gela, 64
Gelon, 9, 61
genitive case, 122, 144, 145
Germanicia, Syria, 337
Germanicus letter, 19, 163
Germanus, 330
Germany, 25
Germe, Mysia, 338, 344
Geta, 225
Gibbon, Edward, 222
Glycon, 116
gold coinage, 32–41, 237, 267
Carthage, 61
Italy, third century BCE, 50
Nero's reduction in weight, 22, 23
reduced fineness in third century CE, 40, 42
Syracuse, 61
Golden Age, 175
Gordian III, 28, 32, 40, 114, 226, 237, 244, 252, 254, 257, 261, 341, 342, 344
Lycia, 172
Gortyn, 109
governor, 111, 112, 117, 120, 121, 122, 126, 132, 147, 158, 176, 304, *See* also proconsul
portraits, 138

grammateus, 121, 122, 149, 234
Gratidianus, xxxi, 81
Graxa, 55
Greek, 187, 188, 194
late spelling, 188
Greenland ice cores, 24, 28, 222
Gresham's Law, 2, 30
Grimenothyrae, Phrygia, 324
Grumum, 55

Hadrian, xxxiii, 28, 31, 166, 175, 342
bear hunting, 215
city foundations, 215
journeys round the empire, 214
Olympios, 199
province coins, 39
visit to Egypt, 212
Hadrianeia, Mysia, 344
Hadriani ad Olympum, Mysia, 324, 342
Hadrianopolis, Caria. *See* Stratonicea, Caria
Hadrianopolis, Lydia, 260
Hadrianopolis, Paphlagonia, 326
Hadrianopolis, Phrygia, 342
Hadrianopolis, Thrace, 342
Hadrianotherae, Mysia, 215, 344
Hadrumetum, Africa, 151
Halicarnassus, Caria, 336, 338, 342
hoard, 32, 99
Hampsicoras, 59, 60
Hannibal, 36, 44, 58, 66, 72, 80, 108
Harpasa, Caria, 342
Heliopolis, Syria, 189, 190, 262, 339
Heraclea Minoa, Sicily, 64
Heraclea, Bithynia, 255, 257, 327
Heraclea, Caria, 143
Heraclea, Italy, 7, 34, 50
Heracles, labours, 214
Heraclitus, 201
Herbessos, 64
Hermeias, 187
Hero and Leander, 236
Herodotus, 209, 336
Hicetas, king of Syracuse, 61
Hierapolis, Phrygia, 122, 143, 227, 230, 324, 336
Hierapolis, Syria, 332, 337, 342

**354** Index

Hierapolis-Castabala, Cilicia, 103, 227, 246, 328
Hiero, king of Syracuse, 9, 61, 65
Hierocaesarea, Lydia, 344
hieromnemones, 121
Hieronymus, 61, 62
Hieropolis, Phrygia, 324
Himera, 64
Hipparchus, 336
Hippo Regius, Africa, 330
Hippodamia, 204
Hipponium, 55
Hirtius, A., 37, 38, 330
Homer, 204, 336
Homonoia, 96
   Homonoia coinages, 176, 206, 207
Hopkins graph, 12
Huesca. *See* Osca
Hybla Megale, 64
Hydisus, Caria, 342
Hydrela, Phrygia, 143
Hyllarima, Caria, 342
Hypaepa, Lydia, 337, 343, 344
Hyrcanis, Lydia, 342
Hyrgaleis, Phrygia, 325, 342
   inscription, 124, 326

Iaitia, 64
Iberian coinage, 14
Iberian denarius, 14, 84–5, 88, 107
Iberian script, 86
Iconium, Lycaonia, 322
Iconium, Pisidia, 337, 339
Iguvium, 317
Iliad, 336
Ilistra, Lycaonia, 342
Ilium, Troas, 178, 336, 344
Iltirta, Spain, 85
imperialism, Roman, 70, 72
indemnities, 6, 10, 36, 68
India, 2, 25, 33, 40
inflation, 41, 182, 184, 223, 264, 266, 267
inscriptions on coins, 144–7, 175, 187–95, 232
Iol, Africa, 330
Ios, 336

Iotape, Cilicia, 246
Irenopolis, Cilicia, 246, 262
Isaura, Lycaonia, 342
Isinda, Pisidia, 246, 250, 344
Istrus, Moesia, 193, 326, 342
Italian asses, 19, 29
Italica, 323, 330
Italos, 94
Italy
   coinage in the second and first centuries BCE, 79–81
   third century BCE coinage, 53–6
Iulia Gordus, Lydia, 122, 143, 344
Iulia Traducta, 323
Iuliopolis, Bithynia, 342

Jerusalem, 190, 227, 342
Jewish War
   First, 20, 150
   Second, 333
Jireček line, 195
Juba I, 149
Judaean kings, 22
Julia Domna, 243, 341
Julia Maesa, 227
Julia Paula, 227
Julia, daughter of Augustus, 141
Juliopolis, Bithynia, 216, 227
Julius Caesar, 79, 93
   conquest of Gaul, 16, 36, 90
   gold coinage, 2, 13, 37
   portrait, 131
   portrait at Corinth, 327
   portrait at Lampsacus, 132, 133
   portrait at Nicaea, 102, 132
   veni, vidi, vici, 102

Kalakte, 64
Kamarina, 64
Katane, 64
Kaunos, 173
Kavalkar inscription, 124
Kelin, 85
Kendreiseia Pythia, 230, 342
Kentoripai, 64
Kephalion, 149

Index **355**

Kephaloidion, 64
Kese. *See* Tarraco
Keynes, J.M., 34
kndrm, 326
Koinon
    Bithynia, 112, 328
    Cappadocia, 328
    Crete, 112
    Cyprus, 112, 195
    Galatia, 112, 328
    Lacedaemons, 96
    Lesbos, 112
    Lycia, 112, 173
    Macedonia, 112
    Paphlagonia, 112
    Phrygia, 112
    provincial, 112
    Thessaly, 112, 164
    thirteen cities, 112
Koraia Aktia, 232
Kraft, Konrad, 179

La Palma, 67
Labienus, 134
Laerte, Cilicia, 246, 250
Lampsacus, Mysia, 99, 100, 132, 133
Laodicea, Phrygia, 143, 206, 210, 228, 233,
    325, 332, 344
    agora, 228, 230
Laodicea, Syria, 19, 103, 189, 190, 217, 227,
    322, 332, 333, 339
Laranda, Lycaonia, 342
Larinum, 55
Latin, 86, 174, 190, 191, 194, 195, 197, 209,
    253, 263, 269, 333
    decline of, 188
Laur., Q., 80
legionary denarii, 94
Leontinoi, 64
Lepcis Magna, Africa, 19, 147, 330
    inscription, 326
    silver, 322
Lepidus, 133
Lepti, Africa, 145, 151, 163
Leucas, Greece, 93
Leucas, Syria, 133, 227, 342

Lex de Gallia Cisalpina, 322
Lexovians, 91, 163
Lilybaion, 64
Limyra, 331
Lipara, 64
litra, 83
liturgy, 80, 111, 118, 119, 124
Livia, 141, 170
Livy, xxxiv, 54
Locri, Greece, 164
Locri, Italy, 8, 50, 55, 70
London, 255
Lucani, 55
Luceria, 55
Lucius Antonius, 133
Lucius Verus, 27
    Parthian war, 204, 210, 212
Lucullus, 92
Lugdunum, 25, 152, 161
    branch mint under Nero, 165
    bronze coinage, 158
    late Roman mint, 255
    mint for Mark Antony, 90
    mint under Nero, 162
    transfer of mint to Rome, 23, 25
Lycia, xxxvi, 27, 29, 99, 113, 123, 163, 172–3,
    191, 253, 342
Lydian, 187
Lyons. *See* Lugdunum
Lyrbe, Cilicia, 246, 250
Lysias, Phrygia, 342
Lystra, Lycaonia, 339

Macrianus, 346
Macrinus, 28, 344
Maeander valley, 142, 182, 249
Maecenas, 128, 158
Maecianus. *See* Volusius Maecianus
Maeonia, Lydia, 342, 344
magistrates, 118, 147
magistrates' names, 37, 91, 92, 115, 120,
    122, 144, 147, 202, 233, 260, 306, 341,
    345, *See* also names on coins, city
    magistrates
Magnesia on Maeander/ Priene inscription,
    32, 322

## 356 Index

Magnesia, Ionia, 114, 122, 148, 240, 325, 343
  inscription, 324
Magnesia, Lydia, 325, 344
Magnetes, Greece, 164
Magydus, Cilicia, 246, 250
Malaga, 66
Mallus, Cilicia, 328, 339
Mamertini, 64
Marathus, Phoenicia, 133, 147
Marcellus, Clodius, 324
Marcellus, Hostilius, 220
Marcellus, M. Claudius, 138
Marcianopolis, Moesia, 232, 326, 342
Marcus Aurelius, 222, 251, 342
  Marcomannic wars, 210
Marcus Aurelius and Lucius Verus
  clasping hands, 211
Mark Antony, 12, 38, 90, 94, 95, 103, 105,
    108, 129, 133, 141
  portraits, 133–4
Maronea, Thrace, 93, 265, 342
Mars, 6
Marseilles. See Massalia
Marsyas, 217
Masicytes, 331
Massalia, 16, 58
Massalia imitations, 81
Mastaura, Lydia, 324
Mat(eola), 55
Matavo, 330
Mauretania, 29
Maximian, 345
Maximinus (Thrax), 234, 342, 344
Maximinus Daza, 269
Maximus, Fabius, 122
medallic coins, 220, 251, 340, 343
medallions, 220, 340
Megara, Greece, 336
Meles, 55
Men, 215
Menai, 64
Menas, 124
Mesambria, Thrace, 342
Messalina, 141
Messana, 64
Messene inscription, 94, 108

Metapontum, 7, 34, 50, 51, 55
metropolis, xxxiii, 114, 202, 205, 207, 261
Metropolis, Ionia, 178, 343
Metropolis, Phrygia, 325, 342
Midaeum, Phrygia, 157, 178
Milan, 255
Miletopolis, Mysia, 324, 342, 344
Miletus, Ionia, 230
Millar, F.G.B., 137
mine coins, 333
Mineia, 80, 325
mint magistrate, 306
Mithradates, 17
Mithradatic War
  First, 93, 99
  Second, 99
  Third, 99, 102, 103, 131
monetisation. See Rome
moneychangers, 126–7
Monte Bibele hoard, 58
Monte Iato, 61, 63, 82
Mopsus, Cilicia, 19, 150, 262, 322, 328
Morgantina, 61, 63, 64, 78, 82
Moschion, 324, 325
Motye, 64
Muziris papyrus, 40
Mylae inscription, 6, 35, 62
Mylasa, Caria, 19, 322, 324, 344
Myra, 173
Myrlea, Bithynia, 322
Mytilene, 154, 251, 336, 344

Nacolea, Phrygia, 328, 338, 342
Nakone, 64
names on coins, 147, 232
Naples, 6, 7, 45, 50, 51, 53, 54, 55, 74
narrative, 228, 234
nauarchis, 216
naval bases, 216
Naxos, Sicily, 64
  hoard, 63
Neapolis, Caria, 234, 324
Neapolis, Italy. See Naples
Neapolis, Samaria, 191, 339, 342
Nemausus, 111, 139, 148, 152, 158,
    161

Nemea, Greece
  excavation coins, 327
Neocaesarea, Pontus, 339, 342
Neoclaudiopolis, Paphlagonia, 338
neocorate, xxxiii, 199, 200, 201, 202, 215, 229, 231, 233, 235, 260, 307
neo-Punic, 86, 147, 170
Nero
  Armenian war, 150
  branch mint in Gaul, 162, 165
  branch mint in Thrace, 162, 165, 194
  British war, 150
  coin inscriptions, 144
  coinage reforms, 12, 22–5, 162
  Greece, 116, 143
  portraits, 142
Nerva, 328
Nicaea Cilbianorum, Lydia, 344
Nicaea, Bithynia, 101, 114, 141, 145, 154, 178, 204, 216, 251, 257, 328, 336, 342
Nicomedia, Bithynia, 40, 101, 114, 141, 216, 230, 235, 269, 326, 328, 338, 342
Nicopolis ad Istrum, Moesia, 342
Nicopolis ad Lycum, Pontus, 338
Nicopolis, Epirus, 19, 139, 143, 164, 198, 257, 322
Nicopolis, Syria, 125, 337, 342
Ninica, Cilicia, 339
Nisibis, Mesopotamia, 190
Noah's ark, 235
Nola, 8
nome coins, 213
nominative case, 122, 144, 145, 189
nomos (Sicilian), 83
Nora hoard, Sardinia, 16, 59, 62
Norba, 8
Novae, 194
Nuceria, 7, 55
Numantia, 85
Nysa, Lydia, 114, 336, 343, 344
  theatre, 198
Nysa, Samaria, 132, 342

obol, 50, 94, 124, 163, 183, 309, 310, 343
Ococleia, Phrygia, 342
Octavia, Octavian's sister, 95, 133

October Horse, 6
Odessus, Moesia, 193, 226, 326, 342
Oea, Africa, 147
Oikoumenika, 232
Oikoumenika, Megala, 199
Olba, 102
Olbasa, Pisidia, 342
onkiai, 83
Onogur, Bulgaria, hoard, 268
Oppius, Q., 153
Orestes, 206
Orra, 55
Orthosia, Caria, 143
Orthosia, Phoenicia, 133
Osca, 14, 323
Otho, 164
overstrike, 54, 78, 268, 307

Paestum, 7, 55, 80, 169, 325, 330
Palmyra, 163, 190
Paltus, Syria, 342
Panemoteichus, Pisidia, 223, 246
Panhellenion, 215
Panormus, 64, 82, 330
Pansa, C. Vibius, 101
panther bronzes, 81
Paphos, 192
para, 122
Paris, judgement of, 336
Parium, Mysia, 145, 323, 328, 339, 342
Parlais, Pisidia, 339
Paros hoard, 334
Patara, 331
Paterna, Africa, 323, 330
Patras, Greece, 134, 143, 164, 210, 337, 345
Patricia, Colonia, 323
Pausanias, 197
Pautalia, Thrace, 251
Pednelissus, Pisidia, 246
pegasi, 61
Pella, Macedonia, 92, 108, 342
Peloponnesian coins, 123
Pelops, 204
Peltae, Phrygia, 342
Pergamos, 201

## 358 Index

Pergamum, Mysia, 98, 123, 141, 149, 199, 201, 228, 251, 257, 269, 337, 338, 340, 342, 344
exchange inscription, 126
neocorate temple, 200, 215
second neocorate, 202
Perge, Pamphylia, 179, 245, 246, 250, 261, 268, 333, 344
inscription, 261
Perinthus, Thrace, 194, 240, 257, 328, 342, 344
Peripoloi, 8
permissu, 116, 118, 165, 175
Perperene, Mysia, 333, 342, 344
Pescennius Niger, 38
Pessinus, Galatia, 341
Petelia, 55
Petra, Arabia, 29, 190
Pharnaces, 102
Phidias, 198
Philadelphia, Lydia, 206, 233, 324, 340, 342, 344
Philetos, M. Aur., 325
Philip, 28, 40, 234, 237, 245, 252, 257, 344
Philip II, King of Macedon, 34, 50
Philip Philadelphus tetradrachms, 18, 21, 104
Philippi, Macedonia, 154, 188
Philippopolis, Arabia, 189, 190, 332, 342
Philippopolis, Thrace, 157, 194, 230, 232, 328, 342
Philistis, 9
Philomelium, Phrygia, 342
Phocaea, Ionia, 251, 344
Phoebus, Aurelius Aelius, 122
Phoenice, Epirus, 164, 328
Phoenician, 147, 187, 207, 209, 334
physical properties, xxxv, 12, 21, 150–7, 250–3
Piazza Armerina hoard, 63
Pigres, L. Aelius, 230
Pinos Puente hoard, 85
Pisidia, 182
Plancus, L., 37
Plato, 327
Plautus, 68, 69
Pliny, 180

Natural History XXXIII, 6, 10
trade to India, 40
Po Valley, 7, 8, 16, 58, 90
Pobla de Mafumet hoard, 171
Poemanenum, Mysia, 342
Pogla, Pisidia, 246
Polemo, M. Antonius, 119, 205, 221
Polybius, 77
Pompeiopolis, Cilicia, 132, 246, 326, 328, 336, 342
Pompey, 17, 77, 79, 102, 103, 104
gold coinage, 36
portrait, 131
Ponte Gini hoard, 56
Poplilius, C., 93
Populonia, 7, 16, 51, 56, 57
Poroselene, Lesbos, 187, 269
portraits, 131–44, 224
Augustus, 129, 131
emperors', xxxv
military, 225
radiate, 143, 144, 150, 153, 173, 226, 229, 310, 328, 342, 344
salutation, 225
and sculpture, 140
Vespasian, 144
Postumus, 257
praetor, 80, 84, 153
Pratica di Mare hoard, 68
Priene, Ionia, 336, 343
excavation coins, 127
prize crown, 227, 231, 232
Proclus, Cl., 336
proconsul, 18, 19, 84, 97, 101, 103, 118, 146, 324, 332, See also governor
Prostanna, Pisidia, 204, 261
Provincia Dacia coinage, 253, 257, 267
Prusa, Bithynia, 101, 216
Prusias ad Hypium, Bithynia, 227, 245, 251, 257, 341, 342
prytanis, 122
psephisamenos, 118
pseudo-autonomous coins, 115, 137, 176
Ptolemaic coins, 152
Ptolemais, Cyrenaica, 90, 320

Ptolemais-Ake, Phoenicia, 133, 135, 190, 208, 262, 339
Pudukkottai hoard, 40
Pula, 60
Punic, 86
Punic coinage. *See* Carthaginian coinage
Punic War
　First, 6, 7, 36, 44, 46, 53, 62, 72, 108
　Second, 6, 7, 8, 9, 11, 35, 44, 49, 54, 55, 57, 59, 60, 65, 66, 69, 75, 78, 80, 89, 108, 169
　Third, 79, 89, 108
Pygmalion, 334
Pyrrhic War, 7, 34, 53, 70
Pyrrhus, 61
Pythagoras, 336
Pythian Games, 227

Quadratus, Aulus Julius, 336
quadrigati, 6, 60, 61, 62, 66, 67, 72
quaestor, 82, 92, 110, 111
quattuorvir, 80
Quietus, 346
quinarius, 66, 94, 172, 309, 320
　bronze, 151
　early, 10, 11
　Gallic, 77, 90
quinquennalis, 80
Quintillus, 261

radiate. *See* Antoninianus
radiate crown. *See* portraits
Raphanea, Phoenicia, 216
Raphia, Judaea, 342
reverse designs, 147–50
Rhegium, 55
Rhesaena, Mesopotamia, 188, 190, 339, 342
Rhodes, 19, 98, 115, 322, 328
Rhodian drachmae, 29, 110, 331
Rhosus, Cilicia, 328, 337
Richborough, 39
right to coinage, xxxiii, 116
Roma, personification, 70, 101, 109, 201, 204
Roman imperialism, 45
Roman pound, 309
Romanisation, xxxv, 79, 87, 130, 308
Romano-Sicilian coinage, 65, 82

Rome
　alliance with Alexandria, 337
　alliance with Amisus, 337
　alliance with Thessalian League, 337
　Capitoline hoard, 58
　first coins, 8, 45, 48–52
　as a foreign state, 204
　Forum coin finds, 69
　as a 'Greek city', 51
　mint building, 165
　transition to monetised society, 45, 69, 80
Rome against Carthage allegory, 72
Romula, 323
*RPC* database, xxxvii, 325, 332
Rubi, 55
Rufinus, Cl., 336
Rufus, Domitius, 121

Sabratha, Africa, 147, 149, 330
Sagalassus, Pisidia, 204, 246, 250, 261
Saguntum, 87
Saitta, Lydia, 341, 344
Salapia, 55
Salonina, 223
Salutaris, C. Vibius, 30, 326, 327
Samnite Wars, 44
Samnites, 8
Samos, 328, 336, 338, 343
Samosata, Commagene, 40, 332, 337, 342
Sanquinius, M., 160
Santa Marinella hoard, 68
Sappho, 336
Sardinia, 16, 59–60
Sardis, Lydia, 113, 121, 215, 230, 240, 324, 337, 338, 342, 344
　excavation coins, 127
Satala, Commagene, 326
Saunitai. *See* Samnites
SC, xxxiii, 112, 160, *See* also Antioch
Scepsis, Troas, 336
Scipio Africanus, supposed portrait, 54
Sebaste, Phrygia, 342, 344
Sebaste, Samaria, 190
Second Sophistic, 174, 197
Second Triumvirate, 96
Segesta, 64, 323

## 360 Index

Seleucia, Cilicia, 19, 322
Seleucia, Pisidia, 261
Seleucia, Syria, 19, 125, 333, 337
Selge, Pisidia, 246, 250, 261, 268
Selinus, Cilicia, 64, 342
Senate personification, 115, 118, 176, 201
Sentinum, Battle of, 56
Sepphoris, Gallilee, 204, 324
Septimius Severus, xxxiii, 28, 235, 252, 342, 344
Serdica, 194, 255
Servilius, C., 95
Servius Tullius, 45
sestertius
    CA coinage, 154
    double, 344
    early, 10
    fleet coinage, 95
    Greece, 150
    influence, xxxv, 130, 151, 153, 154, 155, 157
    Rome, 153, 161
    Spain, 152
Sestus, Thrace, 257, 335, 342
    inscription, 123, 124
Severa, Julia, 123
Severan debasement, 28
Severus Alexander, xxxiii, 27, 225, 226, 237, 243, 253, 344
Sexstos, M. Aur., 260
Sextus Pompey, 133, 134, 141
shipwrecks, 69, 222
Sibidunda, Phrygia, 342
Siblia, Phrygia, 325
Sicca, Africa, 145
Siceliotai, 8
Sicily, 7
    coinage in the second and first centuries BCE, 84
    third century BCE coinage, 61–5
Sicyon, Greece, 143, 164
Side, Pamphylia, 204, 232, 245, 246, 261, 268, 326, 333, 339, 342
Sidon, Phoenicia, 19, 147, 190, 322, 328, 334, 339, 342
Signia, 8

Silandus, Lydia, 210, 211, 252, 344
Sillyum, Pamphylia, 246, 250, 261, 268, 344
silver coinage, 4–32, 168, 175, 237, 253, 267, 322
silver shortage, 12, 25, 36, 88
Silvium, 55
simissos publicos, 90, 163
Simon Maccabaeus, 324
Singara, Mesopotamia, 190, 342
Sinope, Paphlagonia, 245, 257, 323, 328, 339, 340
Siphnus, 342
Siscia, 255
small denominations, 51, 86, 162, 172
Smyrna, Ionia, 119, 121, 122, 157, 176, 203, 206, 215, 240, 251, 257, 260, 336, 337, 344
    Antinous, 221
    declining weights, 247
    neocorate temple, 200
    pattern of issue, 187
    third neocorate, 204
    weights, 184
    workshop, 180
Soli, Cilicia. See Pompeiopolis
Solus, 64
Spain
    coinage in the second and first centuries BCE, 88
    coinage in the third century BCE, 66–7
Sparta, Greece, 134, 135, 139, 193, 243, 244, 247, 249
SPQR mint, 255
SR, 336
standards, miltary, 216
Statilius, 163
Stectorium, Phrygia, 324, 332, 342
stephanephoroi, 121, 122
Stobi, Macedonia, 188
stone, sacred of Emesa, 227
Strabo, xxxiii, 180
strategos, 121, 260, 325
Stratonicea, Caria, 19, 98, 117, 322, 324, 340, 344
Stratonicea, Lydia, 338, 342, 344
Sturni, 55

Index **361**

stylistic similarities, 142, 143, 180
Suessa, 7, 55
Suetonius, xxxiv
suffetes, 147
Sulla, 79
 bronze coinage, 81
 coinage in Greece, 92
 gold coinage, 36
Sun God, 226
Supera, Cornelia, 224
supply, 253
switching, 192
Syedra, Cilicia, 246
Synaus, Phrygia, 342, 344
Synnada, Phrygia, 143
Syracuse, 7, 9, 35, 64, 75, 82
 Democracy, 61, 62
 gold coinage, 61
 hoard, 61
Syria
 changes in the third century CE, 208
 coinage of the first century BCE, 103–6
 coinage of the imperial period, 207
Syrian tetradrachms, 21, 27, 29
Syros, 164

Tabae, Caria, 19, 98, 322, 325
Tabala, Lydia, 342
Tacitus, xxxiv, 200, 268
Tacitus, emperor
 city coinage, 261
Tarcondimotus, 102, 103
Tarentum, 7, 34, 50, 55, 74
Tarquinii, 56
Tarraco, 84
Tarsus, Cilicia, 19, 102, 322, 328, 336, 339, 342, 344
Tartessian script, 86
Tauromenium, 64
 inscriptions, 83, 108, 163
tax, 10, 14, 17, 19, 22, 25, 30, 32, 94, 143, 163, 173, 320, 321
Teanum, 7, 55
Teate, 7, 55
Telamon, Battle of, 58
Temenothyrae, Phrygia, 344

Temnus, Aeolis, 336
temple, xxxiii, 22, 36, 60, 72, 80, 114, 147, 148, 149, 199, 200, 201, 202, 208, 210, 211, 214, 221, 228, 234, 235, 252, 342
 on Alexandrian coins, 213
 Artemis at Ephesus, 198, 199
 Augustus at Pergamum, 199, 231
 three at Ephesus, 338
 three at Nicomedia, 230
 three at Smyrna, 204
 two at Pergamum, 202
Teos, Ionia, 336, 342
Termessus, Pisidia, 246, 249
Thaena, Africa, 147, 323
Thapsus, Africa, 147, 330
Tharros, Sardinia, 59
Thasos, 93
Thebes, Greece, 164
Themisonium, Phrygia, 342
Theophanes, 336
Thespiae, Greece, 164, 328
Thessalian League, 17, 32, 93, 337
 alliance with Rome, 337
Thessalonica, Macedonia, 92, 95, 96, 154, 257, 328, 333, 339
Thessaly, diorthoma, 19, 94, 163
Thurii, 7, 50 See also Copia
Thyatira, Lydia, 187, 251, 269, 337, 344
Tiberiopolis, Phrygia, 342
Tiberius, 19, 24, 25, 42, 80, 137, 138, 169
Ticinum, 255
Tigranes, king of Armenia, 103
Timbriada, Pisidia, 246
Timbrium, Phrygia, 326
Tingi, 139
Tityassus, Pisidia, 342
Tium, Bithynia, 101, 266, 327, 328, 336, 341
Tmolus, Lydia, 340
Tomi, Moesia, 193, 194, 226, 243, 245, 247, 249, 326, 338, 342
Torelló d'en Cintes hoard, Menorca, 85
Toynbee, Jocelyn, 39
Trajan, 27, 31, 174, 175, 228, 342
 Dacian wars, 210
 Parthian War, 123, 201
Trajan Decius, 233, 344

## 362 Index

Trajanopolis, Lydia, 338
Trajanopolis, Phrygia, 342
Tralles, Lydia, 260, 333, 343, 344
Transalpine Gaul, 16, 90
Trapezopolis, Caria, 143, 325
Trapezus, Pontus, 333, 342
Trebonianus Gallus, 125, 344
Trier, 255, 329
Tripolis, Lydia, 143, 338, 342
Tripolis, Phoenicia, 117, 133, 255, 339
tropaikon, 94
Troy, Troas, 327
Tryphon, Po. Ail., 325
Tuder, 317
Turris Libisonis, 323
Twelve Tables, 45
Tyche, 207
Tyndaris, 64
Tyre, Phoenicia, 22, 23, 25, 115, 147, 190, 207,
208, 209, 234, 262, 322, 334, 339

Ulatos, 91
Utica, Africa, 89, 323, 330

Valentia, 109
Valerian, 232, 244, 246, 248, 257, 342,
344
Valerian II, 223, 319
validity of city coins, 126
Velia, 7, 50, 51
Venusia, 55
Verbe, Pisidia, 342
Vercingetorix, 37, 320
vergobretus, 91
Verres, C., 84

Vespasian, 165
and Greece, 116, 163
portraits, 144
Vetulonia, 56
vexillum, 216
Vibo, 55, 80
victoriate, 10, 11, 31, 78, 88, 317, 320
Victory types, 338
Viminacium, Moesia, 253, 254, 255, 257, 267,
339
Volasenna, P., 118
Volaterrae, 56
volume of coinage, 238–43
Volusius Maecianus, 29
vota, 200
vota publica coins, 270

warfare
explanation for coinage, 17, 123, 168
warfare,
explanation for coinage, 316
wealth
display, 316
women
absent from Syrian and Phoenician coins,
207
portrait with poppy, 227, 228
portraits, 139, 227
women's names, 119, 122–3, 225
workshops, 179, 180
wreath
corn ears, 213

Zela, Battle of, 102
Zeugma, Commagene, 332, 337, 342

Printed in the United States
by Baker & Taylor Publisher Services